Empire of Neglect

RADICAL AMÉRICAS

A series edited by Bruno Bosteels and George Ciccariello-Maher

Empire of Neglect

The West Indies in the Wake of British Liberalism

CHRISTOPHER TAYLOR

Duke University Press

Durham and London

2018

© 2018 Duke University Press
All rights reserved
Printed in the United States of America on acid-free paper ∞
Text designed by Julienne Alexander
Typeset in Whitman, Gill Sans, and Bickham Script by Westchester
Publishing Services

Library of Congress Cataloging-in-Publication Data
Names: Taylor, Christopher, [date] author.
Title: Empire of neglect : the West Indies in the wake of British
    liberalism / Christopher Taylor.
Description: Durham : Duke University Press, 2018. | Series: Radical
    Américas | Includes bibliographical references and index.
Identifiers: LCCN 2017045248 (print)
LCCN 2017052446 (ebook)
ISBN 9780822371748 (ebook)
ISBN 9780822371045 (hardcover : alk. paper)
ISBN 9780822371151 (pbk. : alk. paper)
Subjects: LCSH: Politics and literature—West Indies, British—
    History—19th century. | Liberalism—Great Britain—History—
    19th century. | Great Britain—Colonies—Administration—
    History—19th century. | West Indian literature (English)—
    Themes, motives. | America—In literature.
Classification: LCC PR9210.5 (ebook) | LCC PR9210.5 .T39 2018
    (print) | DDC 820.9/358729—dc23
LC record available at https://lccn.loc.gov/2017045248

Cover art: Michel Jean Cazabon (1813–1888), *On the Caroni, Trinidad*,
date unknown. Pencil, watercolor, and gouache on paper.

TO CHRISTOPHER AND GERRI TAYLOR,
MY PARENTS,

&

SARAH PIERCE TAYLOR,
MY NEVER NEGLECTFUL PARTNER

Contents

Acknowledgments

That I have written a book about neglect remains confusing to me; it was written with the love, care, and support of innumerable teachers, colleagues, friends, and comrades. The English Department at the University of Pennsylvania is the only institution I have ever felt any intense investment in, a weird feeling for me that I can explain only by the fact that the department invests so much in its students. This book would not have been possible without the rigorous coursework and professional guidance of Suvir Kaul, Michael Gamer, Jed Esty, Tsitsi Jaji, Jo Park, Heather Love, and David Eng. Still less would it have been possible without the attention and example of my committee. I once wrote in a course evaluation that David Kazanjian taught me how to read; he continues to do so every time I go back to his work. David models for me a way to combine archival sensitivity, theoretical creativity, and political urgency, and I could not imagine a better mentor. I am equally indebted to Ania Loomba, whose ability to combine sparkling thinking with political fierceness and intellectual rigor continues to inspire me. As I moved with her from the classroom to the Occupy camp in Philly, Ania allowed me to encounter the continuities and discontinuities between work in the academy and work in the world, and it is a lesson I hold on to. Along with Ania, Amy Kaplan has always helped in honing my points and my prose. (I'll never forget the howl of Amy's dog one evening as I bloviated about Melville; no doubt my book would be shorter if Amy's dog could read.)

The friends, colleagues, and comrades I met at Penn have been a constant source of help and inspiration; I'm fortunate that my best interlocutors have been my best friends. Dave Alff, Rachel Banner, Jos Lavery, Phil Maciak, and Christen Mucher have all given me invaluable personal and intellectual advice along the way, and I'm truly indebted to all of them. I thank the bartenders of Philly for their patience as Dave, Phil, and I talked too loud and too long about husbandry manuals, disappearing Jesuses, and bears. The brilliance of Christen and Rachel scared me from our very first classes together. Megan Cook has always livened things up, and Mel Micir provided invaluable advice as a teaching mentor and as a friend. Marina Bilbija has been my constant companion in geekery, and I cherish our friendship. I'm grateful to my political science pals—David Faris and Murad Idris—for helping me think across the disciplines I aim to traverse.

My friends and colleagues at the University of Chicago have been inspiring, stimulating, and lots of fun to be around. Even before I met her, my work owed much to Lauren Berlant; I owe much more to her now that I have benefited from her advising, questioning, and critiquing. I have also benefited from the advice of Bill Brown, Jim Chandler, Frances Ferguson, Elaine Hadley, Eric Slauter, and Ken Warren. I have had the ridiculously good fortune to find a gang of interlocutors and co-conspirators in Chicago, at both my university and other universities. In addition to being perfect pals, Zach Samalin and Sonali Thakkar have always pushed me to sharpen my frequently too blunt polemics into actual points. Adrienne Brown has proved the friend and co-thinker I didn't know I needed. In addition to being good pals, Tim Harrison and David Simon have always generously entertained my periodic forays into the early modern. Harris Feinsod and Edgar Garcia continually push my thinking on hemispheric studies. Nasser Mufti has been a hilarious and invaluable friend; I forgive you for making me drink malort with your mom. Pete Coviello and Julie Orlemanski have modeled what enthusiastic, cheeky, committed criticism can look like. I owe all members of the Chicago-area Junior Faculty Working Group for their incisive comments. I am also grateful to the many brilliant students at the University of Chicago, in particular Ajay Batra, Mollie McFee, Cass Picken, and Jean-Thomas Tremblay, as well as to our wonderful departmental staff.

This book was completed with the support of many other institutions and scholars. I owe particular thanks to the Radcliffe Institute for Advanced Study at Harvard University, whose support enabled the completion of this book and put me in contact with a dizzying array of brilliant scholars. Thanks, too, to the librarians and archivists at the Library Company of Philadelphia, the National Archives of Trinidad and Tobago, the National Archives of the United Kingdom, the Regenstein Library at the University of Chicago, and the Van Pelt Library at the University of Pennsylvania. I am especially indebted to audiences and interlocutors at numerous American Comparative Literature Association seminars; the C19 conference; the Tepoztlán Institute for the Transnational History of the Americas; the Franke Institute at the University of Chicago; Harvard University; Brandeis University; the City University of New York Graduate Center; and the University of Illinois, Chicago. My thanks to Tanya Agathocleous, Sunil Agnani, Siraj Ahmed, Erika Beckman, Larissa Brewer-García, Sarah Brouillette, Joshua Clover, Leah Feldman, Adom Getachew, Bilal Hashmi, Peter Hudson, Aaron Kamugisha, Agnes Lugo-Ortiz, Keguro Macharia, Kris Manjapra, Annie McClanahan, Aamir Mufti, Sonya Postmentier, and David Sartorius for stimulating, helpful conversations. In an act of extraordinary charity, Anjuli Raza Kolb read the entire manuscript; thanks, Anju, and I owe you one. Thanks, too, to Geo for approaching me about contributing to this series, the Duke University Press team, and the very helpful feedback of my anonymous reviews.

My friends and ridiculously large family have been a source of constant comfort. I'm thankful in particular to my siblings, Claire, Pat, and Joe, for troubling the friend-family divide. Much love to Nick Bentgen, Ethan Goldhammer, Marci Kwon, and Dave Reilly, land sailors all. This book was written in the fever and fret of various social movements, and my comrades on the streets in Philly and Chicago have always been a source of inspiration and hope. Thanks to my parents, Christopher and Gerri Taylor, who have supported me in ways calculable and incalculable. My father's curiosity and willingness to learn has always been a disposition I have tried to replicate. I would never have begun this course of study at all were it not for my mother, whose constant trips to the local library made my childhood a bookish paradise. My deepest gratitude is pledged to Sarah Pierce Taylor. Being with you, Sarah, has been the best thing to ever happen to me. This book would have been impossible without your constant love and support, as well as our freakish aptitude for synchronized whistling. I love everything about our life together, from nerdy debates over subaltern studies to chilling with Percy and Byron in bed. Nānu ninnannu prītisuttēnc, forever.

INTRODUCTION

The age of empire was dead; that of free traders, economists, and calculators had suc-
ceeded, and the glory of the West Indies was extinguished forever.
—ERIC WILLIAMS, *Capitalism and Slavery*

Empires of neglect emerge when subjects demand the attention of a world
that is indifferent to their presence within it. This book argues that British
West Indian writing of the long nineteenth century emerged in response
to the rise of neglect as a practice of imperial rule. I adopt the term "neglect"
from my archive, using it to describe these transformations in imperial governance, as well as to mark the forms of subjectivity constituted in relation
to these transformations. "Neglect" was the name West Indian writers gave
to a diffuse set of discursive and institutional practices that facilitated the
divestment of economic capital, political care, and popular concern from
colonies that had once been considered the crown jewels of the British Empire. This critical attunement, I will argue, fashioned particular forms of
imperial subjectivity—forms of subjectivity that, outraged by their attenuated
presence in the imperial world, are saturated with normative understandings
and deeply felt fantasies of what empire was, what it risked becoming, and
what it could be. What happens, I ask, not simply when subjects are neglected,
but when they come to conceive of themselves as being neglected?

I link this dialectic of structural transformation and subject formation to
gritty, technical, and at times eye-droopingly boring changes in the politico-
economic fabric of the British Empire. What West Indians decried as imperial
neglect was an effect of novel forms of thinking about and organizing economic relations that emerged in the wake of the partial collapse of Britain's
Atlantic empire after 1776. Beginning with Adam Smith's *The Wealth of Nations* (1776), classical political economy's theorizations of the relationship

between states and markets were all opposed to what Smith called "the mercantile system," or what we today call mercantilism.[1] The mercantilist order of the British imperial state secured to West Indian merchants and planters a protected monopoly over British markets in tropical produce. After decades of political-economic theorization and free-trade agitation, the mercantilist order was more or less dismantled in 1846 with the passage of the Sugar Duties Act, the repeal of the Corn Laws, and the repeal of the Navigation Laws.[2] Through this legislation, Britain disembedded its economic structure from the empire; many of its commodity markets no longer distinguished between imperial and extra-imperial producers but admitted from both at the same tariff rates. These changes in tariff laws might seem rather arcane, but concealed beneath them was a "great transformation" in the modalities by which Britain related to the broader imperial polity—and, in particular, to the West Indies.[3] The mercantilist market protections that free trade exploded were something more than narrowly fiscal instruments. Elite West Indians had long understood mercantilist market protections as materializing what the planter-historian Bryan Edwards called "a fixed and permanent *compact*," which he described as "an arrangement not framed by the colonies, but by the mother-country herself, who has suffered it to grow sacred by time, has recognized it by a multitude of laws, and enforced it by stricter ties and recent provisions."[4] The very term "protection" was saturated with political and affective connotations, harking back to early modern conceptualizations, as well as plebian understandings, of the relationship between subjects and sovereign and to kin-based models of parental oversight.[5] The theory and practice of economic liberalism displaced the idioms and the institutions that loosely structured empire as a polity, unbinding Britain from the inchoate but nonetheless effective normativity of the imperial compact.

This unbinding took place through the decades during which the West Indies were becoming "increasingly negligible," in Eric Williams's words, to British capital.[6] We tend to think of the first decades of the nineteenth century as a time during which Britain invested an overwhelming amount of moral energy and public attention in the West Indies, culminating with emancipation on 1 August 1834. We can even assign a monetary value to this care: Britain paid £20,000,000 to slave owners as part of a constitutional bargain with colonial legislatures for black freedom. Yet the very process of emancipation worked to shunt British capital and British attention from the islands. While the motivations behind Britain's decision to emancipate enslaved West Indians were hardly a reflex of economic determinations, political-economic thought provided the institutional mechanisms that structured emancipation: West Indians were emancipated to the market.[7] The problem was that the value and profitability of the islands had been shrinking through the early nineteenth century and nearly collapsed after emancipation. As the profitability of the West Indian colonies declined, British capital and British imperial attention shifted from the West Indies to more remunerative sites within empire, such as India, or to sites beyond it, such as Cuba and Brazil.[8] Liberalization facilitated this divestment of capital and concern, allowing capitalists to turn from an area that, just a decade previously, had been the object of the abolitionist state's intense moral investment. If West Indians were emancipated to the market, eight years later the market was emancipated from West Indians. Whatever the intentions of good-hearted Britons, liberal freedom *became* a form of liberal neglect. These intentions soured pretty quickly anyhow. Britain's increasing reliance on extra-imperial sugar producers called into question the value of retaining what Benjamin Disraeli would describe as the "forlorn Antilles" and as "millstones" around the collective neck of Britain.[9] Why keep the West Indies at all? Was maintaining the Atlantic empire even worth it? Spectators on both sides of the Atlantic considered free trade "preparatory to a dissolution of the imperial connexion"; in Britain, free traders, fiscal conservatives, and even abolitionists wished that the West Indies would declare independence, that the United States would annex the islands, or that the islands would sink into the sea.[10] None of these things happened; for this reason, the passage of the Sugar Duties Act is frequently treated as a footnote in British fiscal history or a chapter in postemancipation West Indian history, not an epochal event in the constitution of the empire. Yet the combined effect of the discourse and practice of economic liberalism yielded a new, flexible form of imperial rule, one premised on the indifference of empire to the reproduction of its own *imperium*. It yielded, in other words, an empire of neglect.

As is probably evident, my approach to liberalism departs somewhat from that of scholars working across the fields of economic history, political theory, and literary studies. By sticking close to the discursive and institutional process of liberalization, and by tying these tightly to transformations in tariff regimes, I hope to avoid reproducing the vague ways that the adjective "liberal" tends to circulate. Here, liberalism is not a transhistorical philosopheme with an inbuilt tendency toward fashioning self-possessive subjects or excluding infantilized others; nor does it name a voluntary party affiliation.[11] Instead, I explore how the discourse of liberalism was practically *enacted* and trace the looping consequences of these enactments.[12] In so doing, I hope to push back against scholarship that attempts to save the Enlightenment or liberalism from itself by stressing the anticolonial, anti-imperial, or antiracist fundaments of these varied traditions.[13] My problem with this approach is that the political and ethical value of "anticolonial" and "anti-imperial" thinking has transformed across time even as it was heterogeneous across historical space; we cannot fuse our postcolonial political horizons with those of the eighteenth and nineteenth centuries. Adam Smith's critique of empire seems righteous to us—certainly more righteous, if we follow Jennifer Pitts's important account, than the civilizationist and racist imperial liberalism articulated decades later by John Stuart Mill. For the colonial subjects I explore, however, Adam Smith's anti-imperialism was precisely what made him odious. Indeed, as Pitts points out, liberal anticolonial and anti-imperial thought emerged with little reference to the stated desires of imperial subjects, which were for the most part *not* anti-imperial in ways recognizable to us as being such.[14] (Moreover, and as we will see, most nineteenth-century West Indian anticolonialisms were not anti-imperialisms; indeed, opposition to the colonial state form was frequently articulated through the ideological resources of the empire and as a defense of it.) Given that metropolitan anti-imperialisms tended to ignore the thoughts and feelings of imperial subjects in the colonies, the methodology of this revisionist approach—which is more or less a hermetically textualist intellectual history—reproduces the foreclosure of colonial subjectivity, even as the critic reads the tradition as aligning with what the colonial subject might or would have said. At the same time, this textualist mode of interpreting the liberal tradition centers authorial and moral intentions over instituted effects.[15] One need not doubt that Smith sincerely found empire unjust; that the liberal abolitionists whom I explore in this book really cared about enslaved humans; or that Richard Cobden and other free traders truly believed that liberalization would end slavery, increase global plenty, and bring about world peace. But the institutions constructed to translate anti-imperial intentions into worldly action were themselves constitutively indifferent to the sovereignty of moral intention. West Indians lived not in the warm glow of abolitionists' and political economists' hearts but with the effects induced by the institutional structures built by these intentions. Approaching metropolitan thought and practice from the colonial world requires a methodological consequentialism.

This book explores how West Indians responded to the set of transformations that rendered their position in empire negligible, at best, and precarious, at worst. I read across a broad archive of materials—economic treatises and husbandry manuals, plantation novels and planters' books of account, sentimental novellas and pirate romances, emancipation narratives and post-emancipation memoirs—to assay the shaping force of imperial neglect on West Indians' relations to the empire and to the world. It is only through a close engagement with this archive that neglect can become legible as a practice of imperial rule. Admittedly, "neglect" seems like a weird term to apply to empire. The heavy Foucauldianism of colonial and postcolonial studies has yielded a picture of empire as indefatigable, busy regulating, controlling, shaping, and ending the lives of colonial subjects. It is indeed an image that empire solicits: the archive at Kew bulges with metric tons of proof that empire never relinquished attention over the colonial world. Moreover, as seminal texts of postcolonial studies demonstrated, the cultural archive of Britain is structured by an imperial unconscious: even when empire seems far away, it is right there, symptomatically present in the parlor of Mansfield Park.[16] No one was neglected. To describe empire as neglectful seems mistaken for another reason, too: the charge of neglect inscribes empire within a normative framework that much social thought and humanistic critique takes to be inapplicable to the realities of imperial power. Empire, we know, was (and is) always indifferent to the claims of imperial subjects; to postulate that it had a duty it could neglect is to be foolish, at best, and to reproduce a racist-civilizational alibi for empire, at worst. Yet I will argue that there is a stark discontinuity between the forms of attention Britain extended and the kinds that West Indians desired. the practices of governmentality or metropolitan Britons' weak awareness that empire existed did not equate to the form of political legibility West Indians desired. Moreover, to take empire as a form of power that ineluctably excepts itself from normative bindings of the political—one that will achieve form *only* through practices of governmentality or in the metropolitan unconscious—is precisely to recapitulate the emergent conceptualization against which West Indians wrote. From elite plantation owners to their emancipated ex-slaves, from Tory protectionists to mulatto socialists, West Indians across the lines of race and class strove to render legible the subtle institution of neglect and, by so doing, to recompose empire as a political world bound to accord meaning and value to West Indian lives—whatever the economic value of the West Indies.

Etymologically, neglect connotes the activity of not reading, of not gathering together, and (in a maximal philosophical sense) of not gathering something into a given *logos*.[17] Liberalization constituted West Indians as empire's negligible subjects—they could neither compel British attention through the citation of political logics nor gesture to the economic value of the islands and were functionally rendered invisible in the liberal order of things. Published a year after the epochal votes on free trade, Charlotte Brontë's *Jane Eyre* (1847) neatly encodes this shift: the creole Bertha is locked away; Rochester simply ignores the legal ties binding them together; Bertha offs herself in an enactment of free-trade fantasies that the islands would simply disappear; and the moral and narratological horizon of the novel shifts toward St. John Rivers's India. The heterogeneous subjects I mark off as "West Indian" were fashioned through this double play of ignored ties and divested care. My use of the term "West Indian" refers less to a stable identity or a demographic population than to heterogeneous subject positions that emerged as the opposition—and in opposition—to the consolidation of liberal-capitalist logics. Moreover, this was the term that my subjects themselves used; it was only at the tail end of the liberal project, concomitant with Britain's transfer of regional hegemony to the United States, that the neutral geographic signifier "Caribbean" would come to replace the historically and political laden term "West Indies," and then only unevenly. It might be tempting to imagine that these broad political and economic transformations went on above the heads of all but the most elite of West Indians, but they did not. Debates over market liberalization and free trade enflamed both elite and subaltern publics throughout the Atlantic world, just as neoliberal globalization has been an item of popular and elite debate and contestation today.[18] If critiques of free trade were common across classes, however, race differentially allocated the effects of liberalization, differentially patterned responses to it, and opened up different possibilities for managing the rise of neglect as an imperial practice.[19] Binding these different and frequently antagonistic positions together is the normative fantasy that the empire should work to sustain West Indian life and the despair attending the recognition that British attentions were going elsewhere. Rather than marking a coherent form of subjectivity, then, "West Indian" names the incoherence of varied subjectivities de- and reconstituted by the de- and reconstitution of the British Empire.

Drawing as heavily as I do on West Indian self-description to track the imperial practice of neglect, I am interested in the selves fashioned and formed as performative effects of those descriptions. What happens when subjects relate to themselves as if they are neglected? Neglect is a profound experience of nonsovereignty, one that locates the possibilities of one's being in a world in the attenuated attentions of another. Yet a low-grade, subtle optimism underwrites neglect's affective repertoire of loneliness, incompletion, and diminishment. To feel oneself neglected is to inscribe the present tense of another's inattention within an anticipatory horizon of the other's return, enabling one to periodize nonrelation as a brief hiatus, a temporary withdrawal. Neglect thus poses the diminution or even absence of a relation as the grounds for that relation's construction, reparation, or reanimation.[20] Throughout this book, I explore how West Indian critiques of imperial neglect worked to attach subjects to a world that was turning away from them. In many ways, then, complaining about imperial neglect is an inherently conservative act: it retains a particular horizon of political legibility as the only horizon of legibility imaginable or desirable. It is also, however, fantastically, critically utopian. It envisions the reconstitution of a world such that those neglected by it would be accorded legibility within it, a world in which, to follow Rancière, the uncounted might count.[21]

Empire of Neglect explores how this double play of world maintenance and world building would ultimately result in a vexed reorientation of West Indian political and literary imaginaries toward the hemispheric Americas. Indeed, glancing at the figures, generic forms, and imaginative geographies prevalent in this literature, one would hardly be able to guess that subjects of the British Empire wrote much of the writing this book considers. Following Britain's turn to free trade, Simón Bolívar figures more prominently in this archive than Queen Victoria; *Uncle Tom's Cabin* is drawn on more frequently than *Bleak House*; and Boston and Caracas serve more readily as settings than London and Liverpool. This literature might seem to demonstrate West Indian writers' participation in the hemispheric circuits of political, commercial, and cultural exchange that scholars of the transnational Americas have identified in the past two decades. Yet West Indian writers did not approach the hemisphere with the inspiriting, expansionist thrill of building *nuestra América*.[22] Rather, the Americas functioned as a surrogate for the imperial world that West Indians could not inhabit but to which they remained melancholically attached.[23] Unfortunately, scholars have largely failed to include the nineteenth-century British West Indies within hemispheric American studies. This is partly a result of the field's mooring in U.S. literature and American studies departments and its development out of studies of U.S. empire.[24] As an analytic topos, the "hemisphere" tends to be configured by the itineraries of U.S. empire building, and the British West Indies went blessedly unvisited by Yankee gunboats for most of the nineteenth century. The hemispheric itinerary that I trace diverges from these trends, insofar as this creole America emerged less through the dynamics of U.S. expansionism—although these dynamics certainly shaped West Indians' engagement with the hemisphere—than as an alternative to problems internal to the British Empire. Some writers, such as the Trinidadian Michel Maxwell Philip and the Jamaican Mary Seacole, used the imaginative geography of the hemisphere to model postliberal forms of imperial relation: they wrote to empire by writing through the Americas. Others, such as the Trinidadian mulatto radical George Numa Des Sources, who founded a short-lived socialist colony in postcolonial Venezuela, sought to build new, postliberal worlds in the New World. In all cases, the Americas emerged as an alternative horizon of political belonging that promised West Indians (and especially black West Indians) forms of political legibility and social care denied them in the liberalized empire. As we will see, the United States plays but a minor role in this hemispheric formation. The writers I explore looked more to the south than to the north as they sought new worlds.

This book offers an account, then, of the political, economic, cultural, and affective processes through which West Indian writers situated their worlds in the Americas. In so doing, it follows the work of other hemispheric scholars in moving beyond programmatic demands that we take the hemisphere seriously as an analytic frame and beyond geographically determinist models that take the hemisphere as a given unit of analysis.[25] I am rather interested in the historical conditions of possibility that incite subjects to dramatically remap their worlds. The analytic frames that I deploy are thus responsive to the political orientations and reorientations of the subjects I explore: scalar shifts register recompositions of political imaginaries. Indeed, it is perhaps only on the basis of the reorientation I track that the psychic and affective violence of imperial liberalization can become apparent. The occluded violence of imperial neglect becomes most visible when we realize that it so devastated West Indians' worlds that they were impelled to turn to a new one: the New World itself.

Political Economy and One Origin of West Indian Literature

At first glance, it might seem strange that West Indian writers invested so heavily in the arcane knowledge buried in political economic treatises or in the minutiae of debates over economic governance. What could be less susceptible to literary treatment than tariff law? Yet West Indians' literary investment in such topics is so superficially apparent that one need not undertake allegorical acrobatics to find the economic in their literary writing. The white Jamaican Francis Cyrus Perkins's lyric "The Planter's Petition"

(ca. 1846), for instance, laments the inauguration of British free-trade policies; sixty years later, the black St. Kittsian George Reginald Margetson's long
poem *England in the West Indies: A Neglected and Degenerating Empire* (1906)
would lament their persistence. But the impact of economic thought and
practice went far beyond supplying objects to West Indian writers. More decisively, the rise of political economy structured the function of West Indian
literature in local, regional, and imperial public spheres. Indeed, what I have
rather hastily been calling "West Indian literature" emerged as a generic and
epistemological alternative to political economy.[26] This literature offered an
alternative mode of reading the relationship between polity and economy at
odds with the emergent discipline they castigated as neglectful.

To understand how literary genres came to serve in this function requires
understanding the broader discursive and generic ecology of West Indian
writing. It is a little remarked on but nonetheless remarkable fact that no
British West Indian—however broadly we define the term—wrote a book
bearing the title "A Political Economy" throughout the period of the discipline's consolidation or, indeed, wrote anything that would be legible to us
as a treatise of political economy.[27] This archival lacuna is odd for a couple of
reasons. Given the commercial orientation of West Indian life, creole textual
culture was saturated with mundane genres of economic writing. Business
correspondence, plantation books of account, and various forms of legal and
financial instruments were the stuff of the plantation world's scribal ordinary. At the same time, West Indian elites were not the indolent ignoramuses
of abolitionist caricature. It is now well established that elites across the
Caribbean participated in and made contributions to Enlightenment-era
scientific inquiry, that many elite West Indians had high levels of education,
that some were avid readers of political economy, and that a select few even
sat in the same parliamentary chamber as David Ricardo.[28] They wrote both
multivolume tomes of colonial history that rigorously considered economic
development and occasional interventions into pressing economic debates.
They wrote manuals on plantation husbandry and discourses on tropical
medicine. They even wrote poems, plays, and novels concerned with aspects
of economic life. But at no point did a West Indian write a political economy.
Reading the logic of an absence is an uncertain enterprise, but I want to suggest that the lack of a West Indian political economy is the product less of
ignorance, creole indolence, or the contingencies of history than it is itself
an argument—that, in effect, this lacuna in the archive of creole letters possesses a robust positivity and even quietly articulates a fierce polemic.[29]

For West Indians, political economy was an inherently "anticolonial" enterprise—and that was not a good thing.[30] Indeed, almost as soon as Smith published *The Wealth of Nations*, West Indians approached political economy as a unified discourse that achieved coherence and regularity through a devaluation of the imperial world. Bryan Edwards, for instance, takes a moment in his monumental 1793 history of the British West Indies to chastise those "Political economists" who "theorize concerning the utility of colonies"— one of the first usages of the collective noun.[31] Decades later, Alexander Mac-Donnell's *Colonial Commerce* (1828) would decry the "Political Economists who are most in vogue" for their approach to colonial affairs.[32] Between these two, and beyond, the West Indian public sphere lit up with critiques of political economy; as MacDonnell would relate, the possible policy effects of this emergent, increasingly hegemonic discourse had induced an "intense anxiety" in the West Indies.[33] How could the technical idiom of political economy have engendered such intense affective responses? The problem was not, as one might expect, political economy's critique of slavery—which did not really exist.[34] Nor was it solely that political economy's investment in free markets threatened the profits of West Indian planters and merchants— although it did. The problem, rather, was that the very discipline of political economy was built on the destruction of the imperial polity.[35] West Indian critiques of political economy were defenses of their position within empire, as well as of empire itself.

From Adam Smith onward, political economists and their popularizers frequently staged empire's end to limn the existence of an economic order superordinate to the dictates of the state. As the rumble of canon and shot from Lexington and Concord echoed around the Atlantic, *The Wealth of Nations* posed a simple question to its readers: was empire worth it? Smith would answer no: Britain "derives nothing but a loss from the dominion which she assumes over her colonies."[36] Yet the answer Smith gives is less important than the very articulation of the question. Smith takes the corrosion of imperial sovereignty marked by the eruption of imperial civil war as an opportunity to disembed economic logics from political rationalities. Smith had cast economic relations as an epistemic domain autonomous from the political much earlier in his treatise, making a distinction between economic and political power in a gentle critique of "Mr. Hobbes."[37] This theoretical distinction, however, had minimal purchase in a world where sovereign states everywhere aspired to control economic processes to augment state power. As Mary Poovey has written, Smith's political economy is epistemologically riven by the fact that it could not descriptively, empirically render what it sought to theorize: the systematic, natural market.[38] Smith used the collapse of empire into civil war to modulate *The Wealth of Nations*'s latent epistemological crisis: it made empirically intelligible the effective existence of a supersensible, systematic economic order over which no sovereign was truly sovereign. Following Smith, political economists returned again and again to the American Revolution to demonstrate the viability of an auto-regulative commercial order formed by the sovereign state's withdrawal. Political economy cognitively disembedded the market from the polity by staging the dismantling of empire.[39]

For West Indians, political economy's epistemic separation of the economic from the political threatened profound alterations in the political constitution and political imaginary of the empire. As legal scholars have attested, the imperial constitution of Britain's Atlantic empire had always been incredibly indeterminate. Heterogeneous legislatures and legal codes striated the empire; it was composed of largely autonomous spaces that were federated but lacked a coherent and explicit constitutional form.[40] For members of this fragile polity, economic connections frequently stood in for formalized political relations. What we might think of as economic transactions articulated the relationship between imperial subject and imperial sovereign—the export duties that were paid to the Crown, say, or the preferential tariffs that West Indian produce received on Britain's markets. For West Indians, these seemingly "economic" relations materialized empire as a field of reciprocal protections and obligations, a polity by negotiated compact if not by coherent design. This understanding of economic relations underwrote all discussions of West Indian commercial life, from Edward Long's and Bryan Edwards's encyclopedic accounts of West Indian history through petitions and pamphlets addressed to the Crown. West Indians even offered arguments for free trade long before this policy would be identified as anti-imperial in tendency, as a privilege the Crown should extend to deserving subjects.[41] One postemancipation Jamaican peasants' petition to Queen Victoria—the one whose incompetent response from the Colonial Office partially set off the Morant Bay Rebellion in 1865—requested that the Crown establish what was basically a joint-stock company for the landless peasantry in recognition of their condition as Her Majesty's impoverished subjects.[42] Following Louis Dumont's description of mercantilist economic writing, we might take West Indians' approach to empire as "mingl[ing] the phenomena we classify into economic and political. They considered economic phenomena from the point of view of the polity."[43] But we might tweak it, too: West Indians surrogated an imperial political perspective through considerations of economic phenomena, deducing an imperial polity from the multiplicity of economic interactions. As it became hegemonic, political economy decomposed the epistemic and discursive contexts in which such acts of mingling or surrogation would make sense. Take a single keyword, "protection." In the 1780s, it still rang out with early modern, Hobbesian connotations of a sovereign's obligation to his subjects; by 1846, it would more narrowly name the economic instruments that had once mediated that political relation.[44] Empire was functionally depoliticized as a consequence of political economy's analytic disembedding of the economic from the political, leaving imperial subjects without a coherent idiom or imaginary of imperial political belonging.

West Indian literature emerged to create the discursive and epistemic framework within which empire could become legible as a polity that gathered West Indians into it as constituent members. West Indians did not write political economies, no; instead, they wrote novels and poems to theorize political and economic relations. By refusing to think economic affairs through the forms that increasingly claimed an epistemic monopoly over them, West Indian writers enacted a refusal at the level of genre to engage the economic as if it could cohere into autonomous, discrete epistemic field. Literature thus developed much differently in the West Indian from how it developed in the contemporary metropolitan Britain. Whereas metropolitan writers posited an autonomous field of literary value in response to the political economy's autonomization of economic value, West Indian writers never conceded the autonomy of the economic in the first place.[45] Rather, West Indian literature sought to theorize the economic while simultaneously reembedding it as a subordinate component in a broader imaginary of the polity. As a consequence, West Indian writers never posited literature as possessing an autonomous, self-evident value, either; the literature I explore is almost entirely, unapologetically indifferent to literariness. (As you will see, much of it reads that way, too.) The Barbadian writer J. W. Orderson, for instance, would acknowledge that "*West Indian Literature*" had not "climbed the higher steeps of Parnassus, nor . . . [did it] occupy any eminent station in the flowery paths of *Belles Lettres*."[46] But for Orderson, as for others, the value of West Indian literature derived not from its aesthetic quality but from its presentation of "facts"—that is, for its referential relationship to the social, economic, and political world from which it emerged.[47] Obviously, the factuality of this discourse is debatable, particularly through the era of slavery, but that is part of my point: creole writers used literary genres to describe worlds in order to circulate alternative norms and epistemologies for thinking empire.

I thus read this literary archive as articulating a peripheral form of politico-economic theory that is fundamentally opposed to the discursive and epistemological order installed by political economy, generalized through multiple popularizing recensions, and eventually instituted in state practice. While this argument is motivated by a desire to specify more precisely what literature actually did for West Indian writers, another part of my aim is to broaden our sense today of literary genres' epistemic and political possibilities. Literature is rarely content to be literature or content to assume a coherence or stability that could make the very term "literature" something more than a catachresis or a marketing category. I do not mean this in the sense that literature absolves itself from any ontological or epistemological configuration that would ensnare it, although I do tend to keep faith with this deconstructive and postdeconstructive claim articulated differently by Jacques Derrida, Jean-Luc Nancy, and Philippe Lacoue-Labarthe. I mean it in the humbler sense that a great deal of literature intends to push and present knowledge for and within domains of social being, an intention whose aims are irreducible to the aesthetic: it wants to tell us something about race, about politics, about (why not?) tariff law. Indeed, literary genres are sites of epistemological democratization, even communization, for populations with diminished access to the generic and epistemic codes of expert knowledge or (as in the West Indian relation to political economy) for populations whose accession to a particular generic and epistemic code necessitates a violation of their form of life.[48] This is particularly true of much of the (post)colonial world, where the formation of higher institutions of (Western) disciplinary knowledge production developed well after the formation of colonial literary cultures, which even then made themselves available to only small segments of the population. Indeed, as many postcolonial scholars have argued, literary genres might more adequately map the political and social realities of postcolonial life than the social sciences do or can.[49] They certainly map vernacular social imaginaries far better. The enduring maldistribution of access to expert knowledge means that most thought cannot be thought through the epistemic and generic codes that organize what counts as disciplinary "knowledge."[50] And yet, thinking happens, a lot of it, and frequently in the amateurish space of to-hand literary genres: novels, short stories, poems, plays. Literature is the peculiar anti-institution—or even ante-institution—that interrupts settled distributions of knowledge with the otherwise illegible thinking of those about whom disciplinary knowledge is bound to not care. And it was through literary genres that West Indians would make a claim that the emergent discipline of political economy was founded on neglecting: that they were rights-bearing members of an imperial polity.

The Vanishing Horizon of Empire

From the vantage of our postcolonial present, it might be surprising that empire constituted the horizon of political legibility for West Indians. Indeed, I began research for this book hoping to identify a cultural link between the full emancipation of enslaved West Indians in 1838 and the incipiently anticolonial labor rebellions that swept through the region in 1938. My aim was to excavate nineteenth-century proto-nationalist "foundational fictions" to displace the conventional understanding that Windrush generation authors in postwar London originated British West Indian literature.[51] Reading across a handful of recently recovered nineteenth-century texts shattered my expectations of them: I found everything but anticolonial nationalism.[52] That is, I found an intense fealty to the British Empire, on one hand, and an emergent investment in the hemispheric Americas, on the other. Where is the nation? I wondered. It had to be somewhere, but it was not. Reading across imperial discourse of the era—and, in particular, empire-scaling debates over economic liberalism—I came to realize that this archive was offering an account of my own incomprehension of its politics. Like the liberal economic discourse this literature emerged to critique, I neglected to consider these writers in the way they insisted on being considered—as rights-bearing subjects of an expansive imperial polity. What required explanation, I realized, was not why colonial subjects understood themselves as political subjects of empire, but the opposite. How had it become nearly unthinkable to imagine empire as the horizon of subjects' political lives, as the existential framework that gathered their worlds into a coherent order?

Reading empire as a viable state form, one that organized the affective and imaginative lives of colonial subjects, requires rethinking the political epistemologies of the contemporary disciplines. As Frederick Cooper argues, the "standard view of global political history of the nineteenth and twentieth centuries" is one of "a long and inexorable transition from empire to nation-state."[53] As Cooper suggests, focusing primarily on French African decolonization, this narrative evacuates the contingencies of process from the decolonizing transition.[54] Moreover, this narrative inhibits the development of a critical idiom for reading the politics of those who refuse to submit to the iron historical law of nation formation. Colonial subjects are always supposed to be moving out of empire. How, then, do we address those who seem to dwell within it? As David Sartorius remarks, scholars of the colonial world routinely encounter "pro-colonial affinities" in their archives, only to dismiss them "as the misfires of historical subjects acting against their interests: dupes, victims, collaborators."[55] Subjected to functionalist explanation or ideological demystification, conventional approaches to empire occlude what Antoinette Burton calls "imperial facticity," which I take to name the ways in which empire might appear to subjects as their unremarkable, ordinary political world.[56] This occlusion becomes weirder when we consider that most people, for most of world history, built lives within empires. It is the nation-state that is exceptional, the contingent product of the Age of Revolutions that took about a century and a half to become the default unit of sovereignty in the world system.

Yet for a contemporary world system that is epistemologically and institutionally structured by postimperial norms, empires present and past can appear only as anomalous deviations from the proper order of things. In part, our inability to approach empire in its facticity is a product of the decolonization projects of the mid-twentieth century. The anticolonial moment wound up binding popular sovereignty—and so, for a liberal state system, the political itself—to the institutional form of the nation-state. Empire was correspondingly redefined negatively as a foreign polity's direct or indirect intervention into a national people's autonomous administration of its affairs (what I would call imperialism). Yet, as Martha Kaplan and John Kelly have argued, the epistemic, normative, and institutional fabrication of the nation-based state system was not only the outcome of liberationist anticolonial movements; it was equally a "new, global plan for political order" overseen by the United States.[57] Anticolonial movements were ultimately conscripted into a global state order that was entirely functional for U.S. hegemony at the same moment that empire more or less vanished as a meaningful political concept and became instead a term of polemic—and a polemical term that worked to reinscribe the normativity of the nation-state.[58] Ann Stoler has argued that colonial studies subsequently "produced a representational archive of empire" and particular models of imperial rule in which "empire is seen as an extension of nation-states, not as another way—and sometimes prior way—of organizing a polity."[59] Put differently, the rightly critiqued "methodological nationalism" of the social sciences and the humanities is always already a methodological postimperialism.[60]

This methodological postimperialism has informed much scholarship on the British Empire in the age of free trade. While a generation of imperial historians, under the influence of J. R. Seeley, understood liberalization as a watershed moment, scholars today tend to deny that free trade was indeed a "great transformation" in the imperial world.[61] Indeed, empire is largely absent from the signal, much cited theoretical account of the liberal era: Karl Polanyi's *The Great Transformation* (1944). Polanyi waxes apocalyptic about the repeal of the Corn Laws but has nothing to say about the Sugar Duties Act; he laments liberalization's decimation of the social and moral fabric of British life but does not register how it decimated the broader imperial polity. My point is not that Polanyi *should* have assumed a broad imperial optic in assessing liberalization's impact. It is, rather, that the political cartography assembled by liberalization functionally made such an optic unavailable.[62] Similarly, more contemporary scholarship on free trade tends to approach the process as if it is narratable from the perspective of Britons alone. Part of the problem is archive selection: focusing on British policy makers, parties, or parliamentary voting patterns ensures that West Indians will be occluded.[63] Scholars who explicitly address empire do not do much better. John Gallagher and Ronald Robinson's influential "free trade imperialism" thesis reinscribes the narrow analytic perspective of Little Britain even as it tracks the expansion of British imperial involvements throughout the era. While liberal mid-Victorians—like antiliberal West Indians—understood Britain to be anti-imperial, Gallagher and Robinson hew to the fact of Britain's multiform and growing entanglements around the world to argue that the empire of free trade was broadly continuous with the mercantilist empire that preceded it and the neo-mercantilist empire to follow it.[64] The "imperialism of free trade" thesis is more Cobdenite than it would perhaps care to admit, insofar as a narrowly defined Britain serves as the analytic perspective that synthesizes the diffuse and dispersed activities that, for Gallagher and Robinson, constitute empire: investment in South America, wars in China, state building in India, colonization in Australia, the retention of formal colonies elsewhere, and so on. Here, "empire" functions as a catachresis for Little Britain's expansion beyond the small islands in the North Atlantic; it is not a state or a polity so much as what Great (not Greater) Britain did.

Unwittingly, these critical accounts of free trade metaleptically posit an effect of liberalization—an insularly definable British polity—as the process's presiding subject. From Smith on, liberal political economy worked to build the spacing of the political that latter-day historians take as common sense. Thus, in the final paragraph of *The Wealth of Nations*, Smith writes that Britain had accrued the debt of imperial war making through the eighteenth century because "the colonies were *supposed* to be provinces of the British empire." Given the fact that the colonies did not support their defense well enough— they did not pay their own way—Smith declared Britain's empire to be one "in imagination only," a "golden dream."[65] By distinguishing the imperial from the provincial, Smith cognitively scales the political space of Britain down to the Three Kingdoms; moreover, by deriding empire as a "golden dream," he denies it politico-ontological status. The political cartography projected by Smith would gain traction through the nineteenth century—ironically, even as Britain busied itself asserting its "moral *imperium*" in the West Indies.[66] On one hand, political economists would increasingly delaminate Britain from the empire, tending to define colonial trade as foreign trade. On the other hand, political processes worked to consolidate the political at the level of Little Britain. In particular, Reform in 1832 functionally expelled the West India interest from Parliament, with the effect that the islands no longer had secure representation in the empire's legislative body.[67] Finally, the passage of free-trade legislation in 1846 dramatically confirmed the exteriority of the colonial world from the British polity: from the perspective of Britain's liberalized markets, Jamaica was as foreign to Britain as Cuba, or Trinidad as Brazil. The West Indies were conceived of less as political members of an expansive polity than as expensive "property" (as Cobden put it) of the British nation.[68] And not just expensive: free traders such as John Ramsay McCulloch and Cobden described the islands as expendable and recommended simply abandoning them.[69]

McCulloch and Cobden are perhaps limit cases, but the very idea that the islands were detachable, nonintegral components of the British polity enabled the development of a rationale of imperial rule as flexible as the free markets that underwrote it. The liberalization of Britain's markets maximized the mobility of British capital, allowing capitalists to divest from the declining colonies and invest in more profitable sites within and beyond the empire. Claiming imperial subjecthood could no longer compel British capital or British concern to stick around. Indeed, the very status of imperial subject underwent a profound transformation. As liberal economic reason subsumed imperial political logics, liberal jurists and statesmen would attempt to provide a *nomos* for an empire whose ontic persistence could not be squared with its theoretical and institutional dismantling. The emergence of ideologemes of responsible governance for the lighter-skinned colonies made thinkable—as the U.S. Revolution did for Smith—a tendential political division of empire in the name of bestowing representative government to white colonists, allowing for fiscal retrenchment in Britain, and maintaining healthy commerce among all parts. At the same time, statesmen and jurists suggested that empire should persist for the darker folk of the world not because colonial subjects had a political right to inclusion in the empire, but because Britain was bestowing a gift of civilizing governance to prepare the uncivilized for self-rule.[70] Scholars tend to read such rhetoric as providing ideological cover for an empire expanding throughout Asia and the Pacific, and so it did. Yet what served as a justification for the intensified incorporation of Asia into the political and economic world of Britain functioned as an alibi for Britain's turn from the West Indies.[71] The replacement of political with economic logics supplemented by racial moralism as empire's foundation rendered West Indians' relation to Britain precarious, dependent as it was on the moral voluntarism of metropolitan Britons, even as liberalization facilitated the divestment of British capital and British concern from the West Indies to locations elsewhere. By positioning empire in the horizon of the nation-state—even if this horizon was infinitely deferred—the liberalized empire refused to consider empire itself a meaningful location of political relation. In Stoler's terms, liberalization rendered empire a "moving target," a form of relation that evaded capture by political normativities.[72]

From the late eighteenth century until today, metropolitan social theory has been unable to sight the emergence of neglect as a practice of imperial rule precisely because the neglect of empire constitutes the deep structure of its various epistemologies. I want to suggest that the practice of neglect—and thus the crisis it occasioned for West Indians—can become legible only by adopting the perspective of those negotiating their instituted illegibility. Williams's opus *Capitalism and Slavery* (1944) is a key text for opening up this perspective. In many ways, *Capitalism and Slavery* is the West Indian twin of Polanyi's *The Great Transformation*: it supplements Polanyi's fixation on Britain with an emphasis on the empire in ways that enable us to see the polity-destroying gravity of the transformations that Polanyi narrowly narrates as the history of a small island in the North Atlantic. While Williams's text is frequently (and reductively) taken as an economistic critique of hagiographic historiography on abolition, it is more properly read as an account of how the West Indies came to be "forgotten" in the wake of abolition and emancipation.[73] Interpreting abolition in 1807 and emancipation in 1834/38 from the horizon of liberalization in 1846, Williams could not reconcile the intense investment of imperial concern attending the first two events with the neglect instituted by the last.[74] As he goes on to explain, capitalism deploys and produces certain social formations for accumulation in one era (such as plantation colonies during mercantilist empire), only to divest from these forms to enhance the valorization of capital in another (as with liberalization).[75] Williams's account of liberal capitalism's dynamics tracks Randy Martin's account of neoliberal capitalism: "Capitalism's drive for self-expansion forces people together to create forms of life that encumber social wealth, whose limitations capital subsequently flees."[76] *Capitalism and Slavery*'s mix of outrage, melancholia, and sarcastic realism—captured in the pseudo-Burkean epigraph to this introduction—derives from the fact that Britain did not care to sustain the imperial "form of life" that it had violently fostered and then freed. Williams's approach to capitalism is indeed rather economistic inasmuch as he sees the dismantling of the mercantilist empire as a foregone conclusion; yet the normative force of Williams's work derives from his outrage that the imperial polity nonetheless did not block capital from divesting from a world in which imperial subjects were forced to invest. In other words, *Capitalism and Slavery* is a scathing critique of imperial neglect   even if Williams, writing on the cusp of decolonization, did not himself care to be included in an imperial polity.

A century earlier, West Indian writers encountered this depoliticization of empire as a crisis of neglect without the imaginative and affective buffer afforded by the nationalist alternative. As we will see, this refusal of nationalism was overdetermined by multiple conditions, but here I want to foreground the islands' unique histories of settlement and development. By the era of free trade, there were few local frames of political reference beyond the empire within which West Indians, black or white, could emplot their worlds. The political dislocation of the Middle Passage, as well as the fact that by the 1840s most black West Indians had been born in the islands, meant that empire appeared less like a foreign invader than like the quotidian but deep structure of West Indian reality.[77] Empire was "the political reality with which [West Indians] lived," the underived ordinary within whose coordinates West Indians mapped their relation to the world.[78] They were, to supplement David Scott's lovely phrase, conscripts of imperial modernity.[79] When I suggest, then, that liberalization induced a crisis in West Indian political imaginaries, my point is not that West Indians, black or white, loved empire, gladly sang Victoria's praises, or invested much positive affect in the relation—although there was plenty of that. My point is rather that empire served as an assumed horizon of political legibility that the discursive and institutional dynamics of liberal racial capitalism displaced.[80] For West Indians, empire was a "form of life," as Martin might put it. It was created by millions of people forced together (and who forced people together) with differentiated degrees of violence; it was nonetheless the world in which West Indians sought freedom, became emancipated, and imagined themselves as political subjects. Confronting liberalization's disembedding of Britain's polity and economy from the formal structures of empire, West Indian writers attempted to reanimate the empire as a political world to halt the flight of British capital and British concern.[81] In so doing, they generated an epistemic framework through which the dynamics of neglect could be exposed, understood, and critiqued.

Paradoxically, the form of critique developed against liberal political economy functioned to attach subjects to a world that was detaching from them. In many ways, the imperial polity that creoles invoked to manage the crisis of liberalization did not preexist its putative dissolution; the empire creoles desired did not preexist their citations of its loss. For this reason, it is a moot point whether Britons ever recognized West Indians as political subjects of the empire, or whether the imperial state had ever worked according to norms of obligation, reciprocity, and protection. The empire that West Indians imaginatively produced in response to the rise of economic liberalism is irreducibly discontinuous with the empire that actually existed, just as it is irreducibly discontinuous with the ways in which Britons imagined, conceptualized, and practiced empire.[82] West Indians looked to empire for political belonging not because they had it in the past—after all, as enslaved, most of them did not—but because they needed to reanimate a vanishing horizon of political relation in the present. West Indians' insistent invocation of a nonneglectful empire thus functioned catachrestically, as an a-referential formation of an always already lost object that enabled them to articulate political demands to negotiate their disorienting present. Given my insistence on the catachrestical nature of West Indians' empire imaginary, my aim in this book is not to provide a third-person, structural account of what empire was, such as one finds in the work of Alexander Motyl.[83] Instead, I take definitional or foundational accounts of what empire is—both historical and contemporary—to be already and necessarily bound up in a mutating field of situated political fantasies. Tracking these fantasies requires maintaining an analytic intimacy with my subjects, such that the indicative and subjunctive moods of my own writing blur as I come to inhabit West Indians' peculiar structure of feeling. Indeed, neglect becomes legible only from a fantasy-laden perspective that empire was, could have been, or could be different. The critical idiom of neglect functioned analogously to the way that critical keywords generated in response to capitalism's restructuring of the social function of the state—"precarity," "abandonment," "disposability," and so on.[84] These markers of social catastrophe orient the present around the functional absence of a "past" form of the state; in so doing, they conscript critical affects and imaginaries into a cruel optimistic relationship with the state in its present form. The result is a bounded and binding poiesis, a fabulation of a world to come that intensifies the hope subjects have in the mutability of the world that, at the moment, does not care for their presence within it.

The Hemispheric Turn

Liberalization reconstituted the political cartography of Britain such that West Indians could no longer immediately or intuitively assume the British Empire as their political world. *Empire of Neglect* argues that British West Indian writers encoded their subtraction from the empire as an entrance into worlds exorbitant to it. Hemispheric American geographies, histories, and literary genres overtake those of the British Empire in the literature produced in the wake of free trade. These narratives—which are almost always tales of orphans and illegitimate mulatto children—symbolically render liberalization as a process of parental abandonment, one that can be repaired only through the formation of political, kinship, and romantic ties in the hemisphere. For some West Indians, the Americas came into being as an imaginative and practical site through which they could manage their functional expulsion from the imperial polity. I say "some" because, without a more concerted effort at recovery, the to-hand literary record of the nineteenth century is too small to admit generalizations; moreover, the significant literary texts we possess are biased toward Trinidad and Jamaica (with some input from Barbados, British Guiana, and elsewhere). Nonetheless, within the texts we do possess, the Americas functioned as a placeholder for the desires, fantasies, and hopes that could no longer readily or easily attach to Britain. For this reason, the hemispheric reorientation I trace is not a stark rupture with West Indians' imperial past. Rather, West Indians' turn toward and encounter with the Americas was structured by the perduring sense that they belonged elsewhere. Within this discursive, affective, and political ecology, the Americas became a zone of political investment for West Indians insofar as they functioned as a surrogate for Britain—as a displaced repetition of a world West Indians could not have but could not not want.

Part of my argument here is that the usability of the hemisphere as a scale of literary and historical analysis for these materials is dependent on and subordinate to West Indians' relations to intraimperial transformations. As many literary scholars and historians have shown, the British West Indies had long been connected to points in the New World through shared histories of conquest and settlement and flows of commodities, capital, and people.[85] There is, however, a fundamental discontinuity between scholarly and historical subjects' modes of world mapping, and the observable empirics of circulation cannot stand in for the phenomenological, affective, and political orientations through which subjects locate their worlds. Indeed, one source of the frustration that has accompanied hemispheric American studies from the beginning is that it is simply easier to identify "the Americas" as an analytic field materialized by the circulation of stuff than it is to find Americans or Americanos who inhabit the hemisphere as their political world.[86] Thus, while British West Indian subjects routinely interacted with other points in the New World, the density of empirical articulations with American polities did little to affect the contour of West Indian political identifications. Indeed, as Andrew Jackson O'Shaughnessy has argued, the emergence of colonial independence movements in the Americas—and the American Revolution of 1776 first and foremost—reattached planter elites to the British imperial polity, even as they continued to agitate for local autonomy in governmental affairs and for freer rights of trade with American polities.[87] It was only with liberalization in 1846, when they understood themselves as abandoned by empire, that West Indians would begin to consider themselves in a broadly American frame of reference. The hemisphere operates in this book less as a cartographic given or a field of empirical connections than as the imaginative space constituted by a political project. It functioned as a flickering horizon of time-bound social possibility whose value was structured by the negativity of imperial neglect and abandonment.[88]

These projects of hemispheric reorientation were heterogeneous, riven by the multiple modalities by which neglect fashioned subjects in the West Indies. West Indians approached the hemisphere in diverse ways. Elite white West Indians turned to hemispheric frames of analysis to describe the ironic effects and possible consequences of liberalization. As I show in chapter 3, creole pamphleteers argued that liberalization in Britain intensified slavery and territorial imperialism in the hemisphere: imperial neglect would result in the islands' abandonment to reenslavement at the hands of Yankee filibusterers. According to this line of argument, Britain needed to return to imperial protectionism so that plantation owners could both protect black West Indians from U.S. conquest and civilize them through the extension of remunerative wage labor. The expansionist presence of the United States in the hemisphere similarly conditions the political imaginaries of black and brown West Indian writers. Indeed, the absence of nationalist imaginaries is readily explicable by black fears, common throughout the hemisphere, that black sovereignty was impossible in a state system that first and foremost cognized black subjects as enslaveable and in a hemisphere where the space of slavery seemed only to be expanding.[89] Put simply, black West Indians could not reiterate the U.S. declaration of independence in a world inhabited by the United States. (As we will see, black British West Indian authors marked the inadequacy of nationalist projects to their political present by refusing the modal normativity of the Haitian Revolution.) Instead, black West Indian writers gestured to U.S. slavery and imperialism as a means of recalling Britain to the promises that they associated with emancipation. At the same time, however, black West Indians increasingly drew on hemispheric American histories and geographies to model what emancipation, as an incorporation of black subjects into the imperial polity, *should* have been.

Unsurprisingly, then, it was not the United States to which most black West Indians turned in their attempt to manage the crisis of imperial neglect. They instead looked south and mobilized Spanish imperial and Spanish American histories, geographies, and political forms to imagine and theorize modes of political belonging opposed to the neglectful logics of the liberalized empire. To be sure, U.S. print culture played a remarkable role in the development of West Indian literature. The publication of Harriet Beecher Stowe's *Uncle Tom's Cabin* (1852) was perhaps *the* print event in the mid-nineteenth-century West Indies, and black and white creoles also borrowed other genres from Yankee print culture (the dime novel, socialist pamphleteering, and so on). However, these generic forms were mobilized in the service of reorienting West Indian political imaginations from the north to the south, from the anglosphere to the hispanosphere, from a neglectful empire to a new world of care. This work of reorientation is most evident in texts that maintain a link to Stowe—Michel Maxwell Philip's

Emmanuel Appadocca (1854), Marcella Noy Wilkin's *The Slave Son* (1854), and George Numa Des Sources's *Adolphus* (1853)—all historical narratives about Trinidadian slavery in which Bolívarian Venezuela replaces Canada as the realizable, desirable site of fugitive mulatto freedom. More broadly, West Indian writers recuperated Spanish imperial norms—or associated them with postimperial Spanish American polities—to fabulate the existence of multiracial states that accorded black subjects political legibility and secured their material lives with diverse forms of economic protection. Black West Indians contested liberalism by investing (what Anglos on both sides of the Atlantic thought of as) the decaying form of Spanish mercantilist empire with a political and ethical normativity opposed to liberal neglect. The quasi-Fourierist Des Sources would radicalize this fantasy, describing the imperial and postimperial regime of Venezuela as more or less socialist throughout the run of his radical newspaper, *The Trinidadian* (1849–54). As Des Sources's career attests, West Indians' investments in the Americas were not simply figurative: Des Sources would found a short-lived socialist, black autonomist colony in Venezuela in 1853. More famously, Mary Seacole's career as the "black Florence Nightingale" would begin in the isthmus of Panama, where she worked alongside thousands of other West Indians to build and service the infrastructure of transcontinental transportation systems. Des Sources and Seacole simultaneously built hemispheric alternatives to British imperial belonging *and* modeled postliberal modalities of political and economic life for Britain.

In tracing this reorientation, my aim is to argue for the poetic possibilities that accrue in zones of instituted depletion, neglect, and abandonment. Neglect is not simply a position of social death. Rather, it incites acts of worldmaking through which subjects attempt re-enfleshing forms of life that have been stripped bare.[90] By tracing the worlds West Indians formed as they sought to find a place where their presence would be meaningful to others, my aim is not to valorize endurance over exhaustion or mobility over stuckness in conditions where a population is structured as negligible. The poiesis of the world poor cannot be taken as an alibi for their impoverishment. Yet I fear that contemporary critical idioms generated in similar scenes of disposable, abandoned, or negligible life work to subsume the political semiosis of such subjects in the service of maintaining the encounter with life's other as a politico-ethical absolute. As Alexander Weheliye quips of Giorgio Agamben's influential conceptualization of bare life, "What seems to have vanished from this description is the *life* in the *bare life* compound; hence the homo sacer remains a thing, whose happening slumbers in bare life without journeying through the rivulets of liberation elsewhere."[91] As we will see throughout this book, the subtraction of "life" from "bare life," the inattention to the persistence of social vibrancy from scenes of bodily or social unworlding, was entirely functional for the installation of a political order that was neglectful of black life. Approaching life as bare disburdens the critic from listening for the fugitive, otherwise unthinkable forms of life fabricated by those for whom social life is a being toward death. Obviously, the point is not to romanticize such improvisations with structures of catastrophe. Rather, the point is that the neglected project forms of world that are necessarily discontinuous with the desires emanating from the world of the critic, the scholar, or the state.

For neglected West Indians, these worlds to come were figured by and within the New World. But West Indians' political investments in the Americas were fragile, dependent as they were on intraimperial dynamics. Indeed, they ultimately proved ephemeral. By the turn of the twentieth century, Britain would begin a return to preliberal modalities of empire; in 1919, it would reestablish the tangle of protections and preferences whose dismantling in the 1840s induced a West Indian crisis of political identification. Yet this economic reincorporation of empire did not include the political rights that an earlier generation of West Indians imagined underwrote economic relations between free peoples. Instead, this economic reincorporation of empire would relocalize political antagonism within the empire. As Britain reoriented toward and reinvested in the West Indies, West Indians reoriented their political imaginaries toward Britain. In the process, West Indians would come to inhabit the binary mapping of the political that would propel anticolonial nationalism—that of the colonizer/colonized. While West Indians would continue to travel through the Americas—and, indeed, migrate more and more to the United States—the Americas themselves would cease to hold the political meaning with which an earlier generation of writers had invested them. They would become, as V. S. Naipaul would lament decades later, a mere "fact in a geography book."[92] That Naipaul and his generation would more or less forget the writers this book treats makes sense: they inhabited another world.

Outline of Chapters

This book is organized into two parts of two chapters each, with a hinge chapter between them. While each chapter moves across various temporal units, the dominant line of the book unfolds more or less chronologically.

In part, this recourse to a chronological historical structure is an effect of the fact that readers are unlikely to be familiar with much of the material I explore or the historical coordinates in which this material is situated. At the same time, the narrative I offer is one of an accumulating crisis. The first three chapters should be read sequentially; the order matters less for the last two. Situated as this work is between British imperial and hemispheric American frames of reference, it is possible that students of American culture will find it too British and students of British culture will find it too American. I beg patience from both sets of readers, offering as my excuse that the feeling of not being where you would like is precisely the melancholic unworlding of the West Indies that I am tracing.

Part 1, "Managing Neglect," is conceptually organized by morphologies of a plantation's decline. A planter's neglect, urged husbandry manuals, would lead to a plantation's worthlessness, which would ultimately force the planter to abandon it. These keywords—"neglect," "worthlessness," "abandonment"— reappear frequently in the archives I explore as the idioms through which black and white West Indians examined their attenuating relation to the British Empire. These keywords, moreover, map onto key moments in the discursive and institutional elaboration of economic liberalism in the British imperial world: 1776, 1834, and 1846.

Chapter 1, "The Political Economy of Neglect," traces how British political economy constituted itself, in the wake of the American Revolution, through incessantly imagining the abandonment of empire. Reading key texts of political economy alongside an archive of plantation correspondence, planter and husbandry manuals, and the anonymously published novel *Marly; or, A Planter's Life in Jamaica* (1828), I explore how the figure of the planter emerged as an imperial antithesis to the neglectful sovereign of political economy. Where Smith's political economy was epistemologically and politically grounded on the possibility of the state's withdrawing attention from economic transactions, elite West Indians understood the imperial economy as propped up by obligatory, inexhaustible bestowals of attention and care from figures bound together in an incalculable web of relations. The planter emerges as a noncalculating bearer of attentiveness whose presence supplements the necessary inadequacy of any automated, market-based regime of calculable rationality. The planter's imperial gaze gathers together diverse domains of existence, countering political economy's division of the economic and the political, the imperial world and Little Britain.

Chapter 2, "'Them Worthless Ones': Emancipatory Liberalism in Jamaica," explores the vicissitudes of the emancipation process in Jamaica. In an obvious sense, emancipation worked by stripping enslaved subjects of the monetary value that their bodies bore; it worked by rendering their persons worthless and relocating value in transactional labor-power. The four-year period of Apprenticeship inaugurated in 1834 was intended to assist in this relocation of value by fashioning formerly enslaved humans into an industrious, wage-dependent peasantry. Instead, Apprenticeship constellated a durative period of worthlessness without repair, as planters hyper-exploited still-bonded laborers while they retained secure access to them. This chapter explores the divergent ways in which liberal abolitionists and Jamaican ex-slaves navigated the institution of black life as absolutely worthless. Reading across abolitionist pamphlets, I argue that abolitionists always maintained sanguine hopes for black worthlessness, arguing as many did through the 1820s and 1830s that freedom could be quickly obtained by divesting all value from the islands through market liberalization. Confronting the failure of labor markets and market rationality during Apprenticeship, abolitionists attempted to relocate the normative grounds of value from the market to the reproductive labor of Jamaican women. Reading the ex-slave James Williams's *A Narrative of Events, since the First of August, 1834* (1837) alongside the parliamentary inquiry it set off, I argue that emancipated Jamaicans sought to develop idioms of imperial subjecthood as a way to resist their slide into worthlessness. Where abolitionists picked up the figure of worthless life to reconstitute projects of liberal value production, ex-slaves moved through worthlessness to find another horizon of social being that they associated with empire.

Chapter 3, "Imperial Abandonment and Hemispheric Alternatives," examines the collapse of this fantasy of imperial belonging with the liberalization of Britain's sugar markets in 1846. Here I am interested in how liberalization's reconstitution of the politico-economic scale of Britain patterned the modalities by which liberalization would register as an event for Britons and West Indians. The West Indian writers I explore are motivated by a vexing question: how could they show that liberalization was not simply an act of fiscal fine-tuning but a dramatic event of imperial abandonment? Reading the pamphlets of the white absentee planter Matthew Higgins and the pirate novel *Emmanuel Appadocca; or, Blighted Life, a Tale of the Boucaneers* (1854), by the Trinidadian mulatto Michel Maxwell Philip, I argue that West Indian writers turned to the Americas to render legible the occluded violence of imperial abandonment. In turning to the hemisphere, Higgins and Philip fabulate new forms and norms of imperial belonging at the very moment that empire seemed threatened with wholesale dismantling—Higgins, by arguing that liberalization would ultimately result in the conquest of the islands by the United States; Philip, by recuperating fantasy-laden ideals of what the Spanish empire had once been to model a postliberal form of British imperial care. This chapter is a hinge chapter inasmuch as it begins to trace a hemispheric reorientation on the part of West Indian writers, but it is *only* a hinge insofar as this reorientation is incomplete. As Philip's novel explores, the cost of conceiving of oneself as abandoned is a melancholic introjection of the world one purportedly lost as the deep structure of one's subjectivity. Philip's novel warns, I argue, that any critique of imperial neglect or imperial abandonment risks fashioning subjects who are nothing but their wounded attachment, unable to attach to alternative horizons of political belonging.

Part 2, "Building New Worlds," is less tightly structured than part 1. This loosening of structure is a symptom of the fact that liberalization destructured West Indians' imaginative and affective worlds. Chapter 4, "Uncle Bolívar's Children," explores how black and mulatto West Indian subjects attempted to find a world in compensation for their instituted worldlessness. This chapter is centered on *The Trinidadian*, a newspaper based in Port of Spain and edited by the radical mulatto George Numa Des Sources. A vehement critic both of imperial liberalization and the racial-capitalist order of colonial Trinidad, Des Sources would urge his fellow Trinidadians of color to migrate to Numancia, a Fourierist colony he founded in Venezuela. As I argue, Des Sources's colonizing scheme was underwritten by a profound ambivalence about the possibility of black subjects' acceding to any position of political belonging in the world's interstate system, arguing that blacks were fated to political homelessness but still in need of a home. Des Sources wanted both recognizable political belonging and to subtract himself from this very problematic. This ambivalence, I argue, structured his approach to Venezuelan colonization, which was simultaneously coded as a separatist movement from any state *and* as a relocation of citizenship dreams to the postcolony. Arguing that state abandonment rendered black political imaginaries transnational by default, I explore the transnational web of literary transactions that constituted the dialectic of Des Sources's political thinking.

Reading across Des Sources's investments in Spanish imperial law, German and American utopian socialism, and the tradition of sentimental abolitionism opened by *Uncle Tom's Cabin*, I show how Des Sources's Venezuela is a composite rendered ambivalent by his conflicting desires for freedom from and proximity to the state.

Chapter 5, "A Purely 'Mercial Transaction," reads Mary Seacole's *The Wonderful Adventures of Mrs Seacole in Many Lands* (1857), a memoir that details the travels of this sutler, hotelier, and nurse from the edges of the U.S. and British empires in Panama to the edges of the British and Russian empires in the Crimea. A migrant seeking work after Jamaica's economic collapse, Seacole uses her text to valorize forms of material sociality that exceed the "purely commercial transactions" of liberalism's market. Declaring herself "Mother Seacole," she describes her affective labor as a nurse, petty trader, and hotelier throughout the Americas as a model for her mother country, Britain. Seacole's text identifies postliberal potentials that inhere in the interstices of empires. For Seacole, liberal empire depends on decidedly nonliberal economic practices for its maintenance—practices that are organized by ideologies of reciprocity, redistribution, and responsibility. Seacole poses the affective, caring, and marketing labor that she undertakes in spaces only partially incorporated into the British Empire as exemplary for how the empire should be organized. It is only in disaster zones of capital and empire such as Panama, I argue, that Seacole can imagine herself a subject of the British Empire.

This hemispheric reorientation would, however, be of fairly short duration. By way of conclusion, I explore how West Indian political imaginaries were eventually reincorporated into the empire in such a way that anticolonial nationalism became the political horizon of West Indian writing. I examine this shift by focusing on well-known West Indian responses to James Anthony Froude's famously racist travelogue, *The English in the West Indies; or, The Bow of Ulysses* (1888). Scholars tend to read these responses—particularly that of John Jacob Thomas—as inaugural sites in the history of West Indian anticolonialism. This anticolonial nationalism, I suggest, testifies to a broader transformation in the grammar of West Indian political thinking. By the twilight years of the era of free trade, West Indian writers had absorbed the epistemic and political principles of economic liberalism. Assertions of black fitness for political autonomy premised on economic achievement came to overwhelm prior generations' political idioms and imaginaries; the political cartography of colonizer-colonized began to reset the map of an integral empire that creoles strove to realize. This binary mapping occluded the third space of the Americas and all of the fantasies for which the Americas had stood. In time, anticolonial nationalism would render these other modes of being political unthinkable, unimaginable, and, above all, neglected.

PART ONE

Managing Neglect

Chapter 1

THE POLITICAL ECONOMY OF NEGLECT

Jamaica preferred "Yankee Doodle" to "God Save the Queen." Who cared?
—ERIC WILLIAMS, *Capitalism and Slavery*

Scenes of Imperial Abandonment

In his *An Essay on the Production of Wealth* (1821), Robert Torrens introduces his chapter on colonial wealth with a thought experiment. Imagine, Torrens asks, an unmet demand for sugar in the British market. Imagine, too, that in response to this demand, English gentlemen convert land best suited to sheep pasture into plantations of root vegetables from which sugar can be processed. For Torrens, the result would be "a small supply of sugar at great expense." The English proprietor could "obtain a much more abundant supply" of sugar by trading with tropical colonial producers than "by raising it at home"—as, indeed, British sugar consumers did. Theorizing colonial trade through the lens of Ricardo's doctrine of comparative advantage, Torrens's chapter seems poised to celebrate the utility and value of Britain's colonial empire. But a disconcerting question intervenes. If a "territorial division of employment" necessarily optimizes the British economy, is it necessary that this division take the institutional form of a colonial empire? Britain needs the tropics, sure—but does it need colonies?

> Here, perhaps, it may be asked,—If it is by establishing divisions of employment that the colonial trade promotes the formation of wealth, what can be the utility of incurring the expense of maintaining colonial establishments? Might not the trade which is carried on between a mother country and her colonies, be equally extensive and beneficial, though the connection between them were dissolved, and the colonies acknowledged as independent states?[1]

Torrens's questions propose a startlingly transformed world in which Britain would have commerce without colonies, a trade empire without the "expense" of political sovereignty. Yet the great transformation invoked in the passage is obscured by Torrens's resolute evacuation of authorial and political responsibility for the process of withdrawal he projects. Given in the passive voice, Torrens's questions emerge from a discursive possibility ("it may be asked") at a logically necessitated point in his argument ("Here"), a point that is itself immediately qualified ("perhaps"). Torrens's rhetorical evacuation of authorial responsibility functions as a model for the counterfactual regime of postimperial trade that it imagines: although the political bonds between colony and metropole "were dissolved," trade "is carried on" between them. In the world conjured by Torrens's hesitant sentences, the active intentionality of political sovereignty is absorbed into the agentless passivity of everyday commercial relations. Even colonial independence does not arrive with the bang of a political declaration but weakly derives from another's acknowledgment of an accomplished state of affairs. Sovereignty has been evacuated of any decisive effectivity it might once have been held to possess; it cannot even decide on its own abdication. Rather, a market calculus will determine whether West Indian sugar is worth Britain's squeeze of colonial cane.

If Torrens's questions appear revolutionary, they were so in a generic way by their publication in 1822. Imperial skepticism was the stuff of encyclopedia entries. James Mill concludes his supplement to the *Encyclopedia Britannica* (simply entitled "Colony") by wondering how colonies, "so little calculated to yield any advantage to the countries that hold them," continue to court the "affection" of "modern Europe."[2] Indeed, political-economic speculations regarding imperial dissolution had become so common that Torrens, otherwise a promoter of colonial empire, must write the empire's end when writing a political economy.[3] Where a number of intellectual historians have attended to the anti-imperialism that is constitutive of and coextensive with the origins of classical political economy, in this chapter I explore elite West Indian responses to the discipline's accumulating argument that the West Indies could be lost without a loss to Britain.[4] It is only through recourse to colonial responses, I contend, that we can understand the transformations that political economy wrought throughout the empire. Superficially, political economy changed little: the age of political economy was an age of global imperial expansion, not retraction or dissolution. Read alongside the ongoing expansion of Britain's formal and informal empire through the nineteenth century, the anti-imperial orientation of political economy is understood to have been at best feckless. This interpretation tracks broader claims that liberal political economy had minimal impact on the pragmatics of policy framers, who were more likely inspired by evangelical social thought.[5] At worst, the emergent discipline appears as nothing more than a new ideological mask for old imperial aims.[6] In each case, putative structural continuities—between the first and second British Empires, between mercantilist empire and the empire of free trade, between policy makers and, well, policy makers—make ironic any claim that the emergence of political economy marked a discontinuity in the political reality of empire.[7] This historiographical emphasis on continuity has stuck, however, only because it quietly assumes metropolitan Britain as its organizing subject. To put a figure to the analytic frame, we might say that this historiography adopts the gaze of the City banker, one of Cain and Hopkins's gentlemanly capitalists, who is fairly indifferent as to whether his money is invested in colonial Jamaica, colonial Bengal, or Portuguese Brazil, provided the returns are good. For British subjects on the other side of the Atlantic, however, this indifference *was* the discontinuity between imperial dispensations, and political economy incorporated this indifference as its politico-epistemological principle. Of course, this indifference did not register through an abandonment to independence or with anything like the positivity of a big historical event. It registered instead as a deactivation of the discursive and epistemological parameters within which colonial subjects could become legible and exert power as political subjects.

Political economy made a revolutionary break with empire by quietly depoliticizing it. To be sure, this quiet discursive shift was buoyed by and referred back to louder revolutionary transformations in the British Empire. For his British readership, Torrens's generic speculations would have recalled the doubled anti-imperial revolutions of 1776—the year in which the thirteen northern colonies declared independence from the empire, on one hand, and the year in which Adam Smith's *An Inquiry into the Nature and Causes of the Wealth of Nations* was published, on the other. As we will see, these political and discursive events were intimately linked. The American Revolution occupies a privileged position in Smith's inquiry: it offered empirical proof of the market system whose functioning Smith could elsewhere only assume as an aprioristic given to authorize chains of deductive reasoning. In *The Wealth of Nations* and in a position paper written for Parliament in 1778, Smith insisted that the costs of maintaining sovereignty were too high and that Britain's economy would expand following political severance from the colonies.[8] By the 1820s, and even before, Smith's prophecy had been confirmed by reality; it was a bit of common sense to note that British trade with the former colonies had only multiplied in value following independence.[9] This common sense was mobilized to affirm the soundness of Smith's predictions regarding the war's effects and, by extension, to confirm the scientificity of a discipline whose commitments to abstraction and deduction courted scorn from multiple political and epistemological communities— Tories, creoles, statisticians, historians.[10] Political economy's repetitive scenes of imperial abandonment would cite this history, transforming the American Revolution into an "epistemological figure" for the overwhelming sovereignty of the discipline's organizing abstraction, the market.[11] In the process, the aftermath of the American Revolution came to serve as an allegory for the future of the empire's Atlantic remnants—with the difference, though, that this time it was Torrens, John Ramsay McCulloch, or the *Edinburgh Review* declaring independence for the colonies.

Ironically, the West Indies so well served as a present-day metonym for the erstwhile colonies because the islands' economies were so disrupted by their revolution. The year 1776 ushered in a period of profound economic turbulence for the West Indies, which by the conclusion of the Napoleonic Wars would register as terminal decline.[12] As accumulating debt, disrupted commodity chains, reduced market access, and the political force of abolitionism diminished the profitable reproducibility of the islands, British capital began a course of expansion beyond the boundaries of formal empire to sites of high-growth potential such as Cuba and Brazil. Dale Tomich writes, "To the extent that it came to control commerce outside the bounds of its own empire, Britain became relatively indifferent to formal colonialism as the means of defining the nature and direction of commodity flows and the division of labor between core and periphery."[13] Yet the structure of Britain's markets lagged behind commercial possibilities and commercial realities: mercantilist protections in favor of West Indian producers directed capital to these declining islands even as these protections inflated the price of cheaper sugar from extra-imperial producers. Britain had to develop a market structure that could translate the "increasingly negligible" value of the West Indies to global capitalism into an effective economic reality.[14] In this context, political economy's fantasy of a future abandonment of empire functioned less as an institutional program for the present than as a conceptual prolepsis that translated the free market's indifference to political ties into an immediately available and actionable perspective. By thinking empire to its end, in other words, political economy assembled an epistemological framework in which

Britain's markets could be thought (and organized) on postimperial lines, whether or not Britain retained formal sovereignty over its colonial possessions. Provided imperial ties did not tie up Britain's market with preferences and protections, it did not matter whether the West Indies remained within the empire, revolted against it, or sank into the sea.[15]

I want to think about this residual inclusion of subjects within a world that is indifferent to their presence within it as a condition of neglect—a condition, as I noted in the introduction, that carries the etymological connotations of "not being read" and "not being gathered together." I draw this term from the wide range of texts I explore in this chapter, in which neglect names the slow corrosion of the frames of legibility that allow subjects caught up in a world to become meaningful for it. States of neglect do not assemble themselves in dramatic events of political expulsion or pathos-laden declensions into social abandonment. Rather, to recall Eric Williams, neglect is what you have when no one cares if you are humming "Yankee Doodle" or "God Save the Queen"; when a sovereign indifference depletes the very meaning of a subject's dependence or independence, autonomy or allegiance.[16] Almost immediately, elite West Indians lamented the extent to which the emergence of liberal market rationality entailed the dissolution of empire as a robust polity and castigated the emergent political economy for its "anticolonial" impulses.[17] Writing through the boom in Smith's popularity in the 1790s, the planter-historian Bryan Edwards was already complaining about those "Political economists" who "theorize concerning the utility of colonies" and who imagine that "Great Britain might derive advantages from [the West Indies'] commerce" even if the islands were declared independent or allowed to enter into "a state of dependence upon some other nation."[18] These complaints would gain in intensity and volume through the early nineteenth century, as the West Indian economy steadily declined within and Britain's economy steadily grew beyond the political boundaries of its Atlantic empire. Naturally, these complaints were charged as much by economic self-interest as by imperial patriotism. But what concerns me is the anxious sense, accompanying each creole complaint and each creole petition, that empire no longer constituted a politico-discursive horizon within which colonial subjectivity could become legible. Who was listening? Who cared?

Elite West Indian writers responded to the rise of political-economic neglect by attempting to consolidate a political theory of empire. The materials covered in this chapter are generically various; I read across plantation correspondence and husbandry manuals, volumes on colonial history and novels. The multiplicity of genres I treat is part of my argument. For creoles, there could be no independent genre of economic writing because (what we now call) "the economy" was neither a self-sufficient zone of social life nor an autonomous epistemic object; economic relations were always mediated by the political and social structures of empire. The generic ecology of creole economic thought is thus remarkably distinct from that which was emergent in Britain—where the epistemological (and increasingly institutional) separation of the economy from its political, social, and cultural casings resulted in what Mary Poovey describes as an increasing differentiation of economic from other genres of writing.[19] Indeed, *not* writing a political economy was a foundational feature of creoles' argument with political economy: creoles enacted their critique by only ever approaching economic relations at second hand, through forms of generic mediation that could not present the economy as an immediate epistemic object. Correspondingly, literary writing possesses a different function from that which it possessed for their Romantic contemporaries. If, as the old story goes, the Romantics responded to the autonomization of economic writing and economic value by delineating an autonomous sphere of literary value, creoles used literary genres to re-embed the economic within superordinate social and political frames. Like a previous generation of colonial Americans, creole writers "saw their literary productions as potential economic interventions."[20] Indeed, the novel form enabled creoles to theorize political economy without conceding to the generic and epistemic norms of the discipline of political economy.

Elite West Indians came to redefine the exercise of sovereignty as a hermeneutic attunement characterized by an aneconomic, hyper-empirical attention. As I show in the first part of this chapter, political economy's anti-imperialism was intimately linked to its critique of inductive accounts of economic life and its corresponding valorization of methodological abstraction. I am concerned here with the political effects of this epistemological shift: as the market replaced mercantilist theory's sovereign state, empire became illegible within theoretical accounts of the British polity. It appeared, in Smith's terms, as an "appendage," not a constitutive component of a Greater British state. I then explore how, against political economy's curious splintering of the political and the economic, creole writers turn to the plantation to model the subordination of the economic to the sovereign. This representation of the plantation was not merely ideological. As I argue through an archive of epistolary exchange between a widowed plantation proprietress in Jamaica, Catherine Harding, and her metropolitan agent, William Gale, the aneconomic attentiveness of metropolitan subjects to planters was necessary for empire to work. As political economy epistemologically abandoned empire, creole writers saw in the organization of the plantation a surrogate for displaced rationalities of imperial rule. Within this body of work, the planter comes to name a form of sovereign presence that supplements any abstract textualization of the social—be it in the form of a letter to an agent, Custom House receipts, or a treatise on political economy. I conclude with the anonymously published novel *Marly; or, A Planter's Life in Jamaica* (1828), a novel written by a former plantation driver. Narrating the career of a young orphan attempting to reclaim his ancestral plantation, I argue that *Marly* in fact narrates the restoration of the hyper-attentive imperial sovereign to his proper estate.

It doubtless seems odd that West Indian elites demanded a more attentive imperial state. Through the age of revolutions, colonial houses of assembly did in fact assert the islands' freedom from imperial legislation over internal affairs—a kind of constitutional solidarity with the rebellious colonies to the north. Through the era of abolition, West India merchants and planters continued to critique imperial overreach, raging against the closure of the trade in enslaved Africans, the slave registration acts, and so on. Imperial intrusion, not neglect, seems to have been the primary point of antagonism. But elite West Indians' apparent desire for an updated version of "salutary neglect" was materially structured by their wholesale dependence on the governmental and economic apparatus of empire.[21] Attempting to maximize autonomy within empire was in no way inconsistent with hewing to, and defending, its structures. Elite West Indians considered themselves "the citizens of a free and independent empire," as one poet put it, and this underarticulated citizenship was held to convey real rights to imperial support—rights they had no intention of relinquishing.[22] White West Indians continued to feel that they required the policing of docks in Britain, the stationing of British soldiers on the islands, the securing of the seas by British warships, financial assistance from Britain, and, above all, the protection of West Indian staple commodities in British markets. If elite West Indians demanding imperial attention seems to invert expectations, this apparent inversion has something to do with how a historiographical tradition dependent on abolitionism's autobiography has trained us to see the plantocracy as wholly reactive to the activist initiatives of the British public and the emancipatory imperial state. Yet, like most white guys yelling about getting the state off their backs, elite West Indians did not want to let go of the state or have the state let go of them; rather, they wanted to refashion it according to their imperatives. The discourse I track, which discounts pugnacious assertions of autonomy in favor of demands for attention, discloses the extent of the crisis unleashed by the doubled revolution of 1776. Liberal political economy's assault on a weakened Atlantic empire compelled elite West Indians to seize the state—ideologically and materially—to defend that empire and their position within it.

Half Awake in a Fake Empire

Smith closes *The Wealth of Nations* with a long, blustering indictment of empire:

> The rulers of Great Britain have, for more than a century past, amused the people with the imagination that they possessed a great empire on the west side of the Atlantic. This empire, however, has hitherto existed in the imagination only. It has hitherto been, not an empire, but the project of an empire; not a gold mine, but the project of a gold mine; a project which has cost, which continues to cost, and which, if pursued in the same way as it has hitherto, is likely to cost, immense expense. . . . It is surely now time that our rulers should either realize this golden dream, in which they have been indulging themselves, perhaps, as well as the people; or, that they should awake from it themselves, and endeavour to awaken the people. If the project cannot be completed, it ought to be given up.[23]

As a growing cohort of revisionist scholars have insisted, Smith hated empire. But what kind of hate denies the reality of its object? It is striking that the moments at which Smith's anti-imperialism achieves intensity are moments at which empire undergoes an epistemic recomposition: Smith's normative sense that empire should not be is underwritten by a stronger epistemological claim that it does not really exist at all. Empire "exist[s] in the imagination only"; it is a "project," a "golden dream" from which Britain's rulers and Britain's people must "awaken." Alas, ongoing attempts to find a Smith hip to postcolonial times have tended to minimize the epistemological work that his anti-imperial moments do, even when epistemology provides the idiom of his moral and political critique. Yet to think the coextension of Smith's anti-imperial politics with his anti-imperial epistemology is to track the foreclosure of colonial subjectivity—to track, that is, the instituted neglect that sits at the center of liberal intentions to approach imperial affairs more caringly. Elite West Indians such as Bryan Edwards, Joseph Lowe, James MacQueen, and Alexander MacDonnell were all attuned to the extent to which political economy's "anticolonial" impulses marked a point of intersection between its epistemological investment in "abstract reasoning" and its (increasingly diffuse) political investments in natural law and natural rights.[24] I read from out of this creole attunement, arguing that political economy's critique of empire functioned to displace an epistemic regime premised on induction from empirical experience in favor of one premised on deduction from supersensible abstractions. It was only through the collapse of empire that Smith and his heirs could posit the latter procedure as epistemologically valid.

Empire and a methodological commitment to empiricism and induction implied each other because, for the writers of what Smith called "the mercantile system," economic analysis was epistemologically moored in the transcendent and synthesizing perceptions of the political sovereign. The sovereign state not only provided writers with the empirical data they worked over; it also provided the optic from which they composed accounts of economic life. In this discourse, the figure of the sovereign possessed narratological and conceptual function: his exhaustively attentive gaze gathers together diffuse and incommensurable processes. Consider Sir James Steuart's *An Inquiry into the Principles of Political Oeconomy* (1767), the last great work of British mercantilist theory. As Keith Tribe argues, "The Sovereign or Statesman is essential in the structure of [Steuart's *Inquiry*], since in his administration of the aggregated 'polity' he is the sole expression of a unity which is otherwise dispersed among individual units or the categories which articulate these units."[25] For Steuart, the statesman's attention is necessary because economic relations lack an autonomous logic by which they would regulate themselves. This epistemic-political assemblage contained within it a prophylactic against methodological abstraction. Economic processes' lack of an immanent principle of auto regulation meant that economic knowledge could not be generated through recourse to aprioristic reasoning: there was nothing to abstract from, no system to build save one that attends to the persistent undoing of any system. Steuart would declare systems "mere conceits" that "mislead the understanding" in their movement from "induction" to "principle" to a "deduction" that "extends [the principle's] influence far beyond the limits" it should go.[26] He offered an anticipatory critique of Smith's method that would resonate in Thomas Pownall's early response to *The Wealth of Nations* and echo through the nineteenth century in various reactions to political economy.[27]

Indeed, if Smith's "very violent attack . . . upon the whole commercial system of Great Britain" was simultaneously an attack on mercantilism's forms of knowing, it was at the level of the epistemological that Smith's assault was most exposed.[28] The elevation of the "system of natural liberty" over the mercantilist state implied a massive reconceptualization of the subjects, objects, and methods of economic inquiry. Smith was keenly aware of the shaky grounds on which he trod; his text betrays an acute self-consciousness that his postulation of "an autonomous economic sphere" separate from the domain of the sovereign state might appear as little more than fanciful system building.[29] Conceptually, such a postulated separation made sense. As Smith demonstrated in his opening critique of Hobbes, the irreducibility of money to power implied the irreducibility of capital to the state, of the market to the sovereign.[30] The persistent problem, however, was that such conceptual postulations lacked empirical support: nowhere in the world could Smith point to the functional existence of an economic order that was autonomous from political institutions. Read only slightly against the grain, *The Wealth of Nations* is nothing less than an encyclopedic account of the multitudinous ways in which states structured, contained, and intervened in commercial life across space and time.[31] Given the absence of empirical referents, what sense did it make to pose the economic as a discrete epistemic domain, one systemic enough in its functioning that one would argue deductively from it?

Smith managed the epistemological problems confronting his enterprise in a few ways. First, like Hume, Smith downplayed the purchase of empirically oriented and inductively constructed accounts of economic life, famously asserting that he had "no great faith in political arithmetic."[32] Their point was not that the data were bad, but that the data could not be good: however "obvious and simple" it might be, the "system of natural liberty" was supersensible and not available for empirical representation or inductive reconstruction.[33] Any empirical representation of market transactions would simply show unnatural markets.[34] Smith also recognized that his readers had no reason to have any great faith in his system and acknowledged that the epistemic autonomy he ascribed to the economy lacked—and probably would forever lack—institutional supports. He declares, for instance, that calls for a complete "freedom of trade" were "as absurd as to expect that an Oceana or Utopia should ever be established."[35] In so doing, he rhetorically incorporates possible objections to his method by conceding that his system might not ever achieve institutional, and thus empirical, positivity.[36] He therefore had to demonstrate that the systemic logic underwriting his deductions, while not available and possibly never available for empirical representation, was nonetheless real. The American Revolution provided a moment in which the postulated separability of economic from political logics became legible as an imminent, and then immanent, actuality.

The American Revolution served Smith in much the same way that the French Revolution would serve Kant: it empirically signaled the historical effectivity of a supersensible, systemic rationality. It is no coincidence that Smith published *The Wealth of Nations* in the same year that Britain's North American colonies declared independence: Smith seems to have waited for the moment. Having moved from Kirkcaldy to London in 1773 with a largely completed manuscript, Smith became "very zealous upon American affairs," as Hume put it—so zealous that he delayed publication of his text to revise and expand book four, the book on colonial commerce.[37] After the war, Hugh Blair encouraged Smith to remove these long reflections on the imperial troubles from subsequent editions of the work, thinking such writing "more appropriate to 'a publication for the present moment.'"[38] Instead, he added to his critique of empire in the 1784 edition, padding his previous reflections on empire with a scathing indictment of how the empire has "entirely neglected," "burdened," and "sacrificed" the home consumer in favor of colonial profiteers.[39] Smith expands his treatment of an exploded empire to ease the cognitive shift required to transition out of defective "Systems of Political Œconomy" and into the system of natural liberty.

Smith takes the event of the revolution as an opportunity to perform an epistemological sleight of hand that rendered the possible and even emergent reality—that Britain would lose its American colonies—immanent to his evaluation of the empire's unfolding present. In other words, he incorporates the imminent possibility of an Atlantic economic order disembedded from the empire into his evaluation of the empire. In so doing he generates a perspective that, while as yet unrealized and perhaps improbable, nonetheless felt possible and so realistic: that of the nonsovereign market system. The rhetorical composition of this perspective is quite complicated. Considering the possible consequences of Britain's "voluntarily giv[ing] up all authority over her colonies," Smith once again guards against the charge of utopianism: "The most visionary enthusiast would scarce be capable of proposing such a measure [as imperial abandonment], with any serious hopes at least of its every being adopted." In the very next sentence, however, Smith confidently adopts this "visionary" perspective, and for the simple reason that this perspective was hardly visionary in the wake of 1776: "If [a program for imperial dissolution] was adopted, however, Great Britain would not only be immediately freed from the whole annual expence of the peace establishment of the colonies, but might settle with them such a treaty of commerce as would effectually secure to her a free trade, more advantageous to the great body of people, though less so to the merchants, than the monopoly which she at present enjoys."[40] The rhetorical and epistemological thrust of this "visionary" passage is to translate readers' assent to a localized prognostication into a belief in the reality of the system that underwrites his conditional proposition. The perspective that Smith paraleptically occludes converts into the premise of a conditional; by assenting to this conditional, one simultaneously assents to the premise's visionary assumption (that the economic constitutes a systemic order from which deductions from law to case can be made) while still maintaining oneself as something more grounded than a visionary. This complicated epistemological transformation registers less painfully in Smith's shifting of economic analysis's grammatical mood. In the passage quoted earlier, the subjunctive quietly overtakes the indicative as the proper mood with which to assemble economic life: the supersensible virtuality of the "would" or "might" displaces the indicative of induction. In effect, deductions premised on the logic of the immanently possible are rendered as valid as knowledges generated by inductive approaches to the evidently actual—more valid even. After all, by the text's end Smith writes empire off as a fantastical dream, despite its empirical existence. Put differently, Smith distinguishes a political ontology from the ontic political, degrading the latter as a perversion of the former.

In effect, Smith's speculation separated the epistemic order of the market from that of the polity and then deployed the former as the latter's regulative norm. This doubled movement registers as a withdrawal of the empirically oriented, busybody sovereign of mercantilist lore: "The statesman who should attempt to direct private people in what manner they ought to employ their capitals, would . . . load himself with a most unnecessary attention."[41] The market would fill in the space the sovereign evacuated. By costing empire, Smith not only proleptically inhabited this perspective; he also staged the kinds of questions that the state should be asking, posing the postsovereign rationality of the market as the proper rationality for the sovereign. The state should begin calculating the costs of the polity, aligning the space of the latter to the market's demands.

It might be hard to feel the weirdness of this great transformation—or even to feel it as a transformation at all. Economic historians today routinely follow Smith in calculating the value of empire, and such operations do not strike us as weird, barbaric, or economistic: we possess an ingrained assumption that empire was not a robust polity constituted by ties that exceed economic calculation. We can only understand the weirdness and gravity of Smith's intervention if we are willing to understand empire as a state form, one that constituted the baseline, irreducible political horizon of most Atlantic subjects' worlds. To read Smith from the perspective of this polity, as West Indians did, is to see his striking expulsion of empire from the space of the political.[42] Indeed, creole respondents frequently used spatial metaphorics to register their bewilderment at the way in which political economy zoned economic rationality such that empire was outside the noncalculating space of the political. Prior to the rise of political economy, elite West Indians as well as popular metropolitan thinkers had insisted on interiority of empire to the domestic geography of Britain. The planter-historian Edward Long, for instance, would cite Edmund Burke to argue that the West India trade possesses "the nature of a home trade as if all our Dominions in America were fixed to Cornwall."[43] Decades later, and in what must be one of the few positive citations of Lord Brougham by an apologist of colonial slavery, Alexander MacDonnell would recall Brougham's own version of the Cornwall test from the latter's *An Inquiry into the Colonial Policy of the European Powers* (1803): "Mr. Brougham has observed . . . the expenses of national defence for five counties in the south of England amount to more than those of all the rest of the kingdom; and, therefore, if the new rule of economy were followed, the inhabitants of Yorkshire might bitterly complain how essentially they suffered from their connexion with Kent or Hampshire." "How," MacDonnell asks, "are we to decide where dominion should terminate? . . . Again, how are we to estimate distance as regards political dependence?"[44] The epistemological emergence of the abstract, systemic market entailed a clear, though contested, demarcation of political space from economic space. The colonies were placed in the latter.

Indeed, the imperial polity could not survive the disembedding of the market from the domain of the sovereign because the imperial polity was little more than the sovereign state's attentiveness to matters of intraimperial commerce. Imperial subjects were not represented in Parliament; the empire did not possess a constitution that ran parallel to or intersected with that of Britain. Instead, commercial regulations materialized political obligations. Commercial "protections" and "duties" metonymically stood in for the absent constitution, and they served this function so admirably that Britons and creoles would cite an inchoate but nonetheless binding imperial "compact."[45]

By divesting economic relations of the political meanings with which colonial subjects and the mercantilist stated burdened them, political economy left empire without a constitution. Indeed, the abstraction of the economic from the political induced a kind of political formalism: Smith could imagine the retention of the American colonies only on the condition that they were incorporated into Parliament.[46] Political economy performatively aligned the market with formal political-institutional space, leaving the nation—not empire—the default unit of political-economic analysis. (Just think of Smith's title.) We can see this alignment quite clearly in McCulloch's *A Statistical Account of the British Empire* (1837), who begins by defining what he comprehends in the term "empire": "The British Empire, exclusive of its foreign dependencies, consists of the islands of Great Britain and Ireland, and of the smaller islands contiguous and subordinate to them."[47] Beneath the dull sobriety of a political economist delimiting his unit of analysis, however, was concealed a more intense, violent process of expulsion. More than a decade earlier, McCulloch had drawn on the example of the American Revolution to insist on liberalizing Britain's sugar markets: "It is not easy to see how we could sustain any injury from the total breaking up of the colonial monopoly, or even from the total and unconditional abandonment of these dependencies."[48] If McCulloch appears to accord his market rationality an extraordinary, polity-defining power, this power is already precomprehended in the terms of his argument: the "we" for whom he writes grammatically disaggregates Britain from the West Indies, circuitously anticipating the "breaking up" and "abandonment" that economic rationality demands.

Creoles' befuddlement at these broad epistemological and political transformations was not insincere. An abstract market that functions systemically without the guiding hand of a sovereign? A form of value capable of rationally directing flows of capital? The world picture assembled by political economy did not make any sense—as anyone who spent any time on a plantation could tell you.

Infinitely Obliged

Seven years after Smith published *The Wealth of Nations*, just as the imperial civil war came to a close, two metropolitan merchants attempted the difficult but routine task of figuring out how much a Jamaican plantation was worth. It was not going well. "I am at a Loss for the materials respecting the valuation of the Weston Favel Estate," William Atherton from Bristol wrote to

William Gale in London on 4 February 1783. Atherton cannot find the "Books & Papers" that record the course of a long dispute at the Jamaican Chancery between the widowed plantation proprietor Catherine Harding and her deceased husband's creditors. Missing books of account are, however, the least of Atherton's worries. Far more unnerving is the absence of a clear protocol by which Weston Favel could be evaluated. Atherton vaguely recalls that the estate had been valued at £24,000 around 1776, but he does not know how to incorporate the American Revolution's disruptive effects on the Atlantic economy into his calculations: "how far the increase of expenses attending the import of Sugars since that time ought to operate on the value of Jamaica Estates I cannot determine. . . . I feel myself incompetent to give an Opinion of what ought to be offered." Moving from the value of the Weston Favel Estate to the "value of Jamaica Estates" in general, from lost papers to lost protocols, Atherton's practically minded letter attempts the work of theoretical abstraction that would become the hallmark of British political economy. Yet Atherton's aspirational abstraction does not yield a "conceptual grid that enables every phenomenon to be compared, differentiated, and measured by the same yardstick."[49] Instead, Atherton's abstraction from Weston Favel to the "value of Jamaica Estates" reveals the incalculability of this value: the estates are commensurate in their general incommensurability. Atherton experiences this incalculability as an incapacitation ("I feel myself incompetent"), a "Loss" of epistemic sovereignty that he manages by deferentially referring the matter to Gale, whom he acknowledges as "a much better judge of the home['s] Valuation than myself."[50] Atherton knows, moreover, that he cannot recommend simply cutting ties with the estate in the name of economic rationality. Gale was bound to Harding through an extensive Atlantic network of kin and friendship and had obligated himself to assist Harding in refinancing her estate, resolving legal issues before the Jamaican Court of Chancery, and settling an annuity upon her and her children from the plantation's proceeds. The merchants might wind up throwing good money after bad—again, Atherton had no idea what the value of the estate was—but throw it they must.

Read together, Smith's political economic treatise and Atherton's letter reveal the divergent emphases with which Atlantic subjects freighted modes of economic calculation. Smith ascribes an extraordinary power to empire's notional books of account—so much so that, should they reveal the imperial polity to be in the red, Smith is willing to dissolve the entire affair. Yet even as Smith loads economic calculation with a polity-defining power, he is less interested in the mathesis of accountancy than in its morality, less invested in actual calculations than in the rhetoric of calculability. For Smith, the rhetoric of calculability organizes a politico-ethical disposition of national and personal self-care; it demands a reflexivity about and rationalization of Britain's longer-term interests. For Atherton, however, the actual practice of economic calculation reveals both the epistemological inadequacy of plantation accountancy and the nonsovereignty of the plantation's aspirational accountant. Atherton is missing an equation, he does not know how the addition of a quite simple variable—the increased costs of freight and handling—"ought to operate on the value of Jamaica Estates." Yet Atherton recuperates the limits to his ability to count out the economic value of a plantation by socializing the work of accountancy itself. If for Smith the rhetoric of calculability necessitated the division, dissolution, and rationalization of imperial sociality, for Atherton the fact of incalculability impels its reproduction.

In staging this confrontation between metropolitan and colonial forms of economic rationality, I do not mean to imply that plantations were pre-, non-, or anticapitalist economic formations.[51] Plantations produced in and for a capitalist world system, and planters felt the systemic imperative to produce and accumulate surplus value as any capitalist would.[52] Yet if the imperative to accumulate was global, the forms of rationality by which this imperative was made operational were zoned, territorialized, and particularized. Economic historians of the Atlantic world tend to brush aside these epistemic fault lines, favoring narratives of integration organized by a perspective derived from a seemingly neutral world market.[53] While circuits of commodities and capital linked the plantations to metropolitan markets, plantations' spatial and temporal distance from the scene of surplus realization meant that they lacked an adequate view of this process. In Marx's terms, plantations were "formally," but not "really," subsumed into the value circuits of capital, and the formality of this subsumption gave rise to site-specific forms of economic rationality.[54] Planters could not access, see, or respond to the market in the same manner as their metropolitan correspondents, and they knew it. Whereas London-based merchants and political economists could (imagine that they could) count, cost, and calculate the value of imperial commerce, scholars of plantation accountancy have argued that the local and systemic conditions of incalculability inhibited planters from adopting "rational" accountancy practices.[55] It would be more accurate to say that conditions of incalculability gave rise to situated forms of economic rationality and accountancy. Planters understood their plantations as embedded within a dense imperial network organized by both social and political ties that offset their locational disadvantage within the imperial world system. Indeed, the plantation economy was founded on a broader imperial "economy of obligation," one in which narrowly economistic logics were embedded within social logics of reciprocity and protection.[56]

Letters were fundamental instruments of this imperial economy of obligation.[57] As Ian Steele remarks, Britain's Atlantic empire was "a paper empire," and it was through epistolary exchange that creoles devised a form of socialized accountancy that enabled them to paper over the epistemic gaps that left them unable to count, calculate, or cost the value of their enterprises.[58] While the letters I explore here are entirely practical in orientation, the epistolary form would pattern creole theorizations of the imperial political economy, both generically and epistemologically (see chapter 3). Letters reveal economic life as a set of intensely personal relations that take place *between* subjects, not as a homogenous, abstract field that contains subjects. Epistolary exchange localizes and particularizes the epistemological positions of the writers: no correspondent has a totalizing view of the field, no one can assume the aggregating market perspective that political economy adopted. The implied subjects of this creole economy act through a constitutive deficit of actionable knowledge. Unable to reliably access information produced by impersonal, price-setting markets, creoles used letters to personalize and navigate economic life.

The personalization of economic life through epistolary exchange meant that commercial relations were embedded within—or, from a liberal perspective, irrationally freighted with—noneconomistic social logics. Of course, the transatlantic epistolary economy of receipt and response was not immune to varied forms of uncertainty, and it was through their negotiation with the quotidian problems of correspondence that creoles worked out an ethical approach to economic life. Because the responsiveness of each correspondent is a condition of correspondence, because nonresponse is a possible fate of any missive, letter writing thematizes multiple forms of responsibility and accountability. The economy of epistolary circulation presupposes a "you" whose status as recipient and reader is ultimately unstable, leaving the writer uncertain whether the proper addressee has read her words. The letter might err, recovered by an unintended addressee; the "you" whom the letter intends might be inattentive, neglect to read the letter, or (at the extreme limit Jacques Derrida proposes, a limit frequently touched on in Atlantic correspondence) have died.[59] The intended reader can always absolve himself from the responsible attention that the form of the letter solicits. The Atlantic network of circulation presupposed an economy of responsive attentiveness open to the incalculable possibility of error, absence, and neglect. Creoles negotiated the constitutive possibility of neglect in two linked ways. First, creoles' mode of addressing their correspondents attempted to produce the addressee they desired: by figuring merely mortal merchants as godly figures capable of bestowing infinite amounts of attention, creoles obliged their correspondents to fit their fantasies. Second, creoles had to present themselves as deserving subjects to whom their correspondents were obliged to respond.[60] The plantation economy required immense amounts of transatlantic affective upkeep, and the necessity of performing this social labor only intensified after the imperial crisis of 1776. With American independence and its concomitant disruption of Atlantic economic circuits, creoles became acutely aware that merchants might invest their attention—and their capital—elsewhere.

Catherine Harding was quite sensitive to these great transformations, and her letters to Gale are saturated with the anxiety that he might divest his attention from her struggling family. In sociological terms, Harding was hardly representative of the Jamaican plantocracy: she was, after all, a woman.[61] However, Harding's access to gendered idioms of dependence, obligation, and protection more accurately tracks the reconstitution of creole political idioms in the wake of the American Revolution than that staged in colonial houses of assembly. Cranky declarations of creole autonomy were always underwritten by sober recognitions of the planters' structural dependence on Britain—this is in part why only thirteen colonies rebelled in 1776.[62] Conventionally feminine modes of address cast into relief the political position and political desires of elite West Indians in ways that fulminations in the Jamaican House of Assembly do not. At the same time, Harding's letters are not so different than those of, say, the Antiguan planter Samuel Martin or Jamaican planter Simon Taylor, except perhaps for a relative lack of swagger compared with these well-off men. The plantation economy generated the same political, epistemological, and affective problems everywhere it operated. The primary instrument developed to manage these shared, structural difficulties—the letter—was correspondingly a deeply structured, generically patterned object.

Indeed, Harding's letters are so illuminating for their desire to stick close to convention: she attempts to bind Gale's attention by investing standard features of the epistolary form with an excessive meaning. Prior to thanking Gale for the content of his activity on her behalf—lending money, consulting with lawyers, or helping to raise her kids—Harding always thanks him for the fact of her response: "I have the pleasure to thank you for your favor."[63] These utterances are formulaic, but formula is precisely what Harding wants: she maintains the security of her world through the absorption and reproduction of generic and affective norms.[64] But it is not just a question of politeness. The mannered reproduction of lines of communication—what Roman Jakobson would think of as language's phatic function—reinscribed creoles within an insecure scene of address. Atlantic mail moved slowly, and even more so during the American Revolution; fleets arrived haphazardly, and Harding did not know with any surety when she would be able to send or receive letters.[65] The temporal lag attending Atlantic communication helps explain Harding's more exuberant salutations: "I am infinitely obliged by your most welcome letter and the trouble you have taken to make me thus happy."[66]

Yet the purported infinitude of her obligation did not prevent Harding from undertaking a kind of epistolary and affective calculus. Letter exchanges functioned like credit economies, and writers deployed a "careful calculus of barter and sentiment" in their correspondence.[67] Subtly scolding Gale in a letter dated 8 April 1778, Harding writes, "It is some time since I had the pleasure of a line from you but your paragraph concerning my business was very acceptable."[68] It is unclear whether Harding considers Gale at fault for the lag between letters; he had in fact responded to her previous missive on 25 January 1778, and it probably had not arrived in Jamaica by that time. It is clear, however, that Harding counts his concern for her by counting his words, implicitly comparing his "very acceptable" paragraph to her three- and four- page letters. At the same time, Harding's use of a diminutive synecdoche ("a line") for a letter figures his paragraph as graciously exceeding a letter's minimum requirement—the minimum requirement of a salutation, of a formal inscription of attentiveness and responsiveness to another. As Harding writes it, Gale's attention oscillates between the calculable and the incalculable; in giving a little, he already gives too much. Harding thus worries that in taking his time, she gives nothing but trouble: "The necessity of business so frequently obliges me to intrude upon you that I really am distressed by the apprehensions of my being very troublesome."[69] Harding's pro forma apology actually absolves her of responsibility for the insistent intrusions: the frequency with which she writes him is an effect of the "necessity of business." Such invocations of epistolary debt were intended to incite their immediate cancellation. Equally bound by form, the gentleman merchant had to inform the widow that his trouble was no trouble at all, and that the widow should not be apprehensive about his continuing attentiveness to her concerns.

Harding's epistolary oscillation between the rhetorics of calculability and incalculability neatly tracks the plantation's oscillation in and out of forms of economic rationality. Indeed, Harding needed to intrude on Gale's attention because she had extremely limited and belated access to market data. Sugar prices could fluctuate wildly, making any price estimate "vulnerable to the indeterminacy of imputed prices."[70] A resident planter like Harding would not receive price information until the sugar had been carried to a British market and sold and information on the sale was sent back. This circuit took a great deal of time, and a plantation would be able to close its fiscal year only after it was well into the next one. With more immediate access to market data, a metropolitan factor such as Gale was "in the best position to create more complete accounts."[71] Harding, in effect, cannot give an account of herself; she has to rely on Gale. On 5 October 1780, for instance, Harding wrote to the London merchant: "I have the pleasure to acknowledge your favour of July the 6th inclosing our acct current & value of the crop [17]79 which I am happy to find has so well answered the exigencies of our concern for the year."[72] While Gale knew the financial state of the plantation for months, Harding comes to this knowledge belatedly. She indexes the experience of epistemic deficit by describing her emotional reaction to a successful year as "happy." Lacking control over or timely knowledge of distant sugar markets, prices happen to planters and retain a happenstance quality. Planters lingered in a perpetual perhaps, hoping to find that their gains "answered" the exigencies of the year. Figuring the belated knowledge of the market as an "answer," Harding suggests that sugar production is an interrogative practice in which the planter anxiously questions, but cannot know, whether the resultant mass of sugar will translate into profit or loss. The interrogative mood saturates even those moments when Harding decides how to distribute her eventually monetized crop. In a typical conclusion, Harding requests of Gale: "After payment of [the supplies for the Estate & my familys expences] whatever Balances may remain on the above 5-Hheads [hogsheads,] of sugar as well as on the 20 Hheads shipped in the April fleet, you will be pleased to direct may be paid to Mr John Dawes on the Mortgage acct. with the estate of Tho. Harding [her deceased husband]."[73] Here, Harding treats her hogsheads of sugar as if they have already been monetized; she even imagines them as having a remaining balance. Yet she cannot assign a numerical amount to the money that the sugar will have become. Money is thus discussed inexactly, as "whatever Balances." Not yet a realized exchange value, but always already a commodity intended for a distant market, sugar inhabits a strange temporality of anticipatory calculability.

Even with an agent's aid, planters had a limited repertoire of actions available to deal with a shifting economic field; almost all of them involved the extension of production. Debt-trapped planters had little choice but to produce, and to produce as much as possible.[74] The planter "has no alternative," writes one abolitionist, "but, either at profit or loss, to work [his slaves] on."[75] Thus, even as the American Revolution began devastating the Jamaican economy—rendering shipping uncertain, drying up credit, driving up the price of provisions, and disastrously leaving enslaved people without secure or adequate subsistence—the cash-strapped, indebted widow could not halt or reduce production.[76] She had to enlarge it, which necessitated the purchase of more human beings:

> You were so kind as to mention Mr Lawrence having given the Consignments of Weston Favell together with his own to Hibberts house & that I might thence be annually supply'd with Negroes at a small Advance, but as Mr Lawrence did not mention to me his having fix'd the matter with the House in England I thought it would be proper to mention it to Mrs Hibbert in Kingston which I accordingly did, their answer you have inclos'd . . . as to an advance you know my situation & will do the best you can for me and be particular in telling me whether I may draw for more than the value of our Crop next year [and what] arrangement you have made on my behalf with Mr Dawes & tho we are much in want of Negroes I have not been able to purchase any on that account.[77]

Harding relates to Gale the difficulties she has faced in securing "Negroes at a small Advance." Whatever the understanding between the Hibberts in Britain and her friend and relation Richard Lawrence, the Hibberts of Kingston are apparently chary of floating a loan to an indebted widow proprietress whose title to the estate was caught up in a suit before the Jamaican Court of Chancery. Facing barriers in every direction, Harding turns to Gale for a loan. Harding knows that she cannot not plant; that plantation production must be extended. But she also knows that she cannot justify the request based on the current returns of the estate; after all, a third party had refused her request and she lacks information regarding the enterprise's present and future profitability. Harding adopts two strategies in soliciting a loan whose value cannot yet be calculated. First, she acts as if her request is in fact bounded by the parameters of economic rationality: she deferentially yields to Gale's superior knowledge of her "situation" and she establishes a purely notional relationship between the capital she needs and the "value of our Crop next year." Second, Harding embeds this commercial logic—a logic that already failed to secure her a loan from the Hibberts—within a broader grammar of obligation. Referring to next year's sugar as "our Crop," Harding establishes their relationship as one of co-proprietorship while simultaneously extending this economic tie into the future. For Harding, the futurity of their intimacy binds Gale to act in the present, enabling her to shift from the indicative to the imperative mood: "you . . . will do the best you can for me and be particular." If planters like Harding were bound to extend cultivation, merchants like Gale were equally bound to sink their capital.

Even as Harding set imperial obligations to work to secure her plantation's economic vitality, she had to ensure that economistic logics would not recode or transform the thick socialities binding Gale to her enterprise. Harding attempts to downplay the commercial orientation of her plantation enterprise—or, rather, to subordinate the plantation's economic aims to the requirements of domestic reproduction. Keep in mind that participants in the imperial economy understood plantations as both business ventures and domestic units, as both "estates" and "homes" (in Atherton's terms). This understanding was not simply ideological or propagandistic: it structured the logic of plantation commerce as well as modalities of plantation accountancy. Business and domestic expenses went into the same ledger; like most planters, Harding did not distinguish household income from the enterprise's capital. She would continually plead that her ultimate concern was to secure the reproduction of her family's domestic life, not necessarily to maximize the estate's profitability. By stressing her domestic aims and noncommercial goals, Harding figures the plantation economy as an *oikos*, to use the term in the sense developed by Karl Rodbertus in his studies of ancient slave economies. Rodbertus's oikos is a blank term that marks "the concept of an economy in kind under which money, markets, and exchange were at a discount, in spite of the existence of an elaborate organization of production."[78] As in a household, where most labor and exchange is not monetized or quantified, the *oikos* involves a series of transactions that "*lack . . . quantitativity.*" Following Karl Polanyi, these nonmarket economies distribute goods through nonquantifiable acts of reciprocity, which "demands adequacy of response, not mathematical equality . . . transactions and decisions cannot be grouped with any precision from the economic point of view."[79] Harding would in part elicit this incalculable response through sentimental troping. Figuring herself to Gale as "a widow with three children," she draws on the generic codes of sentimentality to code Weston Favel as a locus of kinship, not commerce; Gale is asked to secure a domestic, not an economic, unit.[80] If he did so in quite literal ways, by standing as "security" for Harding's mortgage to Dawes, Gale's labors also figuratively secured the home from the penetration of commercial logics. He would describe himself as the "medium" between Harding and the commercial world, allowing Harding to live a life in which the logic of the oikos and the logic of the economy were relatively separated.

Gale would assume Harding's mortgage in 1783, dissolving this epistemic and ethical separation of the domestic world and the commercial world. For Harding, however, this dissolution is not occasioned by the insinuation of commercial logics into domestic space, as we might suppose. Rather, Harding expands the nonquantitative logic of reciprocity to incorporate the London merchant; the imperial oikos invaginates the metropolitan economy. She tropes Gale's assumption of her mortgage as an intimate and embodied exchange, as if the transatlantic transfer of title involved the touching of bodies. "Bind[ing]" himself to her debt, Harding figures Gale as "taking it up" into his hands: "You are very kind my good friend in saying you will do everything that is necessary towards taking it up, in your hand all woud [sic] be safe."[81] The visible hand of the London merchant makes "safe" and protects that Jamaican widow from the incalculable operations of the market. Continuing the metaphorics of touch, Harding "hold[s]" herself in permanent debt for his care: "I am infinitely obliged my good Friend by your kind congratulations on the happy crisis in my long & perplexing business, whereon I shall ever hold myself indebted to you for the part you have so kindly taken in bringing matters to this issue."[82] The metaphorics of touch bring merchant and planter into an imperial proximity, a closeness produced through the figurative reciprocation of affects and embodied performances. By figuring the transfer of debt as an intimate transaction of touch, Harding transcribes calculable debt into nonquantifiable feelings. Their relationship becomes excessive to the quantifiable debt Harding owes.

Such affective tropologies were not superadditions to a more basic economic rationality. Rather, the embedding of economic relation within an affectively saturated field of social accountability was the engine of plantation economies. Indeed, planters' failure to participate in narrowly economistic logics was not an antieconomic reaction to commercial life. Rather, the zoning of economic rationality meant that the only way for certain subjects to participate in Britain's imperial economy was to rely on incalculable, non-quantifiable modes of sociality to supplement the varied epistemic deficits that they encountered. Such irrationality was functional for the endurance and extension of the imperial plantation economy: plantations pumped millions of pounds of surplus out of enslaved humans while simultaneously contributing to the development of British capitalism's financial apparatus. It was, that is to say, rational within the institutional context of empire. In the wake of political economy, some monetary theorists would attempt to suture this understanding of empire as an oikos to dominant economic thinking. The monetary theorist William Blake would correct the terminology deployed in the British Customs House's ledgers, asserting that the commodities and capital sent from the East Indies and West Indies to the metropole were less "imports" than "remittances"—that is, allocations of goods internal to a dispersed but unified domestic economy.[83] Charles Bosanquet would argue similarly: "The importation of sugar and colonial produce, however large an item in the Custom House books, has no reference to, or connection with, the balance of trade, because it is British property, is not purchased, and no debt is incurred for the surplus beyond export, any more than for the excess of the produce of land beyond the expence of cultivation."[84] In these claims we can hear traces of Long and MacDonnell's insistence that Jamaica was not really so different from Cornwall or Yorkshire, that empire was a domestic polity that contained trade. But we can also detect traces of a broader political and epistemological project—that of viewing empire from the perspective of the planter. Blake's creole colleagues were hard at work on the matter.

Attentive Planters in a Neglectful Empire

Plantation correspondence provided creoles with the epistemological and ethical raw materials through which they would develop their imperial political economy; it also yielded them a genre. As the rate of absenteeism mushroomed through the late eighteenth century, concerned but distant plantation proprietors would routinely send instructions to the plantation's managerial staff. Such instructions could be terse, oriented toward a concrete and immediate end. Some absentees, however, caught up in the era's investment in improvement, would dispatch to the colonies long-winded programs for plantation governance. Some of these planter manuals, such as that of Henry Drax, circulated informally among absentee proprietors, resident planters, and concerned plantation managers.[85] Others, such as Martin's, were printed in small runs on local presses (at least two in Antigua) for the consumption of a given island's planter elite, only to then be printed in London.[86] By the early nineteenth century, writers began publishing manuals of plantation governance with metropolitan presses for audiences in Britain and across the empire. This expansion in implied audience correlated to West Indians' emergent sense that modalities of organizing the micropolity of the plantation should be abstracted to the macropolity of empire. After all, "plantation" had already served as an early modern metonym for "colony." It was in the movement from humdrum instructions regarding plantation management to abstracted exegeses on plantation governance that the figure of the planter would be born.

Through the figure of the planter, creoles attempted to develop a surrogate for the politico-epistemic rationality lost with political economy's displacement of mercantilism's sovereign. Today, scholars tend to read this figure as either a bald idealization mobilized in the "war of representations" between abolitionist and pro-slavery forces in the imperial public sphere or as expressive of a panoptic principle of plantation governance.[87] I suggest, rather, that the aim of this discourse was to develop a new optic for viewing empire in a period during which empire seemed to be vanishing as an organizing unit of political and economic reality. To read elite West Indian writing as engaged primarily with abolitionist publics is both to overstate creoles' commitments to democratic publicness and to understate their strategic savvy. Before Parliamentary Reform in 1832, West Indians ceded the public to abolitionists, recognizing both the difficulties of generating a pro-slavery social movement and the fact that they did not need one.[88] The ideology of planter paternalism that served and serves as an obvious object of critique was a moral corollary of a broader politico-epistemological work undertaken to recalibrate state optics. Instead of trying to foster public support, West Indian writers rather sought to "give a lesson to statesmen," as the West Indian merchant and agent James MacQueen put it in a different context—a reasonable and reasonably successful strategy in the twilight years of Old Corruption.[89] West Indians were less worried about losing their enslaved humans than about losing their protected markets, and for good reason: their legal title to the former was infinitely stronger than their title to the latter. Moreover, political economy devoted much of its effort to arguing away such protections; however, and aside from a few pages in Smith, the classical tradition is almost wholly silent on the superiority of free labor. When creoles *did* mount critiques of free labor, they did so typically as a response to abolitionists' deployment of the figure of free labor as an argument to free markets (typically for British Indian sugar, produced by "free" colonial Indians).[90] The assumption that all elite creole writing was reactive to William Wilberforce makes for great hagiography but poor literary history. Plantation manuals were intended less as bits of propaganda and more as a mirror for princes for the imperial state.

Indeed, the planter cuts a rather Machiavellian figure in these tropical *specula principum*, pitting his virtue against the infinite number of contingencies threatening to overwhelm the plantation.[91] The planter's primary vehicle for this virtue was his attentiveness. As Martin put it, "the duty of a good planter to inspect every part of a plantation with his own eyes."[92] According to Thomas Roughley's *The Jamaica Planter's Guide* (1823), an ever expanding set of potentially destructive "contingencies" always hovered around the plantation; in these conditions of extreme incalculability, "present judicious management may be in a great measure defeated by wilfull neglect."[93] The planter could not economize his attention by treating his enterprise as a mathematizable and calculable operation. The economic data revealed by markets or books of account always required the supplementary, qualitative form of care that the planter personified. The figure of the planter emerges as a subject who undertakes the unlimited task of neglecting nothing. "Neglect," Derrida writes, is an "abyssal word," for one "is always a priori negligent, more or less negligent, and so always too negligent."[94] Like Smith's withdrawing statesman, the planter always knows that he does not know enough; the difference between the two is that the planter assumes the aprioristic finitude and partiality of his knowledge as an incitement to attend ever more closely and exhaustively to the world.

The planter came to model an alternative form of imperial sovereignty in part because the activity of planting was so diffused throughout the empire. If the idealizing discourse on the planter was necessarily conditioned by a lack of social referentiality, creole theorists deployed the catachrestic nature of the term to expand the set of subjects it included, to scale up from the plantation to the empire. For Roughley, the term "planter" includes attorneys, overseers, and bookkeepers resident on the plantation, but it implicitly expands to "the independent, non-resident owners of the land, and capitalists, and all who are interested in the welfare of that species of property" (vii). The plantation thus articulates landed and commercial interests—a point made by Smith but here reworked to establish plantations as unifying mechanisms for the empire. By gathering all of these people into a single term, Roughley abstracts the term "planter" from its colonial particularity and transforms it into a generalizable mode of subjectivity. While the spatial coordinates of Roughley's text appear restricted to the Jamaican plantation, he in fact theorizes empire as if it were a plantation—a dispersed oikos that comprehends "planters" throughout empire in a single domestic unit.

What is being generalized, in the term's referential drift, is a form of empirically oriented hyper-attentiveness. Roughley describes his own knowledge of plantership as derived from "many years" working in Jamaica; his "knowledge of the prevailing system of culture has been matured by experience" (vi). At the epistemological center of Roughley's "practical economy" is a man with his hands in the dirt—or, as he later acknowledges, with a whip in his hand (73, 80). Roughley cannot simply valorize the experiential, for he is specifically theorizing a form of plantership adequate to absenteeism. Rather, his aim is to inscribe the experiential as a dynamic condition of possibility *and* impossibility for attempts to write the plantation. The accumulation of texts necessary for plantation management signifies both the proprietor's attentiveness and the impossibility that acts of attention could stabilize into a systematizable textual arrangement. Roughley suggests that absentees hire a traveling agent, who would sojourn in the colony for a period of time and bring back a dizzying report:

> There should be laid before the proprietor, in plain legible terms, the accounts of the estate to the end of every year, a list of slaves and stock, with their increase and decrease; the cultivation of the estate, with the returns from plant and ratoon, in curing house hogsheads of sugar; the number of acres in cultivation of canes; returns of rum; the condition of cane, grass pieces, and provision grounds; the quantity of acres laid down in a table, whether plant or ratoon; their condition, and when fit to be cut; the names and number of white people on the estate, with their occupations and salaries; the different island accounts, whether paid or unpaid, as they are presented; the shipments and appropriation of the crop; what balance of the crop still remains on the estate, or at the wharf, not yet appropriated or shipped, and the list of clothing and provisions served to the slaves; jobbing and tradesmen's accounts; &c. &c. (28)[95]

The travels of the agent and the texts materialize a circuit of imperial attention, a circuit that concludes under the eyes of the planter. The planter here emerges as a kind of hermeneutic center who voraciously reads and works across various kinds of texts. He reads to stamp out neglect: with this information, the absentee planter will be able to "make his remarks on any errors which have crept in through neglect or otherwise, which demand censure or amendment" (30). Yet even as plantation theorists foregrounded the necessity of writing the plantation, these theorists held that texts of accountancy should not be seen as disburdening or economizing attention or as replacements for the inquisitive intentionality of the planter. The doubled "&c. &c." that concludes Roughley's list of textual forms marks the openness of the series: the work of textualizing the plantation is potentially limitless, without closure. John Lowndes thus reopens his short text *The Coffee-planter* (1807) with a supplementary chapter entitled "Omissions"—as if the fact of neglect requires immediate exposure and immediate repair. For these theorists, the attentiveness of the good planter only reveals the extent of his neglect, which should incite him to even more intense concern for his property. The plantation can never be exhibited "in one view": the planter must read and reread these various texts and even imagine the existence of texts he does not yet have before him.

For these theorists, the circulation of texts served as a means to incite subjects to bestowals of attention that exceed the representational capacities of any text. Texts were thus important less for the information they conveyed than for the subjects they formed. Henry Drax stresses the disciplinary qualities of textual accountancy in his instructions to his plantation attorney. Discussing the estate's sugar curer, Drax instructs, "You must frequently view his Accounts, also daily see his Sugar in every Bay. This Diligence of yours will make him fearful of erring by Neglect or otherwise, well knowing it must be discovered."[96] Drax's sugar curer was an enslaved human, so the consequences of "erring by Neglect" could be fearful indeed. Discussing the plantation's store of implements, Drax recommends that his attorney "charge one of your White-Servants that can Write" with keeping a book that records "what White or Black by Name, he delivers any Particulars to," as well as the date of the tool's return. For Drax, this book will not only stamp out waste and keep down incidental costs; in positive terms it will also instill an attentive disposition in plantation workers: "The oftener you inspect all these Accounts, the more careful you will make the Parties concerned."[97] Text here appears as a technology for fabricating care, a fabrication that ideally refashions literate and illiterate plantation workers, black and white, enslaved and free. Imperfectly materialized but insistently incited through text, attention was understood to hold the plantation—and the empire—together.

It was through the figure of the slave that plantation theorists transformed the epistemological dispositions of the planter into a general theory of government. As Gordon Turnbull put it, "The judgment and discretion of the manager of a plantation, are best shewn by a proper attention to these objects"—the objects being the "government or treatment of the slaves."[98] Plantation theorists deployed considerations of governance of the enslaved to derive a model for an antiliberal imperial constitution. For Martin, it is the presence of the planter who unceasingly bestows his "utmost care and tenderness" on his human property that distinguishes the colonial from the metropolitan form of economic governance. The planter's care secures to enslaved humans food, healthcare, and most radically a "right to civil protection."[99] The class organization of Europe, Martin comments, sadly leaves workers without such a protection: "The lowest condition is no just ground for contempt or neglect, no more than the colour of a man's complexion is for uncharitableness; and whatever Europeans may think of it, the distinction between the vulgar of the most free government and the negroes of our colonies is little more than nominal; for he that is forced to hard labour in support of life, is as much a *slave to necessity*, as negroes are to their owners."[100] The planter's care, Martin claims, protects the slave from enslavement to the necessity of submitting himself to the contingencies of capitalist labor markets. Europe's economization of social care means that its "slave[s] to necessity" cannot rely on material attention when they most need it: "necessity will make no abatement for sickness, or other accidental inabilities; and the tender mercies of the parish-officers, like the miser's largesses [sic], administer but little comfort to a sick man." Planters "are accountable" in a benevolent and caring way that a neglectful, sovereign market cannot be.[101]

A terrifying, if transparent, bit of ideology? Of course. But this argument did something more in the colonial West Indies than it would for later theorists of slavery in the U.S. South such as George Fitzhugh. For an age that would soon witness the declaration of inalienable rights to life, liberty, and the pursuit of happiness, Martin's right to civil protection could perhaps have been claimed only through the figure of the slave—that is, through the figure of a dependent subject who (as the story went) ceded personal sovereignty for guarantees of subsistence. As the American Revolution would reveal, West Indian elites *were* such dependent subjects, willing to enact a Hobbesian bargain of political obligation for politico-economic protection.[102] West Indian elites did not want independence; they needed, and so wanted, to maintain their dependent position within empire. Martin's positive coding of enslaved humans—"rational Beings they are," he writes, "and ought to be treated accordingly"—accordingly bespeaks the awkward consciousness that it was through the slave that the master's right to imperial protection became intelligible.[103] For these theorists, the slave's right to civil protection scaled up: Just as the planter protects the slave from the contingencies of the labor market, so too must the imperial sovereign protect the planter from the contingencies of the commodity market. This right could not be justified through economic logics: it preceded them, was superordinate to them, and when necessary interrupted them.

From its roots in the reams of correspondence that circulated through Britain's plantation empire, the plantation manual became the primary genre through which West Indians theorized the politico-economic constitution of that empire. Although they shed the epistolary form, manuals of plantation governance retained creole correspondence's investment in thematizing responsive attentiveness. Opposed to Smithian political economy's location of social cohesion in the aggregating effects of the market, the creole science of colonial commerce asserted that only the good planter's flexible, qualitative form of attention could gather together the dispersed elements of plantation life into a coherent unity. For these theorists, the planter's persistent attempts to eradicate neglect implied a form of imperial political organization. It also implied an aesthetic.

Planting Sovereignty

Published in Glasgow in 1828, *Marly; or, A Planter's Life in Jamaica* elevates monotony to a formal principle. The novel's excruciating boringness derives from the fact that it does not want to be a novel at all. In the preface to the second edition, the anonymous author writes, " Although he [the author] does not feel himself altogether alive to the mysteries of *fiction* he was determined to avail himself . . . of the fashionable medium of a tale, to convey what *facts* he was enabled to pick up."[104] The novelist's claim that fictionality was merely a vehicle for factuality was successful: even the arch-abolitionist James Stephen would draw on the "descriptive passages" of the pro-slavery text in describing the workings of plantation slavery.[105] Yet the novel's interest in offering a referentially accurate account of Jamaican reality is simply a subordinate part of its broader aim to narrate and valorize a form of subjectivity that, oriented toward empirical particulars, desires to "pick up" such facts in the first place. Little connects the "descriptive passages" composing *Marly*'s investigation into "the real state of slavery" in Jamaica besides the protagonist Marly, whose interest in Jamaican society compels him to attend to diverse particulars, which are then articulated as a coherent social unity through his narratological presence. The narrative time of the novel slows down and dilates as Marly familiarizes himself with Jamaica and as *Marly* familiarizes the reader with a form of caring attunement. Marly exercises, I suggest, a sovereign form of attentiveness dethroned by the epistemological principles of political economy. And if *Marly* is boring— and it is—it is because its sovereign subject just cares too much. About everything.

In terms of style, ideology, and epistemology, *Marly* looks back to the late mercantilist tradition of economic thought against which Smith most immediately responded. The character of Marly functions in much the same way as we saw the "Statesman" function in Steuart's *An Inquiry into the Principles of Political Oeconomy*. In many ways, *Marly* is the narrative of Steuart's States- man reclaiming his rightful place at the head of the imperial polity—just in Jamaica. My reference here is not accidental: just as Steuart's writing was set against the collapse of Jacobitism, so, too, does this history of lost sover- eignty and failed repossession inform the background to *Marly*'s narrative. The novel traces young George Marly's attempt to reclaim his ancestral estate in Jamaica, which unscrupulous executors of his father's will stole from him when he was an infant living in Scotland. The history of Marly's lost family estate is intimately linked to Scotland's loss of national sovereignty, a loss in- scribed in the text through the figure of Prince Charles Edward. First settling in Jamaica in 1746, Marly's grandfather was suspected by his peers of having been "out in the year forty-five" during the Jacobite uprising. (Sir James fled to Paris.) Marly's grandfather always showed "slight symptoms of displea- sure, when the universal subject of discourse was broached, about the rising in Scotland in 1745, especially when any person happened to call it a rebel- lion, and the Prince Charles Edward, the Pretender." These "symptoms" in- vite suspicion that "he had been engaged in the affray, and had eloped, prob- ably afraid of being harshly dealt with" (17). The history of the Marly clan is thus inscribed within a melancholic history of lost sovereignty and failed repossession. Yet Jamaica functions as a reparative scene where the failure of the uprising can have achieved imaginary success. When the grandfather spoke about the event, "he uniformly denominated it the rising, and the

Pretender was always honoured with the name of the Prince" (17). In Jamaica, at least symbolically, sovereigns can be restored to their proper place.

Through its inaugural invocation of the failed Jacobite uprising, *Marly* codes its narrative of the reclamation of lost plantation property as one of the reclamation of lost sovereignty. George Marly embodies this sovereignty, assuming many of the attributes of the Bonnie Prince. Like the prince, Marly was not born in the territory to which he asserts a right; like the prince, Marly cannot speak Gaelic; like the prince, Marly arrives in his native/ nonnative land surreptitiously. Most important, Marly possesses the prince's purported skill at disguise, which enables him to circulate through all ranks of Jamaican society.[106] To maintain this link between the prince's bid for sovereignty in 1745 and Marly's in 1820, the novel exorcises the crisis in imperial sovereignty marked by 1776. According to internal textual evidence, George's father was born in that year.[107] Having left the island to be educated in Scotland, George's father attempts a return in 1797, only to perish at sea with his wife. It is upon his death that Marly's rightful inheritance is stolen. The novel's protagonist is only a year old when his father dies; George Marly, the child of 1776, has no memory of his father. When young Marly finally appears on his ancestral estate, he is taken to be a ghost—not of his father, but of his grandfather. One slave tells another that "within two hours of sun-rise, he saw old massa Marly's ghost, in the shape of a young man, mounted on a fine horse, such as old massa Marly used to ride, galloping along the road past Equity Hall" (110). This genealogical haunting short-circuits Marly's father, establishing a line of disrupted continuity between Marly and his grandfather, between Jacobite Scotland and contemporary Jamaica. The ghost of 1745, Marly inherits the logic of imperial sovereignty that the political and discursive events of 1776 brought to crisis.

Marly embodies this principle of sovereignty through his careful and attentive gaze. From the novel's opening, the narrative asserts that the sovereign attention of the planter is irreducible to graphical technologies that attempt to discipline contingency, to calculate the incalculable. Indeed, an extreme incalculability conditions Marly's enterprise: the orphaned minor travels without letters of recommendation. Marly describes such letters as a form of social insurance to his fellow traveler, a Scotsman named Campbell: "Marly called out—'cheer up my friend, why be disconsolate because we are in a strange land? Our chance is as good as others. . . . Come, come, no drooping, you have a letter of recommendation, which, no doubt, will insure you employment; and although I have none, my spirits are good, and my hopes as sanguine as ever'" (6). Whereas Marly trusts to his virtuous capacity to hold steady before turbulent *fortuna*, his friend's letter of introduction enables him to "insure" himself against social contingency. Such letters were a crucial feature of the Scottish Atlantic diaspora, serving as a kind of nonmonetary credit instrument that insinuated strangers into relations of trust, obligation, and community. Through such letters, absentee proprietors, merchants, estate overseers and attorneys, and the bearers of the instruments formed complex "webs of patronage" held together by common geographic and ethnic provenance, economic favors, and, of course, letter writing.[108] Without any document testifying to his character, Marly is literally not written into patronage networks; unable to discipline contingency, Marly can only hope that chance will throw something his way.

Marly's reliance on his virtuous capacity to realize chance opportunities pays off during an encounter with a merchant named Graceson. He graciously invites Marly to drink a glass of punch, having witnessed a migrant Highlander planter reject Marly's application for employment because he lacks a letter of introduction and cannot speak Gaelic. Sympathetic to Marly's placelessness in the imperial economy of obligation, Graceson declaims against letters of introduction for the calculable, but meager, benefits they bring:

> Letters of introduction! What of them? I know their value to a scruple's weight: for do you know, gentlemen, when I came to the island, some twenty years ago, I brought six with me; and what might their worth be? Why, neither more nor less, than five dinners and one glass of grog—that was the whole value of them; and yet those who received them, acknowledged that they were from very dear and very respected friends, whom they would feel extremely happy to serve. Thus, gentlemen, we are enabled to fix the exact worth of a letter of introduction, as of the value of one dinner at the most, or at any rate of a glass of grog, though I have known many who did not receive even so much. So, a truce with letters of introduction! (10)

Graceson argues that letters of introduction are quasi-monetary instruments with a "value" determinable to a "scruple's weight." The exchange value of these letters is in tension with (and makes ironic) the recipients' claims about friendship and communal obligations. These letters translate obligations to "very dear" friends into the mechanical offering of a meal. As Graceson narrates it, the letter takes on a value that is curiously indifferent to the person bearing it: letters do not so much establish the individual as a unique and creditable person as they set in motion a ritualized and conventional form of exchange. Graceson models (as his name implies) an alternative form of social engagement, premised on the gracious bestowal of incalculable and unforeseeable gifts. He secures employment for Marly, declaring it to be the unmotivated, aneconomic act of a friend.

Writing against the transformations taking place in imperial governance, *Marly* valorizes modes of sociality that oppose accountability to accountancy, the incalculability of gracious giving to the calculability of exchange. Similarly exploring the articulation between creole literature and creole accountancy, Tim Watson has argued for the emergence of a "creole realism," suggesting that this literary epistemology emerged out of "the attempt to narrate the story of the British colonies from the point of view of a planter class defined by their qualities of reasonableness and enterprise."[109] Watson follows Ian Baucom's account of "actuarial historicism" to suggest that these economic texts transformed the plantation world into an abstract and calculable economy, at once sanitizing slavery while departicularizing enslaved humans into accountancy units.[110] Most historians of plantation accountancy would agree.[111] I suggest, however, that West Indians developed a critique of the very mode of textual rationalization of plantation life that Watson understands them as operating. As we have seen, severe epistemic limits reduced the effectiveness of accountancy techniques; if creoles developed a sense of epistemological realism, it was generated at the space where textual forms of systematization broke down. Indeed, *Marly*'s critique of calculating accountancy is inextricably bound up with a suspicion toward writing itself. As we see in Graceson's dismissal of letters of introduction, *Marly* holds that written attempts to produce relations of social accountability quickly devolve into instruments of calculable sociality, fueling automatic rituals of exchange that translate particular objects or relations into a "value" knowable to "a scruple's weight." *Marly*'s frustration with writing emerges out of writing's pretended scrupulousness: it makes objects legible but does so by abstracting them, erasing their particularity, and making them calculable and fungible.

Marly continues its critique of writing through a representation of the functions of a plantation bookkeeper, the employment that Graceson finds for the boy. In the Jamaican plantation system, the position of bookkeeper bore little relation to what we would call an accountant.[112] Bookkeepers were instead part of the plantation's managerial staff, overseeing labor, disciplining enslaved humans, and so on. Marly, unfamiliar with Jamaican terms, does not know this. In the boiling house on the first day of the job, he searches for the book he imagines he is to be keeping:

> He knew he was a book-keeper, but although every place had undergone a narrow scrutiny, he could not find the vestige of a book of any description; nay, there was not even so much as pen and ink in the whole house. He was puzzling himself with thinking what kind of books, or what kind of entries he should have to make, when he observed Brutus, on the completion of emptying a cooler, reach his hand over the table, to a board, a few inches square, regularly drilled with holes, from one of which he withdrew a peg, and placed it in a hole, one degree farther removed. This act at once explained the mystery to Marly, who saw, that this board was the book, which he was to keep, that the peg was the pen, and the number of holes passed through by the peg, in the course of twenty-four hours, was the numeration of the coolers, and which again, was the quantity of sugar made in a day. This mode of book-keeping, it must be confessed, was far from being complex, and in consequence no study was requisite. (34)[113]

The relationship between the writing that Marly expects and the writing he observes is ambiguous. In the text's series of assertions ("this board was the book," "the peg was the pen," and so on), Marly's reiterated "was" simultaneously possesses a metaphorical and a predicative value. Are these boards and pegs improper catachreses of the technologies proper to Eurocentric notions of writing? Or does the "was" establish a predicative relation, enfolding the boards and pegs into the proper of writing? Ultimately, the text declares board-and-peg writing to be a "mode of book-keeping," suggesting that this minimally "complex" writing possesses features in common with more complex accountancy textualities. Marly will go on to use other implements of writing on the plantation: for boards he will use books; for pegs, pens; for holes, numerals. Yet the novel sarcastically establishes this board-and-peg writing as teleologically analogous to the other "modes of book-keeping" that Marly uses: they all render and reduce processes and products to numbers.

By naming the counting slave "Brutus," *Marly* associates the act of counting with the assassination of an imperial sovereign. It is by juxtaposing Marly's scrupulous search for the book to the simple attention required for Brutus's bookkeeping—and, by extension, all graphical forms of accountancy—that Marly demonstrate the superiority of the planter's sovereign attentiveness. The passage begins inside Marly's consciousness ("He knew"), and closely attends to the course of his "narrow scrutiny." Through tracing Marly's scrutiny, the reader is invited to inhabit a generative and transformative mode of attention that adapts to frustrated expectations and unforeseen problems. The paratactical prose conveys a kind of accountancy operation—each item of the process that Marly observes becomes its own syntactical unit, enclosed by commas—but there is nothing mechanical or automatic about Marly's mode of registering the operation. His attention does not passively record objects; it transforms them through metaphoric and predicative assertions. Unlike the debased "modes of book-keeping" that operate through degrees of difference between isomorphic magnitudes, Marly's attentiveness gathers together and holds in relation the apparently incommensurable objects of pegs and pens, boards and books. Marly's qualitative, creative consciousness can hold together varied forms of calculation and accountancy.

For *Marly*, the social cannot be left to its own (graphical) devices. Rather, social and economic relations require a supplementary donation of attention to attain coherence and cohesion. The social "facts" that the novel purports to relate achieve legibility only through Marly's intensive and extensive gaze. But if *Marly*'s insistent interruption of its narrative with the tedium of attentive description formally enacts its critique of political-economic epistemology, these interruptions also open narrative space wherein alternative forms of politico-economic rationality can be articulated. Yet to understand the text's willing dilation of nonnarrative discourse as interruptive is misleading: such dilations constitute the dominant of the novel. Indeed, *Marly* is little more than a string of discourses on economics, plantation management, and imperial governance held together by Marly's being present at their articulation. If *Marly* is an antipolitical economy pretending to be a novel—and it is—it makes use of this generic pretense to re-embed economic disputation into a political, social, and ethical field.

The ever-attentive Marly functions as a recording device for the myriad debates raging through the Jamaican public sphere. Graceson's appearance in the text through a long harangue on letters of introduction is structurally similar to the eighteen-page discourse of Marly's mulatto friend on mulatto rights (161–79) and Mr. Broadcote's thirty-page discourse on improvement and imperial protection (225–55). Marly's exemplary willingness to pause and attend to the words of others allows the novel to give voice to arguments opposed to Smithian political economy. An "elderly gentleman" rages against the "abolitionists" who, having failed to persuade England to emancipate the slaves through moral arguments, have turned to political economy to achieve their aims: "They are strenuously endeavouring to instil into the minds of the people of England, that these Settlements have all along proved a heavy burden upon the country, and that it would be better if the whole West India Colonies were swallowed up in the ocean, than that they should remain, for Britain would then be eased of the heavy load of expense which they annually cost, and sugar and coffee procured cheaper from other sugar countries. This mode of arguing is the order of the day" (277). Against the claims of political economy, this gentleman offers a veritable heap of counterproofs, ultimately asserting that "these Islands are of incalculable benefit to the mother country" (280).

Yet the novel's refusal to concede that the islands could be anything but such an "incalculable benefit" to the empire is belied by its exploration of the proper mode of relating to social forms that have become a "heavy burden." Through the figure of the infirm slave, *Marly* attempts to deduce an analogical grounding for its assertion that empire retains an obligation to maintain robust economic protections for the plantation colonies. Indeed, this claim is articulated immediately prior to the elderly gentleman's description of the merits of the protectionist economy: as the novel's narrative time progresses, its argument scales up, moving from the infirm slave to the declining colony. In this discourse, the "humane" Mr. Broadcote asks how "declaring the whole slave population instantly free" would impact ex-slaves' "claim to the protection of the estate": "It would amount to an order to cast upon the wide world the aged, the infirm, the sick and the orphan, and all who were unable to support themselves. After they were declared free, they could have no claim to the protection of the estate on which they were born, and toiled out the strength of their days, except humanity; and judging from our experience of human nature, how few would be found who would listen . . . to the pitiful and imploring cries of helpless poverty" (249). Read from the perspective of the enslaved infirm, programs of liberal emancipation simply produce precarity: when social legibility (or, in Broadcote's metaphorics, audibility) is pegged to economic value, those defective for value production are institutionally neglected. No normative or legal force will impel postemancipation plantations to attend "to the pitiful and imploring cries" of those who cannot work. To the imminent liberal order, Broadcote opposes the pre-emancipation estate, one wherein infirm bondspeople's "claim to the protection" of the plantation does not depend on the "humanity" of plantation owners. Instead, legal regulations determine the slave's entitlement to subsistence without reference to the master's capacity for humane feeling or to the slave's capacity for production. Where political economists wish that the declining islands would sink into the sea, planters, Broadcote implies, would never abandon their declining, elderly slaves.

Even as *Marly* strives to imagine the alignment of plantation and imperial modes of governance, the novel concludes by marking their divergence. By the narrative's end, Marly has been restored to his plantation, where he promises to bestow on his property his inexhaustible care: "Now that he is seated at his ease, his attention has been devoted to ameliorating the condition of his labourers, by every practicable means, without proving hurtful to themselves or to his own interest" (324). Although the narrator notes that Marly's ameliorative efforts have met with some prejudice, he says that colonial legislatures have become more and more invested in amelioration; Marly's attentive mode of governance, the narrator is certain, will scale up. The novel concludes with the pious hope that, as an effect of this recalibration of the colonial state, "slavery will then gradually cease" and "a virtuous race of peasantry will inhabit these islands, and happiness, contentment, and prosperity, will be the blessings which will crown the whole" (324). Through an appended note, however, *Marly* dissolves its own fantasy of aligning plantation, colonial, and imperial modes of governance. "Since the greater portion of the foregoing sheets was printed," the novel resumes, Jamaica's colonial legislature had in fact promulgated an act of amelioration that abolished the flogging of women, admitted slaves' testimony against whites, abolished Sunday markets, and so on. On review, however, Secretary of the Colonies William Huskisson "has thought they have not gone far enough, and therefore has returned the Act of the Island, without approval, thereby annulling what had been done in favour of the Slave" (325). Huskisson was perhaps the most highly placed free (or at least freer) trader of the era.[114] *Marly* concludes by insinuating that the imperial state's reorientation along the lines of liberal economic theory has already begun interfering with planters' capacity to care, transforming their ameliorative acts into dead letters. The "now" in which the restored Marly sits at ease and attends to his property is a vanishing present.

But, Really, Who Cares?

By beginning this book with a chapter on a collectivity of people about whom we probably could not care less, my aim has been to stretch to their limits the kinds of political and moral energies that gather themselves, particularly in today's theoretical climate, around terms such as "neglect" and "abandonment." If Doctor Johnson thought slave owners yawping about freedom were ridiculous, how much more outrageous were their pathos-laden lamentations that they were not being paid enough attention? Few of us will sigh with Bryan Edwards, "So little has the science of colonial commerce been understood or adverted to!"[115] Fewer of us will sympathetically resonate with the "intense anxiety" that, MacDonnell asserted, "prevail[ed]" amongst owners of other human beings through the era of political economy.[116] We do not care, and we probably cannot.

I want to take this impossibility of investment, this impossibility of putting ourselves in a scene where creole complaints would be worth the hearing, as signaling the deep epistemological transformation that political economy in fact effected. It is comforting to think that we do not care about creole elites; our sympathies are elsewhere, with the enslaved. But when Williams let out his quip—"Jamaica preferred 'Yankee Doodle' to 'God save the Queen.' Who cared?"—an implied question motivated his snark. Why should the horizon of political being be constituted by patterns of affective investment, by conscious donations of care? For Williams, the fact that imperial belonging had become contingent on voluntaristically distributed metropolitan attention disclosed a new truth: in the age of political economy, empire was no longer a factical category of collective experience, a basic principle of worldliness no one had to feel anything about because that is what there was. For creoles, British indifference to the colonies became a problem at the precise moment that flatness was no longer an option—a flatness once derived from the obvious, unremarkable givenness of their imperial world.

Indeed, just his sarcastic asides, few writers have been more elegiac on empire's end than Williams—a fact forgotten today, as much scholarship continues to use him as an example of how quasi-Marxism plus anticolonialism equals bad history. Williams waxed elegiac because he knew it was not planters who would inherit the problem of living within a vanishing polity propped up by the voluntaristic care of a few Britons. It was the enslaved who would briefly feel the warmth of British care, only to be discarded as worthless—inconvenient, haunting reminders of an empire that just could not seem to quit Britain.

It is to this archive of worthlessness that I now turn.

Chapter 2

"THEM WORTHLESS ONES": EMANCIPATORY
LIBERALISM IN JAMAICA

As a slave, the worker has *exchange value*, a *value*; as a free wage-worker, he has *no value*; it is rather his power of disposing of his labour, effected by exchange with him, that has value. . . . His *valuelessness* [*Wertlosigkeit*, "worthlessness"] is the presupposition of capital and the precondition of *free* labour in general. Linguet regards it [that is, the loss of value] as a step backwards; he forgets that the worker is thereby formally posited as a person who is something for himself *apart from his* labour, and who alienates his life-expression only as a means towards his own life.

—KARL MARX, *Grundrisse*

To track enslaved lives through the archive of plantation accounts is to track histories of devastation, decline, and death. Consider London, a person who lived his enslaved life on William Gale's York Estate in Jamaica. In an inventory and evaluation from 1775, London is described as a thirty-eight-year-old "Congo" who served as a "watchman" on the estate.[1] He is also described as "worthless," as recorded in a note under the column "Condition." Despite his worthless condition, Gale's bookkeeper assesses London's value at £40. In an inventory prepared seven years later, London gains a new modifier: "elephantisis [*sic*] worthless." London's ailment explains his steep drop in imputed value, which is updated to £5. That London retains a monetary value is itself noteworthy; some people, such as the "superannuated" (but not "worthless") Andrew, were valued at £0. Others, such as London's fellow watchman Simon, bore an even stranger relationship to monetary evaluation. In 1775, the fifty-eight-year-old "invalid" was appraised at £40. In 1782, it is revealed that Simon has "ulcerated leggs." Yet instead of a monetary figure—even a minimal one such as £5 or even £0—Simon's value is marked as two vertical slashes.[2] At his age and with his health issues, Simon was effectively free from sale; no one would have purchased him. At the same time, legal obstacles would have prevented his manumission: the estate would have had to pay a fee to the colonial state in the likely event that Simon could not support himself.[3] Because he was unable to be removed from the plantation but understood to be unable to work on it, economic value no longer serves as a meaningful way to describe Simon. The lines that occupy the place of value do not mean "no value," as an imputed sum of £0 would. They mark, rather, the nonavailability of a language of value to describe Simon's position in the plantation's world. In Gale's books of account, such vertical slashes proliferate in the sections evaluating enslaved women, particularly for those women—such as Large Mimba (sixty-seven in 1782) and Phibba (sixty-two)—beyond the age of childbearing. The removal of these enslaved people from the language of value is shocking: it encodes, in a grotesquely sanitizing fashion, a lifetime of violence and deprivation that the language of accountancy can index but not render. Yet if tracking lives through plantation records entails a shocking confrontation with the stark absoluteness of wasted life, it also entails grappling with the startling fact that such "worthless" life remains legible at all. Gale's plantation appears as a scene of horrific and horrifically slow violence, but the wasting of Simon's life did not strip it bare. Rather, Simon's insistent presence within Gale's books marks the persistence of sociality beyond value.

The great transformation that emancipation wrought registers in the clearance of "worthless" humans such as Simon from plantations' books of account.[4] Following full emancipation in 1838, planters adopted forms of bookkeeping adequate to the liberalized labor market and the transformed legal relation that obtained between plantations and the emancipated labor force. As slave inventories became wage books, capitalist forms of value mediated the legibility of ex-slaves before the plantations on which they had labored and lived. Worthless humans negligible to the valorization of capital became, in an archival sense, entirely illegible: they simply disappear from the material texts of plantation society. This erasure did not happen all at once. During the period of partial bondage known as Apprenticeship—a four-year period beginning on 1 August 1834 in which ex-slaves were bound to labor for their masters for forty-five hours per week—children younger than six were declared entirely free. They, too, vanish from some plantation inventories, a fact that indexes their broader displacement from the plantation's distributive economy.[5] Planters were no longer required to care for such life, to assign it a juridical or biopolitical value that exceeded the immediate demands of value production, and so they expelled it. Whereas worthlessness once indicated the persistence of a sociality beyond the valorization requirements of capital, in the postemancipation order of things worthlessness marked defective subjects off as disposable. Emancipation had the effect of exposing life without value to the full consequences of its worthlessness.

While the foreclosed figure of the worthless ex-slave limns the ugly underside of emancipation, even those who survived slavery more or less intact had to negotiate becoming free as a stripping of value from their lives.[6] As Marx notes, worthlessness is constitutive of liberal-capitalist value relations: the free wage worker's life has "no value" for capital, which accords value instead to the worker's "life expression," his labor-power. Antislavery activists in the pre-emancipation era shared Marx's postemancipation understanding. In his *West India Question* (1833), Joseph Phillips declares, "The flesh and bones of these Slaves are worth nothing; it is their *labour* alone that is of value."[7] Both Marx and Phillips script emancipation as a liberating disentanglement of a value-creating capacity from the enslaved life that bears it; emancipation entails, in other words, the forced devaluation of the "flesh and bones" of enslaved humans. For both, this divestment of value from life is little more than a vanishing analytical moment, one superseded as valueless but free humans transact with capital and posit their otherwise worthless lives as the telos of their labor. The onset of Apprenticeship forced abolitionists to revise this hopeful narrative. At an anti-Apprenticeship meeting in Birmingham in 1835, the Reverend John Burnett would describe his outrage on discovering "gentlemen sitting down with all the coolness of arithmeticians, calculating the prices of men and the value of blood;—looking to the children rising into life, and to the aged moving towards the tomb, and exclaiming with the voice of oppression, 'These are the men to be disposed of'—and counting the number of their victims as they would the bricks and stones of the palaces in which they dwelt."[8] Starving men, invalids flogged and abandoned to death, women raped, children born as dead due to violence against their mothers, the whole open set of people whom the Jamaican ex-slave James Williams would name "them worthless ones"—these figures crowd the archive, populating a necropolis at the heart of Britain's empire of care.[9] The liberal script of emancipation, abolitionists declared, had gone horribly wrong, and its perversion was nowhere more evident than in Jamaica. Far from functioning as a vanishing analytic moment, worthlessness had splayed out into a durative temporality: imperial attempts to make the socially dead live created a world that let them die.[10]

In this chapter, I argue that antislavery representations of worthless life functioned both to critique and to recuperate the violent process of emancipatory liberalism. Political economy is once more central to this story, both in terms of its precipitation of the crisis and in its impact on the modality by which the crisis was represented. In many ways, emancipation was an "experiment" in applied political economy: the architects of emancipation turned to Jeremy Bentham, Adam Smith, and other political economists to make the construction of a free society both imaginable and actionable.[11] It also provided the cognitive tools through which the results of emancipation were understood.[12] The cognitive frame of political economy conditioned not only statist modes of assaying emancipation but also the popular, activist modes of narrating and representing the ugly effects of emancipatory liberalism. Indeed, the relationship between political-economic thought and the antislavery writing of the 1820s and 1830s is so intimate that we tend to assign an argument developed by the latter (the superior productivity of free over enslaved labor) to the former. (From the opposite direction, Harriet Martineau's "Demerara" (1832) in her *Illustrations of Political Economy* series neatly epitomizes the cross-fertilizations of abolitionism and popular political economy in the era.) Much latter-day antislavery writing was a vernacular genre of political economy—not simply in terms of its explicit ideological commitments but, more important, in terms of its absorption of political economy's epistemology. The texts I explore here were compiled, composed, or collaboratively written by antislavery activists from provincial Britain, the "new people," in George Stephen's terms, who revitalized the quiescent antislavery scene in the 1820s and dominated the movement against Apprenticeship in the 1830s.[13] Evangelical radicals such as James Cropper and his son-in-law Joseph Sturge understood "commerce as an instrument of moral policy," taking Smith's market system as a form of providential ordering.[14] I am interested in how the astonishingly popular texts these men helped produce—the ex-slave James Williams's narrative account of Apprenticeship, pamphlet-size anthologies of colonial dispatches, and so on—render the social effects of emancipation legible *through* narrative and descriptive procedures that derive from political economy's modality of assembling knowledge about society. They provide "models of value," in James Thompson's terms, if only by demonstrating the violent failure of the liberal-capitalist value form to fully subsume Jamaican life.[15]

While this chapter could be read in part as an account of the imperial formation of the "modern fact," I am less concerned with epistemological questions as such than in the political (or antipolitical) ramifications of antislavery activists' approaches to the shattered social of emancipation-era Jamaica.[16] It is a striking fact that the crisis of emancipation never registered as a crisis for liberal political economy, despite the willingness of activists to incriminate themselves and their plans in the social production of worthless life.[17] Even as the utopian hopes for liberal social engineering were dashed by empirical reality, activists reinscribed and recuperated the epistemic grammar of political economy as they assembled knowledge about emancipation. By compiling and composing scenes of worthless life, activists reconfigured liberalization as a recuperative, animating force. Joseph Sturge and Thomas Harvey give us a glimpse of the vitalizing qualities of economic liberalization in their travelogue *The West Indies in 1837*: "Some [formerly enslaved Antiguans] had been stimulated to more industrious habits. One of the most worthless women on the property, once always pretending illness and an inability to work, had become an industrious a laborer as any on the estate."[18] Here, participation in liberal-capitalist forms of sociality marks the accession from putative social death to putative social life. As Sturge and Harvey exemplify, and as I argue, gender became a central lever by which liberal abolitionists imaginatively and affectively managed the crisis of political economy's value form, taking biological reproduction as a point of intervention through which the reproduction of a free-labor, free-market society could become newly thinkable.

This political-economic hermeneutic diminished the legibility of the forms and fantasies of social being that were improvised by ex-slaves in and through the process of becoming worthless. As we will see, fantasies of imperial belonging and imperial justice sustained apprentices through the period. Yet antislavery writing's absorption of political economy's epistemology meant that ex-slaves were primarily rendered as objects to be governed, *not* as political-juridical subjects of an extended imperial polity. While scholarship on colonial governmentality has attended to this coding of the emancipated, it has tended to displace questions of sovereignty entirely, downplaying Michel Foucault's assertion that, with the emergence of regimes of liberal governmentality, the "problem of sovereignty is not eliminated" but "is made more acute than ever."[19] Ex-slaves inhabited this problematic space, setting the symbolics of sovereignty to work to recode themselves as rights-bearing subjects of the empire. They did so by jointly composing letters of gratitude to the Crown; by comporting themselves as good Christians and, thus, good Britons; by appearing before special magistrates to seek justice as rights-bearing subjects of the empire; and by occasionally demanding an audience with the colonial governor himself.[20] It is easy to discount (and, in the case of the missives of gratitude, wince at) these expressions of an imperial political subjectivity. Yet it is important to recall that claims to imperial subjecthood, frequently articulated through Christian subjecthood, had long been the common idiom of subaltern antislavery and anticolonialism in the West Indies; in many ways, the Demerara Rebellion of 1823 and the Jamaican Baptist Rebellion of 1831–32 were rebellions against the colonial plantocracy in the name of imperial freedom and in defense of imperial sovereignty.[21] Moreover, in claiming imperial subjecthood ex-slaves were not so much availing themselves of a secured juridico-political identity as they were laying claim to it through performative utterances that constituted that identity through the very act of demand or complaint. Imperial subjecthood served as a catachresis that organized an insurgent desire to achieve political legibility as something *other than* a laborer, whether enslaved or free. Yet the political-economic hermeneutic underwriting activist approaches to emancipation always already deactivated the discursive conditions by which such performances could be felicitous in rendering ex-slaves legible to and before empire as juridico-political subjects. Jamaican ex-slaves were accorded rights and a position as "fellow subjects" of the empire to the extent that the allowance of such rights was functional for their free subordination to the emergent market regime.[22]

Scenes of worthless life were complex moments at which antislavery writers and ex-slaves articulated different, and even opposed, versions of emancipation's promise. We might think this difference by returning to the two forms of bookkeeping with which I began this chapter. If antislavery activists looked forward to a period in which social worth and economic value—both productive and reproductive—would harmoniously align, ex-slaves sought a form of life in which economic value and social worth were disarticulated, in which sociality persisted through the collapse of economic value, and in which even the worthless stuck around and left their mark. In the coming chapters, we will see how British-led liberal globalization inhibited West Indians from realizing this form of life within the empire, inducing a turn to the New World as a scene of postliberal socialities. I now explore the roots of this foreclosure in the emancipation process itself.

"The Essential Thing Is to Get Rid of Them"

First published in Britain just a few years before the Act of Abolition was passed, Jeremy Bentham's *Emancipate Your Colonies!* (written in 1793 and first published in English in 1830) should complicate our sense of who—or what—was emancipated in 1834. Addressing the revolutionary National Convention of France in 1793, Bentham pointedly asks, "What if colonies, as they are called, are worth nothing to you? What if they are worth less than nothing?"[23] Following the line Smith adopted in *The Wealth of Nations*, Bentham is certain that free trade between independent nation-states would prove more profitable than intraimperial, mercantilist commerce. Yet whereas Smith thought that British pride in possessing colonies, as well as the political power of those interested in colonial trade, would prove radical free-trade schemes to emancipate the colonies little more than a "Utopia" or "Oceania," Bentham's reflections on France were written within a doubled revolutionary conjuncture in which a postimperial utopia seemed realizable.[24] For Bentham, the revolution within hexagonal France had shattered the class power of those invested in Antillean commerce; meanwhile, revolution in Saint-Domingue had driven up the costs of colonial rule and unleashed an intense ideological debate that threatened to divide revolutionary France. If the emancipation of the colonies had long been economically rational, such a measure was now politically possible, and, indeed, expedient: "Great differences of opinion, and those attended with no little warmth, between the tolerators and proscribers of negro slavery:—emancipation throws all these heart burnings and difficulties out of door; it is a middle term in which all parties may agree."[25] Unwilling to live with an empire of slavery, but equally unable to realize an empire of freedom, France should simply do without empire. The moral, economic, and political imperative to give up empire is so intense that Bentham suggests it should be done immediately, without consideration for the mechanism of detachment: "How you part with the poor people who are now your slaves, is after all a subordinate consideration: the essential thing is to get rid of them."[26] Indeed, even after being emancipated from French rule, these "poor people" may remain slaves. So long as France does "not direct the raising" of sugar, French people "need not trouble" themselves about how sugar is raised.[27]

Emancipate Your Colonies! mapped so neatly onto the British discursive environment in which it was published that it was all but redundant. Antislavery activists with a mind for political economy had already hit on Bentham's expedient of liberalizing trade to liberate slaves. What is useful about Bentham is the stark way in which he articulates a disposition of indifference to his *dispositif* of emancipation: it casts into relief the violence of neglect that haunted the many emancipation programs floated by abolitionists who did care to free enslaved humans. These quasi-Benthamite programs of emancipation were a rather blunt response to constitutional and theoretical limits that had always haunted organized antislavery. Scholars typically narrate the history of British antislavery as a telescoping movement: activist energies first fixated on the sphere of circulation (the African slave trade) and then narrowed to the site of production (plantation slavery). William Wilberforce himself authorized this interpretation when explaining his return to organized antislavery in the early 1820s: antislavery activists always knew, he asserted, that interventions in the sphere of circulation were not adequate to the task of ameliorating, or ending, slavery.[28] Yet even as Wilberforce strove to code dashed hopes as part of the plan, the political structures that compelled abolitionists to indirect attacks on slavery remained more or less in place. As Wilberforce knew well, abolitionists initially struck at the slave trade because they could: Parliament had the legal authority to regulate the trade. Conversely, Parliament's authority to legislate the internal organization of colonies that had chartered local houses of assembly was far shakier. Following the abolition of the slave trade in 1807, the juridical terrain of empire did not shift; Parliament's legislative competency to interfere with West Indian property remained weak, as West Indian elites never tired of shouting. The debacle over Wilberforce's Slave Registry Bill in 1815 proved the rhetorical, if not legal, soundness of the plantocracy's constitutional claims to Parliamentary noninterference, even if parliamentarians demurred that they did in fact possess such authority—they just would not use it.[29] Parliament retained, however, a set of fiscal instruments that shaped Britain's sugar market—duties, tariffs, bounties, and drawbacks—and so the parameters of plantation profitability and its authority to regulate intraimperial and British trade through these instruments were indisputable. Whereas West Indians defended their property in enslaved humans with a robust language of rights, they could defend their market protections only through the weak vocabulary of "compact." The mercantilist structure of empire that sustained British West Indian plantations remained juridically and politically weaker than the plantation regime itself: antislavery activism remained on firmest ground when it attempted to control the circulation of commodities through the sea.

They were on theoretically firmer ground, as well. Second- and third-generation political economists never followed through on Smith's rather vague suggestion that free labor was superior to enslaved labor. The cliometric scholarship of the 1970s suggests that classical political economists were reticent with good reason: slave labor was productive and profitable, particularly in the frontier zones of the world system.[30] Indeed, not only did abolitionists fail to find robust support for a free-labor argument in the work of political economy; they found the opposite. Jean-Baptiste Say's *Treatise on Political Economy* (written in 1803 and published in English translation in 1821), the continent's most important and popular work in the line of Smith, was "so disconcerting to British abolitionists that it became the subject of special damage-control efforts at the beginning of their emancipation campaign two decades after its publication."[31] Say was a doctrinaire free trader who excoriated France's mercantilist system. For Say, the high rate of profit that prevailed in the prerevolutionary Antilles was little more than a sign of economic disequilibrium. Unfortunately for antislavery activists, Say located the plantation economy's tendency toward disequilibrium in "unfree trade, not unfree labor"; indeed, Say defended the rationality of plantation production.[32] Adam Hodgson responded in *A Letter to M. Jean-Baptiste Say, on the Comparative Expense of Free and Slave Labour* (1823); other abolitionists would point to the copy-hold experiment of the Barbadian planter Joshua Steele as indicative of the relative superiority of free labor.[33] Even as antislavery activists invented the free-labor argument that popular history would assign to mostly reticent political economists, they incorporated political economy's far more robust critique of mercantilism into the structure of their argument. Mercantilist protections for plantation produce made slavery profitable and thus inhibited free labor from asserting its relative superiority. The withdrawal of these protections, abolitionists argued, would compel plantations to shift to a free labor regime.

The free-trade imaginary of antislavery activists introjected a profound ambiguity into their schemes for West Indian emancipation. Were slaves being emancipated into the British Empire, or was the empire being emancipated from its slave colonies? The very title of the elder James Stephen's *England Enslaved by Her Own Slave Colonies* (1826) suggested that both forms of emancipation were on the table. Indeed, in the first volume of his opus, *The Slavery of the British West India Colonies Delineated* (1824/30), Stephen would suggest that if emancipation could not be achieved within empire, empire was bound to abandon the colonies to hasten the collapse of slavery.[34] For others, emancipation within empire would serve as a prologue for the colonies' emancipation from it, which would have the effect of freeing Britain from them. John Taylor makes this point clear in his *Negro Emancipation and West Indian Independence: The True Interest of Great Britain* (1824). The debate over the desirability of emancipation, Taylor writes, "is at once answered, by [enslaved West Indians'] well known wish to emancipate themselves."[35] This emancipation is both personal and political: through a citation of Haiti, Taylor posits national independence as the horizon of black emancipation from slavery. After emancipation, the West Indies "will, in a short time, become fit to assume the management of their own internal and external affairs," the effect of which is that "Great Britain will be relieved from a heavy burden."[36] Note how Taylor converts his racist and patronizing ascription of a fitness for freedom into a desire for freedom of a particular kind. Indeed, liberal antislavery's absorption of political economy's anti-imperial epistemology meant that programs for imperial emancipation were already patterned by a teleology of freedom that culminated in the dissolution of empire into nation-states. Needless to say, none of these antislavery activists cite any black West Indian articulations of nation-statist freedom dreams: they would not have been able to find many.[37] Rather, the telos of "West Indian independence" marks the terminus of empire's intention to care for emancipated subjects in worthless colonies.

In a barrage of pamphlets published through the 1820s, James Cropper made the most sustained case for dismantling mercantilist empire in the name of securing black freedom. By 1825 the "unofficial philosopher of the antislavery movement," Cropper was a Quaker merchant from Liverpool with a large fortune derived from American cotton and the British Indian trade.[38] The sources of Cropper's wealth would soon prove embarrassing to him, as West Indian antagonists remarked on both his willingness to trade the produce of bonded labor and the possible self-interest motivating his plans for free-trade freedom. According to David Brion Davis, Cropper read Smith at some point in the 1790s, and Smith enabled the devout Quaker to see "the great hand of God in the flow of goods toward their natural markets."[39] Like many of his fellow liberal abolitionists (and, indeed, like Smith), Cropper believed that the value of the West Indies was artificially inflated, that the West Indies were "worth nothing at all," and that mercantilist protections amounted to little more than a "sacrifice" on the part of Great Britain "exceeding in amount the value of all the colonies put together."[40] The liberalization of Britain's sugar market would realign actual value and market value and reveal plantation slavery to be entirely unprofitable. The freedom of slaves would be an effect of the freedom of markets, but only insofar as free markets will so devalue enslaved labor as to make it unprofitable.

For Cropper, slavery is only profitable in spaces where the value of labor is exorbitantly high, in frontier zones of the world system. Cropper suggests that it was probably the "low value of labor" that led to the "gradual and imperceptible decline of slavery" in Britain and other parts of the North Atlantic world: "There can be no doubt that a reduction in price of labour, probably (as in many places at present), to the lowest scale of subsistence, rendered slave labour unprofitable, and produced its abolition in Europe."[41] A similar condition holds in British India: "In a densely peopled district, like that of Bengal, where wages are reduced to the lowest rate of subsistence, what can be the profit or motive for holding men in slavery?"[42] There is nothing special about West Indian labor that should accord it a higher value, as Cropper makes clear: "Labour in the West Indies is of as little value as it can be anywhere."[43] The space of the world market in sugar is as "densely peopled" with producers as colonial Bengal, but mercantilist protections segment and isolate these productive populations, preventing them from coming into competitive contact. By liberalizing and globalizing Britain's sugar market, the crowding of the market will cause the price of sugar to drop, with a corresponding fall in the value of enslaved humans. Freedom, Cropper asserts, will be an effect of the slave's worthlessness.

But how? By liberalizing Britain's sugar market, the price of produce will be regulated by those zones that remunerate laborers at "the lowest scale of subsistence"—that is, zones of free labor such as British India or, at least, what Cropper took to be the "milder systems of slave labor" of Brazil and Cuba.[44] Market pressures will compel West Indian planters to adopt better systems of management, Cropper asserts: "Low prices of produce . . . compel the adoption of the best and most economical systems; and thus lead almost necessarily to an improved treatment of the Slaves."[45] Cropper manages his hesitation about the status of his deduction ("almost necessarily") by recourse to demographic data drawn from the United States. By means of this example, Cropper argues that the slave population will grow as an effect of improved treatment and looks forward to "the time when, from an increase of their numbers, or other circumstances, they would cease to have any saleable value; and when it would be a great hardship on their masters to compel them any longer to hold them in slavery."[46] When slaves "become burdensome," in short, "slavery will cease."[47]

Cropper's program reveals the paradoxes that attend thinking freedom through the optics of liberal political economy. For one, Cropper transforms the lower-cost, higher-profit sugar produced by extra-imperial slave plantations into a technology for West Indian emancipation. British West Indian freedom relies on the allocation and centralization of slavery elsewhere.[48] I will explore this problem more deeply in the next chapter. More important to me now is the epistemology underwriting Cropper's line of argument. Like the classical political economists from whom he draws, Cropper argues deductively from a set of postulates regarding the systematicity of markets toward a particular case.[49] On one hand, this epistemological sharing results in a striking convergence between Cropper's plan to induce freedom within the colonies and, say, John Ramsay McCulloch's program to free Britain from them. The difference between liberal care routed through political economy and disciplinary political economy's indifference is one of accent, emphasis, intention. On the other hand, Cropper's deduction of freedom from the systemic functioning of markets transforms methodological postulates into "almost" ineluctable laws. The empirical figures that Cropper compiles (the U.S. demographic data, for instance) are useful only to the extent that they figure this systematicity; they have the same epistemological status as the examples that saturate Smith's *Wealth of Nations*. Particular results are simply the reflux and reflections of the rule-bound world of the market. By the 1820s, however, political economy's reliance on deduction had come under assault from numerous quarters—from Tory and histori cally minded political economists, statisticians, and, as we have seen, West Indian social theorists.[50] Indeed, in a long-running polemic with Cropper in the pages of Liverpool newspapers, John Gladstone (publishing under the pseudonym "Mercator") would force Cropper to consider another, less providential possibility: what if liberalization's recoding of enslaved life as tendentially worthless did not inspire planters to economically rational bestowals of concern but to intensified exploitation?[51]

Cropper would float the possibility several times:

How unreasonable would it be to suppose, as some of the advocates of Slavery would have us to do, that as the system became less profitable, its severities would be increased; until . . . Slavery, having arrived at the utmost point of severity and oppression, would be transformed at once, by some tremendous shock, into freedom; and that at a time when the Slaves are least of all prepared for it. Such a supposition, would be a monstrous absurdity; and yet, such as it is, the Planters seem to have been able to persuade the people of this country to believe, and to act upon it. This error . . . arises from the [plantocracy's] habit of looking more to temporary, than permanent advantages. There is no doubt, that the Planter . . . will, when the price of sugar declines, be very likely, not only to feed his Slaves less, but to work them harder; but the state of his affairs will soon convince him, that he must change his system, or be ruined.[52]

Cropper effectively manages the possible breakdown of the market's systemic effects by arguing that the unfolding of such effects will take time. The problem that confronts Cropper now is that of thinking how enslaved humans would endure the open duration of the market's pedagogical process. While recognizing that the costs of liberalization might be displaced to enslaved humans, Cropper asserts that the market will penalize creoles' short-term thinking and "convince" the planter that the long-term reproducibility of his enterprise relies on a meliorated "system." Liberalization here functions as a process of persuasion that aims to reorganize slave-owning West Indians' sense of time, their "habit of looking to more temporary, than permanent advantages." This process will itself take time, and thus the problem: enslaved West Indians are, according to Cropper, "half-starved beings, . . . impaired by the want of a sufficient quantum of nutrient, to compensate for the exertions which they are compelled to make."[53] Confronted with an intensification of labor, on one hand, and a squeeze in subsistence, on the other, could these humans survive the time of their masters' lesson? Cropper can at best suggest that the period of induced hyper-exploitation will end quickly, that "the state of his affairs will soon convince him" that good treatment, and even freedom, is maximally conducive to the long-term health of their enterprises.

A tangle of disavowals and assumptions underwrites the temporality of expectant deferral that Cropper opens. For one, Cropper has to ignore liberalization's present tense, the way that worthlessness assembles itself into a "state of . . . affairs." The text is vague on this state of affairs, but it must be a state so disastrous that it could compel planters to convert wholesale to a liberalized regime of management. Cropper abstracts away the violence of lived worthlessness even as it is the concrete effects of this violence that will serve to "convince" planters. Once planters realize that the dead cannot cut cane, once planters realize that the intensity of their exploitation is interfering with the long-term survival of their enterprises, they will adopt rationalized management strategies that will ensure a profitable future. Moreover, Cropper's program of market-enforced amelioration assumes that planters could imagine a profitable future for their enterprises beyond the horizon of mercantilist slavery. Few in fact could, and political economy was on their side.[54] So, too, implicitly, was Cropper, whose very program relied on the declining position of West Indian production vis-à-vis extra-imperial sites of production with or without enslaved labor. Without the fantasy of futurity, nothing prevents liberalization's temporality of intensified hyper-exploitation from converting into a durative present. Indeed, Cropper assigns but the slimmest possible role to the imperial state in maintaining enslaved humans in life through the process of devaluation.[55]

While Cropper's program never became imperial policy, the political-economic thought on which it draws would organize both the institutional process of emancipation and the ways in which antislavery activists interpreted its effects. Important to me here is how Cropper's embrace of the deductive epistemology of political economy and his faith in the providential systematicity of markets enable him to enfold worthlessness into a temporality that ends ineluctably—minus a hiccough or two—with the subsumption of life into liberal value relations. Cropper no doubt would have disputed Bentham's assertion that the "essential thing is to get rid of" the worthless colonies, as well as the humans in them. The difference between the two, however, is not so wide: Bentham's disposal of the colonies is starkly absolute while Cropper brackets, relativizes, and temporalizes worthlessness, transforming it into an abstract moment. Just as important, neither Bentham nor Cropper accords any role to state mechanisms in absorbing the "shock" of liberalization; nor do Bentham and Cropper imagine that emancipation entails the production of a positive political relation with and within empire. Emancipation here appears in its etymological sense, as a letting go.

Cool Calculations and Worthless Life

From the outset, the process of emancipation was riven by a tension between the logics of political sovereignty and the logics of liberal governance. On one hand, emancipation was an extraordinary act of imperial state formation. The Act of Abolition of 1833 dissolved the condition of *imperium in imperio* that chattel slavery introduced into the empire, incorporated eight hundred thousand humans as rights-bearing subjects directly under the Crown's protection, and testified to imperial Parliament's willingness to treat empire as a constitutional space unified under its legislative sovereignty—something it had been chary to do since the years immediately before the American Revolution.[56] Moreover, it set in motion what was perhaps the single largest nonmilitary expansion of the British imperial state in history. It provided £20,000,000 in compensation money to those whose human property was to be set free—at 40 percent of the state's annual revenue, an amount that "would equate to £200 billion today."[57] And it promised a political identity to ex-slaves. As the Marquess of Sligo, governor of Jamaica, informed newly minted apprentices in an address promulgated on 1 August 1834, "You will in a few short years enjoy every privilege which any other persons in this island, being British subjects, possess."[58] In many ways, the emancipation process was an extraordinarily statist measure in an era in which British middle classes continued to "disdain statist solutions" to social problems, as Lauren Goodlad puts it.[59] Indeed, antislavery activists were cognizant that they were in some measure violating tenets of liberal social thought. As the antislavery Member of Parliament Daniel O'Connell wrote to Sturge in 1844, Britain undertook this expansion "for the sake of humanity, but in direct violation of the rules of political economy."[60]

Yet if the causes of emancipation were exorbitant to or in violation of political-economic rationality, it was through this very logic that the imperial state gave effect to its sovereign intentions. As noted earlier, political economy provided the cognitive and institutional technologies through which emancipation became thinkable and actionable. Following Karl Polanyi, we might think of emancipation as a process in which the imperial state worked to disembed a market in labor from the material and cognitive structures in which laborers had previously been embedded.[61] As the New Poor Law of 1834 would in insular Britain, the Act of Abolition instituted a world in which West Indian ex-slaves "would be free, but only after being resocialized to accept the internal discipline that ensured the survival of the existing social order. They would be free to bargain in the marketplace but not free to ignore the market."[62] Indeed, Sligo followed up his promise of imperial subjecthood with an exhortation that was in part a condition: "Pay the most diligent attention to your duties; serve your masters with cheerfulness, and with the gratitude they deserve."[63] Ex-slaves were in effect doubly conceptualized by the imperial state both as rights-bearing subjects of the Crown *and* as a population whose conduct required regulation, correction, and (re)formation. As its name implies, the period of Apprenticeship was understood as a time during which ex-masters and ex-slaves would come to inhabit the forms of liberal subjectivity adequate to the liberal society in formation.

As we will see, the crisis of Apprenticeship was an effect of the imperial state's attempt to refashion plantation Jamaica into an ideal-typical society culled from liberal political-economic thought. What concerns me here is how this tension between the logics of political sovereignty and the logics of political economy made available discontinuous modalities of mapping and responding to the crisis. I work through these discontinuities through a reading of James Williams's *A Narrative of Events, since the First of August, 1834, by James Williams, an Apprenticed Labourer in Jamaica* (1837). Indeed, Williams's text depicts apprentices as suspended in an emancipatory present both durative and unendurable, one wherein the structuring fiction of futurity has withdrawn, exposing apprentices to an ongoing time of being alive without being (of) value. *A Narrative of Events* is a collaboratively written text, and I am interested in the conflictual and divergent ways in which Williams and his editorial team sought repair for this state of wounded freedom.[64]

These divergent interpretations are evident in how Williams and his editors interpretively assemble the present tense of Apprenticeship. On the first page, Williams describes his experience of the new regime:

> I have been very ill treated by Mr. Senior and the magistrates since the new law come in. Apprentices get a great deal more punishment now than they did when they was slaves; the master take spite, and do all he can to hurt them before the free come;—I have heard my master say, "Those English devils say we to be free, but if we is to free, he will pretty well weaken we, before the six and four years done; we shall be no use to ourselves afterwards."[65]

At first glance, Williams's text appears to confirm emergent antislavery common sense regarding the dynamics of Apprenticeship. According to Williams's editor Thomas Price, *A Narrative of Events* demonstrates what metropolitan liberals long assumed: "*slavery has not been abolished*—it exists with unmitigated rigour, in its most ferocious, revolting, and loathsome aspect."[66] Others would similarly claim that, under the "new law," slavery "virtually exists under another name, and that name is Apprenticeship."[67] Yet Williams resists this identification, instead attuning the reader to the substantive differences that render Apprenticeship discontinuous with the social and economic logics of slavery. Williams's first claim is that apprentices have faced an intensification of violence. While partially faulting the affective disposition of his master—Gilbert Senior's "spite"—Williams also opens the unnerving possibility that this seemingly irrational affect is underwritten by a grotesque, but grotesquely rational, calculation. Just as Cropper desired, the master now undertakes acts of cost and labor accountancy; he looks to the long term, four and six years down the line. Yet an intensification of severities, not care, has resulted from his calculations. Williams's text points to the unnerving gap between economic rationality and the moral values with which antislavery activists desired to freight it. By retaining the term "slavery" as a paleonym for the new reality of Apprenticeship, Price and his allies attempt coding the "cool calculation[s]" undertaken by planters such as Senior as deviations from political-economic and juridical law, not as modes of comportment with it.[68]

Yet the imperial act of abolition itself generalized the economic optic that yielded the chillingly cool calculations undertaken by the colonial plantocracy. In the act's preamble, Parliament commits itself to providing "a reasonable Compensation . . . to the Persons hitherto entitled to the Services of such Slaves for the Loss which they will incur by being deprived of their Right to such services."[69] The act carefully distinguishes between the slave's person and the slave's capacity to labor, the slave's "Services." It separates what Marx would call the worker's "life" from the worker's "life expression" and accords value only to the latter. This perspective enables the act to approach black freedom as a problem of lost value, paying masters for the "Loss" of a potential of which slaves were the bearers but with which they were not identical. The production of black freedom subsequently became an actuarial problem, particularly as compensation was to be ad valorem by island, not per capita. Strikingly, enslaved humans whom masters might have described privately as "worthless" were suddenly endowed with a public value. Much of this capital simply fled the island: slave owners, aware of the bleak economic outlook of Jamaica, took the sudden liquidation of their historically illiquid capital as a chance to divest wholesale.[70] Yet the financial fiction that such subjects possessed a losable economic value was coupled with a stripping of value from enslaved life as such: it is the "services," not the "Slaves," that the act evaluates and for which it provides compensation. Indeed, the act realized a long-held but historically frustrated plantocratic dream—one interdicted by imperial regulations and colonial laws, by the post-1807 constriction of the labor pool, and the scrutiny of an antislavery public—of treating bonded black life as nothing more than the accidental bearer of a quantum of labor-power.

The subsequent period of Apprenticeship witnessed the articulation of a liberal-capitalist optic to a regime of bonded labor in the context of a generalized economic decline understood by planters to be irreversible. "Economy in the management of planters has all at once become the order of the day," lamented Richard Robert Madden.[71] This novel "economy" affected, first and foremost, the apprentices: through cost-cutting and hyper-exploitation, planters hoped to "squeeze" as much profit as possible from their plantations before their world collapsed.[72] In effect, planters offset the costs of freedom by initiating an austerity regime that neither the colonial nor the imperial state softened. Antislavery activists cited colonial malfeasance and a will to pervert imperial intentions, but the act itself treated the provisioning requirements for apprentices vaguely and as an afterthought. Indeed, the state actively participated in allowing planters to cut back on subsistence goods—almost always coded as gratuitous "allowances"—that supplemented the caloric intake of plantation laborers. The imperial jurist John Jeremie stressed that such "favours" were better understood as "rights," but the imperial framers of emancipation neglected, and the colonial framers of the Jamaican act in aid refused, to accord apprentices a right to a barrel of salted herring, a measure of rum, or a bit of sugar.[73] Attempts to retrofit the Jamaican act of abolition to incorporate such allowances as rights foundered on weak legal reasoning and weaker legal instruments.[74] At the same time, the state served as the primary actor in the hyper-exploitation of the islands' hungry apprentices.[75] Under Apprenticeship, masters were no longer allowed to enforce work discipline through violence; penality was (or was supposed to have been) deprivatized. A web of state-run disciplinary institutions formed to keep apprentices holing, cutting, and boiling. Exposed to the cool calculations of their masters without even the skein of biopolitical protections afforded by the previous regime of ameliorated slavery, apprentices could be treated as disposable life, as incipiently worthless beings.

Williams's text represents Apprenticeship as a "death-world" given over to necropolitical accumulation strategies, as Achille Mbembe might put it.[76] Indeed, Williams experiences the stultifying, suspended time of emancipatory liberalism primarily through starvation, posing personal freedom as the management of slow decline. As he notes, part of the planters' accumulation strategy throughout Apprenticeship involved a massive cutback in subsistence provisioning: "Apprentices a great deal worse off for provision than beforetime; magistrate take away their day, and give it to property; massa give we no salt allowance, and no allowance at Christmas; since the new law begin, he only give them two mackerel,—that was one time when them going out to job."[77] The shriveling up of allowances in the wake of emancipation is exacerbated by planters' using the imperial state apparatus to punish apprentices by taking the labor time slotted for work on their provision grounds and giving it "to property," the plantation. Williams would constantly suffer such punishments: "They make me pay off the fifty days; them give me no Sunday at all; every Wednesday they give me half a day to work my grounds, the other half them take to pay off the fifty days;—For one year and three months, them keep on take the half day from me every week, and never give me any feeding." [78] Here, Williams undertakes a kind of subsistence bookkeeping that perversely parallels his master's cool calculations. He notes the time owed (fifty days), the way it was disaggregated into parts over time (no Sundays, half-day Wednesdays), and the total duration (one year and three months). These bookkeeping operations also resonate with those ideally undertaken by the responsibilized poor legislated into existence in Britain, who had to engage in calculations of need without recourse to dissolved moral economies or a redistributive state.

Not receiving "any feeding" implies that Williams was starved through his apprenticeship years. He would state as much at the text's conclusion when he meets Sturge, who was in Jamaica for the fact-finding tour that would result in *The West Indies in 1837*, a well-documented comparative account of the emancipation process. Sturge, Williams says, tells him he "musn't discourage, that it only to last seventeen months." Sturge, in essence, adopts his father-in-law's understanding of the temporality of emancipation, asserting like Cropper that it will end "soon." Williams responds, "I tell him, I don't know if I can live to see the seventeen months out; I was quite maugre and hungry that time, quite different to what I stand now, I hardly able to get anything to eat then, my ground all gone to pieces, the time them put in workhouse, and if my father and other people no been give me something, I would have starve. Mr. Sturge give me a shilling, and then I go back home."[79]

Where Sturge attempted to code the temporality of Apprenticeship as one of hopeful expectation, a time wherein one "musn't discourage," Williams asserts that it is better grasped as a period of waning and progressive etiolation. This process cannot be reversed; it can only be temporarily arrested by the gifts given by his "father and other people." Intriguingly, this faint trace of the kin and communal relations that sustained apprentices through the period's punitive austerity is almost immediately suppressed by Sturge's gift of the shilling. Here the text performs that which Apprenticeship both intended and prevented ex-slaves from achieving: a movement from communal self-provisioning through subsistence farming to a derivation of subsistence through monetary transactions with white men, a subsumption of life into the value relation of liberal capitalism. Yet the clipped balance of Williams's concluding sentence—"Mr. Sturge give me a shilling, and then I go back home"—casts the adequacy of this reparative gesture in an ironic light. The gift of the shilling dissolves the scene of complaint, and Williams turns away.

A Narrative of Events is a catalogue of apprentices being turned away from sites of appeal. Consider the case of Henry James, an "old African" of about forty-six years who is flogged by a magistrate when cattle that he was responsible for watching ate corn.[80] James's fate gives insight into how worthless humans—humans such as Gale's Simon—were affected by the transformations wrought by emancipation. Like Simon, James had served as a watchman, an occupational status that derives from and indicates his wasting health. With the inauguration of Apprenticeship, however, James was sent back into the field, as Gilbert Senior attempted to squeeze out every bit of possible profit.[81] By the end of Williams's micronarrative, James has died. Williams's narration does not privilege the event of flogging as the effective cause of James's death. Rather, Williams attunes the reader to the nonpunctuality of his death, to the way in which it is the effect of the diffuse systemic causality of neglect:

> After the flogging, he got quite sick, and began coughing blood; he went to the hot-house [plantation hospital], but got no attention, them say him not sick. He go to Capt. Dillon to complain about it; magistrate give him paper to carry to massa, to warn him to court on Thursday . . . Capt. Dillon say that him don't think Henry James was sick; he told him to go back, and come next Thursday, and he would have doctor to examine him; the old man said he did not know whether he should live till Thursday. He walk away, but before he get out of the town, he drop down dead—all the place cover with blood that he puke up. He was quite well before the flogging.[82]

For Williams, James was bound up in an institutional pattern in which neither mechanisms of political speech (the complaint) nor bodily semiosis ("coughing blood," "puk[ing]" it up) could be felicitous in achieving the "attention" he desires. James wants his complaint to become a medical and legal event, but the administrative temporalities that distribute justice and care absorb the acuteness of his crisis. For James, the promise of care is simply care's mode of withdrawal: the diffusion of responsibility for the biopolitical upkeep of apprentices means that no crisis can register as crisis. In death, the disruptive hard C's that marked his illness resolve into an alliterative and dulling drone—"he drop down dead"—as if his death does not sound, cannot not signify. Indeed, Williams presents James's death as a dying without cause or consequence, as an act of becoming a body that does not matter because it never mattered.

What is intriguing to me is not simply the failure of justice but the retention of its idiom. Confronting the breakdown of imperial mechanisms of law, Williams figures himself as a preserver of imperial justice.[83] (Indeed, Williams's text would even precipitate an imperial investigation, as we will see in the coda.) In an altercation with Gilbert Senior, Senior "raise up his stick three times to lick me down." Williams responds, "You can't lick me down, Sir, the law does not allow that, and I will go to the magistrate if you strike me." Williams is struck and then locked in a dungeon, whereupon he shouts, "*It wasn't a man made this world, and man can't command it: the one that make the world will come again to receive it, and that is Jesus Christ!*"[84] Similarly, after a flogging administered by the magistrate Stanley Rawlinson, Williams opposes the (mal)functioning of legal administration with a higher normative order:

> I went into where the court was sitting, and I said to Mr. Rawlinson; You don't do justice betwixt I and master. . . . Then Mr. Rawlinson say I have been before him eight or nine times already; I say, if I have been twenty times before you, you ought to do justice. He said, He do justice. I told him, You don't do justice. Then he said, If you say another word, I will put you out in the rain; then he made police take and handcuff me, to carry to workhouse.[85]

Here Williams forces himself into the scene of law to condemn it. He presents himself as someone who knows what justice is, insisting that it is not something that can be calculated or reduced to statistical regularities: "If I have been twenty times before you, you ought to do justice." This "ought" is underwritten by a fantasy in and optimistic attachment to a normative regime exorbitant to the local scene of legal administration. This fantasy centers on empire itself, the fullness of whose law Williams hopes will messianically restore justice in the island. Indeed, *A Narrative of Events* is itself a performative enactment of this fantasy: Williams's descriptions of the catastrophe of worthlessness would function as evidence to be used to indict the colonial order for violating imperial law.[86]

Yet Williams's presentation of himself as a rights-bearing subject concerned with preserving the imperial nomos is substantively made ironic by the formal features of the text through which he articulates his complaints and his demands. Williams's *Narrative* is formally structured by the epistemic frames of political economy, a framing that works to displace his positioning of himself as a legal subject of empire. We can see the structuring function of a political-economic poetic in the *Narrative*'s departure from the narrative forms employed by Mary Prince and Ashton Warner in their slave narratives.[87] Williams's *A Narrative of Events* shares many features with these texts: the distributed authorship, the paratextual mechanisms of authentication, a narrative that concludes with a tentative freedom, and entrance into the world of print. It departs, however, from those texts' attempts to apprehend the lives of their authors as a biographical totality. Prince's memories of her relations with her mother were among the most compelling elements of her text; Williams's *A Narrative of Events* offers no account of his life before the beginning of Apprenticeship.[88] Indeed, Williams constantly invokes the Act of Abolition as a historical break and a biographical rupture, frequently employing locutions such as "since the new law come in" or "since the new law begin."[89] Yet the text's narrative structure presents emancipation not so much as a rupture that occurs *within* the biographical time of Williams's life as a separation of Williams *from* the biographical. If, as Marx suggests, the transition from slavery to free labor entails the displacement of value from life to life's synecdoche—the laborer's "life expression"—*A Narrative of Events* replicates this structure by divesting narrative value from Williams's life as a biographical totality and relocating it to that period during which Williams was to be remade as a free wage worker. Indeed, whereas Prince is titularly denominated a "West Indian Slave" and Warner is simply called "A Negro," the title page names Williams an "Apprenticed Labourer." By coding Williams as a creature of the Act of Abolition, the structure of *A Narrative of Events* presents him as a deracinated bearer of labor-power: one frustrated from securing himself in life due to a devastating institutional environment, but one effectively equivalent to any other apprentice. When Price concludes that the "tale of Williams is the tale of near eight hundred thousands of our fellow-subjects," it is a liberal-capitalist social imaginary that presupposes the functional equivalence of abstract bearers of labor-power, that enables Williams's tale to become the common coin of the devastated realm.[90]

Williams's appearance as a juridical subject of empire, in other words, is mediated through a political-economic imaginary that primarily apprehends him as a laboring subject. Indeed, the scenes of worthless life that Williams compiled were read as unintended consequences susceptible to fine-tuning and calibration from *within* the framework of liberal political economy. Williams's editors, for instance, demanded the unconditional and immediate abolition of Apprenticeship, assuming that liberal value relations would fully subsume Jamaican life once the condition of bondage was lifted. Cropper held to the end that only the full liberalization of imperial sugar markets could restore apprentices to a temporality of liveliness.[91] Recognizing Jamaican life only in the garb of Jamaican labor, the crisis of worthless life required for its correction only the generalization and intensification of liberal-capitalist modes of sociality. This generalization was so intensive that it would incorporate the very bodies of female apprentices.

A Stillborn Freedom

"The facts related by Mr Sturge, relative to the treatment of females," relates the editor of *Horrors of the Negro Apprenticeship System in the British Colonies*, "were of the most thrilling description." The text from which the quote is drawn is a transcription of a public breakfast in the Town Hall of Birmingham given upon the return of Sturge from the West Indies. As "nearly 500 ladies and gentlemen" dined, shouted "Hear, hear," or cried "Shame," they were regaled with Gothic tales of violated bodies, sexual assault, and abandoned children.[92] Much has been written about the affective life of activists' "thrilling description[s]" of slavery, the bizarre pleasures and fears simultaneously induced and managed in the act of giving narrative form to social death.[93] Here I am interested less in how these texts construct the moment of horror than in how they prepare for the moment that follows—the moment of reflexivity that follows the encounter with sublime cruelty, the moment that quickly follows the therapeutic utterance of "Shame" or the shedding of a tear. The texts I read here, I argue, were underwritten by a political-economic logic that rendered thinkable and actionable the reparation demanded by the figures of worthless life whom readers encountered with horror. While scholars such as Saidiya Hartman have warned us against recirculating such violence-laden "scenes of subjection," I do so to interrupt the affective to cognitive circuitry through which a poetics of governmentality converted horror into an alibi for its intensification. In no small way, anti-Apprenticeship texts solicit speed reading and an avoidance of horror both to shuttle readers from scenes of worthlessness to promises of a reproducible, reproductive life to come, as well as to evacuate from the scene of worthlessness subaltern articulations of other forms of value. There is a political poiesis in these scenes that a liberal aesthetics of terror—which wants terror to just be terror—strives to occlude.[94]

From the very beginnings of organized abolition, the bodies of enslaved women were invested with extraordinary moral concern. Just as importantly, they were invested with an epistemic capacity to reveal the horrors of plantation slavery.[95] The truth-telling power of enslaved female bodies intensified as a result of a set of legal and social-scientific events that took place in the first decades of the nineteenth century. With the abolition of the slave trade in 1807, metropolitan activists hoped that the constriction of the available labor pool would force planters to undertake reforms conducive to the relative flourishing of life. Importantly, metropolitan observers no longer needed to rely on heavily politicized and potentially misleading accounts from the colonies or on the set-piece laws passed by local assemblies but ignored by planters to determine the welfare of the enslaved. Equipped with theories of population propounded by Malthus and new technologies of demography and statistics, activists could generate an objective and scientific portrait of the health of the enslaved. Pro-slavery writers did not cede the science of population without a fight. West Indian men cited demographic pressures and subsistence squeezes in Africa as a moral justification for the institution of colonial slavery. Meanwhile, as Seymour Drescher reports, pro-slavery statistics were extraordinarily sophisticated, more so than those of the abolitionists: the necessity of apologizing for the irreparable drove the sugar interest to innovate with and fine-tune the instruments of demographic science.[96] For a period, demography appeared to be a pro-slavery tool; a chagrined Malthus had to rush a letter off to Wilberforce on the eve of abolition, asserting that science was on the side of morality. Still, planters ultimately lost the battle for and over demography.[97] No matter the complexity of the variables that pro-slavery thinkers developed, by the 1830s abolitionists could proclaim with grim triumph that neither labor-population pressures nor ameliorative measures had worked. The population of enslaved humans was not reproducing itself.

The effect of these debates was to peg the welfare of the enslaved to rates of reproduction. Other metrics of welfare still loomed large—the Christianization of the enslaved, the availability and rate of marriage, and so on—but these metrics were subsumed into questions about the augmentation or decline of the population. The partial but compelling identification of welfare with reproduction rates enabled new legal and rhetorical strategies for ameliorating and ending slavery. Through an Order in Council scripted by antislavery activists and promulgated for the Crown Colony of Trinidad, leg-islatures throughout the West Indies were pressured to pass a bundle of laws directed toward the reproductive viability of enslaved women.[98] In Jamaica, the amount of rest time extended to prepartum and postpartum women was extended; women with six living children were excused from labor; flogging of women was outlawed. Laws also worked indirectly to cultivate a social environment in which sustainable family lives might be formed: Christian-ity and marriage were legally encouraged; the rape of black women was pe-nalized.[99] In many ways, these laws were impossible to implement, serving merely weapons in the "war of representation" between abolitionists and pro-slavery forces.[100] The cultural work of these laws was supplemented by texts dedicated to investing the bodies of enslaved women with a biopoliti-cal value. Pro-slavery writers set the genres of medicine and plantation hus-bandry to work to delineate proper modalities of care; antislavery activists used images and narrative—such as that of Mary Prince—to demonstrate that slave owners still failed to value properly and care for the value of black female bodies.[101] In sum, black women entered the imperial legal script and the imperial public sphere as a "figure of population."[102]

By the time antislavery activists confronted the crisis of social time in-duced by emancipatory liberalism, then, they had to hand a repertoire of forms for thinking and counteracting the demographic collapse that Williams threatened in his narrative of starvation. Yet demographic arguments were not made with great frequency during the debate over Apprenticeship. This is odd: population rates had long been taken as the most objective data available for determining the health of West Indian populations, but now the "reproductive deficit of the slave colonies disappeared overnight from debates in Parliament and the press."[103] Explaining this disappearance, Drescher continues, "the re-production problem was simply replaced by the labor problem"—by enduring concerns, that is, over the availability of "continuous" black labor during Ap-prenticeship and beyond.[104] Yet concerns over labor did not simply replace the biopolitical problematic of the population. Rather, a social imaginary primed by the liberal-capitalist value relation subsumed and repurposed the modalities by which activists and empire approached the black population as a population. As we saw, this subsumption transformed the laws and prac-tices affecting the provisioning of apprentices; it also affected the parameters through which Williams could make his life intelligible, imaginable, and nar-ratable for metropolitan audiences. Indeed, if explicitly statistical forms of truth telling and claims making waned throughout the period of Apprenticeship, narrative genres picked up the slack, deploying imaginative "figure[s] of population" while routing them through the epistemic frame of economic liberalism. Accounts of Apprenticeship such as Williams's *A Narrative of Events* and its twin text, *A Statement of Facts Illustrating the Administration of the Abolition Law and the Sufferings of Negro Apprentices* (1837), assumed the work of demographic-scientific critique, transforming its epistemology into a poetic to cognize reproduction through the value-form.

Put another way, the concern of a previous generation of abolitionists to determine reproductive regularities and map reproductive rates yielded an imaginary that cognized the female population's capacity for reproduction as a form of value-producing labor. Reproduction became reproductive labor-power. As Jennifer Morgan incisively shows, reproduction was always a form of value-producing work in the plantation world—work that could be speculated on, accounted for, costed, and coordinated.[105] Through annual grants of money and things or the gift of money upon a successful birth, enslaved mothers also participated in the monetization of birth.[106] Yet if reproduction was always a form of work, emancipation "transform[ed] the *mode* in which such work was carried out."[107] The reproductive work of enslaved women directly and immediately yielded a value in the form of a fungible human being; the reproductive labor of women subsumed into capital, as Leopoldina Fortunati argues, produces value through mediation within the entire circuit of capitalist (re)production.[108] What appears, then, as a sudden devalorization of reproductive work in the wake of emancipation—an appearance owing to the demonetization of children—in fact marks a transformation in the ways that this work was cognitively and economically mediated.

We get a trace of this transformation in a key passage from Williams's *A Narrative of Events*, in which he discusses the plight of women incarcerated in Jamaican workhouses. We also see how attempts to subsume Jamaican life into liberal capitalism's imaginary of value produced worthless life as a figurative precipitate:

> The drivers constant try to get after the young women that put into the workhouse,—even them that married, no matter; before day in the morning, when the driver open the door to take the people out of shackles, he call for any one he want, to come to his room, and many of them worthless ones do it. Amelia Lawrence complain to her brother and me, that never one morning pass without the driver after her—she don't know what to do, she quite hurt and dishearted about it—but she did not give way.[109]

Williams's moralistic indictment, articulated to his amanuensis, an evangelical preacher, points toward an important fact: Christianity provided an important resource for the enslaved and apprentices to accord value to their lives and to present as proper subjects of empire.[110] At the same time, Williams's description of such women as worthless is starkly realist. For one, under Apprenticeship sex no longer served as a means of enhancing an estate's value: after 1834, all children were born free. All sex acts were, in a sense, worthless—that is, they were not immediately functional for the valorization of any given planter's capital. Moreover, Williams notes that the workhouse has pulverized the forms of social value that obtain outside of it— "even them that married, no matter." "Them worthless ones," then, is both a descriptive and a prescriptive term: it indicates the workhouse's corrosion of social value, and particularly Christian values, but it also, through debasing this worthless sex, maps out a plan for social repair. "Them worthless ones" become worthless because they misuse and improperly alienate the sexual capacities that give them value; in Marx's terms, the flawed alienation of their "life expression" inhibits their lives from taking on value. It is precisely by understanding the value of this capacity that Amelia Lawrence accedes to a proper name, that she takes property in that which is understood to be most proper to her. "Them worthless ones," on the contrary, are not individuated, are not named, and do not speak. This term, in other words, never marks a concrete, nameable set of subjects. It is instead a catachresis that marks a generalizable, abstract capacity that lacks a determinate and determinable referent. It names a power, not a person, but a power whose proper appropriation and use is inhibited by the structure of Apprenticeship society.

A *Statement of Facts* would hone the poetics of reproductive labor-power at work in Williams's *A Narrative of Events* by developing a form of narration and characterization more robustly indebted to social-science epistemology. The text itself is little more than a sampling of tales from the reams of official and unofficial reports compiled on Apprenticeship. As the author reports, "A vast mass of unquestionable facts have been collected from nearly all the West Indian colonies, showing the true character of the apprenticeship scheme."[111] Indeed, this "vast mass of unquestionable facts" is more accurately "an overwhelming abundance of materials," the "amplitude" of which necessitates judicious "selection." Such a selection, the author hopes, will "give the reader a summary view of the whole system," while also presenting that system in "lively colours."[112] The text, in essence, attempts to do what generations of demographically inclined abolitionists had done before: it attempts to make legible regularities affecting and determining the health of the apprenticed population.[113] In so doing, it hopes to derive a nonnumerical but nonetheless factual "figure of population."

As in Williams's *A Narrative of Events*, abused and violated women figure prominently among the text's "cases," as it calls them.[114] Yet these cases have a peculiar status, for *A Statement of Facts* sets to work a poetics of accumulation. In the course of three pages the text narrates as many stillbirths, each caused by the violence that pregnant women experienced in penal institutions. Apprenticeship is revealed in its "true character" when the reader has added together case after case. This act of addition is an act of abstraction. While each case is composed of a mass of concrete particulars, of "unquestionable facts" that ensure the authenticity of the narrative, the reader's movement from the case of Jane Grey to that of Isabella Douglas and that of Sarah Murdoch necessitates that she or he undertake the cognitive labor of synecdochalization to ensure the cases' commensurability. The particularities of their cases are dissolved as each woman comes to be read as a more or less fungible example of a common and commonly frustrated capacity to reproduce. Although they possess proper names, they are less singular persons than they are personifications, the accidental bearers of reproductive labor-power.

Here I violate the reading protocol solicited by the text and stick close to one case: that of Sarah Murdoch. In so doing, we will see how Murdoch is textualized and cared for as a figure of reproductive labor-power. We will also see, however, Murdoch's resistance to this figuration.

Sarah Murdoch "has had six children, all of whom are dead."[115] Introduced through her reproductive capacity, the reader is called on to mourn the institutional failures that inhibit her potential to produce life from achieving robust actuality. In 1835, Murdoch became pregnant once more. Being "very sickly with it," Murdoch "applied to be excused from labour."[116] Murdoch's request, which was refused, indexes Apprenticeship's displacement of biopolitical protections in favor of necropolitical accumulation. As noted earlier, throughout the amelioration period women with six living children were legally "excused from labour." Murdoch's denied application subtly recollects this legal provision even as it marks its formal and substantive retraction: neither Murdoch's children nor the law have survived into Apprenticeship.[117] It also, however, introduces an almost unmanageable semantic instability into the text. Ostensibly applying for relief from plantation labor, Murdoch can be read as punningly requesting relief from the labors of childbirth, from reproductive labor. She flees to her husband's home on another plantation, where she falls ill with a "severe bowel complaint" that "left her very weak."[118] Apprehended as a runaway, she is sentenced "to fourteen days of hard labour in the workhouse, and to work upon the tread-mill."[119] The hard labor in the workhouse induces labor: "Immediately after coming off the mill, whilst standing with the rest of the penal gang . . . she suddenly gave birth to an infant, which fell to the ground dead."[120] Perversely, the workhouse excuses Murdoch from the pain of reproductive labor: the pain of dancing on the wheel overwhelms the bodily pain of giving birth, with the effect that the baby is "suddenly" born.[121]

For the text, the colonial state has absorbed but perverted the temporality of biological reproduction, aborting the colony's future. Playing on Marx, we might say that the editors pose the violent colonial state as an incredibly ineffective "midwife" of the emergent liberal-capitalist order. Yet in desiring to move Jamaica from a necropolitical state of indifference to a biopolitical regime of care, the text itself divests care from that which has died in the name of that which might live. Like Henry Taylor "drop[ping]" to the ground in Williams's *A Narrative of Events*, Murdoch's infant simply "fell," genderless and nameless; it takes on the relative adverb of "which," not "who." Embodying a lost potential, the dead infant receives textual attention only to the extent that its body gives measure to the derealization of Murdoch's capacity for reproductive labor. The response that the text solicits is similar to the response of the workhouse supervisor, who orders Murdoch to the hospital after her induced abortion: "Be off with you—be off to the hospital."[122] Just as the supervisor wants to repair Murdoch's capacity for productive labor, so the text wants to repair the necropolitical regime of Apprenticeship to ensure that Murdoch can felicitously undertake the labor of reproduction. Murdoch, however, refuses to make the transition from necropolitical worthlessness to biopolitical care without lingering over her loss. Refusing to go to the hospital, Murdoch states, "Mass, me cant lef my dead pickaninny on the ground so."[123] The reader then witnesses Murdoch willfully labor for the first time: "She then, ill as she was, took a hoe, made a small hole in the workhouse yard, and with the hoe, drew her dead infant into its shallow grave, and covered it with earth."[124] The only labor that Murdoch willingly undertakes is a sickly labor, a labor of loss, for and with the failed future her stillborn child figures. She thus models a form of care that implicitly critiques the reproductive futurism of the text: while the text cares for Murdoch to the extent that she figures a frustrated capacity for reproduction, Murdoch cares for that which lacks potential, for that without a future. Whereas liberal critiques of Apprenticeship cared for "them worthless ones" by locating a capacity to realize certain values in them, Murdoch cares for the worthless *as* worthless, without integrating the worthless into a field of value.

Murdoch's performance asks readers to approach the social production of death—and even social death itself—as a complex event that articulates life and death in singular ways, yielding relations of sociality and imaginaries of futurity that do not align with imperial biopolitics or liberal value forms.[125] This "mother and mother-dispossessed," in Hortense Spillers's phrasing, augurs the possibility of a "different social subject."[126] The accumulative poetic of *A Statement of Facts*, however, disassembles these complex assemblages for the metropolitan reader. The concatenation of Jane Grey's, Isabella Douglas's, and Sarah Murdoch's stillbirths abstracts each woman from her particular scene and transforms each into a personification of frustrated reproduction. These scenes of frustrated reproduction are read from the perspective of a life that could have been and, indeed, of a life worthy of living. In reinscribing its image of valued (and value-producing) life, emancipatory liberalism conscripted even those women who wished to be "excused from labor" into the work of recuperating its epistemic and normative frames. This is, of course, the paradigmatic condition of subalternity: to say anything is to (be heard to) restate the norm. The point I want to make is that Murdoch's performance and its textual treatment reveals the nonavailability of a position within emancipatory liberalism to think worthlessness as possessing a sociality and a future that does not convert into and align with the value relations of liberal capitalism. Like these stillborn children, the worthless West Indies would have no legible place in the liberalizing empire. As we will see in the next chapter, the emancipated would live the effects of this inability as imperial abandonment.

The Two Conclusions to Williams's *Narrative*

Upon reading Williams's *A Narrative of Events*, Secretary for the Colonies Lord Glenelg wrote to Sir Lionel Smith, the governor of Jamaica, urging him to investigate the truth of Williams's allegations. Smith ordered two magistrates to Williams's St. Ann's Parish to gather testimony from witnesses. By November 1837, Smith had returned the results, officially entitled "Investigation by Commissioners of Inquiry into the Case of James Williams, and Other Apprenticed Labourers." In his attached note, Smith laments, "The whole barbarous case of that individual is proved and confirmed."[127] Through a mass of testimony and affidavits the committee had authenticated the truth of Williams's discourse. The committee turned William's text into a "case" and, in the process, turned it into an imperial fact.

But it did something more. By soliciting the words of Williams's apprenticed community, the committee opened up a space in which apprenticed Jamaicans could renarrate and supplement the very "material facts" that their testimony authenticated.[128] They leave us with a story of Apprenticeship that is different from the one that was adopted by the imperial public sphere. Their testimony does not deny or rhetorically meliorate the violence of emancipatory liberalism. Yet for these apprentices, the scenes of worthlessness and disposable life narrated by Williams are also crowded with forms of sociality, modes of care, and elaborations of value that Williams's amanuensis did not have access to or did not care to compile or include. Their testimony shows us the social life in and of social death, the ways that apprentices held on and held together to give value to themselves in their valueless world.

Adam Brown, for instance, recalls visiting Henry James in the plantation hothouse and listening to James's complaint that "nobody from the house took any notice of him."[129] It was Brown, en route to serve a sentence of solitary confinement in prison, who discovered James's body in the lonely lane. Like Sarah Murdoch lingering over her stillborn child, Brown stopped and "helped to move the body to the side of the road." He notes that the signs of James's passing were quickly vanishing: "it was raining at the time: the rain would have washed away the blood from the part of the ground where the body was." His own body becomes the archive of James's death, and, in many ways, of his life: "the frock that I had on was all stained with blood which came from Henry James when we were lifting him." As Brown becomes the bearer of James's trace, the first-person singular of the recitation unaccountably opens into a "we"; the reader retroactively realizes that Brown insisted that he had "helped" move the body because he was not alone in his efforts. The lonely road suddenly appears populated with an expansive sociality that the archive cannot quite capture. Brown intimates forms of subaltern care and repair that leave but minimal, ephemeral traces on the documents that remain. We see, for instance, just how many people, free and apprenticed, donated and prepared food to keep Williams from starving to death. We see the social tactics employed by women to keep overseers and drivers from harassing, abusing, or raping them.

Most surprising, perhaps, we see that apprentices persisted in a belief that empire was a fair-dealing, justice-dispensing polity that recognized them as rights-bearing subjects. Apprentices had a keen sense that their rights had been violated and in their testimony describe the kinds of self-help they undertook to ensure that imperial justice might be done—choosing the best special magistrate for a complaint, for instance. Brown relates going right to the top, running away and presenting a complaint to Governor Sligo; he receives a letter in exchange, one directed to his local magistrate, Rawlinson. He relates the indifference with which Rawlinson receives Sligo's epistolary order and Gilbert Senior's scandalous assertion that "he would have a law of his own."[130] Through their testimony, apprentices presented themselves not simply as subjects needing the protection of imperial law, but as subjects concerned with protecting the law itself, preserving imperial sovereignty from local forces that sought to corrode it. Perhaps the most forceful sign of apprentices' maintained attachment to empire is the willingness and fervor with which they participated in the investigation. Apprentices knew that this investigation was an imperial event, that their testimony would come before the highest in the realm, and they eagerly participated in a scene of address that brought them before the crown as wronged but rights-bearing subjects. Their testimonies are carefully constructed and confidently narrated. After years of neglect, privation, and abandonment, they finally experienced empire as a receptive, attentive polity.

Williams, meanwhile, was having a much different experience of empire. After completing his self-purchase with Sturge's financial assistance, Williams traveled back to England with the Quaker in March 1837. According to Sturge's letters, Williams gained nearly "1/3 in weight" by May and reported that he "like[d] England rather better than Jamaica."[131] Yet Sturge had concerns: "he excites so much notice that I fear he will be injured by it."[132] By August, Sturge was complaining that the "comparatively idle life and luxurious living but probably above all the attention James Williams has attracted . . . has I ought certainly to have expected produced an unfavourable effect upon him."[133] For Sturge, the only way to redeem the wayward freedman is to withdraw the social supports that enabled Williams to thrive in England: "The only means of bringing him to a proper sense of situation is for him to be compelled to labour for his bread and though I will of course see that thou art at no loss in contributing to his absolute need I believe he is in danger of being quite unmanageable unless he thinks he must depend upon himself alone for support & this while he is here cannot be accomplished." Indeed, Sturge desires to "cast him off at once," but worries that "the *cause*" might suffer from the fact that free blacks wanted to live freedom differently than their liberal allies desired. Sturge relies on a fear of retribution from the planter class to keep Williams sober and industrious: "the dread of falling into the hands of those from whom he suffered so much may be a good check upon him."[134] Astonishingly, Sturge's treatment of Williams reproduces the very structures of Apprenticeship that Williams's *A Narrative of Events* indicted. Sturge withdraws the forms of social "attention" that restored Williams to life and relies on the twinned forces of a subsistence squeeze and a fear of planter violence to compel Williams to docile labor. And so it was that, just as Williams's apprentice friends provided their testimony to the investigative committee, staging their inclusion as rights-bearing subjects within the empire, Williams was cast out of the imperial metropole for relishing too much in the attention he had received.

The difference between Williams's experience of empire in Britain and that of his apprentice friends in Jamaica stages the tension that had riven emancipatory liberalism from the start. Emancipation ideally intended to incorporate formerly enslaved humans into empire as rights-bearing subjects and as members of an intimate community of "friends," in Sligo's words. But the actual mode by which empire incorporated the emancipated into the polity amounted to little more than allowing them to participate in a scene and mode of address, for the substantive paradigm of imperial belonging came to center on an economic logic of value. As Williams's fate suggests, it was not black creoles' words but their work that mediated their relation to empire, and in a postemancipation world increasingly bound up in the globalizing value-form of liberal capitalism their work was becoming worthless. Emancipation fashioned imperial subjects who attached themselves to a fantasy empire, investing it with hopes and deriving aspects of their political identity from it; but this empire was a mutable and shifting object. The very transformations that rendered imperial emancipation thinkable, in less than a decade, would render empire's emancipation from the West Indies desirable, and even probable.

INTERREGNUM

Between Worlds

Chapter 3

IMPERIAL ABANDONMENT
AND HEMISPHERIC ALTERNATIVES

The Bad Romance of Free Trade

Evincing a commitment to legal procedure one might not anticipate in a lawless pirate, the eponymous mulatto hero of the Trinidadian Michel Maxwell Philip's *Emmanuel Appadocca; or, Blighted Life* (1854) convenes a shipboard court of law to try a white Anglo creole prisoner seized during a raid on a sugar-laden West Indiaman. As the pirate schooner sails through the Caribbean, Appadocca charges the defendant: "James Willmington, before God, and in the presence of these men, and in the name of Nature, I accuse you of having violated one of the most sacred and most binding of her laws; of having abandoned your offspring; of having neglected the being whose existence sprang from yours, and for whom you were bound by a holy obligation to care and provide."[1] The neglected being is Appadocca himself, the son of Willmington and a (possibly enslaved) Trinidadian woman of color. Willmington's crime is having forgotten his "principal duties" to his son, an obligation Appadocca summarizes as a debt of protection: "You owed me as [your] offspring, at least, protection until I was strong enough to provide for myself" (63). Instead, Willmington left the pirate "unprotected," "forsaken," "abandoned," not inquiring if his son was "exposed in the helplessness of . . . privation" or "the humble object of capricious charity" (63). In his defense, Willmington argues that "men are not punished in society for such offences," that Appadocca cannot constitute himself as a valid authority to judge, and that "by the laws, a man cannot redress his own wrongs" (65). Gesturing to the sea, Appadocca suggests that the "waste of water, with no tribunals at hand" is a sovereignless void in which subjects are freed of positive law and natural rights are restored to them (65). Appadocca's shipboard trial is the stuff of cheap fiction, but the text intriguingly stages this melodramatic excess alongside abandonment's unremarkable ordinariness. Not only is Willmington's abandonment of Appadocca not cognizable under law, but Willmington himself seems to have no comprehension that he did anything wrong, or that Appadocca is entitled to the wounded subjectivity of the abandoned. Indeed, that Appadocca can only try his case in his piratical court of natural law demonstrates the excess of his plaint to the normal course of things.

Emmanuel Appadocca's staging of abandonment's doubled structures of feeling dramatically condenses the bifurcated way that Britons and West Indians responded to the liberalization of the empire in 1846. Today scholars understand the bundle of free trade legislation passed in 1846 as part of a "great transformation" in Britain's society and economy, and so it was.[2] While most scholars have focused on the impact of liberalization on an insularly conceived Britain, free trade's effects resonated throughout the entire British imperial world. Lord John Russell's fiscal proposal to allow extra-imperial sugar onto the market at the same tariff rate as British West Indian sugar was interpreted by free traders and protectionists alike to augur the total dismantling of Britain's Atlantic empire.[3] In many ways, then, the parliamentary vote on the Sugar Duties Act in the spring of 1846 was a momentous occasion. Yet the scenography of the event was out of sync with the gravity of its effects. As observers remarked, there was something of a mismatch between the import of the transformations Russell advanced and the mundane fiscal instruments through which this revolution was to be accomplished. In an article titled, "Shall We Retain Our Colonies?" (1851), for instance, the *Edinburgh Review* would later comment, "It is abundantly evident that the question of abandoning an empire such as this . . . is far too momentous to be disposed of at the fag end of a discussion on our annual budget."[4] The problem was not simply that tariff discussions are boring stuff, resistant to poeticizing or rhetorical aggrandizing. In fact, free-trade activists had published ample songs, poetry, and literature in the service of their cause.[5] The problem, rather, was that the political, juridical, and affective value of formal empire had so diminished that "the fag end of a discussion on our annual budget" had indeed become the proper space for discussing the empire's future—or lack of one. What the *Edinburgh Review* understood as a lack of fit between oratorical occasion, rhetorical form, and political decision is best grasped not as an anomalous fluke, then, but as evidence of empire's expulsion from the proper political space of a liberalizing Britain.

How? In simple terms, the liberalization of Britain's sugar markets meant that goods from Cuba or Brazil would enter Britain at the same tariff rate as goods from Jamaica or Trinidad. These technical changes, however, consolidated a new epistemic, imaginative, and institutional approach to the world system. By equalizing tariff rates for imperial and foreign producers, Britain signaled that the provenance of goods, imperial or otherwise, was a matter of indifference to Britain; the new market structure effectively displaced the constricted space of imperial circulation in favor of an open space of global flows.[6] The imperial world was made foreign to the British economy. If, in the era of protection, the sugar markets of London or Liverpool were as much the West Indian planter's as the British merchant's, free trade excised the West Indian claim, leaving the markets simply, insularly British. Globalization through deimperialization, then, had the effect of nationalizing the institutional and imaginative cartography of Britain's political economy. Indeed, the emergent centrality of the nation-state to the world system was not opposed to commercial cosmopolitanism but instead served as both its condition of possibility and its telos. As Henry Dunkley, winner of the National Anti-Corn Law League essay competition of 1852, put it, global free trade was "the charter of nations."[7] Empires had no foundational position in this new world picture.

As we well know, Britain's disembedding of its political economy from empire did not mean that it suddenly went about "abandoning" the colonies, as the *Edinburgh Review* suggested was possible. Instead, free trade mutated the political composition of empire, effectively deconstituting empire as a possible horizon of political relation. Indeed, the scaling down of Britain's representative institutions was a key condition of possibility for the passage of the Sugar Duties Act, the repeal of the Corn Laws, and so on. The reforms of 1832 severely diminished elite West Indians' protectionist presence, virtual or otherwise, in the imperial Parliament. Meanwhile, the political ideals cited by colonial subjects—the "imperial compact" or the norm of "reciprocal protection"—no longer had the same institutional mooring once Britain's markets were disembedded from the empire.[8] The deimperialization of the British state occasioned a variety of questions: What in fact was empire? Why retain formal ties with the colonies? Jurists and statesmen throughout the 1840s and 1850s attempted to consolidate a new nomos for an empire whose ontic persistence could not be squared with its political, economic, and constitutional dissolution; the solutions they arrived at, as we will occasionally see throughout this chapter, all posited the fundamental exorbitancy of the proper political space of Britain from its imperial domains. The free-trade activist Richard Cobden put it simply: imperial domains were useless, costly pieces of "property," not political spaces of British imperium.[9] The political had become postimperial—even if empire continued to exist empirically.

The result of this great transformation was a generalized crisis in the ordinary ways by which West Indians organized and oriented their political worlds. As one petition from Trinidad suggests, West Indians increasingly saw themselves as imperial subjects without an imperial polity: "Your petitioners claim, as British subjects, to have your Majesty's West Indian Colonies considered and treated as integral parts of the British Empire."[10] West Indians described this divestment of consideration, this state of being on the inside but on the outs, as a process of "abandonment." The term might seem a bit excessive—a melodramatizing relation to structure best left to penny dreadfuls. Yet the term was a piece of creole quotidiana, a keyword in the planters' lexicon: in the morphology of decline, plantations were "abandoned" after they had become worthless through neglect, overuse, or bad market conditions.[11] More important, the apparent excessiveness of the term to the mutation it tracks raises importation questions about how events come to be considered and treated as events; how crisis becomes legible as crisis. What thinking needs to happen to see global liberalization as a process of imperial abandonment? Part of the difficulty here is that Britain so successfully abandoned empire as a horizon of political relation that it is difficult to understand how anyone could have imagined it to be that in the first place. The institution of imperial abandonment was coextensive with the dissolution of the discursive, epistemic, and affective conventions that could make this abandonment legible. From the nineteenth century through today, the social sciences have reproduced this illegibility. Free trade conscripted and consecrated the scalar imaginary of the emergent social sciences, for which Britain was a nation that happened to have colonies, not a component part of an expansive empire state.[12] Today, this politico-economic nationalism survives in the methodological nationalism that continues to underwrite scholarship across diverse disciplines. This methodological nationalism is particularly apparent in scholarship on Britain's turn to free trade, but this deworlding of empire is more or less a deep structural feature of social-science epistemologies and the cultural critical work that draws on them.[13] Empire appears as an exceptional deviation from the classically liberal, and then postcolonial, institutional norm of the nation-state, as something lacking the political, social, affective, and ideological density of the latter. We can only understand liberalization as the saturated crisis that it was for West Indians if, in a kind of antiliberal *Verstehen*, we grasp empire as "the political reality with which [colonial subjects] lived," as the quotidian frame of reference by which people organized their relationship to the world.[14]

Responding to an event illegible from the perspective of a political and epistemic dominant that continues to attune our disciplinary epistemologies, West Indian writers mobilized literary and quasi-literary genres to convert the occluded crisis of their ordinary's dismantling into a legible problem of general political import. Indeed, it is perhaps only in West Indian literary texts that the event of abandonment becomes legible as such. Try as hard as you like, you will never find proof positive in the archive, in contemporary British discourse, or in today's scholarship that Britain abandoned the islands. The Union Jack continued to fly; trade continued; and the colonial archive continued to grow fat with the correspondence of the imperial center and the colonial state. Like the father Willmington, we might not get that Britain did anything wrong, that an event occurred. West Indians' attempts to describe their ordinary-in-crisis could (and perhaps can, if I have not done my job) only sound extraordinary, as a burdening of reality with a meaning that exceeded the common sense both constituted and consecrated in dominant political, juridical, economic, and cultural discourse. In the archive as well as in the scholarship, the excess of West Indian speech to the emergent liberal ordinary that incited it is troped as romantic. As I will argue, the very work of West Indian writing was to assemble conventions for reading the West Indian context within which a seemingly excessive complaint could appear as a reasonable response, within which what seemed like a romantic approach to the world could become a realistic assessment of it. We can know that something like abandonment happened only by reading the historical context from the perspective opened by these West Indian texts, by reading through these texts to recompose the shifting contexts within which they were written.[15]

The scenography of the Americas was central to West Indian writers' attempt to invent affective, epistemic, and political frames through which to repair their state of crisis illegibility. The West Indies had always been connected to the Americas through geographical proximity; shared histories of plantation and slavery; and flows of people, commodities, and culture. But these empirical connections did little to inflect West Indian political identifications: we might look back and see such transimperial flows as composing a creole America, but creoles understood themselves to be British subjects. It was in the wake of free trade that the Americas would become foundational to West Indian political imaginaries. West Indian writers, we will see, rendered Britain's occluded abandonment of the imperial polity legible by mobilizing a dense set of hemispheric geographies, histories, and possible futures; they hoped to recompose empire as a political world by writing through the Americas. This chapter traces this process of hemispheric reorientation, beginning with difficulties West Indians experienced before the imperial state, turning to speculative assessments of the dynamics of U.S. expansionism, and concluding with historical and geographic recuperations of Spain's New World empire. For some writers, such as the Anglo-Irish absentee planter Matthew Higgins, free trade abandoned the West Indies to a hemisphere about to be overrun by the U.S. slave empire; for others, such as Michel Maxwell Philip, the hemisphere was a repository of politico-economic norms that provided an alternative to liberal empire. Whether cast as a promise or a threat, West Indians' American frame of reference provided a surrogate for the dismantled, abandoned imperial frame of reference that had propped up their political world. Abandonment thus yields an excess beyond the negativity that occasions it: it opens a position of poetic possibility, one where subjects are incited to improvise new political rationalities, new cartographies of belonging, and to invest seemingly familiar terms—such as empire—with a new content.

Yet the improvisatory and recombinatory possibilities that accrue in zones of abandonment are vexed by the very conditions that produce them. This chapter tracks West Indians' imaginative movement from Britain to the New World, but this movement is arrested, halted. The desire for world maintenance subordinates incipient practices of world building; creoles' imaginative movement through the Americas reattaches them to a horizon of British imperial expectation bound to fail them. Indeed, if the sceneography of the Americas provided an idiom through which the occluded violence of abandonment could become legible, its mobilization also enabled an intensification and a back patterning of Higgins's and Philip's attachments to the empire. "Abandonment," as I have noted, names the dissolution of a political ordinary, of an underived, unremarkable, and unremarked on orientation to the world. It would not do, then, to analytically confuse the disorientation attending the dismantling of this ordinary as evidence of a prior, positive attachment to it: abandonment here names not a shattered love but the shock of losing a world so assumed that one did not realize it was losable. Higgins and Philip mapped their ordinary-in-crisis precisely in those dramatic terms, fabulating excessive attachments as a means of converting their diffuse, nonpunctual, illegible crisis into something else. We might say that West Indians responded to their abandonment by falling in love, but only to show how their loved object had already fallen out of it. They were not reactively romantic in the sense that they persisted in attaching to an object that vanished; rather, they fabulated a bad romance to constitute retroactively the very object they lost. Ultimately, the idiom of abandonment engendered toxic forms of fantasy relations, inhibiting subjects from attaching to new possibilities for world making.

The Creole Complaint and the Colonial Archive

"Oh! Hear a suffering planter's cry, who groans against Free Trade / And do believe him when he says, no sugar can be made." So begins Cyrus Francis Perkins's poem "The Planter's Petition" (ca. 1846–52).[16] The title is something of a double misnomer. A native-born white Jamaican of Canadian heritage, Wesleyan minister, abolitionist, printer, and novelist, Perkins was not really a planter in any meaningful sense. Rather, in speaking for and as a planter, Perkins inhabits a particular mode of address: the creole complaint. Historically, creoles had proved garrulous complainers. Perkins's "groaning" recalls Edward Littleton's important book *The Groans of the Plantations* (1689), an early critique of aspects of the economic organization of the Atlantic. In the absence of a formal or theoretical codification of imperial political subjectivity, West Indians complained their way into it across the centuries, blaming Britain for colonial hardships while simultaneously maintaining faith that Britain would correct them.[17] Free trade occasioned an eruption of complaining, as planters sent petition after petition, memorial after memorial, to the Colonial Office, all warning the imperial state about the probable (and then actual) effects of liberalization—thus, the second misnomer in Perkins's title: in calling itself a "petition," his poem marks both the continuities and discontinuities between the nonliterary, political genre through which West Indians related to the imperial state and the lyric form he adopts. The poem functions as an aesthetic surrogate for an increasingly ineffective genre of political address, even as it queries why this surrogation has become necessary. Why has political petitioning become lyrical complaining? Perkins poses his lyrical surrogation of the political as a reaction to the reading practices employed by every creole complainer's addressee: "Oh Downing Street! Oh cruel [G]rey! Oh listen to his cries / And do not still persist to say, 'The croaking fellow lies.'"[18] The problem identified here is not simply that creoles' descriptions of their reality are not believed. For Perkins, the problem is that the Colonial Office takes their words as descriptions in the first place, as verifiable or falsifiable diagnoses of politico-economic reality. By reading enactments of political subjectivity as descriptions of an economic reality, "cruel" Earl Grey's Colonial Office attenuates the force of the petition: complaining becomes constating; "cries" become "lies." The lyric petition opens a space where the ideal function of the political petition cannot be misread, where the staging of a wounded political subjectivity ("Oh!") achieves priority over the referential adequacy of that subject's description of the world.

In complaining about not being able to complain, Perkins's lyric on free trade directs our attention to how modalities of political representation interact with the mundane mechanics of imperial bureaucracy. The age of free trade intensified the problem of imperial representation by dismantling the institutional formations that had once enabled a kind of imaginary compromise between metropole and colony. Following liberalization, the relation of imperial sovereign to West Indian subject was no longer, even if only notionally, concretized by market protections, imagined as a compact, or virtualized through parliamentary forms of indirect representation.[19] Indeed, Perkins eschews idioms of imperial right or imperial compact in pressing his complaint. Rather, the relation between sovereign and subject was materialized in the reams of paper—dispatches, petitions, memorials, and so on—sent off from various government houses in the colonies and deposited in the Colonial Office in London. But what happened to these documents once they arrived in the metropole? Colonial officials and colonial subjects sent literal tons of paper to Grey's Downing Street Colonial Office, sure—but was anyone actually *reading* the documents that would go on to compose the empire's archive? Who? If so, how? And according to what modes or mechanisms were these documents inserted into public knowledge, policy prescriptions, and broader representations of its imperial world? As processes of documentary circulation and archiving absorbed prior forms of political relation, bureaucratic reading practices worked to draw and redraw the lines of the imperial polity. Thus, to worry about the fate of such paper, to worry about official activities of interpretation, archiving, and circulation, was to worry about the very reality of imperial subjecthood. It was all that remained to the empire's abandoned subjects.[20]

Let us track the fate of one such missive, one that would provide fodder for a minor press war over the colonial bureaucracy and imperial subjecthood: a dispatch sent from Governor Lord Harris of Trinidad to Earl Grey on 5 April 1848. Harris's letter attempts to describe the current state of Trinidad at a moment of colonial decline and global revolutionary antagonism. Remarking on "the depressed state of affairs of the colony," Harris describes how saddening it is "*to see the hearts and the affections of a whole population becoming gradually alienated from the country which he loves.*"[21] Perhaps more than normally, moods mattered in 1848, and as Harris registers the growing political disaffection of Trinidadians, the gap of feeling between metropole and colony threatens to make itself legible as yet another iteration of revolutionary upheaval: "Under the present grave circumstances of Europe and the world in general, I would add that if the power of England and her interests are to be maintained in this portion of it, and I think they are worth maintaining, it would not be impolitic that some sympathy of a practical nature should be shewn, and as early as practicable, by the mother country."[22] Harris is anticipating a future—and, for British elites, a gloomy one at that—by attuning himself to the affective composition of Trinidad's present. As Ann Laura Stoler has shown, colonial archives are riven with the "tensions and uncertainties" that attended state attempts to feel out "what *might yet be.*"[23] Saturated with the "*subjunctive mood* of official imaginings," the archive is a layered, storied site where competing feelings about the future vie to become *the* narrative.[24] Thus, Stoler suggests, not all of these saturated subjunctives achieved the status of the imperial indicative. As papers traveled from colony to metropole, as these papers were gathered together, and as empire undertook the labor of reading its own archive, some apprehensions of the future were given more or less weight, ascribed a greater or lesser realism. As Harris's letter traveled from Port of Spain to London, the protocols for determining "what might yet be" a realist or meaningful assessment of the future could shift. Any document could be consigned to the pile of "colonial debris, unfulfilled visions discarded in process."[25]

And so it was. When Sir Robert Peel addressed Parliament on the subject of sugar duties on 29 June 1848, following a massive, months-long inquiry into the effects of free trade on the West Indian colonies, none of the anxieties or apprehensions that underwrote Harris's missive found their way into his speech. Harris's letter played on fears that were no longer operative. We might blame the lack of effect of Harris's letter on the slow circuits of transatlantic communication, on the way that history can intervene in the interval between address and receipt.[26] The letter was processed by the Colonial Office on 5 May 1848; by then, the revolutionary contagion that official

Britain had so feared had fizzled out with Chartism's anticlimactic end on 10 April at Kennington Common. The anxiety that had consumed British elites converted into arrogance; the 1848 that made Harris anxious makes Peel optimistic. Where Harris anticipated that the depression induced by free trade would induce revolutionary upheaval in the colony, Peel insists that the spirit of 1848 promises the spread of freedom, the end of slavery, and the renaissance of the West Indies.[27] He declaims:

> There have been mighty convulsions in Europe. . . . That man who had said six months ago that the contagious influence of events at Paris would involve Berlin and Vienna in anarchy and confusion, would have been thought a mad speculator on the future. The mighty heavings of those convulsions are already felt on the other side of the Atlantic. . . . There are on every side useful lessons, by which the governments of Brazil, of Cuba, and of the United States, would do well to take timely warning, to foresee that that which has happened in Europe must precipitate the time when there shall be a final extinction of slavery and the slave trade.[28]

Peel's message was simple: no restoration of protection (or Harris's "sympathy of a practical nature") was required, because the slave empires of the Americas were on their last legs. The West Indies just had to bide their time—even if, as Harris suggested in his letter, they did not have much time at all.

We might blame Harris's and Peel's discrepant interpretations of the West Indies' future on the divergence between one horizon of epistolary expectation and a shifting horizon of reception. The absentee planter Matthew Higgins had a simpler solution: Peel never read Harris's dispatch. In four public letters he wrote to Prime Minister Lord John Russell—letters that were basically compilations of opinion pieces he had written for British newspapers—Higgins would claim that Earl Grey's Colonial Office had never forwarded Harris's letter to a parliamentary committee then sitting to determine the effects of free trade on sugar and coffee cultivation in the empire. The Select Committee on Sugar and Coffee Planting of 1848 was chaired by the protectionist Lord George Bentinck and populated by an ideologically mixed crowd of members of Parliament (MPs), including James Wilson, the free-trading founder of *The Economist*).[29] The archive of evidence accumulated by the committee is simply enormous, amounting to thousands of printed pages of depositions, inserted Colonial Office documents and dispatches, and various charts and figures. The sheer volume of this archive bespeaks a plantocratic and Tory commitment to an exhaustive empiricism that refuses to neglect any fact or detail.[30] Yet the exhaustive quality of the committee's documentation process also poses problems of reading—not the least of which being, as West Indians lamented, the difficulty of finding an MP who could be bothered to invest the time in, and attention to, sifting through the details.[31] Higgins would insist, however, that this already teeming archive was still incomplete. Not only were documents, such as Harris's dispatch, missing. More troubling, functionaries from the Colonial Office, including Earl Grey, frequently "mutilated" the meanings of documents written by colonial officials and colonial subjects when they proffered such writing as evidence in their testimonies and speeches before Parliament.[32] The fact that most people would not read stuffy data in Parliamentary reports conspired with the fact that some did, allowing the Colonial Office to circulate partial narrative as the whole picture.

Yet the problem for Higgins was less that of misrepresented facts than the fact of misrepresentation itself. Indeed, he assumed that everyone assumed the West Indies were all but ruined: the accumulation of more information did not matter.[33] Instead, Higgins was concerned with the modality of relation and mediation between imperial sovereign and colonial subject. By querying the ways in which colonial knowledge circulated (or did not) through the Colonial Office to Parliament, Higgins carves out a critical space at the ragged edge of the archive where documents become actionable knowledge; where reams of colonial documents are or are not read, cited, sutured together, and transformed into public narrative. This space, where the open totality of the archive becomes a necessarily partial public narrative, is the discursive zone in which abandonment happens. Here, abandonment is both a product and a practice of interpretation: it names the ways in which official readers differentially allocate the political salience of heterogeneous speech acts. Some words matter and are transmitted from 18 Downing Street to Parliament. Others do not and live the remainder of their textual life as debris in the overstuffed Record Department in the damp basement the Colonial Office called home.[34] For Higgins, the fact that words from West Indians could be suppressed, selectively cited, or distorted at will—that creole subjectivity could be left behind in the archive, as it were—marked the dissolution of the last, meager form through which colonial subjects mediated their relation to, and thus participated in, the imperial polity.

At stake in this critical inquiry into Colonial Office reading practices, then, is an inquiry into what imperial belonging meant in the age of free trade. Biographically, Higgins was well positioned to assess the impact of liberalization on the political rationalities of empire's peripheries. Born in Ireland in 1810, he inherited an estate in postemancipation Demerara, which he visited in 1838–39; he returned again in 1846–47. After his second visit to Demerara, he returned to Ireland, where he assisted in famine relief.[35] Despite his seeming integration into the webs of empire, however, Higgins constantly decried British failures to integrate the empire on a political-economic scale. The disintegrative effect of liberalized capital on empire has disintegrating effects on its subjects, right down to their bodies. In a letter to an absentee owner of Irish property, Higgins chastises him, "[Your tenants] are daily dying from sheer famine, and rotting in the cabins where they die. . . . They have no one to look to for aid. . . . You, who have for many years derived your resources from hence, abandon those whose labour has supplied those resources the moment they cease to be profitable to you for a time."[36] The mobility of capital leaves the tenants negligible while it simultaneously leaves them with no one from whom to demand redress: "They have none to look to for aid." This critique of imperial abandonment, then, dialectically recuperates empire as a normative site of care; indeed, the imagined relation of responsibility and the imaginative object of empire may not have preexisted the citation of its loss.

Liberal globalization, however, profoundly affected ideologies of imperial care and so transformed the meanings that imperial officials extended to colonial solicitations for aid. With the Cobdenite proposal to "abandon . . . empire as a measure of economy" structuring public discourse about the West Indies, imperial officials were frequently at a loss to justify why, precisely, empire should stick around.[37] The idiom of care provided a compelling language to account for this breach of economic rationality. Yet its very deployment reinscribed an imaginative cartography that located empire beyond the proper political boundaries of a shrinking Britain. Consider the apologia for empire that Earl Grey offers in his memoirs, *The Colonial Policy of Lord John Russell's Administration* (1853). Noting that the "abandonment of the ancient commercial system of this country" has led many Britons to insist that it "would be better to abandon" the colonies tout court, Grey insists that such an abandonment would violate the obligations Britain occurred by building an empire in the first place.[38] "[The] British Colonial Empire ought to be maintained," he writes, "principally because I do not consider that the nation would be justified in throwing off the responsibility it has incurred by the acquisition of this dominion . . . the Nation has incurred a responsibility of the highest kind, which it is not at liberty to throw off."[39] In other words, Grey proffers Britain's civilizational responsibility, not colonial subjects' political rights, as the constituent grounds of empire's persistence. The effect of such reasoning was the abandonment of empire as a possible horizon of political relation. For Grey, empire is not a polity of subjects but a form of benevolent governance for those colonial populations "too ignorant, if left themselves, to care for" the minute, practical affairs of their political and social worlds—for colonial subjects, in other words, whose putative racial and civilizational debilities inhibit their accession to the political.[40] Here, imperial care functions paradoxically as a technology of political abandonment: the dispensation of imperial care is premised on stripping or foreclosing subjects from the position of political subject and converting them into objects of benevolent governance.

This subsumption of the imperial polity into mechanisms of imperial governmentality accounts for Higgins's hard-nosed investigation of Colonial Office practices: the textual fabric of governance constituted the last field where colonial subjectivities achieved any positivity, however attenuated, before the imperial state. His *The Real Bearings of the West India Question* (1848) opens by linking official reading practices to free trade's corrosion of imperial belonging and imperial sovereignty. Higgins opens by deriding the ways in which, through the course of the sugar committee, "the truth was suppressed—important documents withheld—and facts either actually invented (as in the instance of Beet-root sugar) or distorted and unscrupulously adapted to argument . . . by men in high places." Motivated by free-trade ideology, these "freebooters of the Manchester school" pillage the archive through practices of distortion, suppression, and invention.[41] Just as freebooters in the age of mercantilism constituted a vexatious limit to the realization of unitary imperial authority, contemporary archive pirates interrupt the circuit of sovereignty linking colonial subjects to the imperial state. These freebooters deploy a reading practice corrosive to empire to ornament anti-imperial economic policies with a veneer of realism. In fact, however, the tale liberals tell is little more than a bad romance, a penny dreadful, a pirate yarn.

Yet this epistemologically angled critique of liberal reading practices is itself underwritten by a romantic approach to the state. Who really expects that the totality of any text, of all texts, stuffed into the archive passes under the gaze of attentive statesmen? After all, communicative efficiency—the winnowing of facts to their most basic components—is the pragmatic ideal of bureaucratic governance. This was, in effect, Earl Grey's defense of Colonial Office procedures. In June 1848, Grey addressed the House of Lords in response to charges—such as those brought forward by Higgins—that an ideological orientation toward free trade had affected the evidence that the office had provided to the select committee. Two charges in particular stuck out. The first was that Grey had intentionally withheld colonial dispatches (especially those from Harris) from the committee. The second was that Grey had cited a memorial from planters in Jamaica to Parliament in a "mutilated form," transforming a plea for assistance amid economic distress into proof that there was no distress in Jamaica.[42] Grey took two approaches in refuting the charge. First, he suggested that the possibility of negligence inhered within the functioning of the office precisely because it attempted to multiply the number of readers for every single document. The Colonial Office was in fact a site of zealous over-reading:

> When a despatch arrives it is taken to that division of the Colonial-office to which it belongs, where it is opened and registered, and all the correspondence relating to it is placed with it. It is then forwarded, in success, first to the permanent Under-Secretary of State for the Colonial Department; from him it passes to the Parliamentary Under-Secretary of State; and, lastly, it comes to the Secretary of State himself. Each of those whom the despatch reaches makes his minute upon it . . . and it is desired that those minutes should . . . contain suggestions of what . . . ought to be done with regard to that despatch, so that all the ordinary business of the office may be disposed of by the Secretary of State himself by simply signifying his approval, or otherwise, of those suggestions.[43]

Asserting that without such a schema "it would be absolutely impossible for the great mass of papers that come under the consideration of that department to be disposed of," Grey suggests that the possibility of neglect or the appearance of documentary suppression is immanent to the process of this apparatus of hyper-attention.[44] Tracing the career of each of the documents he supposedly suppressed, he describes how the appearance of suppression was merely an effect of a temporary breakdown in the office's procedure. A clerk forgot to forward a letter; a verbal order was not carried out; contingencies led to the delayed transcription of solicited documents. Grey suggests that attempts to overcome the finite limits of attention necessarily produce and reproduce neglect as a possible effect. The system through which the Colonial Office economized its finite attention to those to whom it was responsible created a condition in which no one was responsible for failures of attention. The very impossibility of assuming a sovereign reading position absolved all from sovereign responsibility.

The charge that Grey willfully misrepresented a memorial sent from Jamaican planters was stickier, inasmuch as Grey could not simply allow misfiring bureaucratic mechanisms to absorb responsibility for his actions. Once again, however, Grey gestured to the pragmatics of statecraft. If the possible suppression of documents is part of the ordinary of bureaucratic governance, selective citation is a very ordinary part of interpretation:

> It is said that I have quoted from a memorial of certain persons in Jamaica a passage in support of my own argument, and without reading the rest of the paper. Undoubtedly I did so, and I wish to know which of your lordships ever made a speech in this house without quoting only those parts of a document which he thought important to his case. . . . Those persons were complaining of the existing state of things in that colony, and of the distress under which they were suffering. My argument was, that the parties making that complaint had themselves admitted facts which, according to my views of the case, made for my opinion. I did not trouble the house with reading the passage at length; I read the passage which I thought important and nothing else; but that despatch, together with every other paper, was laid before the House of Commons.[45]

Grey was not freebooting in the archives; he was simply presenting his "views of the case," offering a necessarily partial reading of a document available to any MP who desired to read it. The interpretive act of arguing, Grey insists, does not require that the argument totally reproduce its factual bases; the necessary partiality of the arguer means that information will enter his discourse according to how "important" it is. The criterion of importance means that much of the archive will remain silent; many texts or parts of texts will remain unread. With a parting shot at Higgins's own method of citation and collation, Grey insists that he is the real victim of selective citation: "If any person had chosen to exercise a plausible ingenuity in collating passages from speeches in *Hansard*, with extracts from dispatches in volumes of blue books, he would have had no great difficulty in making out a plausible case upon which to found such a charge as has been ground against me."[46]

In his *Third Letter to Lord John Russell*, Higgins cites Grey's jibe and "plead[s] guilty" to the charge but confesses that "the high-flown rebukes of Lord Grey had very little effect on my spirits."[47] Higgins would in fact intensify his practice of selection, citation, and collation as his polemic continued. Indeed, in compiling his journalistic writing into small pamphlets, Higgins created textual space in which he could produce a public counterarchive, circulating all of the material that never made it to the Select Committee. Higgins's invest-ment in reprinting full documents is not the product of a reactionary archi-val positivism any more than his critique of Grey is reducible to the fact of selective citation. Rather, Higgins is concerned with the modality of citation, with the ways in which parts of addresses are deemed worthy of citation or not. Grey's defense did him no favors, for implicit in his description of his citation practice is the assumption that the interpretations that West Indians make regarding their own conditions constitutes *the* negligible portion of the document. Grey reads their memorial as providing raw factual material to which was superadded more or less misguided interpretation; the subjec-tive activity of complaining and appealing could be (and was) disarticulated from the data, leaving pure information to be interpreted by Grey. The creole complaint becomes an object of purely technical knowledge. West Indians and colonial state functionaries are reduced to mere "fact collectors," Hig-gins sniffs. "Lord Grey has announced that his system of colonial govern-ment is, to disregard the opinions of the distinguished men who govern our colonies—whom he professes to view merely in the light of fact collectors for himself . . . and reserves to himself the privilege of suppressing and dis-regarding such of these facts as do not chance to tally with his preconceived opinions, formed without either practical or local knowledge." [48]

In freebooting for data about the effects of free trade, Grey ignores the pri-mary fact of the memorial itself: that of its enunciation, that it establishes a relation between political subjects and their sovereign state. As Higgins puts it, "[Grey] entirely suppressed the fact, that the sole object of the Memorial-ists in addressing him, the Minister to whose especial care their destiny was confided, was to lay before him the details of their 'desperate and hopeless condition.'"[49] Grey's "especial care," in effect, amounts to a reading for tech-nical data contained in creole signifying; he does not listen for the subjects who signify. Opposing Grey's elision of the fact of address, Higgins's archival positivism—his incessant citation; his emphasis on reprinting memorials and dispatches—insists that the fact of address is superordinate to the facts communicated. It is no mistake, then, that Higgins writes letters instead of a political-economic treatise. While the treatise functions in the third per-son (which Benveniste defines as a "non-person"), the letter embeds what it communicates within a scene of enunciation and address.[50] Where Grey attempts to diffuse responsibility for the dismantling of this scene of address by invoking a kind of bureaucratic realism, Higgins asserts the priority of the political relation over any epistemological or institutional justification that would generate a limit to whose subjectivity counts. For Higgins, the creole complaint arrives only when the event of its address shatters bureaucratized economies of time and attention that stabilize an order of reality by detaching the subjectivity of enunciation from the facts communicated.

Higgins's desire to engender a form of political relation in the scene of bureaucratic procedure, to uncover a kind of lyrical subjectivity in the mess of papers in the Record Department, is by turns ordinary and extraordinary. It is ordinary because complaining about bureaucracy is precisely the most common mode of address people assume in relating to it.[51] It is extraordinary because few of us, for all our complaining, go to state agencies imagining that we achieve political recognition from the functionaries we meet over counters, through windows, or in the restless shuffle of paper. Indeed, the embeddedness of bureaucratic apparatuses within a broader terrain of representative and political institutions enables citizens of liberal nation-states to distinguish between mobilizing state instrumentalities and being political subjects. Things worked differently for imperial subjects in the West Indies in the wake of free trade. Liberalization had effectively disembedded the space of the British political from the empire; West Indians could no longer imagine that they had their political being elsewhere. All they had was the complaint, the Colonial Office, and its rule of paper. Higgins thus overly invests in these mechanisms as a means of maintaining the fantasy of imperial political belonging. This fantasy of political belonging, however, was underwritten by a speculative narrative of a much different sort. Should the Colonial Office persist in freebooting facts at the cost of considering West Indians as subjects, should Britain fail to hear the creole complaint, the islands would be subjected to freebooting of a much different sort: that of an expansionist U.S. empire.

Enslaved by Abandonment

Higgins's nerdy explorations of parliamentary citational practices achieved melodramatic heightening through their implication in a speculative narrative that saw liberalization as resulting in the West Indies' eventual reenslavement. For Higgins, slavery translated the politico-juridical position of those subordinated to a power but possessing no political presence for it. Of course, political movements throughout the Anglo Atlantic had long mobilized tropologies of slavery to mark just such despotical relations. The idiom of "political slavery" was available to anyone pressing antityranny demands since the emergence of British political modernity—including, of course, owners of enslaved people.[52] Yet Higgins's mobilization of the figure departs from this rhetorical and ideological tradition in important ways. For one, political rhetoricians typically deployed the trope of political slavery in conditions where cutting ties was neither possible nor desirable; in such contexts, emancipation *from* a tyrannical state intended the democratization *of* that state. For creoles, in contrast, liberalization had so diminished the political ties between Britain and the West Indies that they worried that a demand for political emancipation could be heard only as a bid for political exit: to articulate a desire for emancipation from their anomalous politico-juridical state risked registering as a desire for emancipation from that state entirely. Indeed, the language of political slavery was unavailable to creoles because Britain was relatively indifferent to maintaining imperium over the islands. Higgins manages the unavailability of a binding imperial political idiom by mediating critiques of what others would call political slavery through the ideological and affective affordances of antislavery politics. In Higgins's texts, speculative futures of an impending U.S. conquest mapped the present contours of West Indians political relation to Britain *and* established a moral argument for the politico-economic reconsolidation of empire. Liberalization had so diminished empire as a political world that creoles could argue for empire's repair only by staging the catastrophic consequences of its total loss.

Through their attempt to convert antislavery into a rationale for imperial state formation in the age of free trade, conservative West Indians such as Higgins helped to consolidate an enduring mythos of liberalism: that emancipation was impelled by a purely moral or political, but decidedly not economic, causality.[53] For Higgins, British imperial policy through the age of abolition had been vexed by an antinomy between morals and economics. Britain wanted to support freedom, but it wanted cheap sugar, too. In a world turned by slavery, it could have one (by not purchasing sugar at all or by purchasing only expensive "free sugar") or the other (by purchasing cheaper "slave sugar"), but not both at once.[54] Higgins interprets the logic of emancipation in light of this antinomy, presenting the freeing of enslaved West Indians as an econocidal decision for the moral. Emancipation was underwritten by an understanding that sugar "*is* adventitiously invested with a character not its own . . . calculations enter into our resolutions concerning it as foreign to the conclusions of simple commerce as those which attend a Brahmin's purchase of butter or rice."[55] Emancipation was a process in which the sovereign imperial state excepted a sacralized sugar from the rule of the economic. Protection, Higgins insists, was never logical on economic grounds. It was rather the institutional form taken by an exceptional, *antieconomic* decision to sustain black freedom: "We have always considered even a moderate degree of protection to the West Indian colonists utterly indefensible on the grounds of economic science. It was a tax levied on the British empire for the suppression of slavery."[56] Like many before him, Higgins here invests tariff mechanisms with a logic that they could not possibly possess. Taking effect for cause, he infers an animating intention to protect freedom from the fact that such tariffs had been functional for freedom's protection.

Yet this intentionality is fabulated only to underscore its fragility. With liberalization, the brief coincidence of emancipationism and mercantilism came apart. Much as Eric Williams would a century later, Higgins uses Britain's apparent unwillingness to protect the produce of free labor as a basis to query its commitment to freedom in the first place. Britain *had* emancipated its own colonial subjects, but then, but in less than a decade, it assembled a market order that absorbed the sugar produced by more enslaved humans from Cuba and Brazil. Liberalization amounts to a moral and economic externalization of slavery: "[Britain's] humanity revolts at a system which its economy proves. With an adroit compromise of decency and license, it goes out of its own house to gratify its propensities."[57] The turn to liberal globalization thus appears as a *return* to a pre-emancipation economy of slavery— the difference here being that British West Indian planters were prevented from participating in this reversal. Logically, Higgins insists over and over again, Britain should relegalize slavery in the West Indies: "*If the sugar bill of 1846 was right, the slavery bill of 1832 [sic] was wrong.*"[58] The converse implicitly holds true, as well: if emancipation was right, liberalization was wrong. In effect, it does not matter whether Britain maintained protection in the wake of emancipation with the intention of sustaining freedom or not. The fact was that freedom could be sustained only through maintaining such protections, and Britain had to norm its intentions and actions by this fact.

The decline of the West Indies, however, was simply one mode by which the contradictions between freedom and slavery engendered by Britain's turn to liberal globalization achieved phenomenality. The darker underside of liberalization's ruination of the islands' economies was its intensification of slavery elsewhere: "The ruin of the West Indies was the making of slavery."[59] In response to their fluid incorporation into Britain's economic geography, Cuban and Brazilian planters began extending their operations—bringing new land into cultivation, incorporating new technologies into the production and distribution process, and enslaving more and more people from Africa to work on the booming plantations.[60] Indeed, the intensification of the slave trade through the 1840s was well documented, and it intensified despite British naval patrols and international legal treaties designed to stop it.[61] In effect, the chance of massive profits in the new market opened to slave producers throughout the Americas made the risk of losing cargoes of enslaved Africans to British naval schooners worth the while. For protectionists, planters, and anti-free-trade abolitionists alike, the slave ship came to figure the realities of liberalization in a world turned by slavery.[62] "*Cheap sugar means cheap slaves*," Higgins would inform Lord John Russell, when wondering aloud whether the slave sugar the minister put in his tea was in fact drenched with blood—a common trope from the era of abolition to which West Indian planters suddenly (and somewhat gleefully) had access.[63]

The future inaugurated by free trade amounted to a temporal recursion to a pre-1834 and even pre-1807 past: enslaved labor remained the linchpin of the liberalizing world system. Yet Higgins's point was not simply to call attention to the hypocrisy of an empire that abolished slavery in one zone and intensified it in others. Many protectionists and antislavery activists (such as Perkins) *had* made that case, but free traders easily dispatched the argument by gesturing to the inextricability of slavery and other forms of bonded labor from almost any form of capitalist production: sugar was not exceptional.[64] Instead, Higgins would further suggest that free trade's reanimation of slavery had the ironic effect of reanimating the putatively surpassed logics of imperial territorial expansion. Free traders imagined the withering away of territorial imperialism; for Higgins, the spatial dynamics of liberalization were more complicated than free-trade cosmopolitanism allowed. If free trade implied that Britain (at least notionally) would turn away from formal territorial acquisition in favor of the deterritorialized logics of commerce, in the Americas free trade positively spurred the territorial expansion of the U.S. slave empire.

Liberalization had the ironic effect of converting Yankee expansion into conditions for British growth. Indeed, U.S. legislators revamped the structure of the U.S. economy to better fit into the emergent order of liberal globalization. Anticipating Britain's repeal of the Corn Laws, U.S. Secretary of the Treasury Robert J. Walker proposed a free-trade tariff schedule in 1846 to integrate the United States into the British-instituted global division of labor.[65] Put simply, Walker intended for the western United States to feed

Manchester with cheap grain while the South supplied its cotton. As Philip McMichael shows, this subordinate incorporation of the United States into Britain's globalized economy had the effect of extending slavery throughout the South. Even though "British free trade policy consciously promoted the western granary of the United States as a rival frontier to the slaveholding South," cheap grain lowered wage costs in Britain, thereby increasing industrial profitability, which in turn spurred the demand for cotton and so slaves.[66] Slavery subsequently expanded. New land was brought into cultivation; more spectacularly, formal and informal agents of the United States conquered more land that could be brought into cultivation. It is no accident that the United States invaded Mexico the same year that Parliament repealed the Corn Laws and Congress passed Walker's tariff.[67] Britain's postimperial political economy assumed the extension of agrarian imperialism elsewhere. From this perspective, the liberalized markets of Britain functioned as the absent center of what Michael Rogin called the American 1848—that is, the process by which the United States deferred but intensified sectional antagonism by playing Ahab to a Mexican Naboth's vineyards.[68]

In this context, Higgins's figure of the "freebooters of the Manchester School" assumes another layer of meaning, condensing the systemic links between liberalization, liberal reading practices, and the expansion of the U.S. slave empire through formal and informal state agents throughout the Americas.[69] Should Britain fail to reintegrate the islands into a British imperial state, the West Indies will be easy prey for predatory Yankees. In a skeletal outline of the chain of anticipated events, Higgins writes that "the result [of free trade will be]: the ruin of the planters; the abandonment of the islands; the seizure of them by the United States; their renewed cultivation by a slave population; and our own ultimate dependence on our former colonies for slave-grown sugar—a sad termination of all our labours,—the fruit of the expenditure of so much blood and treasure." The replacement of verbs with substantives ("ruin," "abandonment," and so on) removes any processual temporality from the narrative; U.S. extension and the reenslavement of black West Indians seem to be less a historically contingent, timebound possibility than a fact simply awaiting realization. Higgins's explains the eventuality of this "seizure" in two ways. First, the loss of protection will leave the West Indies "destitute and deserted, at the feet of a greedy and aggressive state, in whose eyes the institution of slavery would be as great an ornament as in ours it proved a blot."[70] Yet this aggressive seizure also indicates a level of care—however violent—not shown by the imperial center: "The land of stars, slaves, and stripes lies at no great distance. American sympathy will become strong as British interest grows weak. The Antilles will be taken into cultivation again on the slavery principle, and restored to their former degree of productiveness. Free trade will ruin colonists exposed to a competition so unequal, and slavery will follow in the steps of free trade."[71] The weakening of "British interest" leaves the islands exposed to the perverse "sympathy" of Yankee slaveholders. Liberal globalization will instantiate a new political-economic cartography, but it will not be the unified, postimperial world Cobden imagines. The flat world of free trade will be striated by massive slave empires, and the West Indies, negligible to British "interests," will fall into the ambit of U.S. "sympathy."

The empire Higgins seeks to reanimate comes not from the past but from the future. He does not cite the constitution, imperial compact, or customary ideologemes of political slavery; rather, he cites the possible consequences of liberal abandonment as the juridical and moral basis for an empire to come. Eric Williams's dismissal of such imperial attachments—that planters "demand[ed] a seventeenth century position in a nineteenth century empire"—thus misses the curious realism of planters' premises. As Higgins shows, the hemispheric world assembled by the pressures of liberalized markets oddly re-created the geopolitical logics of seventeenth-century mercantilism. The midcentury Caribbean *was* populated by slaves, freebooters, and expanding empires, leaving black West Indians exposed to kidnapping, violence, and the threat of mass reenslavement.[72] Bizarre sub-state sovereignties proliferated even as the United States continued to extend its dubious "protection" to more and more sites in the hemisphere.[73] West Indians might seem romantically attached to empire because their reality had become romantic.

More important, to understand the creole relation to empire as reactively romantic is to ignore the extent to which West Indians such as Higgins recognized that the past provided no compelling idiom to address their rapidly shifting present. The condition of abandonment, as I have suggested, is engendered by an attachment to a relation that persists beyond the dismantling of normative and epistemic frames that once configured it. It is this anomic, barren relation that Higgins attempts to capture when he figures West Indians' political present through the figure of the prospectively reenslaved West Indian. Like the slaves that they would possibly become, West Indians lacked discursive resources to formalize and normalize their attachment or to bind the world to their fantasies of it. But Higgins does not simply invoke slavery to diagnose West Indians' political death to empire; he moreover sets this figure to work to convert the stark fact of political death into a self-evident rationale for political incorporation. By grounding the imperial polity on the persistent threat of reenslavement, Higgins disburdens himself of the necessity of attaching his apparently retrograde argument for empire to the weighty but increasingly unavailable idioms and institutions of law and polity. Higgins's approach to empire is hardly romantic, in other words, because the figure of the slave paradoxically frees Higgins from the citational logics that underwrote backward-looking creole invocations of an imperial compact or imperial constitution. Under the threat of reenslavement, it simply did not matter whether the West Indies were ever part of empire, whether West Indians had a right to political presence within it, or whether a "compact" existed. The figure of the reenslaved human negates the import of law's sedimented historicity, suggesting that if no such ties previously existed, they must be fabulated now. Higgins's projections of catastrophic loss operate as mechanisms of political poiesis.

English Abandonment and Spanish Care

Higgins's speculative reconsolidation of the imperial polity on antislavery grounds had clear limits for the subjects whose oscillating status underwrote his attempt: black West Indians. Higgins's imperial polity is founded on the moral imperative that white Britons protect and preserve the freedom and level of civilization of black subjects—a whitening of the imperial constitution that necessitated infinitely deferring the recognition of blacks as political subjects of empire.[74] Such a move both tracked and anticipated transformations in imperial jurisprudence in the era of free trade. Consider the liberal jurist George Cornewall Lewis's *An Essay on the Government of Dependencies* (1841). Anticipating the emergence of a world system that was institutionally grounded in free-trade nation-states, Lewis wondered what would happen to the colonies once "the motive for the acquisition and possession of dependencies . . . would no longer exist."[75] Empire, Lewis noted, was not a one-way imposition of force; thus, it could not be dissolved unilaterally. The dissolution of empire requires the "consent" of imperial subjects in the colonies: "It is obvious to remark, that the dominant country ought not to abandon its authority over a dependency, unless the people of the dependency consent to the cession." Here, Lewis seems to open the possibility that imperial subjects in the colonies have a juridical and contractual right to empire. He is thinking quite clearly of the Canadas, where discontent with the political form of empire had exploded into open rebellion a few years earlier. Yet the sentence concludes with a rider, and follows with another, both of which distribute the possibility of contracting with (or out of) empire along racial-civilizational lines: "and are capable of forming an independent community. [The imperial state] is bound morally, not to throw off a helpless dependency, although the possession of it should promise no advantage to itself."[76] Within this framework of racial sovereignty, the nonwhite imperial subject's claim to a political relation conflicts with liberalism's normatization of self-care; the subject's demand thus registers as a humiliating admission of "helpless dependency," a racial incapacity to live an autonomous life. Black subjects cannot contract into or out of empire, because they are cognized not as juridico-political subject, but as objects of civilizational care. Lewis thus figures the maintenance of empire as a state form as a gift bestowed by a powerful subject to disabled subjects ("although the possession of it should promise no advantage to itself"), instead of seeing empire as a shared discursive and material construction—one, indeed, given more by colonial laborers to metropolitan appropriators than vice versa. In effect, West Indian demands articulated in the idiom of right could only be heard as black supplications for white beneficence. In Philip's words, liberal empire's inability to cognize blacks as political subjects rendered them "the humble object[s] of capricious charity" (63).

Philip himself had experienced firsthand the effects of such caprice. Philip was the illegitimate child of a white Trinidadian planter and a black mother; his life as a mulatto son with ties to a well-heeled Afro-French Trinidadian family was relatively privileged. He attended school in Scotland as a child and sojourned in London in the early 1850s to study law. It was as a law student that Philip would encounter the legal formlessness of the relations that nonetheless propped up his world. C. L. R. James relates, "While in England he had occasion to write to his father asking for help. It seems that his father refused, or at least neglected the appeal and Maxwell Philip never forgave him." *Emmanuel Appadocca*, James claims, "shows the powerful effect with which the misfortune of his birth weighed upon his mind."[77] We might take this biographical detail as little more than contextualization that enables us to read *Emmanuel Appadocca* as a family romance charged by the racial codes of plantation kinship, but I want to suggest that it also demonstrates the intimate and quotidian ways that liberalization impacted ordinary life for West Indians of diverse classes and colors. The plantocratic and parliamentary archive I worked through earlier may give the impression that the withdrawal of protection was an abstract problem confronted and experienced by creole elites alone—as if the North American Free Trade Agreement or General Agreement on Tariffs and Trade were simply the concerns of global elites.[78] By the early 1850s, the loss of imperial protection had wrecked Trinidad's economy; gone were the days of lavishly supporting children—illegitimate or not—in the metropole. Philip's precarious relationship to his capricious father neatly tracks the broader relationship of West Indians to the empire. They had no legally recognizable entitlement to protection, as Philip the lawyer and Philip the illegitimate son well knew.

Emmanuel Appadocca works to improvise an alternative legal framework in which Britain's withdrawal of protection from West Indians could be judicable as a violation of right. Its generic status as a romance is crucial to the development of this framework. For one, the affective heightening and imaginative excess associated with the genre allows Philip to recast the obscured, ordinary processes of imperial abandonment as a dramatic confrontation between right and wrong. The romance intensifies parliamentary wrangling over the schedule of tariffs into an affectively saturated shipboard trial on a pirate ship, making legible a wrong that was both produced and occluded in the institution of liberal empire. It would not do, then, to read Philip's romance as an exercise in "wish-fulfillment," as Frye might put it, or as a "resolution of real political conflict in the realm of the imaginary," as Belinda Edmondson writes of the genre's effects.[79] Instead, Emmanuel Appadocca opens a "real political conflict," deploying the romance against creoles' condition of crisis illegibility. It does so, moreover, by mobilizing the flexible relation to space and time characteristic of romance in general and pirate romance in particular. As Geraldine Heng argues from a much different context, romance is "the name of a desiring narrational modality that coalesces from the extant cultural matrix at hand, poaching and cannibalizing from a hybridity of all and any available resources, to transact a magical relationship with history, of which it is in fact a consuming part."[80] Emmanuel Appadocca's "extant cultural matrix" is the interimperial world of the southern Americas, and the romance works to cobble together a new imperial normativity out of the heterogeneous political and ideological resources that palimpsestically accumulated around colonial Trinidad. Emmanuel Appadocca seeks to derive an alternative constitution for the British Empire out of the "entangled world" that contained it, pirating from Spanish, French, U.S., and British imperial histories to indict and repair British abandonment.[81] Thus, even as Philip's recourse to the figure of the pirate indexes West Indians' precarious position within the politico-juridical order of empire—they are more or less outside the law—*Emmanuel Appadocca* recuperates this precarity by posing subtraction from the law as an entrance into a terrain of multiple legalities out of which a law that could cognize abandonment might be cobbled together.

Yet *Emmanuel Appadocca*'s indictment of British abandonment is accompanied by a reflexive hesitation over the form of subjectivity constituted in this process of juridico-political improvisation. Appadocca achieves justice from Britain by imaginatively becoming a bearer of Spanish imperial law, but it is only justice from Britain that he desires. If the romance's flexible approach to time and space enables Philip to assemble the various cultural and political resources of the Americas into a hybridized politico-juridical frame, the text's "structure of desire" remains configured by and centered on the British Empire.[82] Indeed, Appadocca's very movement into times and spaces exorbitant to the British Empire enables him to maintain this structure of desire despite the absence of political, legal, economic, or kin structures that could sustain it. *Emmanuel Appadocca*, I argue, reveals its politico-juridical innovations to be a disabling improvisation: the new imperial normativity it fashions allows Philip to decry the occluded crime of abandonment, but it also rebinds subjects to the fantasy that justice could be done if law could find a proper idiom. Emmanuel Appadocca is ultimately rendered a worldless subject, unable to live in Britain but unable to desire a life elsewhere.

This doubled orientation of *Emmanuel Appadocca* is evident in the romance's opening pages, which generate two different kinds of interimperial spaces. Its paratexts situate the romance between London (the site of its writing and the home of its dedicatee), Trinidad (the home for which a maudlin Philip declares a nostalgic attachment), and the United States (whose slave society is the stated object of Philip's critique). We can think of these paratexts as charting the romance's imagined field of circulation, in which Trinidad participates in an Anglo-centered Atlantic world. Indeed, even the preface's reference to the passage of the Fugitive Slave Act in the United States is intended to find a British audience. "Uncle Tom mania" was well under way in 1854, and the best way to be British while brown was to stick to conventions enthusiastically consumed by the metropolitan public.[83] This Anglo-centered orientation is reiterated with the epigraphs, drawn from Shakespeare, that introduce each of the book's chapters. The use of such epigraphs recalls another romancer, Walter Scott, whom Philip read while studying in Scotland. Scott himself wrote a pirate romance—*The Pirate*

(1822)—and it is possible that Philip intended to draw on Scott's cultural authority to secure the status of his own text, generically akin to a penny dreadful as it is, from the charge of being lowbrow.[84] Yet the very first sentence of the narrative interrupts this Anglo-centered Atlantic circuit by inscribing Trinidad within the Americas: "Between the north-west coast of Venezuela and the Island of Trinidad lies an extensive expanse of water, known as the Gulf of Paria" (11). Locating Trinidad by describing its proximity to Venezuela, the London reader is forced to look north from the south, reorienting the basis of her gaze from an Anglo-Atlantic world moored in London to a hemispheric world moored in Venezuela. Similarly, the chapter works to reorient the reader from a proper English lexicon to more hybrid, fluid linguistic practices: the trite formality of the Shakespearean epigraph coexists uneasily with the New World linguistic mixtures of Amerindian and Spanish and the caricatured speech of poor blacks. From the outset, the British presence in the novel is reduced to mere formal convention, a textualization of the insubstantial formalism of the English presence in Trinidad.

The merely formal presence of Britain in the novel tracks the insubstantial presence of Appadocca's father in his life. It also aligns with what Appadocca sees as the increasing thinning of British sociality as an effect of liberal capitalism. Shortly after trying—and trying to execute—James Willmington, Appadocca is captured by a British naval ship fortuitously manned by an old university friend, Charles Hamilton. Explaining to Hamilton how a promising student became an unscrupulous pirate, Appadocca links his father's crime of abandonment to broader transformations throughout Britain. He recalls encountering a woman in London as she attempted suicide and infanticide by drowning: the young woman, "left motherless and fatherless," was "abandoned" by her lover when she became pregnant (102). Appadocca describes how her body materializes her abandonment: "Her auburn hair floated loose over her shoulders and her pale emaciated face. . . . Her lacklustre eyes were as sunken as if animation had already ceased; a tattered dress hung about her skeleton frame, and her fingers were more like those of a dead than living creature. The babe was as pale as the moon that shone upon it" (102). Philip's description of an abandoned urban populace is akin to that of Friedrich Engels in *The Condition of the Working Class of England* (1845). For both, liberal capitalism reconstitutes social institutions of care (such as kin relations, the Poor Laws in England, or protection in empire), producing a socially thin world that inscribes itself as the emaciation of the bodies of those who can be abandoned. Meanwhile, the possessive individual of liberal capitalism becomes the self-possessed subject. No Londoner save Appadocca notices the abandoned widow, whose career as a piratical avenger is inaugurated when he gives her his shoe buckles to pawn for food.

The violence of liberalized social relations cannot be localized to London. Rather, liberalism is a global and globalizing form of world. As it would for Higgins, in Philip's text liberal capitalism in Britain materializes as slavery in the Americas. Philip's preface begins by linking his own biographical abandonment, as well as that of his romance's hero, to slavery in the United States, stating that the book was "written at a moment when the feelings of the Author are roused up to a high pitch of indignant excitement, by a statement of the cruel manner in which the slave holders of America deal with their slave-children"—in particular, the putting to work of their illegitimate children (6). The novel, Philip claims, is an attempt "to sketch out the line of conduct, which a high-spirited and sensitive person would probably follow, if he found himself picking cotton under the spurring encouragement of 'Jimboes' or 'Quimboes' on his own father's plantation" (6). In many ways, it is a ludicrous claim: Appadocca was born free and never put to work on any plantation. The same goes for Philip. We could take this collapse as an opportunistic attempt to dramatize the quotidian, undramatic violence of liberal abandonment through the affectively saturated signifiers of slavery—again, Philip is writing to and within *Uncle Tom's* London. Yet even the charge of opportunism requires us to get a grip on the conditions of possibility for this conflation. The challenge that the text levels, in its conflation of slavery and abandonment's structures of feeling, is to see both as deriving from the articulated politico-economic, juridical, and cultural structure of racial-liberal capitalism.

Emmanuel Appadocca is a text of counter-globalization that turns to hemispheric resources to imagine alternatives to the globalization of racial-liberal capitalism. The pirate ship is, of course, one such resource, and this ship houses a community formed in, through, and against the normalization of neglect and abandonment. The crew "had seen every natural tie break asunder around them," driving them "to seek shelter in that desperate solitude which is relieved, but, by the presence, and cheer, but, by the sympathy of the few . . . like themselves"; they had "abandoned the entire world for the narrow space of their small vessel, and the inhabitants of the vast universe for the few kindred spirits who were their associates" (43). Philip's description of the *Black Schooner*'s crew recalls Ishmael's description of the "Isolatoes" aboard Ahab's *Pequod*, but Philip's abandoned pirates would hardly fit in with Melville's republican "Anacharsis Clootz deputation."[85] Indeed, by casting his story as a "tale of boucaneers"—a phenomenon of the seventeenth century—Philip conjugates a heterotopic time-space asynchronous with that of political modernity. *Emmanuel Appadocca* doubly displaces political modernity, first through a critique of the effects of the French Revolution on idealized kin structures, then through a motivated disavowal of the Haitian Revolution. Appadocca informs Hamilton that he recruited his pirate crew from the ranks of former French aristocrats exiled to "San Domingo" who brought with them "a strong hatred for their then democratic country" (109). The temporal coordinates of the romance become incredibly scrambled here. The narrative suggests that Appadocca had been born in Trinidad after its British conquest in 1797, meaning that by the time the twenty-something Appadocca arrived in London to recruit his aristocratic exiles, the French Revolution and the Haitian Revolution had long since completed themselves, with the latter leaving few Frenchmen behind. The text, it would seem, bends every which way not to say "Haiti." Philip is not, however, simply silencing the past; rather, Philip's disavowal of Haiti should be read as a refusal of the modal normativity of anticolonial nationalism.[86] Free trade's normalization of national sovereignty functioned as a technology of imperial abandonment. While free traders certainly did not desire the violence that attended the Haitian Revolution, many desired its effects— the cost-saving externalization of sovereignty.[87] *Emmanuel Appadocca* thus brackets the Haitian Revolution to find a means of critiquing postimperial modernity that does not dialectically recuperate imperial abandonment with the promise of national autonomy. In so doing, Philip opens West Indian political imaginaries to affiliations and associations occluded by the couplet of free-trade nationalism and revolutionary anticolonialism. Philip's pirates want to reestablish empire, not destroy it.[88]

Emmanuel Appadocca finds this critical idiom not in Trinidad's future but in Trinidad's Spanish imperial past. The romance's attempt to get its British readership to look north from the south, from Venezuela to Trinidad, intended a legal-historical reorientation. Trinidad had been conquered by Britain from Spain in 1797, at the tail end of a decade of intensive development. The island was long neglected by the Spanish empire, and a series of reforms integrated it into the administrative and legal apparatus of the newly formed Capitanía General de Venezuela in 1777. At the same time, Trinidad's final

Spanish governor, José María Chacón, issued a famous *cédula* (decree) that extended various incentives to Catholic slave owners throughout the Caribbean to settle on the island. The primary emigrants were French—first, those displaced by the British conquest of Granada, followed by refugees from the Haitian Revolution. A sizable cohort of francophone free mulattoes migrated to Trinidad, as well, for Chacón's decree similarly provided free black Catholics with incentives and offered them legal protections.[89] When Chacón surrendered the island to Ralph Abercromby, the terms of capitulation ensured the maintenance of Spanish law, a term that aligned with the British jurisprudence of conquest anyhow. In effect, British colonial administrators ruled over a predominately French and African population through the instruments of Spanish law. Trinidad, as V. S. Naipaul put it, was a "foreign colony" in the British Empire.[90]

For many writers of Philip's generation, viewing British Trinidad's present from a Spanish perspective was to witness the legal abandonment of the island's mulatto subjects. Confronting the liberalization and Anglicization of Trinidadian society, Trinidadians of color developed a *leyenda blanca* that fancifully posed Spanish rule as a period of racial equality and economic justice. Indeed, almost immediately after British conquest, subaltern and elite Trinidadians alike set the affordances of an increasingly residual Spanish law to work to critique the British state's dismantling of their rights and protections.[91] The most famous example of this interpretive tack comes from one of Philip's older relatives, Jean-Baptiste Philippe, who wrote a petition to protest how the recodification of colonial law disinherited free people of color of rights secured to them by the articles of capitulation.[92] This leyenda blanca retained force through the 1850s, as we will see in chapter 4. Philip's own Emmanuel Appadocca takes his name from Vice Admiral Don Sebastian Ruiz de Apodoca, the Spanish naval commander who sank the fleet defending Trinidad, preventing the ships from falling into English hands but enabling the conquest of the island in 1797.

This reactivation of the residual neatly aligns with Frye's insistence that "the inherently revolutionary quality in romance begins to emerge from all the nostalgia about a vanished past."[93] By turning to Trinidad's Spanish imperial past, Philip recuperates a politico-economic model in which the axiomatics of care are not opposed to a subject's independence or autonomy. This past offers a world where "dependency" does not correlate with the racialized "helpless[ness]" of liberal imperial jurisprudence; it thus provides *Emmanuel Appadocca* with an imaginary through which abandonment might be critiqued without impugning the abandoned's capacity for autonomy. By assuming the name of a Spanish admiral, Appadocca recasts an illegitimate son's outrage at his practical and legal abandonment into a contest between competing imperial normativities. Spain is thus the prop that keeps Appadocca's project afloat, as is made literal in the text: Appadocca flees the British naval ship on which he is imprisoned by seizing "a large Spanish pitcher of clay," jumping out a porthole, and floating atop the pitcher through the Gulf of Paria to Venezuela (167).

Venezuela occupies a privileged place in *Emmanuel Appadocca*, for it figures the persistent effectivity of norms that the Trinidadian Appadocca could only recall as residual. Appadocca arrives in Venezuela after nearly drowning. (His clay pitcher, as you might expect, did not last very long.) Cast ashore, the insensate pirate is discovered by "two Llaneros, their lassos . . . coiled in wide circles around one arm" (171). In "their spirit of native hospitality," the cattle ranchers save Appadocca the pirate, lassoing him and conveying him to their employer's ranch (172). Venezuela is presented as a space adjacent to liberal modernity. As it is about Haiti, the text is silent about South American independence movements; we are far from Bolívarian republicanism. We are instead located in an unsettled imperial frontier, where the "rude accouterments" used for cultivation index a distance from modernity and where settled hierarchy patterns the social (174). "Esta un hombre de cualidad" (He is a man of quality), remarks one of the Llaneros of Appadocca, according the pirate a recognition he could not achieve in Britain or Trinidad (172). The emphasis on Venezuelan hospitality, moreover, contrasts sharply with Appadocca's description of liberal Britain. The rancher orders his daughter, Feliciana, to attend to the "pallid, wasted, and haggard" stranger: " 'Que se haga toto necessario por eso infeliz,' 'Let everything be done for this unhappy man,' said the Ranchero, who even in the half barbarous life that he led, did not entirely lose the distinguishing politeness of his people" (174). The primacy the text accords to Spanish here is not simply an authenticating gesture; it stages the foreignness of the imperative to aneconomic hospitality to the liberalized British imperial world. In a scathing indictment, the British West Indian is accorded a more homely welcome in the Spanish empire than in Britain. Appadocca's entrance into this new world of care is coded as a moment of epistemic and affective disruption; he falls victim to a "passing madness," as if he cannot compute the welcome he receives (174). Indeed, his hosts do more than offer him shelter: the pirate, "under the care of the fair Venezuelan," falls in love with Feliciana.

The Venezuelan interlude of *Emmanuel Appadocca* is brief. The pirate soon rejects Feliciana, and his growing attachment to her, to resume his quest. Even as the interlude underlines the availability of alternative regimes of care and belonging to Appadocca, its brevity poses a question: Why can Appadocca not remain in a world that is like the one he wants, even if it is not *the* one he wants?

We (Almost) Found Love in a Hopeless Place

Moments after Emmanuel Appadocca tries his father, sentences him to death, and has him pinioned to a cask to float adrift on the sea until he dies of exposure, the narrator directly addresses the reader.

> Reader, have you ever felt the absorbing love that sank and merged your existence into that of a cherished object, and have you ever felt the gall of sneering ridicule from her? . . . Have you ever demanded bread from a parent whom you may have loved to excess and received a stone, or have you ever asked water from the author of your existence and received poison? Then you can fancy the captain's sentiments, or have you ever, while straining your industry and energy to the utmost, been ground down to misery and despair by him from whom nature taught you to expect love and protection, while he himself was rioting in profuse abundance? (70)

Such a plea for readerly empathy makes sense in the wake of the sentence Appadocca metes out to his father. But the forms of relation the text adduces to render Appadocca's violence understandable do not adequately translate the circumstances of Appadocca's relationship with his father. The captain may feel like a lover frustrated by his indifferent "cherished object"; he may feel like a child who had "loved" a parent "to excess" with no corresponding attachment. But Appadocca is neither. As the text relates, Appadocca could hardly have "s[u]nk and merged" his existence into his father or "loved [him] to excess" for the simple reason that Appadocca lived most of his life unaware of his father's existence. Loss is the primary modality through which Appadocca experiences his kin relations—an unsurprising fact, given plantation slavery's generalized production of social death—but his experience of bereavement is always a retroactive production. Appadocca does not know he has been "abandoned" until, as a young adult studying in London, he receives a cask when his mother dies that relates the truth of his paternity. Having believed his father dead, he now learns his father was actually indifferent:

the "dead" father is resurrected as a negligent one through a letter. Taking his mother to have been "treated with injustice" and desiring "vengeance," he writes to his father to "give the offending party an opportunity of remedying the wrong he had done": "I described to him the utter distress in which I, his son, was then placed, and besought him to send me a pittance to sustain the life of which he was the cause" (100–101). His father does not respond, literally neglecting Appadocca, who descends into a life of poverty in London, ultimately becoming a pirate.

Abandonment, *Emmanuel Appadocca* suggests, is not just an event in structure; it is also a fantasy by which subjects relate to it. The narrative of epistolary receipt and nonreceipt I have described stages Appadocca's conscription into this fantasy relation. Appadocca only discovers that he "lost" Willmington's protection as a child when he receives a letter as an adult; the norm of paternal protection to which Appadocca intensely binds is a belated textual effect that compels Appadocca to reread what was according to a new sense of what could have—and should have—been. Thus, even as he condemns his father for withdrawing his protection from his child, Appadocca never experienced this loss *as* a child. Abandonment, in effect, has no present tense: it is a scenario conjured by an active and retroactive assessment of the past from the perspective of an attachment that was never binding—normatively or affectively—in that past. (Indeed, the reader learns the specifics of Appadocca's abandonment only when he narrates his history to Charles.) Appadocca is not simply melancholically attached to a lost object, a lost relation, a lost father. Rather, the fantasy of abandonment induces a kind of melancholic poiesis that fabulates a prior relation only in the wake of its putative loss.[94] Scholars have described such melancholic relations as "laden with creative, political potential," and surely such is the case in *Emmanuel Appadocca*.[95] The romance assembles a novel political, juridical, and literary cartography for the West Indies, centered on the New World, in the name of rendering Appadocca's loss legible; in so doing, moreover, it imagines a new set of norms for a postliberal British Empire. At the same time, however, *Emmanuel Appadocca* is recursively skeptical about the effects of inhabiting this form of relation. The "creative, political potential" that accrues in Appadocca's zone of imperial abandonment cannot be fully accessed, for Appadocca's "structure of desire" remains imperturbably organized by a desire for recognition and justice from his father. Conscription into a fantasy relation of abandonment results in the constriction of its subject's attachments to a single source, site, or horizon of belonging.

In one of the romance's more utopian moments, Feliciana attempts to undo these psychic and affective constrictions by relocating Appadocca within an alternative line of descent. When Appadocca flees Venezuela to continue his course of vengeance, she follows him while attempting to assemble an alternative filiation for Appadocca to annul the drama of paternal abandonment. While visiting a Trinidadian obeah woman to receive a prophecy about Appadocca's fate, Feliciana's Trinidadian guide narrates to Feliciana her recollection of the night that Admiral Don Sebastian Ruiz de Apodoca set fire to the Spanish fleet. He sank the fleet, she claims, because the ships were "laden with gold" and "he would not let the money fall into the hands of the English" (217). In a moment laden with possibility, Feliciana implies that Appadocca may be the son of Apodoca:

> "And what became of the admiral himself?" the lady inquired again.
> "I really cannot say," answered the guide.
> A short pause ensued.
> "Had he any son, do you know?" asked the lady after a time.
> "I do not know, madame," answered the guide.
> "The money that I spoke of just now, has all been lost. They say that sometimes the fishermen manage to bring up a portion. I don't think that is true," said the guide. (217)

The guide appears to misinterpret Feliciana's question, thinking that she is inquiring whether some son could have inherited the sunken wealth. Instead, Feliciana is asking whether Appadocca might be heir to a life that does not require him to seek vengeance against the English. What if Appadocca's relationship to the Spanish empire was one not of nominal affiliation but of genealogical filiation? What if Appadocca could see himself not as the abandoned son of England but as a temporarily lost child of Spain? The text has already assured us, however, that no such link of descent exists. Appadocca's mother declared Willmington the father; Willmington himself recognizes Appadocca as his son; and later we discover that Appadocca possesses a "peculiar mark" that his half-brother recognizes (212). Appadocca's identification with the Spanish admiral remains ungrounded in lineage or biological kinship. His patronymic is an improper name that places the possibility of an alternative affective and political affiliation under the sign of an impossible filiation.

For Appadocca, however, this possibility is blocked. The text translates the impossibility of vertical kinship between admiral and pirate into a frustrated romance between the pirate and Feliciana. In staging this relationship, *Emmanuel Appadocca* encodes the effects of the pirate's conscription into the fantasy of abandonment as an attenuation of the pirate's receptivity to love. While explaining to Feliciana why he cannot stop his pursuit of his father, Appadocca calls attention to the emergent attachment between the Trinidadian and the Venezuelan. He is, he remarks, "sensible to the existence of [her] sentiment, and can only say, from that self-same affection, I am capable of appreciating and responding to yours" (181). But Appadocca is in fact *not* capable of responding to Feliciana's love, as he relates:

> For my own part senora, I have long sacrificed myself to one object. I have long banished away Emmanuel Appadocca, from Emmanuel Appadocca: it boots not to tell the reason why. The world to me, it is true, is the world; the stars, the stars; but the halo that once surrounded them is gone—the feeling with which I may have regarded them is gone from them, and has centered itself in the now single end of my existence. . . . My heart is wasted and its tenderness gone; gratitude for you, senora, is all I dare encourage in my bosom. (181–82)

Sacrificed to his one object, to his one objective, Emmanuel Appadocca banishes himself from himself. That is, he abandons himself to his fantasy of abandonment, and the lost object of the English father is introjected as the deep structure of Appadocca's subjectivity. Appadocca's heart is not simply "wasted"; he *is* his wasted heart.[96] Yet as the passage reveals, this identification of subject and wound is tenuous. The presence of Feliciana, and Appadocca's avowed affection for her, suggests that melancholia may convert into mourning, that Appadocca may reorganize his world by attaching to new objects. Appadocca must therefore actively abandon these emergent attachments to maintain the fantasy of his abandonment. These abandoned attachments include not only the one that emerges between Feliciana and Appadocca but also Appadocca's attachment to his pirated Spanish patronym: he has "banished away Emmanuel Appadocca, from Emmanuel Appadocca." (Indeed, Philip subtly truncated his own name in publishing the book, putting space between himself and his francophone lineage: Michel Maxwell Philip became Maxwell Philip.) We might take the dissolution of Emmanuel Appadocca into his object as staging the relationship between the British world that the romance critiques and the hemispheric world through which the idiom of critique is derived. The hemispheric, hispanophone signifiers are empty vessels for a narrative whose "structure of desire" remains centered on Britain; they are taken up and then abandoned.

Appadocca's inability—or refusal—to form new attachments renders him monstrous. Most critics of the book have missed this component of the text. Reviewers decried *Emmanuel Appadocca*'s "atrocious metaphysics," while some scholars today valorize the retributionist ethic (recoded as anticolonial) that they see as implicit in what Appadocca calls his "social physics" (104).[97] Taking the protagonist's discourse as the degree zero of the romance's discourse, both readings treat the novel more like a two-volume harangue (à la *Marly*, discussed in chapter 1) than as a text invested in problematizing Appadocca's psychic and affective binding to his fantasy of abandonment. But the romance codes Appadocca as being as bestial as the society he condemns. Not only is his leitmotif a serpent, but after fleeing Feliciana he kills a jaguar with his bare hands, consuming the raw, "still quivering flesh" of his victim (187). The mono-purposiveness and self-imposed instrumental quality of his career of revenge ironically mirror those lonely Londoners who "like gruff animals . . . hurry in silence to their separate lairs[,] each . . . intent on his own pursuit." Moreover, the very "social physics" that underwrites Appadocca's ethos of vengeance mirrors the liberal market sociality that he otherwise impugns. Justifying his career of vengeance by claiming that organic and inorganic matter possesses a systemic "mechanism and order" that automatically regulates interactions between persons and things, Appadocca insists that he is simply the instrument of law's will toward equilibrium (104). Single-mindedly "intent on his own pursuit" to the neglect of the care Feliciana extends, Appadocca reveals himself to be the true son of Willmington, as his friend Charles claims: "Such characters as that Willmington, unluckily for humanity, make as many Appadoccas" (205). The text's critique of Britain's abandonment centers less on the fact of Appadocca's abandonment than on how this abandonment so determines Appadocca that he cannot not think of himself as abandoned—even when inscribed within an alternative horizon of love and legibility, such as that offered by Feliciana in Venezuela. Locked in the madness of abandonment, Appadocca cannot reconfigure himself as a subject who is actually receiving the protection he desires.

For *Emmanuel Appadocca*, then, abandonment marks a position of political potential, of political poiesis even, but this potential remains inaccessible due to the psychic and affective violence constitutive of abandonment itself. The illegitimate and outlawed Appadocca's freedom is also his loss, a fact starkly related when Appadocca finally succeeds in killing Willmington. A hurricane has wrecked the pirate ship, and his imprisoned English father drowns with it. Appadocca and his crew swim to safety on the Venezuelan shore. The pirate captain becomes curiously melancholic at the moment of his success, stating to his lieutenant Lorenzo: "The pursuits that engross us during an entire lifetime, and lead us too frequently, to sacrifice health, happiness, and sometimes even draft us into crime, must all—all end in this—in nothing" (242). Once again, according to any simple biographical metric, Appadocca's course of revenge hardly consumed his "entire lifetime"; the point, however, is that Appadocca has no "lifetime" before his course of revenge. Or after. Revealing the location of his treasure trove, he tells Lorenzo to use half of it to fund "a college for abandoned children" and to distribute the other half to his men. Then, bequeathing his sword to Lorenzo, "with a spring Appadocca jumped from the rock and threw himself headlong into the thundering waves below" (244). Appadocca had so "sacrificed [him]self to one object" that the loss of that object is equivalent to a total loss of self: nothing places him in or tethers him to the world. Indeed, this placelessness is made neatly literal with Appadocca's suicidal plunge into the Gulf of Paria. He has no place in the British world that abandoned him, but the dynamics of that abandonment bars him from assuming a place in Venezuela. Cast outside the empire but unable to form new attachments, the pirate is engulfed by the psychic and affective violence of abandonment.

Emmanuel Appadocca queries the costs that West Indians assume in relating to Britain as the empire's abandoned subjects. Just as an adult Appadocca retroactively produced his father as the failed protector of his youth, so, too, may the imperial protection that creoles claimed to have lost be nothing more than a fantasy that madly conjures a responsible empire that never in fact had any presence. As this fantasy is introjected, it gains an impossible reality: subjects relate to themselves as subjects of loss and demand the restoration of what they never had. Such "loss," however, inhibits subjects from recognizing—and desiring recognition within—alternative horizons of legibility, care, and protection. The violence of creoles' (auto-)constriction of their worlds becomes clear that the end of *Emmanuel Appadocca*. Feliciana, who "fell mad over Appadocca's grave" when she discovered his death, now tends to the tombs of the pirate and his mother: "Twice a-year she might also be seen on her pilgrimage to Trinidad, when she plucked the weeds off his mother's tomb, and tended the sea-grape tree that grew over the lonely grave of EMMANUEL

APPADOCCA" (245, 248). Melancholically attached to the English protection he never experienced, Appadocca can receive the care that the Spanish world offers only after his death. *Emmanuel Appadocca* is both a critique of imperial abandonment and a critique of how it fashions subjects who believe themselves to be abandoned, of Britain's liberal globalization and of those whose structured inability to globalize otherwise prevents them from participating in new worlds of care.

PART TWO

Building New Worlds

Chapter 4

UNCLE BOLÍVAR'S CHILDREN

What sentence will posterity pronounce against the Government of the parent state, whose indifference shall have impelled thousands of souls devoted to British Empire to fly their country and seek refuge in a foreign land?

—GEORGE NUMA DES SOURCES, *The Trinidadian*, 29 March 1851

No Country for Young Mulattoes

In the summer of 1851, a notice appeared in *The Trinidadian*, a Port of Spain newspaper oriented toward the island's people of color: an enslaved Venezuelan had been emancipated. José Francisco Paulo was "employed" as a sailor on the *Amacili*, a Venezuelan launch. When it drifted into the waters of British Trinidad, colonial authorities "caused [Paulo] to be put on shore" and "handed over to the Magistrate," presumably through a writ of habeus corpus.[1] He was subsequently "set at liberty." The announcement might have ended there, as such journalistic micronarratives of freedom usually did. But *The Trinidadian* refused to celebrate the event of Paulo's liberation. The predominance of the passive voice is telling: Paulo hardly seems to be an agent in his own emancipation. Indeed, the legal mechanism by which he comes to be free (being "handed over to the Magistrate") establishes an eerie similarity between being policed and being freed. To be "set at liberty" in Trinidad, the small narrative implies, is to be subjected to an authority indifferent to the political agency of the ex-slave.

In a brief commentary on the notice, the mulatto editor of *The Trinidadian*, George Numa Des Sources, makes this critique explicit for his readership. If British Trinidad is a land of liberty, its liberty is not of a quality that even an escaped slave would desire, as is evident from the Venezuelan slaves who had refused "similar liberation": "We have known certain of these slaves refuse similar liberation, and return to the family of their masters. We think that the period fixed by the Venezuelan constitution for the emancipation of slaves is near expired. . . . Whatever be the case, there certainly does exist as great a difference between Venezuelan slavery and that of the slaves of this colony in 1830, as there exists disparity between the condition of *English citizen* and that of *British subject* of our days."[2] Des Sources's invocation of humans who choose enslavement within a thick kin structure to the thinness of liberal freedom anticipates, in outline, the "Anti-Toms" that would soon be published by pro-slavery ideologues throughout the anglophone Atlantic in response to Harriet Beecher Stowe's *Uncle Tom's Cabin* (1852).[3] Yet in tracking enslaved Venezuelans' reversal of the progressive script of liberty, Des Sources intends not to valorize slavery but to highlight alternative paths from it. The institutional processes of emancipation in the British Empire freed enslaved humans but opened—or, as we saw in chapter 2, by opening—a gap between "*citizen*" and "*subject.*" It is this "disparity," Des Sources suggests, that Venezuelans who return to slavery refuse. Implicitly, these Venezuelans are equipped to mark this disparity due to "differences" in the institutional process of slavery in Venezuela, on one hand, and Trinidad, on the other. If a Trinidadian slave opting into slavery in 1830 would have struck a British observer as an outrageous return to a Pattersonian social death, Des Sources anticipates Frank Tannenbaum by suggesting that these Venezuelan fugitives return to a kind of social life.[4] That is, these enslaved humans turn back not to their "masters" but to "the family of their masters," a reentrance into a thick sociality heterogeneous to relations of domination that had constituted Trinidadian slavery. Marking the constitutionally determined termination of Venezuelan slavery, Des Sources suggests that these fugitives return to a scene of potentiality where they might soon realize a different articulation of personal freedom, social belonging, and political status. Why remain in the dystopia of free Trinidad when one could return to the Venezuelan utopia soon to come?

Des Sources would continually pose this question to readers of *The Trinidadian*. Indeed, his narration of enslaved Venezuelans flight from a liberal freedom to an alternative freedom to come was articulated at a moment when he had begun urging his emancipated readership to follow Paulo's peers' lead—to break with Britain and make for the Main. Des Sources understood the difficulty his readers might have in making this political and affective reorientation; the dramatic figure of the slave who chooses enslavement, even if for a different kind of freedom, discloses the possible unthinkability of the politics he endorses. *The Trinidadian*'s ideological trajectory bears witness to the difficulties of simply quitting Britain. Founded by Des Sources in the revolutionary annus mirabilis of 1848, *The Trinidadian* was a bilingual newspaper (the second half of each issue was in French under the header *Le Trinidadien*) characterized by its fierce opposition to colonial corruption and its staunch advocacy for mulatto and black rights.[5] *The Trinidadian* emerged out of a previous paper for which Des Sources had worked, the *Trinidad Spectator*, which was politically moderate and oriented toward reform. Des Sources radicalized the *Spectator*'s program, becoming what British colonial elites feared most: a francophone person of color with republican—and then socialist—politics.[6] British officials described *The Trinidadian* as "a most violent Radical Paper" and Des Sources as "the principal Political Agitator" in Trinidad.[7] Yet, and like much of the West Indies' black print culture, *The Trinidadian*'s critical project was at first animated by an ideology of empire loyalism.[8] For the first couple years of its run, *The Trinidadian*'s demands for a robust extension of citizenship to subjects of color were articulated as defenses of the British constitution against its perversion by Crown Colony rule and the racialized jurisprudence of the liberalized empire. In time, however, Des Sources would come to see his project of suturing citizenship to subjecthood as an impossible dream for his comrades of color. By the time that Des Sources narrated Paulo's dubious "emancipation" in 1851, he had been using his paper to enlist supporters to return to Paulo's Venezuelan home to build a colony there. Using the newspaper's full discursive and generic range, Des Sources made political, legal, historical, and economic arguments in editorials, letters, advertisements, poems, and a serialized adaptation of *Uncle Tom's Cabin*—*Adolphus: A Tale* (1853)—to project the different kind of freedom that could be enjoyed in the "refuge" of Venezuela. Des Sources's insisted that his project of political reanimation was "no Utopia," and his readership agreed: between 1852 and 1853, more than seven hundred Trinidadians migrated to the colony, christened Numancia.[9]

This chapter explores what, precisely, Des Sources and his fellow colonists hoped to find in Venezuela. Des Sources's turn to the utopian asylum of Venezuela was a direct response to Britain's turn away from the West Indies during the period of imperial liberalization. Des Sources asserts that it is imperial "indifference" that "shall have impelled thousands of souls devoted to British Empire to seek refuge in a foreign land." To this indifference, Des Sources counterposed both the putatively paternalistic order of Spanish imperial slavery and the putatively color-blind dynamics of postcolonial republicanism in

Venezuela. Venezuela offered, most simply, citizenship within a state that cared—a far cry from subjection within an empire of neglect. As Belinda Edmondson argues, Venezuela functioned as a kind of "postcolonial space" for Des Sources and other members of his race and class.[10]

But things were not so simple, and could not be. Even as Des Sources valorized the Venezuelan state and the citizenship it supposedly offered, his colonization project was motivated by a pessimistic understanding of how blacks might fit into the institutional fabric of the world's state system.[11] This pessimism was common to many black separatists throughout the New World. By the 1850s, after all, blacks in the West Indies had witnessed their doubled foreclosure from achieving a political world in either the residual (i.e., imperial) or emergent (i.e., national) state forms that centered the world system. On one hand, the liberalization of Britain's empire had as an effect the erection of a cordon around the political nation of Little Britain; as Des Sources's remarked, Trinidadian blacks could be "British subjects" but never "English citizens." However, it was not clear that belonging to other states within the Americas promised much for black folk. Des Sources's protestations to the contrary, postcolonial republics in Spanish America were deeply suspicious of black subjects.[12] Moreover, the imperial impulses of the United States—whether in the form of state-sanctioned land grabbing or informal filibustering—rendered the possibility of national sovereignty for enslaveable subjects in the New World a gamble not worth the staking, even if Britain's black subjects desired to make it.[13] Finally, the example of Haiti loomed large. The Haitian Revolution demonstrated the extraordinary heroism and bravery of black subjects fighting for freedom, but for some it also demonstrated how the institutional form of the state and the interstate system could contort personal and political freedom into conditions of hyper-exploitation.[14] Just as Michel Maxwell Philip would, Des Sources stages a motivated disavowal of Haiti in his novella. Thus, even as Des Sources desired political belonging within a state, this desire was sapped by the recognition that Westphalian idioms of state sovereignty and state belonging never worked very well for black subjects—and that, perhaps, they were not supposed to. The "homeless Sons of the West," as Des Sources named New World blacks, had "no protection anywhere," as the U.S. separatist J. Dennis Harris lamented.[15]

In turning from the diminished political subjectivity available to free blacks in his zone of imperial abandonment, Des Sources was not simply endorsing a return—or advance—to the statist logics of sovereignty and citizenship, this time staged just across the Gulf of Paria. Rather, Des Sources's flight to Venezuela assembled itself as a lateral movement out of the political frameworks of sovereignty and state recognition and into alternative frameworks of survivability, maintenance, and even hope. That Des Sources's turn from dominant political logics of sovereignty and citizenship expressed itself as a movement through a transnational field is hardly accidental: both the excess and the abandoned remnant of the world of states, the space of black freedom, as Richard Iton suggests, is always already incipiently transnational.[16] For Iton, the transnational functions within black emancipatory projects not simply as an analytic topology but also as a political philosophy: to recontextualize black political and cultural production in a transnational field is to "render citizenship itself as less than the ultimate recognition of an individual's value and other than the only recognized marker of meaningful membership."[17] Read in these terms, the black transnational names the remainder of a political subtraction, but a remainder that nonetheless recasts the violence of abandonment as generative of new potentials for a politics otherwise. My point is not to suggest that Des Sources was in some ways an anarchist. He was not. He desperately wanted to belong to a state. It is rather that the nineteenth-century black transnational was a deeply vexed, ambivalent space, where ties to states—and the state as such—were aspirationally reaffirmed, but one also where forms of poststate life came to glimmer with a utopian promise.

The textual affordances of the colonial newspaper proved central to Des Sources's capacity to stage this ambivalence in all of its complexity. Due to Benedict Anderson's still necessary work, we have come to view "provincial creole printmen" as the privileged fashioners of a proto-, and then full-blown, nationalist consciousness.[18] Certainly, Des Sources was amply critical of the colonial order of things, and this critical disposition was animated by a patriotic attachment to the island. Yet *The Trinidadian*'s patriotism was embedded within an affective and imaginative field composed of a multiplicity of loyalties, attachments, and interactions, none of which were hierarchically ordered. Indeed, the paper's seriality presented a diverse array of transnational and transimperial affiliations in a noncontradictory synchrony.[19] Colonial editorial practices of reprinting are crucial here: in the space of a single issue, readers would be apprised of Trinidadian, British, British imperial, West Indian, French, Antillean, U.S., and Spanish American news. Like Trinidad itself, then, the textual world of *The Trinidadian* was dizzyingly global. This globality yielded productive cross-fertilizations between seemingly incompatible political ideologies: empire loyalism, mercantilist statism, Spanish imperial paternalism, French republicanism, multiple strands of socialism, black separatism, and eventually U.S. sentimentalism. The expansive globality of *The Trinidadian's* editorial vision enabled Des Sources to cultivate alternative horizons of political possibility, forms of attachment and affiliation that enabled his readership to unbind from their cruel optimistic relationship to the empire that had abandoned them. Venezuela thus amounts to something of a double trope for Des Sources: it tropes both the world Des Sources imagined as a desirable alternative and the turning of Trinidadian political and cultural sensibilities toward the Americas.

A precipitate of the interaction of these varied ideologies, Des Sources's Venezuela is an uneasy hybrid of political grammars, an unstable assemblage of conceptual part objects that bespeaks both the indeterminacy of black Trinidadians' position in the world system and the creative potentials that such indeterminacy generated. The utopian "wish-image" of Venezuela condenses a varied range of antiliberal longings and ideologies under a single catachrestical name.[20] In this chapter I pry this catachresis apart and explore the diverse chains of which it is composed. I begin with a consideration of Des Sources's relationship to the colonial state and liberalized empire to establish the negativity out of which Venezuela would come to gleam as a utopian alternative. I then trace how, in confronting his bleak present, Des Sources turns to Trinidad's Spanish imperial past, recovering an alternative set of political and governmental norms that stood in stark contrast to Britain's instituted neglect. Importantly, however, the political and economic protections guaranteed to people of color in Spanish Trinidad were not just a thing of the past; imperial mercantilism, Des Sources averred, found a surrogate just across the gulf in Venezuela's multiracial republic. Yet Des Sources's apparent investment in republican citizenship is constantly ironized by his desire to put distance between himself and the state. Turning from Des Sources's valorization of the Spanish imperial and postcolonial Venezuelan states, I explore the impact of varied forms of utopian socialism on his thought. I do so by tracing the ideological and geographical itinerary of a group of utopian socialists through Germany, Britain, the United States, Venezuela, and, ultimately, Trinidad. The transnational quality of this world of utopian print and performance, I suggest, mapped neatly on to a key feature of midcentury socialism: a deep skepticism regarding the value or possibility of statist solutions to social antagonism. If Des Sources's republican Venezuela figures as a site of a robust political subjectivity, it at the same time is constituted through a desire for a sustainable form of postpolitical life. Routed through this socialist optic, the Venezuelan state functions less as a scene where blacks might participate in the exercise of collective self-governing than as an apparatus that promises to maintain New World blacks in a kind of nonsovereign autonomy. I then turn to *Adolphus*, an anonymously published novella set in slavery-era Trinidad serialized even as Des Sources had struck out for utopia; it was, however, most likely written by Des Sources himself.[21] I read *Adolphus*, an adaptation of *Uncle Tom's Cabin*, as condensing—but not resolving—the seemingly contradictory desires that Des Sources invested in Venezuela. On one hand, Bolívarian Venezuela is figured as a multiracial republic that actively seeks to cultivate black subjects as citizens. On the other, the novella enacts a lateral move into a zone of sustainable nonsovereignty that registers as black subjects' reincorporation into the affective and distributive unit of the family—the kind we see in Paulo's peers' return to "the family of their masters," to be sure, but more dramatically in Simón Bolívar's concluding adoption of the eponymous hero of Des Sources's novella. The juxtapolitical idiom of the sentimental novel, to use Lauren Berlant's term, unstably mediates between the hyper-political idiom of postcolonial republicanism and the postpolitical idiom of utopian socialism.[22]

This chapter is not interested in ideological contradiction—not as such. After all, that black subjects in the nineteenth-century Americas would have contradictory, oscillating, unstable political desires seems rather intuitive. Rather, I am interested in how the appearance of ideological contradiction can clue us into foreclosed subaltern political possibilities. Des Sources wrote through a moment when the Westphalian order of territorialized state sovereignty was still an aspirational project throughout the Americas. Indeed, if black subjects fit but poorly into the Westphalian order, so did the Americas, and it is important to recall the sheer amount of labor it took state builders to subsume the hemisphere into the Euro-centered polity of nations.[23] For Des Sources, the Americas is not so much a geographic topos as it is a utopian project. It is a politics, not a place—an important reminder for a hemispheric studies that always threatens to teeter into a geographical determinism. V. S. Naipaul guards us against such determinism and recalls this other, lost future for our Americas in the conclusion of *The Loss of El Dorado*. Having spent hundreds of pages describing the historical intimacy between Trinidad and Venezuela, he sadly recalls of his childhood in Port of Spain, "Venezuela, of which the island once formed a part, was just across the Gulf and could be seen on some days. But Venezuela was a fact in a geography book."[24] Just like Naipaul, we might think of our hemispheric scholarship as saving utopias from becoming mere topoi, as gathering the fragments of failed worlds to imagine the construction of new ones.

Le citoyen anglais est noble et grand

On 1 October 1849, a crowd of Trinidadians of color an estimated five thousand-strong approached Government House in Port of Spain. They accompanied a delegation headed by Des Sources, who bore a petition addressed to Governor Lord Harris. The petition requested the retraction of a recently promulgated ordinance that "petty debtors in the Royal Gaol were to have their heads shaved like common criminals."[25] The regulation was desperately unpopular: given the scarcity of cash endemic to the West Indies but intensified after the liberalization of Britain's sugar markets in 1846, the majority of the island's black population survived on petty debts.[26] This mode of stigmatizing debtors recalled slavery-era penality, in which the shaving of heads—particularly women's heads—was a humiliating technique in the state's carceral repertoire.[27] In a final turn of the screw, the regulation promulgated by Harris was unadorned with even the formalism of popular consent; because it was a Crown Colony, legislative power was concentrated in the governor's hands, not in a representative assembly. When Des Sources and his fellow petitioners approached Government House, petition in hand, they were protesting the oligarchic colonial state's repetition of slavery-era penality in an era of liberal globalization. Whatever hopes propelled the petitioners to the scene of the political, however, were quickly dashed. A rumor spread that Harris had refused to accept the petition. The angry crowd threw stones. The Riot Act was read; shots were fired; and several of the petitioners were killed.[28]

In the press war that followed, Britishness provided the idiom through which the riot was interpreted. Holding Des Sources's *Trinidadian* particularly responsible for the event, the state-sponsored *Port of Spain Gazette* took the chance to indict Trinidad's sizeable francophone black population more broadly. Imbued with all the conservatism colonial elites could muster in that era of proletarian dreaming, writers for the *Gazette* wrote *The Trinidadian* off as a radical organ disseminating foreign republican feelings to an otherwise peaceful populace.[29] The complaint had been common since Britain first conquered the island in 1797: British Trinidad was too French.[30] For Des Sources and his coterie, however, the riot was a symptom of an opposite problem: the political institutions of Trinidad were incompletely British. Indeed, in both its English- and French-language sections, *The Trinidadian* posed itself as preserving the British constitution from colonial corruption. "*Le citoyen Anglais est noble et grand,*" Des Sources wrote a week after the riot, and the presentation of the petition was intended both as an enactment and a defense of this citizenship.[31] Indeed, his fellow organizer Edward S. Hobson had insisted that his comrades "must proceed in a constitutional mode of action."[32] And what could be more British, more constitutional, than petitioning? For *The Trinidadian*, the *Gazette*'s inability to see the Lord Governor's humble petitioners as anything but barricade-building Parisians disclosed the un-British, despotic nature of the colonial state. Publishing as "One of the People," one letter writer insisted that black Trinidadians' use of the petition was both a symptom of black Trinidadians' unconstitutional exclusion from political life and their unshakable attachment to those constitutional forms. Instead of revolting against the Crown Colony's unconstitutional form of rule, those marching to Government House kept faith with the political culture of Britishness, taking "recourse to the only means to which as British Subjects we are not debarred, that of petitioning." Des Sources argued that the elites' interpretation of British petitioning as republican rioting disclosed their "longing for the erasure of our names from the list of British subjects." He refused to accept this erasure without a fight, promising that "we shall still appeal to the British Constitution" to right wrongs.[33]

Through his public appeals to the British constitution, Des Sources attempted to enact an uncodified imperial citizenship. Indeed, what is at first so striking about *The Trinidadian*'s discourse is the faith it evinces in black Trinidadians' capacity to performatively reiterate the terms of the British constitution to incorporate those who had been neglected by it into the "list of British subjects." This faith was in some measure justified. Less a stable political object or juridical instrument than a diffuse cultural repertoire, citations of the British constitution created rhetorical space in which subjects abandoned by the political could resituate themselves within it. The idiom of British constitutionalism was so sticky throughout the colonial world because the constitution was, in Dicey's late Victorian phrasing, so flexible: the constitution worked by being incessantly reworked.[34] Des Sources's performative citations of the constitution thus opened a peculiar political space: by proleptically coding himself as an imperial citizen, Des Sources could critique the conditions that impeded his being recognized as a full member of it. But this powerful political prolepsis also worked to bind—and by binding—Des Sources to a constitutionalist fantasy that normalized colonial life as abnormal. Indeed, as Des Sources's stated fidelity to its terms attests, the "British

Constitution" worked equally well when it apparently failed to work at all. Juridical-institutional failures could (and did) attach subjects all the more securely to the constitution's cultural paradigm, a paradigm that offered a compelling vision of a normative Britishness superordinate to any particular institutional codification of it. Interpreted in light of this unwritten, always rewritten constitution, being shot at by the colonial police appears as an aberration of the law, not an ordinary and immanent enactment of it; being erased from the list of British subjects appears as a perversion of Britishness, not simply what it was.[35]

In the years following the riot, however, Des Sources began to lose faith in constitutionalist paradigms of political mobilization: "British subject! Magnificent soap bubble . . . you are simply a word!"[36] In part, he had come to recognize that the bundle of juridical, political, and cultural transformations that overdetermined the process of imperial market liberalization had displaced the discursive conditions in which such rearticulative performances could matter. Utterances that reiterate and rearticulate political convention—such as, say, claiming British citizenship in French from Trinidad or, in Judith Butler's example, singing the "Star-Spangled Banner" in Spanish in the United States—acquire their efficacy through their location within a common political or public space, one in which co-belonging subjects extend the minimal recognition of listening, reading, and responding to one another.[37] In conditions of structural neglect and political abandonment, however, the minimal donation of attention requisite for rearticulative utterances to force a shift in convention has been withdrawn. For Des Sources, the liberalization of the British Empire had created a global condition in which Britain, turning from empire to worlds beyond, no longer bestowed any attention on its erstwhile subjects: "The policy of the mother country, dictated by its own important and complicated interests, embracing the commerce of the world, cannot stoop to notice the operation of its measures upon the destinies of its Colonies."[38] This divestment of sovereign attention transforms discursive rearticulations of political belonging into ineffective monologues. Imperial subjects in the West Indies have been "neglected and abandoned to the pernicious influence of laws in the consideration of which they have no voice."[39] This denial of voice incorporates but is irreducible to black Trinidadians' minimal access to the representational media of the colonial or imperial state. It is a denial of voice so complete that even critiques of the absence of representational political rule cannot be heard; so complete that the "neglected and abandoned" colony cannot even compel the imperial state to undertake the prepolitical—and so constituently political—act of "stoop[ing] to notice" its subjects.

For Des Sources, Britain's sovereign inattention to Trinidad was deeply ironic, insofar as Trinidad had been constituted as a Crown Colony precisely so that the imperial state might attend more responsibly and effectively to colonial affairs. An abolitionist improvisation with the imperial constitutional order, the West Indian Crown Colony was developed to prevent the two components of English common law most functional for the preservation of unmeliorated slavery from taking root in Trinidad: representative assemblies and English property law.[40] Because Trinidad was a settlement of conquest (versus one of settlement), the English constitution did not immediately transplant itself into the new territory.[41] The conquered territory was thus constitutively exterior to the jurisdictional space of the British constitution; citations of the British constitution were legally, if not rhetorically, a priori inoperative. The Colonial Office framers of the Trinidadian constitution seized on this fact to create a legal order that violated the positive precepts of the British constitution in the name of extending British freedom—or, at least, British fairness—to enslaved blacks. The Crown blocked the formation of a colonial assembly even as it elected to retain the legal regime of Spanish Trinidad on the assumption that the Spanish law of slavery was more ameliorative than British common and colonial law. The legal code of British Trinidad was intended to be exemplary for other slave colonies; in many ways, the metropolitan-led period of amelioration intended the hispanicization of slave law throughout the West Indies.[42] As demonstrated by Philip, as well as by his activist relative Jean-Baptiste Philippe, black and mulatto activists were attached to the Crown Colony, and thus Spanish, legal order, which was perennially threatened with Anglicization.[43]

By the 1850s, however, emancipation and liberalization so flipped the political script that Philippe's fellow Francophone mulatto Des Sources was more or less reanimating the constitutionalist rhetoric of the slave-era plantocracy. For Des Sources, a limited colonial legislative sovereignty was necessary to negotiate the deleterious, depressive effects of imperial liberalization: "The only hope of the Colonies rests on the sagacity and prudence of the measures emanating from their local legislature, for mitigating the evils of Imperial Government."[44] While lack of a popular legislative body was in fact a "deprival of the rights of citizenship, which the British constitution has guaranteed to all British subjects," Des Sources insisted that Crown Colony rule was "not only a grievous injustice"; it was also "destructive to [Trinidadians'] well-being."[45]

With the Crown's attention turned elsewhere, a revanchist plantocracy had begun to mobilize the apparatus of Trinidad's antidemocratic, ersatz Spanish state to displace the effects of liberalization onto the island's poor. The articulation of a liberalized economic structure to an illiberal political state meant that the only British liberty Trinidadian workers enjoy is the state's indifference to their welfare: "One has the right to die of hunger and misery on the high road without any fear of the Government troubling itself about this privilege."[46] Moreover, the white plantocracy had simply seized apparatuses of the colonial state to extract wealth and labor from black Trinidadians.

If colonial rule in Trinidad once looked like an aberration from the script of Britishness, liberalization's transformation of the institutional and discursive constitution of empire made it harder for Des Sources to oppose British imperial normativity to colonial reality. For Des Sources, Trinidadians had begun reading the imperial state's cruel indifference to the colonial state's depredations as contributory negligence. Poor Trinidadians had begun to conflate empire in general with the deviant form it took in the Trinidad: "The tears of despair which silently and bitterly course down the cheek of the poor, are imputed to the Crown, whose name is degraded by the local fisc."[47] With the "ruin of 1854"—the year set for the full liberalization of Britain's markets—fast approaching, Des Sources wonders about the political options that remained for folks so poor they were deprived even of the fiction of the abnormality of their reality.[48] The October riots had demonstrated the anger of an abandoned populace detaching from fantasies of right, but they also demonstrated the capacity of the state to meet force with heightened force. Nonetheless, Des Sources did have revolution on his mind, one that would be enacted not as an overturning of the British order but as a turning away from it. Advancing the slogan "Reform or Emigration," *The Trinidadian* would come to suggest that, just across a thin stretch of water, postcolonial Venezuela exemplified all that colonial Trinidad could have been.[49]

Entangled Worlds

Des Sources's valorization of the Spanish Main found its conditions of possibility in the deep historical entangling of Trinidad and the world to the south. Until Britain conquered Trinidad in 1797, the island administratively was part of the Capitanía General de Venezuela, a political unit formed in 1777 as part of the Bourbon reforms.[50] It was during this period that the island, long neglected by Spain, experienced its most sustained growth since Columbus conquered it. The centerpiece of Spain's program for developing Trinidad was the Cédula of Population, proclaimed in 1783. Negotiated by Phillipe Rose Roume de Saint-Laurent, a French planter whose native Grenada had been conquered by Britain during the Seven Years' War, the Cédula invited Catholics of all nations to settle the islands. Under the Cédula's provisions, white settlers would receive thirty-two acres of land, plus sixteen acres for each enslaved human they brought; free black settlers would receive sixteen acres, plus eight acres for each enslaved human they brought. The island's population rapidly grew, and as it did, it grew French: the majority of free settlers, black and white, had French colonial backgrounds. (It was during this time that Des Sources's family moved from Grenada to the island.) Reviewing this history, Eric Williams quips that Trinidad had become a "French State within a Spanish State"—and, soon, a British one, too.[51]

Trinidad was thus a zone of intense interimperial interaction, a world composed of the accumulating, palimpsestical traces of multiple peoples and polities. Eliga Gould uses the term "entangled worlds" to describe zones, such as colonial Trinidad, whose political and cultural histories cannot be resolved neatly into imperial or national analytical frameworks. As Gould argues, for many in the Atlantic world the "community that mattered most" was never reducible to a single, demarcated polity (such as the British and Spanish empires). It was, rather, "the entangled community that included both."[52] What might thus appear from one perspective as a zone of anomic statelessness or as a borderland zone of diminished sovereignty appears, from another, as a zone of state*fullness*—an everyday scene of political potentiality to which creoles might attach. This perspective should afford us an opportunity to rethink the political space of blackness in the anglophone New World. Throughout the anglophone Americas, blackness was forged through and as an ongoing political abandonment that worked to convert human subjects into objects of governance or things of commerce. Yet as the work of social historians has suggested, this abandonment did not mean that black subtraction from a given political world rendered them politically dead. Rather, blacks' functional expulsion from the states in which they found themselves oriented black political thinking to an incipiently and implicitly transnational field of possibility.[53] As Jane Landers puts it, "Atlantic creoles"—and enslaved creoles in particular—"became adept at interpreting political events and manipulating them," comparatively thinking across empire to "determine the possibilities for freedom that each offered."[54] This cognitive mobility was the product of practical movements in, across, and through the New World's multiple, frictive empires.[55] It would, of course, be ridiculous to celebrate this mobility as a joyful Deleuzean nomadism, charged as it was by the knowledge that staying in place might result in enslavement. My point, however, is that we might see black political practice as inflecting the incomplete Westphalianization of the New World with a kind of anarchist potentiality—a condition of life in which subtraction from the state is not a fall into a state of political nullity but into a field of vexed and vibrant "possibilities for freedom."

The colonies of the Spanish Americas had long served as sites where these possibilities could be actualized. While received hemispheric geographies of freedom continue to point north—north of Mason-Dixon, north of the United States—southern routes to freedom were well traveled. In making "reasoned and informed choices in their attempt to win and maintain liberty," many Atlantic creoles came to the same conclusion in practice that Tannenbaum eventually would in theory: Spanish colonies offered blacks "certain rights and protections not found in other slave systems."[56] The Spanish governor of the Floridas, for instance, had promulgated a policy of sanctuary and freedom for blacks fleeing British (and then, for a period, U.S.) masters in Georgia and the Carolinas. Yet as Landers suggests, fugitive blacks were attracted to the Spanish empire not simply for the personal freedom it offered, but for the formal and informal norms and requirements that bound sovereign to subject.[57] The Spanish empire extended—or, at least, was understood to extend—political subjectivity to New World blacks. Des Sources's writings on, and eventual travels to, the Spanish Main followed in a historically well-worn epistemic and political groove. Indeed, a certain anachronism fuels Des Sources's approach to Venezuela: his understanding of postcolonial Venezuela is mediated by a historical comparison between British Trinidad and Spanish Trinidad. Through a motivated reading of Trinidad's entangled history, Des Sources presents Venezuela as the Spanish empire in postimperial garb.

Des Sources turns back to the late eighteenth century to the period during which Venezuela and Trinidad were part of the same administrative unit of the Spanish empire. It is a time, he writes, that "everyone must remember," for it was during this period that "the Council of Castillo caused Ordinances to be promulgated, protective of the slaves of their colonies. . . . Under Chacón, the law was in full force, and the slave protected. We have seen negroes and mullatoes, officers of the militia troops."[58] As we saw in chapter 3, the last governor of Spanish Trinidad, José María Chacón, had entered into the unofficial memory of Trinidad's black and mulatto populations as embodying principles of paternalistic, caring governance. Indeed, the 1850s witnessed an intensification and extension of this figuration. Chacón would be similarly lauded in the Irish émigré Marcella Noy Wilkins's *The Slave Son*, a sentimental novel published the same year that Des Sources's *Adolphus* was serialized; *The Slave Son* similarly returns to Spanish Trinidadian history and resolves its plot in Venezuela. For Wilkins, Chacón "carefully watched the carrying-out of every law to protect the slave" and "extended his merciful protection" to mulattoes and the island's indigenous.[59] Contesting the Black Legend, Wilkins declares, "We are apt to revile the Spaniards. Let us take a glance at their laws. . . . [P]erhaps we may find something to admire, perhaps even to learn from. Though feudal and despotic their government, they nevertheless framed their laws studiously to protect the friendless."[60] Yet Wilkins's desire for jurisprudential recovery itself bespoke a fact that she and Des Sources would both lament: British conquest put an end to the "feudal" protections offered by the Spanish imperial state. As Des Source puts it, "Since the conquest by the English the pyre and gibbet took the place of the paternal code of Spain." The status of people of color consequently shifted: "The negro up to [full emancipation in] 1838, and the mulatto up to 1820, were considered as brutes—dangerous—and the prey of hardships; and, at the present day, the Government deprives them of the civic rights." His point is clear: "Before 1800 Spain had already recognized us as men, as citizens."[61] Forced incorporation into the British Empire, with its strikingly Inquisitorial "pyre," registers as an ongoing political death.

Then, without noting the spatial and temporal dislocation, Des Sources shifts focus to postcolonial Venezuela, as if Venezuelan independence did not produce a political or legal culture discontinuous with that of the Spanish empire. He performs this shift, once again, through the figure of the enslaved Venezuelan on the run, one who escapes to postemancipation Trinidad, only to find "Venezuelan slavery . . . preferable to the liberty of Trinidad." In Trinidad, these escaped slaves had "but one right—that is, to toil for the all powerful Lords of the Budget, or, like Coolies, die on the high roads and in the gutters." By returning to Venezuela (even if to slavery) they escape the legal and political nonpersonality ascribed to them in British imperial spaces. The implication for Des Sources's fellow "homeless Sons of the West" is that an escape to independent Venezuela would be a return to the paternalistic protections once enjoyed in Spanish Trinidad.[62]

If Trinidad's political separation from Spain introduced a significant discontinuity into the island's conception of citizenship, rights, and legal protections, Des Sources posits that Venezuela retains the Spanish empire's conception of citizenship despite its willed separation from Spain. This citizenship is expansive inasmuch as it is putatively multiracial, but also for its articulation of economic protections with civic and legal personhood. Ideally, Des Sources writes, "The prosperity of a country consist, not in that of a small number of its inhabitants, but in the largest possible amount of protection and ease disseminated amongst the population."[63] Britain had removed such economic protections, enabling the further concentration of "ease" among the island's elite, leaving Trinidad's "resources . . . stultified by the present system of political administration." Venezuela, by contrast, "is fostered by a paternal form of government, ever zealous to protect the national interests."[64] This paternalistic governance takes the institutional form of import duties that amount "almost to prohibition" on foreign goods that might "enter into competition with the proceeds of national industry"— goods such as flour and other quotidiana. The protections afforded national industry, moreover, are not simply negative; Des Sources describes a policy of free land grants and industrial bounties.[65] The import of these descriptions of material life was not simply that Venezuela promised the easier accumulation of greater quantities of stuff. Rather, Des Sources understands economic privileges as materializing political belonging: cheap flour and cheaper land mark a lively political relation. As he puts it, it is through the extension of economic protections that the state builds its "paternal" authority and "augment[s]" itself with "citizens and friends." To emigrate to Venezuela would be to emigrate to a point of potentiality, to a period before England's "great political economists . . . diverged from [the] paths" of offering "enlightened encouragement" to "national industry."[66] It would, in other words, be to emigrate back in time to arrive at a future black Trinidadians might have had as citizen-subjects of a multiracial, mercantilist empire.

Indeed, Venezuela had readopted one notable economic policy of early modern Atlantic empires: colonization. Translating an article published in the *Correo de Caracas*, *The Trinidadian* remarks on the Venezuelan public's "approval" of their colonization scheme, anticipating that prospective settlers might "number among our colonists many Venezuelans." All of this good feeling materializes through the extension of economic and legal protections. "Every measure," Des Sources claims, "calculated to benefit the new Colony has been taken with the Venezuelan Government."[67] According to the prospectus for his "Fraternal Colonizing Association in Venezuelean Guyana," these measures included equal legal protection, proportionate taxation, and that "every citizen" might be "truly free" through the possession of "a voice in the Council of the Republic."[68] At the same time, Des Sources insists that his colony would have maximal local autonomy. He hoped, after all, to "implant into the solitudes of the continent a vigorous nationality," *not* fuse Trinidadian emigrants into the Venezuelan nation-state.[69] While the Numancian colony would derive its authority through its relationship to the Venezuelan state, Des Sources insists that the colony will possess its own "constitution," recognized by the national government.[70]

Des Sources's descriptions of colonial life in postcolonial Venezuela pre-scribe a model constitution for an imperial polity, one that tracked what cre-oles desired the British Empire to be and one that tracked what Des Sources thought the Spanish empire was. To be sure, his identification of this robust citizenship with Spanish imperial subjection, as well as his displacement of this form of citizenship to postcolonial Venezuela, bore only a tangential relationship to the norms and practices of (post)colonial Spanish polities. As Jeremy Adelman argues, Spanish American postcolonies' mobilization of economic instruments such as tariffs was a symptom of the difficult pas-sage that these states made through forms of imperial and postcolonial sov-ereignty. The instability of postcolonial sovereignty led states to intervene into economic life as a means of enhancing their authority vis-à-vis a slowly, unevenly cohering national populace.[71] In other words, the bundling of eco-nomic protections with political citizenship indexed not the persistence of empire but its chaotic collapse. Reading Venezuelan state formation from the recently liberalized British Empire, Des Sources sees an interventionist state seeking to shore up its authority as one fulfilling imperial obligations to protect its subjects and their livelihoods.

Thus, if Des Sources returned to Spanish Trinidad's past as a means of turning Trinidadians' attention to postcolonial Venezuela's present, this com-plex process of temporal mediation risked foundering on the very anachronism that animated his gesture. The rise of the nation-state coupled with liberal globalization to effect a marked discontinuity in the temporal, territorial, and political logics of the world system. A gulf had been carved between the institutional and normative order of imperial-mercantilist and postcolonial states, a divide that could not be crossed simply by sailing across the Gulf of Paria. Yet Des Sources's untimely revalorization of state inverventionism and economic protectionism was not simply an atavistic return to the days of mercantilist empire. Rather, his mediation of Venezuela's present through the Spanish empire's putative past was itself mediated by his embrace of the science of the future. Numancia was not to be just any kind of colony. It would be, Des Sources declared, "a community of labor, of equality of production, of communism, in fact."[72]

Quitting the Political

In many ways, the foundational role of communism in Des Sources's program for Numancia served to resolve a simple problem confronting the would-be colonizers: they were poor. The "principle of communism," Des Sources would write, is "the most fertile [principle] in a Society which, such as ours, is without capital."[73] Alongside these concerns with the practicalities of colonization, Des Sources's turn to "socialism" and "communism"—terms that are only minimally distinguished in his discourse—marks a subtle mutation in the theoretical and political fabric of his project. Indeed, his attempt to suture mercantilist theories of sovereignty and subjecthood to postliberal theories of utopian socialism evinces a hesitation over the very desirability of blacks achieving any legible political subjectivity, whether British, Spanish, or Venezuelan. If the movement from British Trinidad to the Spanish Main intended the resumption of a foreclosed legal and political subjectivity, Des Sources's turn to utopian socialism opens an alternative order of possibilities in which the value of citizenship loses its obviousness. For utopian socialists such as Charles Fourier, Robert Owen, and Étienne Cabet, the political was itself little more than what Des Sources wrote off as a "soap bubble"; they anticipated the harmonization of political antagonisms through a postpolitical order of rational social engineering. While today we tend to associate socialism with state interventionism, and while utopian socialists did indeed regard themselves as developing an "interventionist social science," many utopians did not typically understand the primary agency of intervention to be the state.[74] Indeed, they eschewed contention within or against the state, especially in the form of revolution, in favor of what today we might think of as "prefiguration"—an exemplary living of the future in the present.[75] This utopian withdrawal from the time of the state implied a spatial withdrawal, as well: utopia was prefigured in "colonies" constructed as contiguous to but not subsumed into the space of the state.[76] And so Des Sources's turn to utopian socialism introduces a new aspect of his project. Routed through the idiom of utopian socialism, Des Sources's voyage back to the land of the political is simultaneously a voyage to an asylum from the political. Where New World blackness marks a political death into the social, as Fred Moten suggests, the "socialism" I exfoliate here names a liveliness that persists in and as a black turning away from the political.[77] By converting the mere life of political abandonment into the more life of postpolitical freedom, socialism made it unnecessary for black subjects to conceive their worlds in relation to the antiblack logics of the political state.[78]

Des Sources's encounter with socialism probably begins with Conrad Stollmeyer. Born in Ulm, Germany, in 1813, Stollmeyer migrated to Philadelphia in 1836, where he worked as a printer of a German-language newspaper and books in German and English. Stollmeyer's interest in colonization expressed itself quite early in his U.S. sojourn: his name is found on the lists of the original board of managers of the Deutsche Ansiedlungs-Gesellshaft zu Philadelphia, a society dating from 1836 that attempted to found a colony in Hermann, Missouri. Stollmeyer ultimately stayed in Philadelphia, where his quiet life as an expatriate printer would soon be disrupted by the politics of slavery. Like many German emigrants of his generation, Stollmeyer was committed to abolitionism as an extension of broader republican investments. And so it was that when an antiabolitionist mob burned Pennsylvania Hall to the ground in May 1838, Stollmeyer published a "severe article against the perpetrators" in his German National Gazette, admonishing them for their breach of republican norms.[79] In exchange, the mob nearly dealt Stollmeyer the same fate as Elijah Parish Lovejoy, the abolitionist printer murdered in Illinois the previous year. Stollmeyer's brush with the antiabolition mob did not scare him off from abolitionist politics.[80] It did, however, qualify his faith in the efficacy of republican political forms. Were republican political institutions, or indeed any political institutions, adequate to undoing slavery?

No, the Fourierist Albert Brisbane argued in his Social Destiny of Man; or, Association and Reorganization of Industry (1840). Stollmeyer published Brisbane's foundational text of American Fourierism from his shop in Philadelphia, and its effects on Stollmeyer were extraordinary. For Brisbane, slavery is simply a "symptom" of a broader "social malady."[81] Dominant forms of abolitionism, however, symptomatize abolitionists' deficient knowledge of social logics.[82] Bereft of this knowledge, abolitionists approach slavery as a political problem susceptible to political intervention; they mobilized various idioms and instruments of political right to make their case. The problem with this approach, Brisbane maintained, is that slaveholders could similarly mobilize idioms of political right; indeed, they mobilized them with perfect right. Even as Brisbane found slavery abhorrent, he insists that slavery could not be resolved politically without violating someone's right. Politicians sought to resolve the antinomic character of U.S. political society by "looking backwards" to the Revolutionary period with the hope that the "doctrines of republicanism" might "be carried out in all their purity"; Brisbane holds that "irreconcilable" and explosive antagonism is precisely what a pure republicanism looks like.[83] The resolution of these antagonisms thus requires turning from a reorganization of the state—tinkering with the "superstructure," as he called it—to a reorganization of society.[84] By reconstituting units of kinship and material production, the material and social conditions that animated contemporary political antagonism would simply vanish.

Stollmeyer's encounter with American Fourierism decisively shifted his publishing and activist concerns. He printed several German-language utopian tracts following his publication of Brisbane's work and traveled to Brisbane's New York in 1840 to attend the Fourierist Society celebration of Fourier's birthday.[85] There, Stollmeyer met John Adolphus Etzler. Born in Germany, Etzler (like Brisbane) had studied briefly under Hegel. He was jailed for publicizing pro-emigration material, an episode that brought him into contact with John August Roebling on his release. Together, the two appear to have published anonymously *A General View of the United States of North America, Together with a Community Plan for Settlement* (1830), founded an emigration society, and in 1831 sailed for Philadelphia.[86] The pair split soon after their arrival: Roebling's desire to form a simple farming village (as he would at Saxonburg, Pennsylvania) struck Etzler as a betrayal of the utopian potentials of the New World.[87] Roebling would go on to manufacture wire rope and build the Brooklyn Bridge; Etzler, like Stollmeyer, settled into the fringe world of American utopians. Residing briefly in Pittsburgh, Etzler published his first program for Yankee utopia, *The Paradise within Reach of All Men, without Labour by Powers of Nature and Machinery* (1833). Neither an audience nor paradise materialized, and Etzler spent the subsequent years "as a kind of itinerant secular evangelist preaching about a new kind of Millennium to be brought about through human reason and effort."[88] It was in New York, in the figure of Stollmeyer, that Etzler found his first enthusiast.

On the surface, the theoretical architecture of Etzler's program departed little from that of his fellow Fourierists. Yet where Fourier and Brisbane insisted on making labor "attractive," Etzler would suggest that labor should be abolished.[89] Technological innovation would enable this abolition of work. Etzler designed, acquired patents for, and tried building two machines: the Satellite (something like a massive, self-propelling tractor) and the Naval Automaton (a wave-powered ship).[90] Stollmeyer would publish a manual for their construction, Etzler's *The New World; or, Mechanical System* (1841). Henry David Thoreau would mock Etzler's techno-utopianism in an essay entitled, "Paradise (to Be) Regained": "It would seem . . . that there is a transcendentalism in mechanics as well as in ethics." For all of his spiritualizing of the mechanical, Thoreau holds, Etzler simply "aims to secure the greatest degree of gross comfort and pleasure merely."[91] More accurately, Etlzer's aim was subsistence security for the world's population. More radically, Etzler transcendental mechanics and antiwork orientation displaced the political idiom of republican ideology. As many scholars have demonstrated, labor was central to Jacksonian republicanism: it secured the material independence of the laborer, and this material independence was the basis on which he could assert a civic identity as a free white man in the polis.[92] Despite its antipolitical orientation, conventional Fourierism's valorization of an attractive labor was functional for Jacksonian republicanism in a way that Etzler's antiwork imaginary could never be. As Stollmeyer would later write in England, "The people *do not want work*. Work is not the *end*. The end is provisions, happiness, the satisfaction of all our rational desires."[93]

Unsurprisingly, Etzler's message failed to resonate with Jacksonian mechanics and laborers; nor did Jackson himself respond to Etzler's petition that the U.S. state invest in his machines.[94] Etzler, Stollmeyer, and Stollmeyer's family migrated to England, armed with a new program: tropical emigration. The pair quickly established the Tropical Emigration Society (TES), whose program and constitution were published in *Emigration to the Tropical World, for the Melioration of All Classes of All People of All Nations* (1844).[95] The work purported to show to "people who are dissatisfied with their circumstances and the world, that the world is not such a poor narrow crowded place as ignorant unreasoning people suppose."[96] They need only look to the New World. The TES proposed to form a settlement in Venezuela, which offered "some of the best chances of the globe for selection of extensive tracts of land for a colony on a great rational plan, to ensure success and progress for the greatest happiness of a society that will make use of it." The social technology of the colony was central to this plan, as a Wakefieldian Etzler explained: "All migrations have been but individually, without combination. If a thousand emigrated, they scattered in all directions."[97] Combined with Venezuela's hyper-fecund soil and Etzler's gadgets, a socialized colony could easily put an end to the world's subsistence crisis. The world, Etzler wrote, would live on sugar—not from cane, but from maize. High-fructose corn syrup would be the colony's manna.

To demonstrate how the pair's utopian program could peacefully resolve pressing political problems, Stollmeyer looked to the debates gathering around free trade, protection, and the postemancipation West Indies in his *The Sugar Question Made Easy* (1845). Anticipating the triumph of free trade, Stollmeyer aims to elaborate a "just" solution for "*ruined* West Indians." The state, however, could not be the source of this justice, for "the Sugar Question is—Not dependent upon legislative measures of Parliament, which neither increase nor decrease the quantity of sugar grown."[98] Stollmeyer urged a two-part technological fix, one that would appeal to planters, Codben's Anti-Corn Law League, and abolitionists alike. First, the West Indies should grow maize instead of sugar: the former yields more sugar per plant and more crops per year. Second, sugar producers should do away with human labor, enslaved or otherwise, and more fully embrace advances in mechanization. As to the minimal human labor required to oversee these iron slaves—machines that would be used in the crystallization of sugar but also in the reaping of maize—Stollmeyer recommends that planters incorporate their free workers as shareholders in a harmonious cooperative.[99] The plantation becomes a phalanstery. This socialist plantation's harmonization and association of interests prefigures the harmonization of imperial class interests—a harmonization that the plantation will have brought about. Stollmeyer's ideal plantation "will abolish that unchristian and abominable system of human slavery," enable "British subjects at home to feed on something sweeter than water-gruel and saveloys," and "pay the proprietor of the plantation a very handsome profit."[100] Sheer volume of production would render archaic those political-economic models, such as Ricardo's, that understood relations of income distribution and the division of labor as necessarily antagonistic. Politics would be a thing of the past.

The TES attracted significant popular support in Britain—and, as Home Office officials would suggest, among a broad array of Europeans. Per Etzler's program, the society was established as a joint stock company on 13 October 1844, and the society's extensive network of agents, as well as the positive notices Etzler received in both the Owenite and non-Owenite socialist press, helped sell an impressive thousand shares a mere twelve weeks after the society's foundation.[101] The popularity of the society owed, however, not only to savvy use of plebian print and distribution networks; its message resonated with battered, exhausted Chartists, licking their wounds after two grievous setbacks in 1839 and 1842. As letters to the society's paper *Morning Star* demonstrated, erstwhile Chartists delighted over the Fourierist message that political transformations, however deep, were deeply superficial, and hardly worth working (and dying) for.[102] The TES offered an exit—and a technologically avant-garde one at that—from the useless antagonisms of political life. And, as Stollmeyer's pamphlet dramatically concludes, humanity's way out was already in the making: Etzler and two agents, Taylor and Carr, were already in Venezuela, deciding on plots of land.[103] The society imagined that they had secured a grant of land, although it would be unclear to British officials with which state authority they had transacted—the regional assembly of Venezuelan Guayana, the municipality of Upata, the federal state, or perhaps all three. Aware of pro-emigration policies common to the postcolonial Americas, they also petitioned Venezuela's President Carlos Soublette for a loan of £10,000 for the transportation of the society's members to their settlement.[104] They were ready to build paradise.

But things did not go according to plan. When he arrived in Venezuela, Etzler and his two associates were shocked to learn that the society would not receive the grant they thought they had been promised. With the departure of the first ship of utopian migrants from Britain imminent, the society's agents decided to purchase land. Using his personal funds, Etzler purchased a plot in Valencia, Venezuela; his two associates purchased 120 acres in Venezuela at a site called Guinimita, thirty-five miles from Port of Spain and on the Gulf of Paria. A party of fifty-seven settlers arrived in December 1847, Stollmeyer among them. Stollmeyer and Etzler remained in Port of Spain and formed a railroad company, soliciting the British state for £50,000 for the venture. The remainder of the party traveled to Guinimita, where things went from bad to worse. The settlers had inadequate numbers to clear the land, Etzler's Satellite did not work on the terrain (or on any terrain, really), and disease quickly consumed the population. Some managed to return to Port of Spain. Governor McLeod, hearing of the colony's plight, sent a surgeon; he discovered only two adults and two children remaining at the settlement. The project was falling apart. Communications among the British consul at Caracas, the Venezuelan government, McLeod, and the Foreign Office and Colonial Office reveal that President Soublette had no intention of supporting the colonists; the British state, meanwhile, worked hard "to put a stop to proceedings which entail misery and destruction upon the victims of the delusion, and which cannot probably, be productive of any real benefit to the Projectors [i.e., Stollmeyer and Etzler] themselves."[105] Thus, when a party of 193 settlers from Britain had arrived in Trinidad on the ship *Condor*, the colonial press publicized reports of the pioneer settlers' fate, probably at the behest of the colonial state. Most demanded passage to the United States or return to Britain. The *Condor* sailed to New Orleans; it sank en route.[106] Etzler likewise disappeared and was never heard from again. Of the society members who remained in Trinidad, several attempted to form a cooperative farm; others would find livelihoods as "Utopian and unmanageable" artisans, in the words of the British travel writer Charles Day.[107] The group retained its socialist identity over time: in detailing his travels to Trinidad from the United States, W. G. Sewell would record in 1863 that a "few exiled Chartists came to the island some years ago, and are doing well."[108] Stollmeyer would also remain in Trinidad, undertaking public works projects, preaching temperance (his new cause), and forming a relationship with the new governor, Lord Harris. At the close of 1852, he returned to the newspaper business, working as printer and editor of *The Trinidadian*. The spot was open: Des Sources and his coterie had just embarked for their own Venezuelan utopia.

The transfer of the newspaper indexes deeper, albeit more difficult to trace, exchanges of knowledge and affect between these utopian socialists and Des Sources. Stollmeyer's eventual proprietorship of *The Trinidadian* was but the capstone of an intimacy that had begun almost as soon as the German arrived on the island. Beginning in February 1845, Des Sources sold both Etzler's *Emigration to the Tropical World* and Stollmeyer's *The Sugar Question Made Easy* from the offices of the *Trinidad Spectator* and advertised this fact in his paper.[109] Moreover, like the other island newspapers, Des Sources's *Spectator* covered the collapse of the utopian colony; unlike the other papers, however, the *Spectator* was sympathetic to the colonists. "Its project is humane," writes Des Sources, and the sole reason it collapsed is because "Guinamitta [sic] . . . is not a locality suited to European constitutions."[110] While Des Sources refuses to sermonize about the risks of utopian dreaming, his encounter with Stollmeyer and Etzler hardly amounted to an instantaneous conversion to socialism. As we have seen, Des Sources's idiom became more resolutely constitutionalist and intensely republican in the years after the collapse of the Guinimita settlement. It was only after coming to the limits of constitutionalist critique in a zone of political abandonment that Des Sources turned to socialism.[111] And yet this turn to socialism occurs without much reference to Stollmeyer. Indeed, Des Sources never mentions Stollmeyer in connection to his colonization project when boosting it in *The Trinidadian*. This makes sense: citing the influence of a failed colony probably would have been bad for business. It was only after Des Sources left for Numancia, and left *The Trinidadian* in the hands of his fellow Numancians, that the paper would mention the TES alongside the Numancian Fraternal Colonization Society as comparable, but by no means identical, movements. It was only when Stollmeyer became the paper's editor that someone would pose the relationship between his utopian socialist scheme and that of Des Sources as one of continuity, and even identity. In one of his first editorials, Stollmeyer wishes the Numancians well in their quest for a "PARADISE WITHOUT LABOR," a citation of Etzler's tract that frames the black colonization movement as a surrogate for his own failed utopia.[112] It is a rather violent misreading of the movement: Des Sources at no point articulated an antiwork program. What influence, then, did Stollmeyer and Etzler's project have on Des Sources?

We might detect Stollmeyer's influence in the technical aspects of Des Sources's program. Like the TES, the Fraternal Colonization Society used a subscription model to acquire capital.[113] Like the TES, Des Sources hoped to colonize Venezuela. Like Fourierists, Des Sources "counsel[ed] the principle of association; of community of labor, of equality of production, of communism in fact."[114] Directly invoking Fourier's idiom, Des Sources exclaims, "Let labor be rendered productive by diversifying it, and it will become attractive."[115] Above all, what utopian socialism yielded Des Sources was a means of turning sour imperial lemons into Fourierist lemonade—of converting the negativity of black political abandonment into a position of fecund potentiality. Failed as it was, Stollmeyer and Etzler's movement demonstrated the possibility of movements for collective betterment that were autonomous from and not reliant on a state that could not be relied on. As Stollmeyer put it at the conclusion of *The Sugar Question Made Easy*, solicitation of state support is humiliating and hopeless: "Cease from dancing in the ante-chambers and the lobbies of Parliament, begging for delusive means of retaining or increasing your wealth."[116] Stollmeyer's Fourierist reduction of political relations to social relations allows him to recode the drama of state neglect and political abandonment as a needless melodrama. Here, the state is nothing more than a mechanism for the absorption of social energies that could be better invested and spent elsewhere—a lesson he learned from Brisbane and that the society's former Chartists learned from Etzler. Des Sources would disseminate this lesson to his mulatto and black audience, urging those Trinidadians who "throw themselves at the feet of the throne and cry for justice" to unbind from the British state and invest their energies in an autonomous project for collective flourishing.[117] By redescribing political relations as ontologically void, this creolized Fourierism effected an affective and cognitive reorientation for which the reality of imperial abandonment did not really mean anything at all: it does not matter if you are politically immaterial if the political does not matter. Thus, where "tears of sorrow" once expressed black Trinidadians' frustrated political relation to the empire, socialism unbinds these creoles of color from this cruel optimistic relation with raucous laughter. That is, at least, how Charles Day puts it. "The recent events in Europe," he writes, in reference to the continental 1848s, "have done much to unsettle the negroes; they laugh—they dance—they sing: 'De poor buckra! dey soon be obliged to gib up dere estate, den all de land come to the blacks.' This is what they *do* say now. The doctrines of Communism, Socialism, and all the worst of French delusions are spreading amongst them to a dangerous degree, and they will, ere long, be ripe for any movement."[118] For Day, that black Trinidadians express their encounter with "the worst of French delusions" as a bodily animation functions to disqualify black subjects further from the rationality of the political. But we might read this scene against its grain as disclosing the joy of coming into contact with a projected form of life that disburdens black subjects of the compulsion to assume a position vis-à-vis irreducibly antiblack formations of the political. Instead of the choreographed, sad dance in the antechambers of empire, they move joyfully in their zone of imperial abandonment because they have already abandoned frustrated fantasies of imperial care.

Yet even as utopian socialism enabled a dissolution of Numancians' cruel optimistic relationship to imperial politics, it introjected a profound, productive instability into Des Sources's description of their prospective Venezuelan home. As we have seen, Des Sources coded Venezuela as a multiracial republican paradise; it figured as a site where black Trinidadians could resume an active and meaningful public political presence. But viewed through utopian socialism's postpolitical—and even antipolitical—perspective, Venezuela functions less as a horizon of positive political belonging and more a space conducive to the elaboration of projects at a remove from and autonomous from the state. Venezuela emerges as a figure encrusted with the simultaneity of a desire for proximity to and for distance from the political. We might read this ambiguity as contradictory, even as incoherent; I would rather suggest that our paucity of terms for naming Des Sources's oscillating relation to the political points to a significant limit to our residual Westphalian imaginary. Indeed, Des Sources's project both parallels and prefigures a multiplicity of New World movements that demanded recognition from the state *and* complete autonomy from it: maroon communities throughout the circum-Caribbean to the Yucatecan Maya prosecuting their war through the nineteenth century against criollo elites, all the way up to the Zapatistas' transformation of Chiapas into an autonomous—but not sovereign or secessionist—region in Mexico following the coming into force of the North American Free Trade Agreement on 1 January 1994. Writing through (and against) the moment when nation-statist sovereignty was becoming the institutional norm of postimperial globality, Des Sources himself lacked an intelligible idiom for articulating the varied forms of nonsovereign autonomies once sheltered in the incoherent political fabrics of empires past. He found an unlikely resource for rendering his project intelligible in one of the primary cultural forms of midcentury liberalism: the sentimental novel.

Sentimental Socialism

The Trinidadian printed the first installment of *Adolphus* on 1 January 1853, shortly after Stollmeyer had assumed proprietorship of the paper. The serialization of *Adolphus* began in the wake of "Uncle Tom mania," a transatlantic enthusiasm for *Uncle Tom's Cabin* on which Stollmeyer, now printing *The Trinidadian*, hoped to capitalize. As the 1 January issue of *The Trinidadian* remarks, "Uncle Tom's Cabin has been translated into French, and produced enormous excitement." The same issue includes the "Preface to the German Translation" of the novel, no doubt translated by Stollmeyer.[119] Publishing *Adolphus* alongside these materials, *The Trinidadian* poses the narrative as yet another translation of *Uncle Tom's Cabin*, a translation of Stowe's antislavery narrative into Trinidad's postemancipation historical context. But *Adolphus* would also translate *Uncle Tom's Cabin* into the ideological context of Des Sources's colonization project, deploying the representational and narratological resources of Stowe's narrative to critique the British program of liberal globalization and to animate Des Sources's economic and political descriptions of Venezuela.

Reading Des Sources's translation of *Uncle Tom's Cabin* requires reframing the novel from a transnational perspective. I mean this in two ways. First, I intend "transnational" to name a form of collectivity that is subtracted from the sphere of official politics marked by the state. Within Stowe scholarship, this space of political subtraction is typically named the domestic; in rewriting the U.S. novel from Trinidad and by narrating the flight of a mulatto from Trinidadian homelessness to a Venezuelan home, Des Sources puts this space on the move, presenting the domestic less as a sociological site than as a mode of collective belonging resistant to subsumption within the state.

Second, I intend "transnational" to name a mode of imagining the circuits of capital that unevenly incorporated and affected zones of the Americas. In the hands of Des Sources, as well as that of many contemporary commentators, *Uncle Tom's Cabin* was less a story of the United States so much as it offered a figurative index of the global dynamics of economic liberalism. Here I seek to uncover the material structures and political grammars that made *Uncle Tom's Cabin's* critique of domestic slavery appropriable by creoles of color reckoning with the contradictions attending Britain's integration of global markets and corresponding disintegration of mercantilist empire. Read from this global perspective, the liberalism of *Uncle Tom's Cabin* is converted into an emancipatory autonomism: Des Sources mobilizes *Uncle Tom's Cabin* to figure the dissolution of his imperial home into the anomic space of the global market but retains *Uncle Tom's Cabin's* suspicion of the political state to refuse the subsumption of black political possibility into the antiblack order of the emergent nation-state system.

Des Sources was not alone in using *Uncle Tom's Cabin* to illuminate the heteronomous effects of British liberalization. For the U.S. political economist Henry Charles Carey, the fate of Uncle Tom renders legible the ironic systemic effects induced by the linked tariff schedules passed by the United States in 1845 and by Britain in 1846. Where U.S. Treasury Secretary Robert Walker intended to restructure the U.S. economy to capitalize on Britain's anticipated liberalization of its markets in grain, Carey's *The Slave Trade, Domestic and Foreign* (1853) insists that Britain's liberalization was little more than a refined form of mercantilism. Britain desires to be "mistress of the world," the "sole buyer of raw products" and the "sole seller of manufactured commodities," equipped with the power "to fix the prices of both" and to "impose taxes at discretion" on global producers and consumers. Or, as Carey summarizes it, "Modern British theory looks directly to the enslavement of man."[120] Mapping the looping effects of liberalism, Carey demonstrates that global liberalism perpetuates literal "enslavement" within the United States. Spurred by Britain's liberalized grain markets, U.S. farmers increased production intensively and extensively. The lowering cost of grain and the consequent decline of wages in Britain spurred industrial production in Manchester, which in turn spurred intensive and extensive increases of cotton production in the slave South. In Carey's hands, *Uncle Tom's Cabin* becomes not simply the story of one enslaved human being sold down the river; it more generally demonstrates Britain's economic sovereignty over the United States: "The less the power of association in the Northern slave States, the more rapid must be the growth of the domestic slave trade, the greater must be the decline in the price of wheat, cotton, and sugar, the greater must be the tendency to the passage of men like Uncle Tom, and of women and children too, from the light labour of the North to the severe labour of the South and South-west—but, the greater, as we are told, must be the prosperity of the people of England."[121] Here, the fictive travels of a slave metaphorizes the factual subordination of the United States through an international division of labor to British markets. Arguing that the United States should retake economic sovereignty through a program of neo-mercantilist, state-supported industrialization, Carey offers a counterfactual telling of *Uncle Tom's Cabin*: "Uncle Tom might have remained at home had the powers of the land been maintained and had Virginia been enabled to avail herself of her vast resources in coal, iron ore, water-power, &c.; but as she could not do this, he had to go to Arkansas."[122] Carey's "might have" is ambiguous: even had the United States retained economic sovereignty in the form of neo-mercantilist policies, "men like Uncle Tom" still "might have . . . had to go to Arkansas." These moments reveal a frustrated desire to displace political and ethical responsibility for domestic slavery to foreign machinations. Yet in spite of (or even perhaps because of) Carey's apologetic tendencies, his use of *Uncle Tom's Cabin* poses the novel as a tale of forced migration in the era of liberal globalization. Viewed from a world-system perspective, the policies of liberal globalization translate into a reanimated American slavery, rendering Carey's trope of "enslavement" both metaphorical and literal.

If Uncle Tom's forced migration south maps the deleterious effects of liberal globalization, *Adolphus* rewrites George and Eliza's flight north to represent a utopian escape from it—although, in *Adolphus*, its eponymous mulatto protagonist flees from slavery-era Trinidad to Bolívarian Venezuela. The world-system articulation between economic liberalization and a reanimated slavery (what Dale Tomich calls the period of "second slavery") enabled Des Sources to appropriate the cultural productions of U.S. antislavery as local instantiations of a broader culture of hemispheric antiliberalism. In a context in which the hemisphere's subordination to globalized markets translated as the reanimation of chattel slavery, Des Sources uses the narrative of George, Eliza, and Adolphus's flight from the latter as a way of making flight from the former intelligible. In this way, Des Sources codes his utopian colonization of Venezuela as a continuation of an emancipation project whose radical possibilities were foreclosed by a world-system reallocation and intensification of slavery in other zones in the Americas.

Adolphus begins by staging a dialectical tension between black attempts to secure sites of relative autonomy and an expansionary British Empire's tendency to dismantle these makeshift sites. The novel introduces the reader to Mr. and Mrs. Romelia, free and relatively well-to-do mulattoes. When *Adolphus* opens, the narrative's time is located about a decade after Britain had conquered Trinidad. Suffering under the racial order of British Grenada, the Romelias were "tempted . . . to seek an asylum in Trinidad" along with "numerous inhabitants of the neighbouring colonies."[123] In migrating to British Trinidad, the Romelias and their fellow migrants imagine that they are exiting the normal juridical order of the West Indies. As the narrator explains, the "great inducement" accounting for this mass immigration was "the provision which the benevolent and philanthropic [Spanish governor] Chacón had made, at the capitulation of the colony, for the proper treatment of the coloured people by the English government"—they imagine, in other words, that they are traveling to a zone of Spanish law, albeit one under British rule (7). The Romelias were unfortunately deceived in thinking that Chacón's agreement remained in force. The "fatherly provision of Chacón [had been] trampled under foot" by the British, "slavery with his sword of fire ruled more tyrannically [in Trinidad] than in any other part" of the Caribbean, and "coloured skin was held as inferior to a soul black with corruption and skin, if that soul was only cased within a white body" (7). The Romelias remain, however, and "make the best of a bad affair," constructing a domestic asylum from racism and slavery in an island whose economic and juridical order was constituted by both (7).

Adolphus's valorization of the domestic thus marks a compensatory alternative to the form of Spanish political and legal subjectivity that the Romelias had sought. Importantly, this domestic surrogate for an unavailable Spanish politico-juridical subjectivity is subtly but decisively accompanied by an invocation of a utopian socialist imaginary of affective abundance. It is certainly true that the pleasurable affects that the sentimental novel associates with the domestic transcode, underwrite, and indeed form the telos of the freedoms available to men within the public sphere.[124] For subjects who do not have and cannot want access to publicness, however, the status of the domestic shifts. For *Adolphus*, the domestic names a site removed from the antiblack public order of colonial Trinidad; the narrative's positive valorization of the domestic transforms this condition of violent subtraction into one of affective and aesthetic abundance. The Romelias thus find their asylum in a small cocoa plantation in a "lonely spot," one cut off from the public, but the compensatory virtue of this isolation is beauty: their "small estate shewed a most picturesque scene." The narrative stresses, though, that the picturesque quality of the scene owes to labor, not nature. In "conformity with a plan," before the home is a "large arbour covered with the luxuriant vines of the granadilla. . . . On another side laid a flower garden" (7). The gardener is Antonia, the Romelias' daughter: "Every shrub receives her attention, wherever she passes she leaves behind her the footsteps of order" (10). Antonia seems to be at once the reproducer of the kind of domesticity idealized in *Uncle Tom's Cabin* and an embodiment of the type of planter idealized in plantation husbandry manuals. We can also read the traces of Des Sources's Fourierism in this portrait of domestic horticulture. Indeed, gardening neatly metaphorizes two aspects of this strand of socialism. First, the emphasis on the "order" produced by the "plan" and the attentive labors of Antonia is implicitly opposed to the disorder of unattended, unregulated markets. Second, the labor of gardening is attractive to the laborer—one goal of Des Sources's Numancia—and yields a diversified, highly attractive scene. The forced removal of free black subjects from the public order of plantation Trinidad yields a form of life characterized by beauty, "comfort," and "love" (8).

This asylum cannot sustain itself: no matter how "lonely" the site, zones of black autonomy are precarious and vulnerable to the incursion of racist forces backed by the colonial legal regime. The Romelias exposure is dramatically revealed when Antonia is abducted by the "white mulatto," DeGuerinon. Wealthy and passing for white—he is the son of a Corsican father and a mother who is later revealed to have been a black slave—DeGuerinon delights in both tormenting and lusting after Trinidad's people of color. He sets to seducing the virtuous and beautiful Antonia, but her affections are pledged to Adolphus, leading a frustrated DeGuerinon to kidnap her on a road near her home. Declaring "you are mine" as he carries her away, DeGuerinon rhetorically casts his bodily possession of Antonia as an act of enslavement (33). Imprisoned at DeGuerinon's house, Antonia learns how thoroughly racial capitalism has absorbed the colonial state, rendering the colony effectively lawless. She innocently queries, "Is the majesty of the laws so much fallen as to deny protection to the helpless and innocent?" DeGuerinon responds, "Pooh! pooh! talk about laws, eh! . . . Laws, my dear child, were made for slaves, and aw—petty fellows. But we *whites* (!) [*sic*] do not bother our brains about them. In this country you see, my child, it is all money—money can make the stiff laws to bend—and make you love me too. . . . [W]e have but to imagine a thing, and to us it is law and everything else you choose" (38). The sovereignty of money produces social disorder: it perverts affective relations, softens law, and even whitens mulattoes. This disorder is reflected in the arrangement of DeGuerinon's house, which is lavishly decorated with Chinese porcelain, South Asian carpets, and Caribbean mahogany—an artificial, globally produced world so fantastic that Antonia initially "believed herself to be in a dream" (34). Antonia is far away from the harmonious world of her garden, and the remainder of the narrative works to repair Antonia's wounded autonomy.

This work of repair has to take place at a distance from the legal and disciplinary apparatus of the state, for, as DeGuerinon himself suggests, the state is unavailable as an instrument for blacks seeking to secure freedom. More intriguing, the novella also insinuates that the state is unavailable to blacks as a horizon of political desire. In a brief episode entitled "A Night in Port of Spain, or Common Occurrences," a drunk and marauding DeGuerinon sets the colonial state against Trinidadian blacks by inciting a bout of "Haitian fear." Noting that black Trinidadians were furious at the idea" that a mulatto in prison was to be whipped for being "impudent to one of his superiors," DeGuerinon recommends that they "concoct a placard—threatening fire and blood to all the whites if that prisoner be whipped. This placard we will affix to this house, it being the house of an Alcade, and mark well, if we only keep up the secret it will bring down the whole weight of Sir R[obert Woodford]'s power upon them" (27).

And so they do. The placard, however, does not simply appeal to generic white fears about black revolt; it explicitly inscribes this possibility in the shadow of the Haitian Revolution. "Let us have it à la Des Saline," DeGuerinon exclaims, and proceeds to dictate a message recalling the bellicose style of Toussaint's Tiger: " '*Fire and blood! whites, take notice! that if any free man is put in the tread mill, this house shall be burnt down, and every other house like this*' " (27; italics in the original). The placard had the desired effect. White Trinidad buzzed with worry; troops were called up; and the state offered a reward of 250 pounds for information on this Trinidadian Dessalines. The narrator simply remarks, "The dreams of the mighty whites were nothing else but scenes of San Domingo" (27). The point here is not simply that white elites manipulated anxious fantasies of black revolt to intensify colonial disciplinarity; it is also that the very idea that black Trinidadian intended to follow enslaved Haitians in seizing a doubled emancipation is *only* a white fantasy, one with minimal grounding in a black political imaginary.[125] (Indeed, the Trinidadian E. L. Joseph's picaresque *Warner Arundell* [1837] is perhaps the only literary work from the time that is comfortable with working through the revolutionary period; Joseph was white.) Des Sources is not so much disavowing Haiti as he mobilizes this privileged figure to displace the assumed centrality of state seizure to black politics.

The novella's skepticism about the efficacy of state solutions—a skepticism that Des Sources earned through his years of pressing for constitutional reform in Trinidad—illuminates the second facet of *Uncle Tom's Cabin* that *Adolphus* sets to work. Throughout the Anglo Atlantic, readers of Stowe's work understood it to make intelligible a form of collective politics whose aims neither originated in nor concluded with official state politics. For the British political economist Nassau Senior, Stowe's novel created a nonstate medium through which political relation was possible without the corroding influence of the politics of slavery. As Senior suggests in his review of the novel, the political event of *Uncle Tom's Cabin* was hardly exhausted by antislavery effects it might induce at the level of the state; indeed, Senior anticipated that slavery would persist in the United States for centuries to come. Rather, *Uncle Tom's Cabin* opened a space adjacent to the antiblack, pro-slavery U.S. state, a juxtapolitical scene of collective autonomy. Senior's *Uncle Tom's Cabin* does not so much pressure the sovereign state to do the right thing as it sovereignly inaugurates a new form of right. "As far as the Northern States are concerned," he writes, "*Uncle Tom* has repealed the Fugitive Slave Law."[126] Senior's lack of faith in state solutions was in part a product of his pessimistic sense that the U.S. public sphere no longer constituted an efficacious site of mediation between people and state—an assessment similar to that which Des Sources made of the function of the Trinidadian public sphere's relation to the colonial and imperial states. Other writers with ties to the West Indies—such as Stephen Bourne in *The Uncle Toms and St. Clares of Jamaica* (1853) and Wilkins in *The Slave Son*—would similarly use the novel to imagine forms of juxtapolitical collective emancipation. None of these texts are particularly radical. My point is that in the horizon of slavery, white liberalism unwittingly opens space for thinking a black anarchism—or, more properly, a black autonomism.[127]

Adolphus sets the juxtapolitical orientation of the sentimental antislavery novel to work to illuminate a variety of forms of collectivity autonomous from the state. As I have already argued, Antonia's domestic order was coded as an ersatz Fourierist phalanstery. Upon her "enslavement" by DeGuerinon, the novel suggests, her only hope for "emancipation" derives from the mobilization of still more forms of autonomous, nonstate collectivity. Adolphus is predictably the ultimate agent of Antonia's emancipation; he also figures these forms of autonomous collectivity. For one, his very name amounts to a quiet reference to John Adolphus Etzler; like his namesake, Adolphus will eventually flee to Venezuela. Moreover, Adolphus's biography gestures back to a privileged form of New World black autonomy. The son of a white slave owner and his enslaved "mistress," Adolphus was born just after his mother ran away from her owner/rapist and fell in with a community of maroons (16).[128] From his birth into this maroon community, Adolphus soon passes into another form of nonstate collectivity—the Catholic Church. With Adolphus's mother dying in childbirth, the leader of the maroons arranges for a Spanish priest, Padre Gonzalvez, to administer last rites; he also ultimately prevails on the priest to adopt and educate the infant Adolphus. Gonzalvez's adoption of Adolphus inscribes the mulatto hero within a hemispheric political and cultural circuit that British imperial expansion stressed but, as the novella suggests, did not break. The priest "was in the island previous to the Capitulation" of Spanish Trinidadian officials to the British expeditionary force. Gonzalvez is thus positioned as the bearer of an alternative principle of imperial racial governance that *The Trinidadian* had long associated with the Spanish empire. Knowing "the privileges which were allowed the coloured inhabitants," the narrator explains, the priest's "grief was therefore great when he saw the change which had taken place after the cession of the island to British Rule" (12). Even as the British Trinidadian state rendered people of color juridically homeless, Gonzalvez paternally takes the orphaned mulatto into his home.

While fabricated kin relations serve as a social supplement for subjects that the British colonial order treats as politically and juridically dead, this kinship is also functional for the inscription of abandoned subjects into alternative political orders. The doubleness of kinship is most evident in the events following Adolphus's rescue of Antonia from DeGuerinon. Adolphus shoots—but does not kill—the rapist in the process, leading his mulatto accomplice Ernest to insist that the pair flee Trinidad for Venezuela. Leaving Antonia behind to care for her parents, they make their way to the Main. Arriving, Adolphus marvels, "He had left a land where prejudice against colour had destroyed many of the social ties,—where the soil was daily watered with the tears of slaves,—and where none whatever of the descendants of Ham could claim the rights of a man and a citizen. Another picture was now before him—all was free, all men were equal. Joy reigned in every dwelling,—Liberty had given life to all" (71).

While *Adolphus* codes its hero's movement from political death to free life as a shock, it also suggests that Venezuela's multiracial republicanism is continuous with the imperial paternalism figured by Padre Gonzalvez. Ernest reminds Adolphus that, as luck would have it, Gonzalvez was "an intimate friend" of Simón Bolívar, and they hasten to Caracas to secure an audience (72). Des Sources was shot at when he delivered a petition to Governor Harris; republican Venezuela is so hospitable, however, that the penniless pair immediately gain access to the Liberator. Importantly, Bolívar receives not Adolphus as a stranger but, rather, as a lost child whom the Liberator recognizes and is pleased to adopt as his own.

The scene of recognition turns on a ring that Adolphus presents to Bolívar. As the text informs us, Bolívar had given this ring to Gonzalvez as a token of gratitude; Gonzalvez subsequently gave this token of affection to his adopted child. When he recognizes the token, Bolívar delightedly "seize[s] the young man's hand" and states, "You are thrice welcome to Venezuela; and since I may never have the pleasure of embracing my old friend and companion, let me at least embrace him whom he loves." He then "tenderly threw himself on the young man's neck" (73). The circulation of the ring coordinates a series of fictive filiations. Through Adolphus, Bolívar embraces a remnant of Spain's imperial past. When Bolívar declares Adolphus his "son" immediately thereafter, another substitution occurs: Bolívar stands in for the Spanish priest, serving as a foster father (73). Within this sentimental economy, the Spanish priest serves as a constitutive absence—the hole at the center of the ring—through which Bolívar and Adolphus mediate their relationship. Yet the priest himself is a surrogate for the last governor of Trinidad. The priest's paternal care for Adolphus substitutes for the lost care of Chacón, whose "fatherly provision" had secured rights for mulattoes of Trinidad (7). Bolívar similarly makes "fatherly provision" for Adolphus, offering him his protection, giving him a job as a secretary, and even playing the humble role of letter bearer. The affective circuitry renders Bolívar's postimperial state continuous with the very Spanish empire against which Bolívar then struggled. Space and time translate each other—the movement to independent Venezuela is like a move back in time to Spanish Trinidad—and settlement in Venezuela would enable figuratively orphaned mulattoes to forget that Britain ever intervened in Trinidadian history.[129]

These substitutions may appear to subsume the familial into the political, but *Adolphus* is interesting precisely for its insistence on the discontinuities between the juxtapolitical order of sentimental sociality and the political order of the republican state. Indeed, the narrative concludes by posing Adolphus's domestic and political life as entirely fractured, a fracturing first evident in the space that separates Adolphus from Antonia, who remained in Trinidad when Adolphus fled. This spatial separation opens up a conventional horizon of narrative expectation: the novella wants to conclude with the lovers' reunion. Months after his escape to Venezuelan freedom, Adolphus receives glad tidings in two letters delivered by Bolívar. The first is from Antonia, who reports that, like Adolphus, she is now an orphan and that she also has been adopted by Padre Gonzalvez. Claiming that Romelia assaulted him, DeGuerinon has used the corrupt Trinidadian legal system to send Antonia's father to prison, where he dies. In another letter, Gonzalvez reports that DeGuerinon himself has been imprisoned for debt; moreover, his African ancestry has been exposed. Adolphus is now faced with a choice: he can safely return to Trinidad and there wed Antonia, or the couple can permanently reside in Venezuela. Ernest urges Adolphus to remain: "I will never allow you to leave this abode of safety until we shall have heard further from Trinidad. For my part, if ever I again leave Venezuela, it will not be to return to Trinidad" (81). Ernest describes the advantages of Venezuelan life: "I am very well situated here, highly esteemed by my employers. I have all the comforts that life can desire, and to complete my happiness . . . I am in love!" Indeed, Ernest is to be wedded to the daughter of his employer, symbolically cementing his citizenship in his new home. Here, Venezuela—the economic opportunity it offers, the legal protection it extends—enables the reproduction of heteronormative domesticity.

Yet the text never presents the consolidation of this projected domesticity. The novel ends a few paragraphs after Ernest reports his news, leaving it open whether Adolphus returns to Antonia or Antonia comes to Adolphus. Antonia herself never appears in Venezuela; nor is the reader introduced to Ernest's fiancée. Indeed, while Venezuela is celebrated for providing the economic and legal protections that make possible black heterosexual couplings, women appear solely in mediated form: in the letter Antonia sends and in the declaration Ernest makes. The only ring exchanged is that which circulates among Bolívar, the priest, and Adolphus. While we do not know where Adolphus will settle, we know where Adolphus will be that night. When he delivers Antonia's letter, Bolívar commands the pining lover to "be at my residence this evening. I await you there"—strikingly paralleling the sentiments expressed in Antonia's letter, who awaits a time that their separation will be ended (78). The liberation that Bolívar offers is double: it frees Adolphus and Ernest to complete the typical romantic narrative arc even as it frees them from having to do so. By romancing the masculinist state itself, Des Sources transforms Venezuela into a paradise of bachelors. The possibility that Venezuela signifies remains closed to Antonia, who stays in Trinidad as the adopted daughter of Padre Gonzalvez.

How can one explain the narrative's failure to resolve its animating romance? One possible reading is that *Adolphus does* harmonize the romantic energies circulating through the text: it does so by substituting Adolphus's love for Antonia with a newfound love for the Venezuelan state (and its preeminent statesman). This reading would align neatly with the irreducible homosociality that underwrites republicanism, perhaps even especially multiracial republicanism. Indeed, by keeping Antonia and her foster father Padre Gonzalvez at a distance, the narrative may be striving to reproduce the historical and ideological gulf that it simultaneously sought to traverse. Perhaps the "paternal code of Spain" that the priest embodies and that Des Sources eulogized is in fact irreconcilable with the "community of fraternal interests" that holds together both the fictive republic and the Fraternal Colonization Society.[130] Thus, even as *Adolphus* attempts to render Spanish imperial and Venezuelan republican culture continuous, this gendered geography of political signifiers suggests that they cannot inhabit the same space simultaneously.

I would suggest, however, that the space *Adolphus* puts between the state Adolphus has and the romantic consummation he wants marks a refusal to subsume black sociality into the domain of the state—even a state that embraces black subjects as fraternal citizens. There is, of course, plenty of historical justification for Des Sources's suspicions of the Venezuelan state; indeed, he would soon find that Venezuela was not nearly so hospitable to black subjects as he had fancied. But Des Sources is not just skeptical of how black subjects fit into the state and interstate order. Rather, his refusal to subsume hetero, reproducible black sociality into the state marks an embrace of the radical world-building possibilities of New World blacks. Antonia is not simply excluded from the political. As we have seen, she transforms conditions of political abandonment into conditions of social(ist) flourishing. By keeping Antonia outside Venezuela in the juxtapolity of an abandoned Trinidad, *Adolphus* keeps black futurity open, asking readers to imagine a world to come whose contours resist representation in the political genre of the state or the literary genre of the sentimental novel.

Trinidad: Graveyard of Utopias

Even as the final chapters of *Adolphus* were being published, Numancians were fleeing the colony. Intended to encourage black Trinidadians to build a new world, *Adolphus* serves instead as a headstone for a utopia that has already died—and that, in many ways, was doomed. Des Sources had invested Venezuela with a utopian possibility that the country had no interest in sustaining. When Joseph Riddel, the British consul-general for Venezuela, informed the Foreign Office in 1853 of "Dessources' Scheme [for] the foundation of a Colony on Socialist Principles in the Venezuelan Province of Guayana," he also related that the Venezuelan government actively opposed the project:

> [A Resolution] was issued by the Government, not only declining to encourage Dessources' Project in answer to a Petition presented by [Des Sources] sometime since to the Carácas Immigration Board, but declaring the class of Immigrants he proposed to introduce into Venezuela prejudicial to the interest of the Republic, and consequently prohibiting their admission within its Territory, and moreover directing the Governor of Guayana, to whom the Resolution is addressed, forthwith to report certain particulars respecting the colonists who had already arrived, so as to enable the Government to take such steps in the matter as may hereafter be thought advisable.[131]

This is not exactly a hug from Bolívar. Yet Des Sources was not entirely deluded in imagining that he would receive the support of the state: he had obtained a land grant, as Riddel reported, although it was unclear to the diplomat from which state agency. In any case, it was decidedly not made by the federal government, and for a simple reason: the state simply did not want any (more) black people in its territories. This reasoning puzzles Riddel, who declares the government's anxieties to be misplaced: "This decision of the Government . . . is to be ascribed rather to a dread of the increase of the Coloured Population in Venezuela than to any well-founded apprehensions of the pernicious effects likely to result from the Utopian ideas of the Colonists or the subversive principles professed by their Leader."[132]

In a context in which Numancians were learning that they had no meaningful place in the encroaching Westphalian order, Riddel's attempt to distinguish blackness and utopianism hardly makes sense. But his assumption that nonutopian forms of blackness were possible—that black Trinidadians *did* have a place in the new imperial order of things—perhaps derives from the way in which erstwhile Numancians reinscribed themselves in that order. In a bitterly ironic turn, utopians disgruntled with Venezuelan reality were forced to call on the state they had fled for assistance. Writing to Kenneth Mathison, British vice-consul at Ciudad Bolívar, the colonist Charles Leonidas explained his situation:

> Sir, A great number of young men of Trinidad, subjects of Her Majesty . . . petition to you, being the British Consular and the protector of the nation at Venezuela. . . . Our present state is awful: we are unable to procure ourselves food—we are half starving; we cannot even supply ourselves food to return to our families in Port of Spain. We do hereby beg and pray, as British subjects, for an embarkation to our maternal home. Furthermore, we have left our native land, not to abandon our love for patriotism, but with the idea of making an avenue for our family, as our leader informed us; but, to the contrary, what we have met with is starvation, sickness and ill-treatment. We therefore beg and pray for protection.[133]

The supplication is difficult to read; it must have been excruciating to write. The rhetoric of loyalty, however, was effective. Mathison was authorized to provide money for food and return passage to Leonidas and his companions. The consular official closest to Numancia, Mathison traveled to the colony, where he discovered that Leonidas and fifteen others had already left. He extended his aid to all Numancians, and eight took up his offer; 133 remained with Des Sources. Hundreds of others had already left, most simply returning to their abandoned island "as British subjects."

Des Sources would ultimately return to Trinidad sometime in 1854, eerily repeating the itinerary established by Stollmeyer. Their paths, however, would significantly diverge—indeed, they had already begun diverging even as Stollmeyer published *Adolphus*. Embittered by his own experiences with Venezuelan colonization, Stollmeyer tempered his support for the project with a belief in its imminent collapse. The reason for the colony's impending doom was Venezuela itself, as he claims to have experienced: "Venezuela, with all its decrees and promises to Emigrants, has never fulfilled a single one. Empty promises and hypocrisy are the order of the day—corruption the malady under which all Venezuelan Government Officers suffer."[134] By September 1853, Numancians had begun to return to Trinidad, fleeing utopia. Stollmeyer seems to relish their disenchantment; it reflects his own. He offers the consolation that those returnees disappointed in not finding "an Eldorado of equality, fraternity, ease, and comfort" have gone through a valuable character-building exercise. In December 1853, Stollmeyer sold *The Trinidadian*'s press. He used his final editorial to deride a polity whose civic spirit was so low that it could not support three newspapers. It was enough to try the faith of even Conrad Stollmeyer, phalansterian. Utopia behind him, Stollmeyer would undertake a host of philanthropic and capitalist enterprises, ultimately becoming extremely wealthy. His son and heir, Charles Fourier, would perversely realize Conrad's scheme to build a Fourierist phalanstery in Venezuela by building a mansion, Stollmeyer's Castle, in Port of Spain. It is today one of the "Magnificent Seven" mansions in the city, and perhaps the sole way in which the Stollmeyer name continues to impinge on public consciousness.

Des Sources was less fortunate. A popular song memorializes his inhospitable reception in the home he wished to leave forever: "Creoles charrier bois / Creoles charrier bois / Creoles charrier bois / pour nous brûler Papa Dessources" (Creoles bring wood so we can burn Papa Dessources). He escaped immolation, but only of the most literal kind. His life's work was effectively burned to ash: his press was sold off; his Venezuelan fantasy was dashed; his reputation in Trinidad was ruined. He was at home nowhere. And so it was that at the time of his decease in 1880 he worked daily among the dead, employed as Port of Spain's Keeper of Lapeyrouse Cemetery. The occupation is somehow fitting—after all, Des Sources's utopia was cobbled together with parts he exhumed from the hemisphere's history. And on clear days, he could see Venezuela just across the Gulf of Paria, just beyond the headstones and mausoleums.

Chapter 5

"A PURELY 'MERCIAL TRANSACTION"

Before I left Jamaica for Navy Bay . . . war had been declared against Russia, and we were all anxiously expecting news of a descent upon the Crimea. Now, no sooner had I heard of war somewhere, than I longed to witness it; and when I was told that many of the regiments I had known so well in Jamaica had left England for the scene of action, the desire to join them became stronger than ever. I used to stand for hours in silent thought before an old map of the world, in a little corner of which some one had chalked a red cross, to enable me to distinguish where the Crimea was; and as I traced the route thither, all difficulties would vanish. But when I came to talk over my project with my friends, the best scheme I could devise seemed so wild and improbable, that I was fain to resign my hopes for a time, and so started for Navy Bay.

—MARY SEACOLE, *The Wonderful Adventures of Mrs Seacole in Many Lands*

Those who are failing and falling in the world excite but little interest; and so it is at present with Jamaica. From time to time we hear that properties which used to bring five thousand pounds a year, are not now worth five hundred pounds fee simple. . . . If we have young friends whom we wish to send forth into the world, we search the maps with them at our elbows; but we put our hands over the West Indies—over the first fruits of the courage and skill of Columbus—as a spot tabooed by Paradise. Nay, if we could, we would fain forget Jamaica altogether. . . . But there it is; a spot on the earth not to be lost sight of or forgotten altogether, let us wish it ever so much. It belongs to us, and must be in some sort thought of and managed, and, if possible, governed.

—ANTHONY TROLLOPE, *The West Indies and the Spanish Main*

Between the imaginative maps drawn by Anthony Trollope and Mary Seacole there is a world of difference—indeed, a difference in worlding. The British novelist charts the world according to a globe-scaling hermeneutic of value; monetary information determines what locales will "excite . . . interest" in metropolitan Britons. Contrarily, the attentions of the brown Jamaican nurse, sutler, and memoirist are distributed by the contingencies of military crisis and so by solicitations to care bounded by the imagined community of empire. Red crosses, not pound signs, striate the globe. In the high era of economic liberalism, when, as Trollope suggests, "it is necessary to take in the whole world, in order that the courses of British trade may be seen," Seacole opposes a cartography of care that cuts across, and is indifferent to, the cartography of capital.[1] Yet it would perhaps be more accurate to say that Trollope opposes the concerns of capital to Seacole's care. By the time that Trollope's travelogue appeared, Seacole's memoir had been published to wide acclaim in Britain and translated into multiple languages. Seacole had become a celebrity.[2] Not only was Trollope aware of Seacole's public persona; he had even stayed in the lodging house of Seacole's sister in Jamaica. His scene before the map reads like a polemical act of writing back, one that attempts to reabsorb Seacole's cartography of care into a liberal-capitalist cartography of value.

The necessity of this writing back is explained by the very scene Trollope sets. Economic liberalism, as many scholars have pointed out, does not simply happen; it requires ongoing processes of world making and subject formation, processes that are prone to misfire or fail.[3] Thus, while Trollope posits that an awareness of a global differential distribution of value (what he calls "interest") *should* norm the attentions of his young friend, he worries that it may not.[4] A rational actor should refrain from seeking a career in a "falling and failing" Jamaica; Trollope knows that something less than rational may propel his friends to the island. Simply by virtue of its persisting as an imperial possession, Jamaica solicits attention, despite not being worthy of attention. "There it is," Trollope laments, impossible to forget, and this "imperial facticity" creeps into the fictive scene where Trollope and his friend consult their map.[5] Residual imperial attachments threaten to interrupt economic normativity: the market may not script attention as neatly as one would hope, and against all reason Trollope's friend may take a post on an island that is better left alone. And so it is that the invisibilizing hand of Trollope supplements the invisible hand of Adam Smith, artificially preserving the distribution of attention and investment that the market normalizes but cannot fully realize. The liberal dominant does not sustain itself automatically; rather, it requires the incessant suppression of residuals "defective for capitalism" to acquire the appearance of ineluctability, of naturalness.[6] *The West Indies and the Spanish Main* works to defuse the possibility that residual British imperial attachments might overwhelm rational economic interests, to manage the possibility that old or emergent imperial cartographies might striate the emergent "spaces-of-flows" of a liberalized global capitalism.[7] Trollope's text facilitates the "primitive construction of capitalist subjectivities," but this construction is set to work in a world where competing organizations of sociality, polity, and economy threaten to interrupt normative liberal-capitalist modes of relating to value.[8] When Trollope hides Jamaica with his hand, he is not simply covering over a bad field of investment; he is obscuring alternative forms of politico-economic relation that troublingly persist into, and were even forged within, the liberal present.

Seacole's memoir vibrantly described one such alternative politico-economic form of social organization. It is only recently that scholars haven taken note of the importance of economic concerns to Seacole's text; the first generation of Seacole scholarship focused on Seacole's practices of self-representation in the imperial public sphere to determine the extent to which she accommodated or resisted empire and to explore the strategies by which she, in Simon Gikandi's phrase, "claim[ed] her Englishness."[9] As I argue, Seacole's attempt to secure imperial belonging by representing herself as a model Victorian woman is less important than her attempts to refashion liberal conceptualizations of empire through representations of her socioeconomic practices. Teeming with descriptions of selling goods and proffering services in scenes of political and social crisis, Seacole's memoir reads like an autoethnographic account of the workings of a peripheral socioeconomic formation.[10] There is one underlying feature of the formations Seacole describes that enables her to reconceptualize empire: they do not operate according to the institutional logics of market exchange. Indeed, the market does not integrate the varied collectivities that Seacole's varied enterprises helped to reproduce. This claim may surprise readers of Seacole's memoir; after all, when she is not busy nursing, she is busy selling. Or so it would appear. Yet to subsume much of the transactional activity that Seacole undertakes under the category of market exchange—as most scholars have—says more about the epistemic limits of our still too liberal understanding of economic phenomena than anything substantive about Seacole's social practice or self-understanding.[11] Seacole's text demonstrates the vibrant life of non-market-based modes of material transaction and commercial sociality in the era of liberal globalization and equally demonstrates the centrality of such nonliberal economic forms to the maintenance of the British Empire, British bodies, and the very fantasy of economic liberalism.

That scholars today have a difficult time noticing Seacole's heterogeneity to the practical categories of liberal economic thought is unsurprising; even her contemporaries had a difficult time determining what she was about. The epistemic limits imposed by a liberal-capitalist culture become most clearly visible when we consider the wildly opposed ways in which the British public understood Seacole's activities. These divergent interpretations owed to difficulties readers encountered in relating the diversity of employments that Jamaican women undertook. How did Seacole's care work as a nurse relate to her commercial activities as a hotelier, her nursing to her selling? In general terms, readers responded to the imbrication of care logics and commercial logics in Seacole's text by stressing one over the other. Thus, many reviewers took Seacole as a figure for an aneconomic, deeply feminine imperial patriotism.[12] Others opted to deflate this figuration of Seacole in favor of posing a crass acquisitiveness as the underlying basis for her travels through many lands.[13] Seacole is either a ministering angel shining the pure white light of a Florence Nightingale or a crassly commercial Manchester Man cut from the cloth of a Richard Cobden. While these readings are superficially opposed, each pole implicitly posits the irreducible, binaristic separation of logics of a gratuitous, charitable care from logics of commercial acquisition. Whichever side of the binary one adopts, to think within it is to naturalize the price-setting market as an autonomous epistemic-institutional domain *and* to dematerialize care entirely so as to retrieve it from the taint of economizing.

Not all readers, however, submitted so unthinkingly to the epistemic dictates of liberal capitalism. W. H. Russell, the celebrated *Times* journalist who provided the introduction to Seacole's text, would voice a different understanding of the relationship between the caring and the commercial on the very first page of Seacole's memoir. Seacole, he writes, "is the first who has redeemed the name of 'sutler' from the suspicion of worthlessness, mercenary baseness, and plunder."[14] Traditionally, sutlers were seen as small-scale war profiteers; in many ways, the figure of the "mercenary" sutler is a caricature of *Homo economicus*. The space of sutlering is outside and in between states, in zones of militarized crisis unplugged from normal flows of commerce. The sutler steps in to fill the void left by the state and the market and profits on that void: indifferent to the unmaking of lives and polities around him, the self-interested sutler offers petty goods at inflationary prices and so extracts hyper-profits from a deprived soldiery. What Russell presents as sutlering with a heart, I will argue, marks a paleonymic attempt to give a figure to a form of material transacting that is at once motivated and auto-limited by nonmarket determinants. Seacole's sutlering is not "mercenary" to the precise degree that its institutional logic is not that of the market; rather, the non-market-based institutional logics of redistribution, reciprocity, householding, and (in extreme cases) gift giving propel and sustain her enterprise.[15] Within Seacole's text, social relations such as friendship, maternity, and citizenship structured, regulated, and expressed the nonmarket institutional logics through which her sutlering integrated an ephemeral but vibrant collectivity in Panama and the Crimea. From the perspective of this institutional arrangement, the market-based distinction between exchanging and giving, caring and transacting, does not hold. Seacole's enterprise aims "not to make a profit." She intends, rather, to "create debts"—debts susceptible to greater or smaller degrees of calculability and quantification; debts that organize care work and peddling in a common frame.[16]

My primary concern in this chapter is to explore how Seacole mobilizes this alternative mode of socioeconomic transacting to interrupt the worlding of liberal capitalism and to reconstitute the political borders of the British Empire. Her attempt to forge a life beyond liberalism was hardly a purely theoretical affair; like tens of thousands of Jamaicans, she left the island to eke out a living in the Panama transit zone after Jamaica's economy collapsed in the late 1840s.[17] Nonmarket, illiberal modalities of securing a livelihood are more the rule than the exception for those expelled from capitalism's accumulation process, and Seacole is exemplarily normal in this regard.[18] But economic precarity was not the most frightening aspect of liberal globalization. Rather, the imperial political illegibility of West Indians that liberalization both indexed and intensified, combined with Britain's ongoing policy of avoiding confrontation with the United States so as not to interrupt trade, combined once again with the parceled and partial sovereignty of postcolonial Panama, exposed isthmus-dwelling creoles to the barely limited violence and exploitation of Yankee racial capitalism. It was in Panama that a large mass of West Indians, more or less expelled from the imperial homes, first concretely experienced what U.S. hegemony over the Americas might look like. As both Seacole and Trollope well knew, it was Britain's liberal mode of imperial governmentality that facilitated the United States' ascendance to the position of hemispheric hegemon. As I argue in the first part of this chapter, Trollope's efforts to naturalize the epistemology of liberal capitalism functioned dually as efforts to naturalize Yankee imperialism. He had no doubt that if Jamaica was erased from the map of Britain's interests, it would reappear on that of the United States. By fashioning an anti-liberal political economy for the

British Empire in the interimperial space of Panama, Seacole attempts to build an epistemic and institutional order in which creoles would appear as subjects requiring and deserving imperial protection from the United States, whatever the market value of the islands to Britain. Through her wonderful adventures, Seacole materializes an empire founded not on value but on obligations, of gifts and countergifts, of debts and deferred payments. Lacking the quantifiability of capitalist value, these incalculable accounts cannot be balanced, even if Seacole does keep accounts: "I have a book filled with hundreds of the names of those who came to me for medicines and other aids."[19] Eschewing the punctual exchange of equivalents, Seacole articulates imperial citizenship as a practice of mutual, incalculable, and unending reciprocation.[20]

Making this argument requires recalibrating the ways in which we literary scholars generally relate to economic phenomena in the texts we read. Those of us who work on and within the cultures of capitalist modernity have very few conceptual resources for thinking through non-market-based modes of economic provisioning, much less market-based but noncapitalist economic structures. We tend to approach any form of exchange as *capitalist* exchange, to see any transaction as an instantiation of (capitalist) market logics. From this perspective, scholars have critiqued Seacole's enterprise for her "commercialism," her "economic opportunism," and her entrepreneurialism.[21] Yet, as I have suggested, the market does not organize Seacole's enterprise, and so the conceptual and critical purchase of such terms is rather slight. The second half of this chapter seeks to recover the institutional-logical specificity of Seacole's sutlering by shaking up the epistemic primacy of the market; it does so by supplementing close readings of Seacole's text with the insights of substantivist economic anthropology. Indeed, the hermeneutic orientation of literary studies aligns neatly with substantivists' mode of unpacking immanent logics of socioeconomic organization across space and time: they read instances of what might look like "economic" behavior as motivated and constrained by tangled webs of normativity, materiality, and sociality.[22] From this perspective, the economic is not an autonomous domain of thought or practice; it does not possess its own rationality and is not susceptible to abstract formalization. Rather, the economic is conceived of "as *a component of culture* rather than *a kind of human action*, the material life process of society rather than a need-satisfying process of individual behavior."[23] Seacole's sutlering, I will argue, makes sense as a component of a peripheral imperial culture, a culture that was at once residual and emergent, reconstituted and improvised.

The Ends of Hospitality; or, Capitalism from the Black Below

Anthony Trollope traveled to the West Indies in the autumn of 1858 to regularize the postal system in the region. The problem with administering the mail service in the West Indies, he recalls, is that "our West Indian islands have never been regarded as being of themselves happily situated for residence"; no aspiring bureaucrat with means or talents would consent to a post there.[24] While Trollope's book on his time in the region does not go into any great detail about the process of regularizing the mails in the circum-Caribbean, he does doggedly query the transformations that rendered the West Indies so inhospitable, so undesirable for career men and second sons.[25] Ostensibly a travelogue, *The West Indies and the Spanish Main* reads more like an archaeology of a quickly vanishing present, one in which prior regimes of creole sociality dissolve through contact with liberalized economic systems. Hospitality is the key social practice whose disappearance augurs the entrenchment of a new order of the world. Trollope locates a waning "spirit of hospitality" within the vanishing time-space of a racialized imperial formation, embodied throughout his text by the white planter (31). The declining but hospitable planter bursts into Trollope's text as an archaic residue of a noncommercialized past. Trollope's mobilization of this figure simultaneously enables a mournful nostalgia for the social displacements occasioned by liberal globalization even as it casts this process as irresistible. Like the white plantocracy, hospitality is that which, for better or worse, will disappear as rational commercial logics reconstruct and dismantle the reciprocative and redistributive structures of mercantilist empire. Trollope thus establishes a binary between a waning white-racial hospitality and a globalizing economic rationality, and this binary inaugurates the hermeneutic grid through which all aspects of economic life become legible in the text. Economic actors in the text are either aneconomic, anticommercial subjects who give hospitality without calculation, or economistic, calculative profiteers. Yet given the nostalgic temporalization of this binary, the way in which the bearers of aneconomic hospitality are slated to disappear, the economic can be encountered only in one way: all economic life becomes legible as tendentially participating in a debased, but necessary, economistic rationality. The antiliberal force of Seacole's sutlering diminishes as we realize, after the fact, that she was just another rational economic agent. She was a hotelier, not a plantation host.

Trollope links the dissolution of hospitality to the reconstructed political economy of the British Empire. He understands the liberalization of the

West Indian economy as an economic and moral necessity and never strays far from liberal common sense: "I beg it may not be thought that I am an advocate for such protection" (90). Yet if free trade was necessary, it was nonetheless ugly in both its means and effects: "The West Indians were, I think, thrown over in a scurvy manner, because they were thrown over by their professed friends" (90). Tracing the plantation's classical "ontogeny of debt," Trollope prognosticates, "As regards him himself, the old-fashioned Jamaica planter, the pure-blooded white owner of the soil, I think his day in Jamaica is done. The glory, I fear, has departed from his house" (91).[26] While Trollope laments this passing, he naturalizes it through analogy to weavers thrown out of work by industrialization: "The hand-loom weavers have been swept into infinite space"—and so must it be with white Jamaican planters.

Yet even if the material bases that made hospitality possible have eroded, hospitality survives as a social practice. The planters whom Trollope encounters maintain the welcoming practices of their wealthier forebears:

> And they are very hospitable—and hospitable, too, under adverse circumstances. In olden times, when nobody anywhere was so rich as a Jamaica planter, it was not surprising that he should be always glad to see his own friends and his friends' friends, and their friends. . . . An open house was his usual rule of life. But matters are much altered with him now. . . . But, nevertheless, the hospitality is maintained, perhaps not on the olden scale, yet on a scale that by no means requires to be enlarged. (28–29)

As Trollope implies, the West Indian plantocracy had long been celebrated (and had celebrated themselves) for their hospitality. Trevor Bernard goes as far as to describe the emergence of an "all-embracing cult of hospitality."[27] In the era of slavery, this normative sociability helped consolidate a white colonial order that linked up estates isolated by country miles and bad roads, even as it diffused tensions resulting from intra-white socioeconomic differences.[28] The "altered" situation of postemancipation and postliberalization planters, however, seems to purify the ethical dimensions of the practice. Planters greet the era of free trade and free labor, and the insuperable impoverishment and provincialization that were its consequences, by maintaining the aneconomic, archaic practices of Jamaica past.

These archaic, vanishing enclaves of rural hospitality are opposed to Jamaican urban spaces. While Trollope "never met a wider and kinder hospitality" than he did in rural Jamaica, he "neither ate nor drank in any house in Kingston except [his] hotel"; nor did he "enter any house except in the way of business" (17). Hospitality is reconstituted by concerns of "business"; the "hotel" replaces the welcoming "house." Yet due to the undercapitalized political economy of postliberalization Jamaica, such sites of commoditized hospitality are hard to find. The Jamaican city is, in effect, a space of capitalism without capital, a place without hospitality *and* without hotels. Trollope, confronted with empty time in Spanish Town (a place "like the city of the dead," where "no human inhabitant is to be seen"), registers this concatenation of lack as bodily disorientation: "What should I do? Where should I go? Looking all around me, I did not see as much life as would serve to open a door if I asked for shelter. I stood upon those desolate steps till the perspiration ran down my face with the labor of standing. Where was I to go? What was I to do? 'Inhospitalem Caucasum!' I exclaimed, as I slowly made my way down into the square" (20).

In part, Trollope converts his unfamiliarity with the social life of the city into evidence of its absence. At the same time, the sparse population of the city mirrors the thin peopling of the countryside—with the important qualification that, in an urban commercial center set in a world of declining commerce, Trollope cannot count on a hospitable reception even if he were to find someone, anyone. The cultural axiomatics of liberal capitalism entail the rise of the hotel at the expense of hospitality, but the decapitalization of Jamaica means that there are few hotels to be found. Musing on this dynamic a few pages later, Trollope writes:

> Hotels, as an institution, are, on the whole, a comfortable arrangement. One prefers, perhaps, ordering one's dinner to asking for it; and many men delight in the wide capability of finding fault which an inn affords. But they are very hostile to the spirit of hospitality. The time will soon come when the backwoodsman will have his tariff for public accommodation, and an Arab will charge you a fixed price for his pipe and cup of coffee in the desert. But that era has not yet been reached in Jamaica. (31)

The hotel is "comfortable" precisely because it reverses relations of power between host and guest. The guest at the hotel is not a debtor but a consumer: instead of "asking," the guest "order[s]" and reserves the right to complain. Yet the commoditization of hospitality becomes a problem in those spaces where a hospitable reception would (or should) have an incalculable value: in the "desert" of the "Arab," the forests of the "backwoodsman," or the hot empty streets of Spanish Town. The spirit of capital globalizes faster than capital itself: even in these inhospitable zones, seemingly delinked from the circulation of capital and regulation by price-setting markets, one can still "charge . . . a fixed price" for subsistence goods. This projected globalization of calculative logics, opposed to the "spirit of hospitality," constructs a binary grid through which all sociality becomes legible, even if anticipatorily. One either gives unconditionally (as white planters do and as "an Arab . . . in the desert" should) or one calculates and charges (as, implicitly, everyone will do). The full commercialization of Jamaica has "not yet" occurred—but it soon will.

The emergent of liberal globality is proleptically coded as dominant so that alternative emergents cannot appear. Through the repeated application of his reductive hermeneutic grid (the "spirit of hospitality" versus the spirit of capitalism), Trollope precomprehends the economic life of urban Jamaicans of color as insistently capitalist. For Trollope, the emergence of liberal capitalism from the black below is no more apparent than in the class of mulatto female hoteliers, already stock figures around the West Indies.[29] These women are delinked from the affective bonds of home and kin: "They are always kept by fat, middle-aged coloured ladies, who have no husbands" (195). Trollope's de-kinning of these women works to differentiate operating a hotel from offering hospitality; it is not familiality, or familiarity, that grounds the institutional logic of the hotel but commercial exchange. Hoteliers' derivation of life from deracinated and deracinating commerce mirrors what Trollope takes to be the ontological condition of New World blacks: homelessness. "But how strange is the race of Creole negroes . . . !," he writes. "They have no country of their own, yet they have not hitherto any country of their adoption. . . . They have no idea of country, and no pride of race" (55). Deterritorialized and rootless, cosmopolitan by subtraction, black West Indians lack a home in which to welcome guests.

The upshot of black subjects' affective, social, and even ontological homelessness is that the empire, too, is no home for them. Trollope makes this clear in his account of his sojourn in the hotel of a "sister of good Mrs. Seacole" (23). Seacole's sister's failed dwelling in the empire registers through her failed performance of Britishness. The "patriotic lady," Trollope jokes, could not be "induced to abandon the idea that beefsteaks and onions, and bread and cheese and beer composed the only diet proper for an Englishman" (23). Here, as we will see, Trollope not so subtly writes back to Mary Seacole, who, by provisioning soldiers with "beefsteaks and onions," came to signify Britishness on the field of battle. In Jamaica, however, Seacole's sister's inability to stretch the script of Britishness in her discharge of hospitality distinguishes her as foreign, as non-British. But it also renders her non-Jamaican. Seacole's investment in serving British cuisine comes at the cost of a devaluation of Jamaican food: "It is to be remarked all through the island that the people are fond of English dishes, and that they despise, or affect to despise, their own productions" (24). Trollope's black West Indian subjects are constituted in a chiastic negativity. They desire to be but cannot be British; they desire not to be but ineluctably are Jamaican. Dwelling nowhere, subjects of no land—or, to nod to Mary Seacole, subjects of too "many lands"—black Jamaicans can only simulate hospitality and that in order to sell it.

Hoteliers' commercialization of hospitality raises the possibility that they may offer other intimate services that are equally corrosive to domesticity. Trollope recycles a time-worn understanding that takes the West Indian hotel to be a covert brothel: husbandless mulatto hoteliers "have a knowledge of the world, especially of the male hotel-frequenting world, hardly compatible with a retiring maiden state of life" (195–96). Black subjects' alienation from any home, and their corresponding commercial alienation of homeliness, intensifies into a voluntary alienation of black women from their bodies. Trollope best articulates this link among black homelessness, bodily intimacy, and petty capitalist rationality in an anecdote he records regarding the romantic troubles of a black Jamaican Baptist woman named Josephine. She has just broken with her Jewish lover, Captain Isaacs, whom she had anticipated would propose marriage to her. As Trollope plays it, Josephine is intensely commerce-minded. He explains that she teaches children at a Baptist school, and she asks Trollope for a donation; when Trollope declines, she remarks that her non-Christian *amour* had given her a dollar. "But perhaps you gave him a kiss," Trollope declares (38). For an anti-Semitic Trollope, this bodily intimacy bespeaks a dispositional identity: the black Jamaican and the Jamaican Jew belong together, because each encounters the social as a field for potential transactional gain. Exchange itself emerges as the idiom of their romance. And if money fuels interracial intimacy, it also enables sociability without affect. Trollope meets Josephine in Port Antonio while Josephine waits to secure passage back to Kingston. Unfortunately for the jilted lover, Captain Isaac's coasting vessel is the only ship available for her return. Given their past, Josephine anticipates that " 'twill be so odd like" to ride with him (39). Trollope suggests that it might be a good time to make amends, to which Josephine responds, "Bah! . . . I'll pay him my pound for my passage; and den it'll be a purely 'mercial transaction" (39). Here, calculable exchange colonizes the romantic, disburdening participants from the weight of affective bonds and the aneconomic work of affective upkeep.

Emerging from the social death of slavery always already oriented toward liberal-capitalist animacy, Trollope's black and mulatto entrepreneurs stage market subjectivity as humanity's anthropological default: to be (or become) human is to be for and in the market.[30] Blackness is lived as a catallactics (as Richard Whately had recently redefined the field of political economy).[31] Trollope's discussion of the disappearance of the plantocracy's hospitality protests this fact even as it attests to its effectiveness. Whatever one feels about it, all social life will be soon comported as "a purely 'mercial transaction." The task, for Trollope, is to work out a capitalist-realist subjectivity that can be charmed by the trace of the precapitalist in the present but one that will not overly attach to them, for such traces will soon be effaced anyhow.[32] The subsumption of aneconomic socialities into the market marks the generalization of a formalist exchange as the basis of human relations. Two linked effects stem from the abstract narrative of capitalism that organizes Trollope's text. First, this narrative disburdens Trollope from paying careful attention to the transactional modalities of black Jamaican life. Exchange is exchange, and they are exchanging. Second, black Jamaicans' putative embrace of liberal-capitalist logics, coupled with the decline of the island's white plantocracy, liberates Britain itself to norm its policies according to the market logics that black subjects so enthusiastically endorse. The work of *The West Indies and the Spanish Main* is to make it acceptable to Britons to treat the West Indies as little more than a question of economic interest—even if, or especially if, doing so means ceding the islands to the United States.

Affective Management at the Ends of Empire

Trollope's mournful staging of the decline of white hospitality in Jamaica poses the subsumption of the imperial periphery into the postpolitical value form of liberal capitalism as an ongoing but inexorable process. Trollope believed that a liberalized Britain should dissolve ties with the West Indies—if not immediately, then soon. Yet, and like Adam Smith nearly a century earlier, Trollope knew that residual imperial attachments might inhibit the political and economic dictates of imperial liberal governmentality. In Trollope's telling, Britain's relation to Jamaica is indeed pathological: "Though the utter sinking of Jamaica under the sea might not be regarded as a misfortune, it is not to be thought of that it should belong to others than Britain. How should we look at the English politician who would propose to sell it to the United States; or beg Spain to take it as an appendage to Cuba?" (99). Britain cannot simply abandon the West Indies, for the islands might become the property of some other empire. In a scene of triangulated desire, interimperial reputation and imperial patriotism infuse the islands with a value everyone knows they do not possess; the possible desire of others reenergizes Britain's cathexis. The aim of the second half of *The West Indies and the Spanish Main* is to decathect Britain's relation to its imperial periphery so that Britain might truly be ruled by its interests.

Central America serves as an imaginative geographic fix for this problem, a place where the requirements of capital and empire might be worked through without working up his audience. Central America is a space more or less unburdened by prior British imperial cathexes. Trollope's discussion of the region enables him to anticipate the all but ineluctable consequences of hemispheric liberalization without triggering residual metropolitan attachments to New World empire. In so doing, he stages a *translatio imperii* of hemispheric rule from Britain to the United States, which itself enables a symbolic transfer of the British West Indies to the U.S. hegemon. Thus, where Trollope elides Jamaica from the world of British imperial interest in the book's first act, Jamaica reappears in the cartography of U.S. imperial ambition in the second. "I saw the other day a map," Trollope records while en route to Panama. "'The United States as they now are, and in prospective'; and it included all these places—Mexico, Central America, Cuba, St. Domingo, and even poor Jamaica" (225). In part, the work of Trollope's book is to convert this "prospective" into a present-tense perspective, such that Jamaica would be ruled as if it is already lost to the United States. Yet Trollope's aim is not simply to consolidate the epistemic outlines of this world picture, which by 1860 was more or less official common sense. Rather, his text is an exercise in affective management: he seeks to deprive New World territorial empire of its affective charge so that the known interests of Britain might dictate policy in the region unimpeded by residual attachments, patriotic fantasies, or a masculinist militarism.

The cultural logic of Trollope's text more or less tracks British policy toward the hemisphere. While Britain's midcentury policy in the Americas was at times ad hoc, incoherent, and even contradictory, it came to be regulated by the principle of avoiding antagonism with the United States in the name of facilitating flows of capital, commodities, and people. In broad terms, Britain opted for joint stewardship with the United States over the region to maintain free channels of circulation across Central America. This policy was enshrined in the Clayton-Bulwer Treaty, in which Britain and the

United States pledged to forgo "exclusive control" of passages across Central America, to maintain the neutrality of transit zones, to hold joint stewardship of these transit zones, and to refrain from colonizing or claiming suzerainty over Central American territory. In the end, neutrality and nonintervention were but a prologue to British territorial cession. When the United States first grumbled over Britain's retention of its long-standing Mosquito Coast protectorate after the signing of the treaty, and then Britain's formation of the Bay Islands Colony in the early 1850s, Britain would capitulate to U.S. desires, ceding the Mosquito Coast to Nicaragua and Honduras and the Bay Islands to Honduras.[33] While this cession was resisted by some Bay Islanders and the Mosquito, many metropolitan Britons—those who knew of the colony's and protectorate's existence, that is—had agitated for it.[34] "People here," wrote Lord Clarendon to Palmerston, "don't care two straws about Central America or Mosquitia or the Bay Islands or Honduras boundary—all they wish for is freedom of interoceanic [communication]."[35]

The figure of the hotel organizes Trollope's felt relation to the spatio-temporal dynamics of liberal capitalism in Central America; it allows Trollope to mourn the passing of the archaic while ironically commenting on the instabilities of the emergent. For Trollope, Central America is a land of hotels, of rootless residing, a pure space-of-flows. The problem, however, is that "Spaniards" do not do hotels very well. Ruminating on the possibility of finding a decent hotel in San José, he writes, "The Spaniards are themselves in their own country not at all famous for their inns. No European nation has advanced so slowly towards civilization in this respect as Spain has done" (258). Note here that even as we have seen Trollope decry the hotel's destruction of "the spirit of hospitality," hotels still index "advance[s]" in "civilization." Central America simultaneously lacks access to the deactivated codes of premodernity *and* facility in the emergent rationalities of liberal capitalism. Indeed, the hotel in which Trollope stays is run not by a Costa Rican but by a German expatriate, a hotel "German in everything" (258). Bizarrely, the condition of possibility for hospitable reception in Central America is that local Central Americans not offer or sell it—that, in effect, Costa Ricans and Panamanians have already been denied the position of host. Central America appears as a totally deterritorialized space in which Europeans from one polity welcome Europeans of another.

The ascension of Euro-American migrants to the position of host functions as a quotidian sign of the precariousness of sovereignty for postcolonial Central American states. Constituted as a space-of-flows by and for Euro-

American capital, commodities, and travelers, Central American states are not at home with themselves. Their territory is thus susceptible to seizure by any taker, guest becoming host. It is for this reason that, within Trollope's figural economy, the hotelier metonymically touches on a far less genial and far more exciting character: the U.S. filibuster. Like that of the hotelier, the figure of the filibuster provides Trollope with a means of exploring the ambivalent dialectic opened by liberalization. The filibuster initially appears in Trollope's text as an anachronistic romance figure. As the etymology of the term would suggest, the freebooting filibuster was slotted into the imaginative space opened by the myriad pirates who populated sensational dime novels and adventure stories. The difference, of course, was that filibustering was a phenomenon of the contemporary moment, an actually existing example of life lived, at least for a time, beyond law's reach.[36] Indeed, Trollope's lengthy discussions of filibustering intend, in part, to suture the romantic affects that the figure engenders to his rather staid discussions of travel routes, trade, and small towns. Yet the contamination of the contemporary with apparent vestiges of the past poses a problem for Trollope, as these lawless figures, corrosive as they are to the authority of the states they invade, threaten the security of liberal capitalism: "The weak governments of the country have been able to afford no protection to [merchants], and placed as they were, beyond the protection of England or the United States, they have been completely open to attack. The filibusters for a while destroyed the transit through Nicaragua" (343). Here, the very fact of filibustering marks off the fiction of Central American states' sovereignty; only England and the United States are capable of maintaining the sovereignty of these "weak governments," which more or less positions them as meta sovereigns. Yet even as filibustering interrupts trade and shows Central American claims of sovereignty to be ineffective pretensions, Trollope absorbs the unevenness of the contemporary by posing it as a moment in the projected extension of U.S. hegemony throughout the region. "We reprobate the name of filibuster," Trollope remarks but declares such reprobation somewhat unjust: "Have we [Britons] not annexed, and maintained, and encroached; protected, and annexed, and taken possession in the East—doing it all of course for the good of humanity?" (132). Britons "begrudge" U.S. extension into California and Texas, and "Englishmen, as a rule, would wish to maintain Cuba in the possession of Spain" (132). And yet, "What Englishman who thinks about it will doubt that California and Texas have thriven" since conquest "or can doubt that Cuba . . . would gain infinitely by such change of masters?" (132).

"Humanity," he insists, "would be benefited by such a transfer" (136). For Trollope, the interruptive incursion of preliberal logics of militaristic territorialism will ultimately resolve into a secure, profitable peace.

As his relativizing apologetics for filibustering make clear, Trollope is striving to square liberal globalization with the transfer of regional hegemony from Britain to the United States and to make the United States palatable to his readers. If the notional transfer of Cuba to the United States still rubbed Britons the wrong way, Trollope turns to an imminent act of abandonment, the probable relinquishment of the Mosquito Coast protectorate, to dedramatize the cession of hegemony: "Now it is believed that, in deference to the feelings of the United States, and to the American reading of the Clayton-Bulwer treaty, and in deference, I may add, to a very sensible consideration that the matter is of no possible moment to ourselves, the protectorate of the Mosquito coast is to be abandoned" (314). What concerns me here are the ways in which Trollope modulates his readers' subjectivity to bring it into conformity with the requirement of "deference" to the ascendant hegemon. Crucially, the sentence contains no subject agents: Trollope reports on a generalized belief in the passive voice, a syntactical structure that is replicated when he describes the substance of that belief. This grammatical play distances Britons from the scene of sovereign cession. On one hand, this distance from decisiveness confirms Britain's diminishing agency in the hemisphere; on the other, however, it performs Britons affective and imaginative distance from the polity in question. The probability of abandonment can be reported in the passive voice not simply because deferential Britons are taking orders, then, but also because few Britons care (or know) to actively debate it. Indeed, Trollope only insinuates his own voice into the chain of reasoning to comment ironically on how indifferent Britons should be (and, indeed, probably were) to maintaining suzerainty over the Mosquito Coast. Having dedramatized the maintenance of imperium, the possibly humiliating deference to the United States is recuperated as Britain's sensibly deferring to its own best interests. Britain, Trollope maintains, does not require territorial rule; its globally hegemonic position derives from trade, which has enveloped the "whole world" (322). So why not let the United States play hemispheric hegemon, absorbing the costs of securing trade? After all, "The world is wide enough for us and our offspring, and we may be well content that we have it nearly all between us. Let them fulfil [sic] their destiny in the West, while we do so in the East" (137).

If the fate of the Bay Islands Colony and the Mosquito Coast protectorate demonstrates something of the realism that sparked West Indians' enduring fear of neglect and abandonment, for Trollope it serves as a nondramatic example of how Britain might nondramatically relate to the abandonment of empire. Britain's abandonment of colonies and peoples who had generated a limited metropolitan cathexis provides the outline for a program of imperial decathexis. Trollope intimates this early on in his book, where he explicitly poses abandonment as the ultimate telos of Britain's rule over the West Indies: "A certain work has been ours to do there, a certain amount of remaining work is still probably our lot to complete. But when that is done; when civilization, commerce, and education shall have been spread; when sufficient of our blood shall have been infused into the veins of these children of the sun; then, I think, we may be ready, without a stain to our patriotism, to take off our hats and bid farewell to the West Indies" (82).

Postcolonial scholars tend to take such civilizing rhetoric as opening a temporality of infinite deferral and thus as providing a moral alibi for an empire that never really wanted to quit.[37] Here, however, the logic of deferral works not to obfuscate the gritty mechanics of maintaining rule but, rather, to open a pedagogical time in which Britons will learn how to let go of empire without feeling it as "a stain to [their] patriotism." The reality of global free trade requires the management and attenuation of residual imperial attachments; rule is practiced as a letting go, a work of mourning that paradoxically kills that which has not yet died. The result then would be that, even if the "prospective" United States that Trollope had seen mapped should be realized, even if Jamaica should fall to the Yankees, Britons would know to not feel anything—or, at least, not to feel too much—about it. This prophylactic attenuation of imperial affect works to obviate the possibility that such an object might be fabulated in the event of its putative loss, that the weak patriotic sting that might be felt should the Stars and Stripes rise over Jamaica might convert into a patriotic defense of a land that is already more or less excluded from the *patria*. Indeed, Trollope's ultimate point is that there is no one, from the West Indies to the Spanish Main, to feel anything about. The declension of the planter class and its gentry-style hospitality, combined with the ascendance of a crass black commercial class as foreign to the proper of empire as the Mosquito Coast protectorate, means for Trollope that any such attachments lack a proper object. There is no empire in the West Indies—at least, no empire that would be recognizable to Britons as British.

Marketing before the Market

Trollope's suggestion that Britons imaginatively and affectively detach from New World empire tracks his broader insistence that economic life had already detached itself from the political, cultural, ethical, and affective norms that once burdened it. Britain should be ruled by its interests, for interests are all that remain—"the spirit of hospitality" has all but vanished from the earth. In the confrontation between aneconomic giving and economizing exchanging, between an empire held together by uncalculating affects and a globe networked by interested transactions, the latter terms will always have won: like any binary, Trollope's is hierarchically structured. Yet Trollope's insistence on this binary bespeaks an awkward recognition of its fragility, just as his erasure of Jamaica from his map discloses his awareness that some residuum of imperial sociality might striate the world picture assembled by liberal capitalism's value form. Indeed, Seacole's *Wonderful Adventures* articulates an alternative modality of material sociality that undoes the formalistic subsumption of any and all modes of transaction to the category of market exchange. And yet, as my brief review earlier of Seacole's public reception shows, midcentury Britons had limited resources with which to describe—or even notice—the functioning of an economy that was not ruled by the market. In effect, Seacole's text served as one moment in which the binary that Trollope takes as given was generalized as a pop hermeneutic of the economic. The popular figural economy that posed Seacole as either a small-scale war profiteer or a ministering angel symptomatizes a binary division of sociality into, on one hand, a domain that includes any activity that is formally legible as exchange and, on the other, a nontransactional domain of charitable care. By reducing any transaction to the formal logic of market exchange, liberal economic thought and its popular recensions simultaneously occlude non-market-based modes of transaction and the ways in which these occluded modes might materialize alternative economies of care.

Seacole is the *différance* of this liberal economic thinking, the trace of alterity that must be effaced so its postulates might be secured. In Seacole's text, the opposition between aneconomy and economy comes to crisis. This crisis occurs because Seacole's memoir conjugates political, cultural, affective, and transactional relations in a complex order that is not integrated by or subsumed into the institutional logic of the market. Karl Polanyi's rather schematic discussion of non-market-based modes of economic integration is heuristically useful here. If market exchange entails a "two-way movement of goods between persons oriented toward the gain ensuing for each from the resulting terms," as he puts it, Seacole's enterprise is equally involved in the institutional logics of "redistribution" and "reciprocity."[38] For Polanyi, redistribution begins with a centripetal movement, as goods are centrally collected; they are then dispensed "by virtue of custom, law, or ad hoc central decision."[39] Reciprocity is decentralized and founded on a principle of adequacy: "The right person at the right occasion should return the right kind of object."[40] Reciprocity substitutes equity for stringent calculability, opens a temporality of indebtedness in the place of the punctuality of two-way exchange, and socializes the scene of transaction: the person to whom one gives is not necessarily the person who gives back. Importantly, as part of their immanent functioning, the logics of reciprocity and redistribution incorporate aspects of social being that can appear as noneconomic externalities only from the perspective of the market. Here, political identities, kin relations, custom, laws, and affects function without mediation to enable, pattern, and even complete transactions.

Seacole's participation in these nonmarket forms of transacting was not the result of a voluntary refusal of liberal norms. Quitting capitalism is not so simple. In part, Seacole's British Hotel is an adaptation to the material, social, and economic realities of life in zones of crisis, where cash can be scarce; supplies, uncertain; and prices, unstable. As the architects of liberal globalization employed impoverished laborers to remold the earth to facilitate the free circulation of goods and people, this process relied on subalterns' nonmarket forms of transacting. However, these transactional modes are not simply reactive to liberal capitalism, either. Contra Trollope's claims regarding the declension of the aneconomic and the rise of black commercialism, Seacole establishes the vibrant persistence and rearticulation of mercantilist- and slavery-era social practices that distort the narrative of liberalization. Liberalization *reanimated* nonliberal practices. In the next two sections I trace out how Seacole models an alternative political and economic constitution for a caring empire on the basis of these practices. Here, I investigate how Seacole inherits these nonliberal forms of social transacting and mobilizes them in the founding of her various British Hotels.

My use of the trope "inherits" is advised: Seacole's book begins by linking both her attraction to the marchlands of empire and the social practices that she undertook there to her parents. Writing that she has "good Scotch blood coursing in [her] veins" from her father, a Scottish soldier, "to him I often trace my affection for camp-life" (11). She traces her interest in medicine and hospitality work to her mother, who provided these services to soldiers stationed around Kingston. Seacole describes "assist[ing] her in her duties" and "very often sharing with her the task of attending upon invalid officers or their wives" (12). The practices for which Seacole would become famous are here established as a matrilineal inheritance, a repertoire of acts and knowledges that Seacole learns from her mother. Seacole would also pursue a variety of commercial enterprises alongside her care work: traveling to Britain and returning with pickles for sale, traveling to New Providence and importing "rare shell-work," and so on (14). We might take the work of caring for sick soldiers as discontinuous with importing shells for sale, but the gendered political economy of colonial Jamaica organizes and articulates these apparently discontinuous practices. Before she became an imperial sutler, Seacole was a Jamaican higgler.

Today, the term "higgler" is "commonly used by Jamaicans to identify a particular kind of street vendor—a so-called lower-class black woman who sells a range of items on the streets or in government-appointed market areas and arcades." A higgler is an "informal commercial importer" whose livelihood depends on the kind of exchanges that Seacole made when she took pickles to London or shells to Kingston.[41] Such microtransactions were the stuff of the black Atlantic ordinary: just think of Equiano and his bags of oranges. Higgling, however, has come to be seen as "vulgar, unfeminine, and contaminating," because higgling "boldly inserts itself—or intrudes—into economic spaces not intended for it."[42] Deeply "unfeminine," the higgler takes leave of the domestic oikos and penetrates the masculine world of commerce. Yet, as Winnifred Browne-Glaude discusses in her elaboration of the groundbreaking work of Sidney Mintz, this feminine penetration of the economic in Jamaica is nothing new. Throughout the period of slavery, enslaved and free black women sustained the informal market system that linked urban marketplaces to the rural provision grounds tended by enslaved workers.[43] It is for its infrastructural importance that the colonial state tolerated the higgling of provisions very early on, even as it sought to bar black subjects from vending other goods.[44] Moreover, higglers infused cash money into the economy of the enslaved. Indeed, in the late eighteenth century, Edward Long estimated that enslaved people held about two-tenths of the hard currency circulating in the island.[45] We should take care, however, that we do not pull a Trollope and read this history as charting the emergence of possessive individualism from the black below. For one, the marketplaces where these higglers vended their goods are heterogeneous to "the market" of liberal lore.

These marketplaces were embedded within particular legal and social formations. Moreover, market prices were determined by socialized understandings of just pricing.[46] Finally, these market exchanges took place alongside and through affective, cultural, and political exchanges; the marketplace was a scene of reputation, disputation, and pleasure. Commerce was inseparable from these other modalities of social relation.

The importance of these socially embedded markets would only increase as Britain disembedded its sugar market from empire.[47] The consolidation of "the market" in Britain led to an intensification of marketing practices in Jamaica. Within the division of labor of the emergent peasant households, women retained their slavery-era role as marketers of surplus produce.[48] Thus, even as multiple processes of liberalization attempted to generate a gendered division between public and private, the economy and the oikos, the peasant family's gendered division of household labor meant that this line was insistently crossed—or, indeed, made no sense. This division of labor affected the substantive logic of marketing and higgling. Higgling was an adjunct of domestic production; while a necessary supplement, the marketing of surplus provisions was never an end in itself, never a form of economic activity with an autonomous rationality. Indeed, James Scott suggests that peasant production "has little scope for the profit maximization calculus of traditional neoclassical economics."[49] The profit margins were too slim, and the work of gathering and transporting goods were too time-intensive, for the provisions market to backform the peasant production process. The postemancipation household aimed not at profit but at subsistence; higgling was a means of getting the bit of cash required to purchase necessaries that could not be produced within the household. Marketing, then, was the socialized means by which women reproduced their households in a precarious economic climate.

Like those of these higgling women, Seacole's movements articulate oikos and economy, home and market. These two spheres are neither separate nor opposed; rather, they derive from a common, feminized matrix of (re)productive activity. Within Seacole's text, the hotel becomes the privileged figure for this productive non opposition between home and market, dwelling and circulating, giving and exchange.[50] As we have already seen, hotel keeping, like higgling, was a deeply feminized practice; we have also seen Seacole inscribe her own hostelry practices as a maternal inheritance. This maternal inscription will only gain in intensity: throughout the text, Seacole's hotel keeping allows her to serve as "Mother Seacole" to her British "sons." Indeed, the text locates the mother in the hotel, a site that oscillates between home and market; it names a matrix of sociality out of which these determinate locations would be disembedded, carved out, and treated as autonomous sites. From the perspective of Seacole's memoir, the maternal hotel figures a moment of potentiality that precedes the separation of market and home, of economy and aneconomy, of commercial calculation and affective incalculability. It thus becomes the bearer of an alternative social logic—one illegible according to the hermeneutic biases of economic liberalism.

Seacole turns to hotel keeping abroad following a series of calamities that render Jamaica unhomely. Shortly after the death of her husband (a man who weds Seacole and dies in the space of a single paragraph), Seacole loses her mother. This event leaves Seacole "alone to battle with the world as best I might" (15). Soon thereafter, she writes, the "great fire of 1843, which devastated Kingston, burnt down my poor home" (16). Luckily, Seacole reports that she "never thought too exclusively of money" and was affectively prepared to rebuild her home, which doubled as an infirmary for British soldiers stationed at Newcastle or Up-Park Camp (15). In 1850, a cholera epidemic "swept over the island of Jamaica," testing Seacole's skills as a nurse and devastating her community (16). Seacole's brother decided to migrate to Panama that year, following thousands of Jamaicans who sought a livelihood building the railroad across the isthmus after liberalization decimated the island's plantation economy.[51] Seacole follows him, reasoning, "I might be of use to him (he was far from strong)" (17). As Browne-Glaude writes, black Jamaicans "rejected" the liberalized Jamaican economy by "emigrating to areas such as Panama, the United States, and Central America."[52] Seacole's migration instances one such rejection. In the absence of her mother, far from her motherland, with her first home destroyed by fire, at a time that British inhospitality to West Indian produce pushed myriad Jamaicans from their home, Seacole would set up "The British Hotel," her first hotel abroad.

In so naming her hotel, Seacole does not simply "claim her Englishness," as if a stable form of such an identity was to hand. Liberalization had transformed "the historical and cultural referents that define[d] Englishness"; claiming such an identity required reconstituting that identity, not simply fitting into one.[53] Seacole's British Hotel amounted to an effort to "surrogate" a form of Britishness that had been deactivated through the sequence of political, economic, and cultural shifts that attended liberalization. As Joseph Roach puts it, surrogation is a "process" that "continues as actual or perceived vacancies occur in the networks of relations that constitutes the social fabric."[54]

Multiple "actual or perceived vacancies" constitute the context in which Seacole opens her hotel on the edges of empire: the loss of her mother, the loss of her home, the liberal expulsion of Jamaica from the British Empire. The British Hotel is itself a surrogated form of the home Seacole literally and metaphorically lost. The point here is that the Britishness that Seacole references has no clear referent—it does not point to existent forms of British imperial practice. Rather, the "British" of the British Hotel works as a paleonym that Seacole invests with new content, a surrogate for a vanished modality of socioeconomic relation that Seacole reactivates. This new mode of social relation that Seacole calls "British" will be founded on and materialized through an economic sociality derived from higgling—microtransactions in a world abandoned by capital that prioritize the reproducibility of the household over an autonomous impulse toward profit maximization. Neither for profit nor not for profit, Seacole's British Hotel surrogates an imperial world in which economic value is embedded within a thick field of social relation and where a diversity of transactional modalities flourish alongside the formal simplicity of commercial exchange.

The substantive socioeconomic rationality that would regulate Seacole's British Hotel presided at its founding. When she first arrives in Panama, Seacole helps her brother run his own eating establishment in Cruces, where he caters to gold-rushers and employees of the U.S.-based Panama Railroad Company; a few months later, she sets up her own hotel in Gorgona. The Panama Railroad Company imports prefabricated houses from Maine to house its employees; Seacole, of course, has nothing like the resources of a Yankee firm.[55] Instead, she relies on various social relations to construct the house she requires:

> With the aid of an old Jamaica friend, who had settled at Gorgona, I at last found a miserable little hut for sale, and bought it for a hundred dollars. It consisted of one room only, and was, in its then condition, utterly unfit for my purposes; but I determined to set to work and build on to it. . . . The alcalde's permission to make use of the adjacent ground was obtained for a moderate consideration, and plenty of material was procurable from the opposite bank of the river. An American, whom I had cured of the cholera at Cruces, lent me his boat, and I hired two or three natives to cut down and shape the posts and bamboo poles. (50)

Here, we see Seacole mobilize a range of transactional modalities to get her hotel going. There is simple exchange: the hundred dollars for the hut, the bribe to the government official, the wages to the "two or three natives." But we also see a logic of reciprocity at work. Seacole's Jamaica friend, as a friend, freely gives his "aid" to the aspiring hotelier. Meanwhile, the American repays his existential debt to Seacole for her nursing activities by lending her his boat. (As we will see, this arrangement was common. Seacole allowed people to pay for her nursing expertise how they could and when they could.) Finally, the environmental commons (or what Seacole takes to be a commons) gratuitously yields the materials she requires. Calculable exchange is just one element in a complex assemblage that articulates a diversity of material socialities—exchanging, gift giving, reciprocating, appropriating, and so on.

My point here is not to assert the superior moral value of this assemblage so much as to insist on the persistence of nonmarket modalities of transacting through the era of free trade. Indeed, it was not simple persistence: throughout the hemisphere, liberalization conjured as its illegible obverse scenes of relation where market logics corroded. As Seacole's text reveals, the process of liberal globalization in fact relied on nonmarket modalities of transacting carried out from below. The work of Seacole's text is to suture this mode of subaltern transacting to Britishness—indeed, to pass it off *as* properly British. The necessity for this move is ironically encoded in Seacole's description of how she built her hotel. Note the functional noninvolvement—minus the Jamaica friend, perhaps—of Britons in the scheme. It is a fundamentally American affair, with a Yankee settler lending his boat and Panamanians selling their labor. Seacole precariously converts this American space into a British outpost by the mere application of a name. I say "precarious" because, as Seacole demonstrates, Yankee ascendance threatens to absorb the entire region into its sovereign possession. The only way for Britain to block this unsettling possibility would be to fashion a postliberal empire in which value does not autonomously regulate the bestowal of immaterial attention and material care—a postliberal empire that looks not a little like the British Hotel.

The British Hotel between Empires

Seacole models her alternatives to liberal globalization in spaces of incomplete sovereignty, where multiple empires and nations frictively rub against one another, where trade bursts through imperial and national controls. As Aims McGuinness argues, the construction of the transit zone marked "a transformation in the political order of the Americas" inasmuch as "no overarching empire in the Americas could aspire to impose its will on the vast network of trade."[56] It is precisely such an imposition of political will that Seacole desires, and she mobilizes her interimperial setting to make a sequence of linked political claims. First, she shows that necropolitical accumulation tactics prevail in spaces unevenly incorporated into the geography of interstate sovereignty. For Seacole, laborers in Panama are unsupported by states capable of regulating the valorization requirements of capital; they are entirely subject to capital, which treats them as disposable. (Indeed, the Panama Railroad Company for whom these workers labored and died had achieved—through negotiations with the Neogranadan state and by virtue of the weak sovereignty exercised by the quasi-autonomous Panamanian state—a kind of corporate sovereignty in the transit zone.)[57] Seacole highlights the anomic aspects of life in the isthmus to reinscribe, by outlining its negation, the vital importance of political belonging. To that end, she figures U.S. Americans as embodiments of the logic of necropolitical capitalism, to which she opposes the British Empire she seeks to surrogate. She maps the interimperial field through a friend-enemy distinction that incipiently repoliticizes the anomic field and enables her to claim a British imperial citizenship. Finally, she uses this formal reinscription of the British Empire into the sovereignless space of global capital to determine how the empire should operate. In other words, she first asserts formal inclusion in empire through the friend-enemy distinction, then invests this formal inclusion with substantive content.

For Seacole, the Panamanian transit zone appears first and foremost as an inhospitable space. Caught in an interweaving field of empires, nations, and capital, people live there only to die. Narrating her travels from Navy Bay to Gatun, Seacole reflects: "Every mile of that fatal railway cost the world thousands of lives. I was assured that its site was marked thickly by graves, and that so great was the mortality among the labourers that three times the survivors struck in a body, and their places had to be supplied by fresh victims from America, tempted by unheard-of rates of wages" (19). The total number of workers' deaths has never been conclusively tabulated; the Panama Railroad Company did not keep records of mortality rates for its largely Jamaican and Chinese labor force. A colloquial (and, as Olive Senior contends, certainly inflated) understanding held that one laborer died for every railroad tie laid.[58] For Seacole, the catastrophic working and living conditions render the terms "labourers," "survivors," and "victims" equivalent to one another. Laborers in Panama do not appear under the horizon of life (as in Marx's "living labor") but always already maintain a relation to an imminent death. Even the workers' strike is not encoded as an attempt to enhance their living and working conditions but as a more basic attempt to survive.

Like Trollope, Seacole links the inhospitality of Panama to the failure of the Neogranadan state to assert its sovereignty over the area: the "weak sway of the New Granada Republic, despised by lawless men, and respected by none, is powerless to control the refuse of every nation which meet together upon its soil" (18). This is in part due to the ease with which "lawless men" could manipulate legal apparatuses through bribes to avoid punishment. Justice is not dispersed but vended: "I generally avoided claiming the protection of the law whilst on the Isthmus, for I found it—as is the case in civilized England from other causes—rather an expensive luxury" (45). Neogranadans are, as it were, bad hosts; they fail to provide a clear and effective set of rule to conduct the comportment of their guests. Yet Seacole shows that the Republic of New Granada is not so much a bad host as it is forced to entertain bad guests—U.S. Americans. For Seacole, Yankees come to figure a propulsion to accumulate that is unregulated by any ethical or political normativity. Frontier life renders them defective for political belonging: "The difference between the passengers to and from California was very distinguishable. Those bound for the gold country were to a certain extent fresh from civilization, and had scarcely thrown off its control; whereas the homeward bound reveled in disgusting excess of licence [sic]" (26). Seacole ties this uncertain, petty mode of capital accumulation to gambling, the U.S. pastime in Panama. Here, capitalism appears less as a civilizing force than as a stupid game of chance organized by unruly gamesters wielding guns.

This critique of the United States enables Seacole both to produce an alliance with New Granadians negotiating an aggressive Yankee presence *and* to position herself as firmly British. "The citizens of the New Granada Republic," Seacole writes, "had a strong prejudice against all Americans"; she will elaborate multiple reasons that this should be so (51). Foremost for Seacole is that "this and the other States of Central America" provide a "refuge" for a number of fugitive slaves from the U.S. South (51).[59] Inscribing Central America within the same southern cartography of freedom invoked by George Numa Des Sources, she writes that there "every profession was open to them" and "they soon rose to positions of eminence in New Granada" (51). Fugitive ex-slaves from the United States naturally came into contact with white Yankees, and Seacole insists that this had an effect on their hosts: Neo-granadans, "influenced naturally by these freed slaves, who bore themselves before their old masters bravely and like men," became "strongly prejudiced against the Americans" (51). Of course, Seacole's Panamanian hosts' distaste for Yankees had other motivations. They "feared [U.S. Americans'] quarrel-some, bullying habits—be it remembered that the crowds to California were of the lowest sorts, many of whom have since fertilized Cuban and Nicaraguan soil—and dreaded their schemes for annexation" (51).[60] Seacole suggests that the United States might seize on the recent "Watermelon Riot" as a "reason-able excuse for exercising a protectorate over, or in other words annexing," Panama (67).[61] Desirous of keeping the sovereign state of New Granada open as a "refuge" for fugitive ex-slaves, Seacole will link the Neogranadan con-stitution to that of Britain as a means of fostering British opposition to U.S. imperialism: "It is one of the maxims of the New Granada constitution—as it is, I believe, of the English—that on a slave touching its soil its chains fall from him" (52). Note the complicated narrative trajectory of the pronouns: the depersonalized possessor of chains ("its chains") becomes, through their removal, a person ("fall from him"). Yet Seacole laments, the constitution is rarely mobilized to assist things in becoming men: Neogranadans do not wish to "irritate so dangerous a neighbour as America, [and so] this rule was rarely supported" (52). By establishing a parallel between a British and Neogranadan jurisprudence of freedom, Seacole demonstrates how Yankee imperial expansion is in fact destructive of values that Britain claimed to uphold.

Seacole invokes the British Empire as the sole actor capable of materially inscribing political community into an anomic world of utterly free capitalism. For Seacole, the mere presence of Englishmen is enough to temper the "bul-lying habits" of U.S. Americans. Describing the behavior of Yankees toward local laborers, she writes, "Terribly bullied by the Americans were the boat-men and muleteers, who were reviled, shot, and stabbed by these free and independent filibusters, who would fain whop all creation abroad as they do their slaves at home. Whenever any Englishmen were present, and in a posi-tion to interfere with success, this bullying was checked" (43). Here Seacole poses the isthmus as a battleground between the United States and Britain, between slavery and freedom, between lawless extractors of wealth and a regulated approach to economic life. Her insistence on the bodily violence of filibustering—the shooting, the stabbing—interferes with Trollope's abstrac-tion of this violence through recourse to analogies with Britain's past or by gestures toward the pacific future to come. The only solution to the embodied violence of Yankees is the bodily presence of Brits. Indeed, while Seacole writes in the indicative ("this bullying was checked") as if simply reporting, she is in fact beginning to make a demand that Britain impose its might in the region to manage the anomic effects of necropolitical capitalism. Political demands saturate her seemingly neutral narration of events.

Seacole's norm making achieves explicit articulation when she describes her reaction to a group of Yankees celebrating "the anniversary of the declaration of American independence" (48). Importantly, Seacole will implicate herself in this scene; she opposes U.S. imperialism in the name of Britishness. A "thin, sallow-looking American, with a pompous yet rapid delivery," intones:

> Well, gentlemen, I expect you'll all support me in a drinking of this toast that I du—. Aunty Seacole, gentlemen; I give you Aunty Seacole—... God bless the best yaller woman He ever made—, from Jamaica, gentlemen—, from the Isle of Springs—Well, gentlemen, I expect there are only tu things we're vexed for—; and the first is, that she ain't one of us—, a citizen of the great United States—; and the other thing is, gentlemen—, that Providence made her a yaller woman ... , and I guess, if we could bleach her by any means we would. (48–49)

Note the orthographic parody: the Yankee, not the creole of color, speaks a debased form of English. Moreover, the proliferation of dashes marks "the time expended" between periods as the speaker "turn[s] over his words with his quid before delivering them, and clear[s] his mouth after each sentence, perhaps to make room for the next" (48). The crude, uncivilized modality of delivery replicates the crude, uncivilized content of his speech. Seacole responds by asserting race pride, denying any desire to become a U.S. citizen, and gesturing toward alternative determinations of social value:

> Gentlemen ... I must say, that I don't altogether appreciate your friend's kind wishes with respect to my complexion. If it had been as dark as any nigger's, I should have been just as happy and as useful, and as much respected by those whose respect I value. ... As to the society which the process [bleaching] might gain me admission into, all I can say is, that, judging from the specimens I have met with here and elsewhere, I don't think that I shall lose much by being excluded from it. So, gentlemen, I drink to you and the general reformation of American manners. (49)

Seacole refuses to become white to become a citizen. Through this refusal, she can negate the entire value of such racial citizenship. She will not "lose much by being excluded from it." Instead, Seacole gestures toward another locus of racial, social, and political belonging, one where even if her skin had been darker, she "should" have been "as much respected by those whose respect I value." Seacole suggests, in short, that the respect of Yankees does not matter; she belongs elsewhere, in a world where it is British respect alone that matters.

Yet Seacole is not celebrating the Britain as a race-blind, multicultural guarantor of imperial citizenship. While the Yankee offers Seacole citizenship, Seacole can only solicit British "respect"—she cannot claim to inhabit a position within the British Empire symmetrical to the one that the Yankees offer her. Seacole takes her July Fourth dispute over the value of U.S. citizenship as a chance to subtly recast her position vis-à-vis empire, a recasting that takes place under the horizon of the term "citizen." This is marked textually: the jussive "should" reorients the normative aim of Seacole's speech. If she were darker in complexion, she "should"—not would, because Seacole has already informed the reader about the racism she met with during a teenage visit to London—"have been . . . as much respected by those whose respect I value." Seacole charges her British readership with the task of becoming a collectivity whose respect she should value and, indeed, whose respect would be formally assured to her. If Seacole's British readership would like to assume Seacole's critique of Americans as their own, they must not only chastise the crude racism of the Americans. They must also include Seacole within the British Empire in the same modality as these Yankees offered to include Seacole (if only she were white) in the United States.

Seacole's own practices as a caregiver in New Granada provide a blueprint for how this imperial political community should operate. Seacole offers her account of her caring labor reluctantly; she hopes that "my kind reader . . . will not . . . think that, in narrating these incidents, I am exalting my poor part in them unduly" (30). Yet she also must narrate them, "for my share in them appears to be the one and only claim I have to interest the public ear." To read Seacole's text as modeling alternative imperial norms, I take her depersonalization of her account at face value: far from self-promotion, or even self-writing, she offers an ethnography of crisis in the imperial periphery. Seacole recognizes that she must temporarily embrace her status as celebrity to access the "public ear." In so doing, however, she attempts to displace their fascination and "interest" in the minimal set of attributes that compose the social text of "Mary Seacole" in the name of promoting alternative modalities of sociality. We are encouraged to read *through* the figure of "Mary Seacole" to access the set of social practices that she embodies.

Seacole's labor of care itself begins, as it did in Jamaica, with a cholera epidemic. She alone is able to combat it: "There was no doctor in Cruces; the nearest approach to one was a little timid dentist . . . who refused to prescribe for the sufferer, and I was obliged to do my best." The cholera epidemic induces an aneconomic approach to time. "In so great request were my services," she writes, "that for days and nights together I scarcely knew what it was to enjoy two successive hours' rest" (30). While Seacole's distribution of her time verges on the aneconomic, her disposal of her labor and of her materials—mustard emetics, plasters, calomel—raises the problem of the reproducibility of her enterprise. How did Seacole continue to provide care over time? How did she procure all of the materials that treating cholera required? Importantly, while Seacole did not provide her services gratuitously, the provision of care was not normed by price. Rather, Seacole's care fetched the price that her patients could pay: "It must be understood that many of those who could afford to pay for my services did so handsomely, but the great majority of my patients had nothing better to give their doctress than their thanks" (31). Here, care does not appear as a nonmaterial affect or object that one can give endlessly. There is an economics of care, here premised on a diffuse practice of redistribution. Those who pay for Seacole's services "handsomely" indirectly fund Seacole's ability to care for and cure those who can offer only "thanks." Those who consume Seacole's care are not the formally equivalent, abstract consumers enshrined within British free-trade policies. Instead, the particularity of their class position determines their costs. Moreover, the exchanges that propped up Seacole's caregiving were hardly terminated in a transactional instant; rather, her caregiving opened up a temporality of indebtedness. Thus, when Seacole herself falls ill, "it was difficult to keep out the sympathizing Americans and sorrowing natives who came to inquire after me; and who, not content with making their inquiries, and leaving their offerings of blankets, flannel, etc., must see with their own eyes what chance the yellow woman had of recovery" (38). Here we see an economy functioning through reciprocation: the precise exchange of equivalent values is replaced by a diffuse sense of a normative "adequacy" that regulates the fit between what was initially given and what Seacole tropes as her former patients' "offerings."[62] Seacole's illness, in other words, marks a brief crisis that signals the necessity of debt redemption. She consequently (and humorously) finds herself almost overburdened with care, "almost inclined to throw something at them, or call them bad names" to get them to leave (38).

For Seacole, care does not follow market logics; rather, care is materially embedded within redistributive and reciprocative networks of sociality. It is not that Seacole's care is not exchanged; it is. But these exchanges cannot be disembedded from the material, affective, and social contexts that constitute their possibility; nor can the values exchanged be calculated as if care were a commodity on a price-setting market. Seacole indicates the quotidian life of this distinction when she remembers her relationship to U.S. American women. Seacole had a far from "pleasant" relationship with Yankee women, she recalls, "as the majority of them came from the Southern States of America, and showed an instinctive repugnance" to the colored Jamaican hotelier (51). It is at this point that Seacole offers her sole statement of approval of the formal exchange logics of the liberal market: "Not that it ever gave me annoyance; they were glad of my stores and comforts, I made money out of their wants; nor do I think our bond of connection was ever closer" (51). Seacole's point here should not be mistaken for a (neo) liberal adulation of the capacity of formal exchange to ground a race-blind scene of sociality that might or could or should invaginate the entirety of the social. Rather, her point—one that was at that moment being worked out by Marx in the notebooks we know as the *Grundrisse*—is that the logics of formal exchange should be reserved for those who are beyond the boundary of one's community, for those with whom one would like nothing more to do, for those with whom becoming "closer" is unimaginable.[63] If you are engaged in exchange, you are probably not engaging a friend. Yet Seacole's sentence closes by displacing the logic of exchange in the imminence of crisis: "Only this, if any of them came to me sick and suffering (I say this out of simple justice to myself), I forgot everything, except that she was my sister, and that it was my duty to help her" (51). Once again, this does not mean that aneconomic care simply displaces economic calculation; it means, rather, that crisis induces a modal shift in Seacole's transactional disposition, with the effect that even these racist Yankees are located in the diffuse network of redistribution and reciprocity that animated her enterprise.

Seacole's recollection of her time as a hotelier and healer in the Panama transit zone amply documents the quotidianness of violence, grievous vulnerability, and death that went into making the liberalized world system. One Jamaican would reminisce before a Commission of Inquiry in 1879, "After that sugar bill came into operation . . . there was not a day's work to be found[.] Many thousands of tradesmen and labourers were forced to seek employment elsewhere; they went to the Isthmus and completed the Panama Railway, and nearly all of them died there, indirectly the victims of the free traders and sugar refiners of England."[64] And so they were. Yet as Seacole's memoir also reveals, liberalization insistently generated its dialectical opposite: liberalization's "victims" reactivated nonmarket modalities of exchange to survive the anomic world that capitalism conjured. Within the crisis-laden, undercapitalized, overly capitalist space of Panama, Seacole's British Hotel reanimated transactional logics that were opposed to liberal capitalism's market system. On the battlefields of the Crimea, Seacole would set these logics to work to succor and save Britons.

Toward an Empire of Care

As I am arguing, Seacole's labors cannot be emplotted within a narrowly construed sphere of activity we call the economic. Rather, the British Hotel works by reembedding the economic in affectively, culturally, and politically saturated social relations, which regulate and shape transactional logics. Seacole returned to Jamaica from Panama in 1853; her narration demonstrates how the liberalized British Empire itself continued to rely on archaic logics of redistribution and reciprocity. The occasion for this demonstration was once more a social crisis—yet another cholera outbreak. In a gesture of hospitality, Seacole opened her house to feverish Brits: "My house was full of sufferers— officers, their wives and children" (58). It is on the basis of this caring labor that Seacole would stake a claim to imperial belonging.

To begin this claims making, Seacole thematizes the relationship among caring labor, calculable values, and the British Empire. First, she recodes British deaths in Jamaica as imperial opportunity costs: "Indeed, the mother country pays a dear price for the possession of her colonies" (58). Construing empire as a field of bad investments, Seacole temporarily inhabits the analytic perspective of British free traders; she outlines a debased calculus in which the British mother exchanges the death of some of her sons and daughters for the possession of the colonies. But Seacole will suggest that this perspective is incomplete. Seeing British deaths as pure expenditure elides the caring labor of West Indians: "Creoles . . . [possess] an affection for English people and an anxiety for their welfare, which shows itself warmest when they are sick and suffering" (59). Seacole's text works to render legible the value of creoles' caring labors to the value of empire as such. The caring labor of creoles of color appears as a necessary externality for the success of the British Empire, yet this labor cannot—or should not—be computed as if it were susceptible to the same kind of market-based calculations as a hogshead of sugar. What, then, constitutes adequate reciprocation for this labor? For Seacole, recognition of the centrality of caring labor—and thus of creole caregivers—provides adequate reciprocation. Indeed, Seacole will rewrite empire as a social network through which reciprocated and recognized acts of care circulate among imperial citizens.

Seacole's empire of care is not simply a product of unidirectional acts of caregiving. This would amount to material and affective theft. Rather, Seacole comes to define empire as a network of reciprocation in which citizens care that other citizens care. This becomes clear in Seacole's discussion of a young surgeon who is dying in her house. She pities to see "the poor worn heart long[ing] to see once more the old familiar faces of the loved ones in unconscious happiness at home" (60). Seacole attempts to transform her own home into something recognizable as home to this British surgeon and ends up calling him "My son—my dear child." Later, as the surgeon prepares to die, he beckons to her and says, " 'Let me lay my head on your breast'; and so he rested. . . . 'It's only that I miss my mother' " (60). He dies with Seacole serving as his surrogate mother. It is not this act of surrogation alone that is important to Seacole. Just as important is the recognition bestowed on her act of maternal surrogation. A few months after the surgeon's death, his "real" mother sends Seacole a letter with a token:

MY DEAR MADAM—Will you do me the favour to accept the enclosed trifle, in remembrance of that dear son whose last moments were soothed by your kindness, and as a mark of the gratitude of, my dear Madam,

Your ever sincere and obliged,

M—S—(61)

It is a striking coincidence that the "real" mother, "M—S—," bears the same initials as Mary Seacole. It is as if, by occupying a similar position vis-à-vis the same "son" they have become equivalent; the initials index an identity in social function. Note that M—S— never claims possession over or property in the dead surgeon. He is instead described as "that dear son," as if Seacole's surrogate motherhood has made him, and his memory, common property, shared out across and through empire. The circulation of tokens (the letter itself, the "enclosed trifle") materializes M— S—'s recognition of Seacole's surrogation; her caring labors are reciprocated as equivalent to the labors of this imperial mother.[65]

Seacole traces an affective economy that concatenates the material and the immaterial via performances of labor, recognition, and reciprocation. Yet this alternative imperial value form that Seacole models is beset by a paradox: the empire of care she seeks to make normative can be activated only in moments of exception, when crisis overwhelms the systemic logics of capitalism or empire. The articulation of care, crisis, and imperial citizenship places her recognition as a caring imperial citizen under a particular temporal horizon. The end of the crisis and the return of the liberal ordinary uproot the conditions in which Seacole's care gains a political value that is exorbitant to the value form of liberal capitalism. Ironically, then, *Wonderful Adventures* demonstrates both the viability of nonmarket modalities of exchange *and* the fragility of the caring imperial citizenship that she derives from it. The imperial value form constituted through care interrupts the value form of liberal capitalism, but this interruption is ephemeral and bound to place. Pound signs will always have replaced red crosses.

Seacole negotiates the dissolution of her value into the liberal ordinary by sticking close to scenes of crisis. What Seacole calls her "inclination to rove," her bounding from adventure to adventure, is perhaps better glossed as an inclination to the political—a desire to be somewhere in the world where people will care that she cares for them (11). And yet, as Seacole learns when she tries to serve in the Crimea, the racial protocols of liberal empire block her access to the circuits of recognition that would enable the fact of her care to matter to the British state. After arriving in London in the fall of 1854, she applies to the War Office to become a nurse, only to be rebuffed (72). She then applies to serve as a nurse with Florence Nightingale's corps but is once more denied. Here, Seacole's problem declines from but also overlaps with the one that confronts Des Sources. Whereas Des Sources's project emerged out of a critique of an imperial state that would not secure black subjects' politico-economic autonomy, Seacole confronts a British state and British civil-social organizations that do not care to capacitate black subjects to care for metropolitan Britons. When she receives a final rejection, this time for passage fare from a private Crimean fund, Seacole wanders the streets weeping and wondering, "Was it possible that American prejudices against colour had some root here?" (73).

Seacole's racial foreclosure from the affective circuitry of imperial citizenship impels her to resume, once again, her career as a hotelier and sutler: "If the authorities had allowed me, I would willingly have given them my services as a nurse; but as they declined them, should I not open an hotel for invalids in the Crimea in my own way?" (74). While the British state did not incorporate Seacole into its war machine by distributing funds to her, Seacole trusts that the soldiers serving in the Crimea whom she knew from Jamaica will reciprocate her intentions with "welcome and kindness" (74). Affective debt precedes and prepares for the web of transactions that the British Hotel will have enabled. Seacole intends to discharge the debt in two linked ways: through helping the "kind-hearted doctors" and sutlering hard-to-find goods to troops. After forming a firm with Thomas Day (whom she had met in Panama), Seacole writes, "A great portion of my limited capital was, with the kind aid of a medical friend, invested in medicines which I had reason to believe would be useful; with the remainder I purchased those home comforts which I thought would be most difficult to obtain away from England" (75). Seacole describes the division of her funds this way for somewhat strategic reasons: she is quite aware that some of the British public viewed her more as a mercenary sutler than as a ministering angel, so needs to substantiate that nursing was always "the main object of my journey" (75).

More subtly, Seacole pushes back against the very idea that care labor simply transcends questions of economizing materials, time, and attention. She describes how her nursing activities engaged logics of simple exchange, redistribution, reciprocity, and debt so that her care enterprise could at once sustain itself and reach the largest number of soldiers possible:

> I cannot . . . conscientiously charge myself with doing less for the men who had only thanks to give me, than for the officers whose gratitude gave me the necessities of life. I think I was ever ready to turn from the latter to help the former, humble as they might be; and they were grateful in their war, and as far as they could be. They would buy me apples and other fruit at Balaclava, and leave them at my store. One made me promise, when I returned home, to send word to his Irish mother, who was to send me a cow in token of her gratitude for the help I had been to her son. I have a book filled with hundreds of the names of those who came to me for medicines and other aids. (117)

As in Panama, the munificence of the well-off (officers) funds Seacole's subsistence and her ability to extend care to those who lack means (enlisted troops). This redistributive thrust opens up a diffuse set of reciprocative practices, which are nonmonetized (apples and fruit) and temporally dispersed (the cow she will receive, perhaps, one day). These items that materialize reciprocity function less as a kind of barter currency than, in Seacole's terms, as "token[s]"—objects that metonymize a dense social relation.

If care labor in the Crimean War theater engaged economic logics that were nonetheless irreducible to simple exchange logics, the sale of "home comforts" there took on a value exorbitant to economic determinations. Seacole explores how the very possibility of material exchange generated an affective surplus:

> When a poor fellow lay sickening in his cheerless hut and sent down to me, he knew very well that I should not ride up in answer to his message empty-handed. And although I did not hesitate to charge him with the value of the necessaries I took him, still he was thankful enough to be able to purchase them. When we lie ill at home surrounded with comfort, we never think of feeling any special gratitude for sick room delicacies which we accept as a consequence of illness; but the poor officer lying ill and weary in his crazy hut, dependent for the merest necessaries of existence upon a clumsy, ignorant soldier-cook . . . often finds his greatest troubles in the want of those little delicacies with which a weak stomach must be humoured into retaining nourishment. (111)

Here, Seacole attempts to denaturalize commodity culture in Britain. War alters the phenomenology of exchange and consumption that obtains "at home." In the scene that Seacole describes, "home" is subtly redefined: it is no longer a container of affects and objects but the effect of material and affective circulation. The institutional space of the hotel remixes the an-economy of the oikos and the economy of the market: the hotel exchanges itself for a home space putatively untouched by economizing logics. Thus, Seacole's insistence that the soldier was "thankful enough to be able to *purchase them*" should not be taken as prefiguring nostrums about market access. Her point, rather, is that the exchange of materialities always already constitutes homeliness, and that such exchanges materialize the immaterial—they serve as "tokens." Seacole herself comes to stand in as a token of home: "Their calling me 'mother' was not, I think, altogether unmeaning. I used to fancy there was something homely in the word; and, reader, you cannot think how dear to them was the smallest thing that reminded them of home" (112). Sandra Gunning argues that her "self-generated public image as Mother Seacole sentimentalizes her economic opportunism," all part of an attempt to "represent her commercialism as a patriotic act."[66] But that is not quite right. Affect is not superadded to the transactions Seacole describes. Instead, affect composes these value relations, regulating the worth of the object or service, determining the temporality and form of repayment, and at times serving as the medium of repayment as such—the "thanks" she receives from troops who cannot pay.

Seacole thus simultaneously inverts, extends, and perverts Marxist feminist theories of reproductive labor to incorporate reproductive, domestic, and affective labor into the fold of classical political-economic notions of value (even if only as a transitional demand).[67] Instead of suggesting measuring, if only to shift perspectives, the value of reproductive labor through the optic of a labor theory of value, she poses quantifiable transactions of care and commerce as materializations of an immaterial, unquantifiable affectivity. At the same time, she moves this theory of value from the sphere of the intimate or domestic into that of circulation (she remains, after all, a hotelier). This mode of transacting worked for Seacole, but a structural problem shadows this nonmarket economy of affect: it can maintain itself only for as long as crisis inhibits the market from allocating goods in conformity with their value. When the war ends, and the liberal ordinary takes over, value delinks from the affective and political determinations through which Seacole's enterprise operates. Tokens of home become disenchanted commodities. It is in the context of the liberal ordinary that Seacole appears to be sentimentalizing her commercial transactions or (perhaps) deluded about the intensity of her exploitation; her economy of affect becomes, retroactively, an intense form of affective exploitation. Reflecting on this conundrum, Seacole rages against the reversion to capital's value form:

> The poor old British Hotel! We could do nothing with it. The iron house was pulled down, and packed up for conveyance home. . . . All the kitchen fittings and stoves, that had cost us so much, fell also into their hands. I only wish some cook worthy to possess them has them now. We could sell nothing. Our horses were almost given away, our large stores of provisions, etc. were at anyone's service. It makes my heart sick to talk of the really alarming sacrifices we made. The Russians crowded down ostensibly to purchase, in reality to plunder . . . for wine, for which we had paid forty-eight shillings a dozen, they bid four shillings. I could not stand this, and in a fit of desperation, I snatched up a hammer and broke up case after

case. . . . It may have been wrong, but I was too excited to think. There was no more of my own people to give it to, and I would rather not present it to our old foes. (167)

Here, the peculiar imperial value form generated by the exigencies of war collapses. The material objects that once gleamed as tokens of an imperial sociality become, once again, simply commodities that only communicate a price—and their prices are tanking. In an orgy of expenditure, Seacole smashes her goods to inhibit this reversion. In so doing, she tropologically reactivates the friend-enemy distinction that peace had dissolved, gesturing to the political determination that had only too recently regulated the immaterial value of her goods. Her hotel ruined, deprived of a home to which to return, the end of the war depresses Seacole. "Now and then," she relates, she "would see a lounger with a blank face, taking no interest in the bustle of departure, and with him I acknowledged to have more fellow-feeling than with the others, for he, as well as I, clearly had no home to go to" (164). "Had I not been happy through the months of toil and danger[?] What better or happier lot could possibly befall me?" It is only through the articulation of crisis and care that Seacole can accede to the status of imperial citizen, of Mother Seacole. The end of war leaves Seacole just another creole from an island Trollope will erase from the world.

Indeed, the very writing of her *Wonderful Adventures* works as a final attempt to surrogate a form of British imperial belonging premised not on market value but on politically and affectively saturated logics of reciprocity. Seacole returned to London bankrupt and mired in a legal dispute with her former partner, Day; her story is quite literally the last thing she has to sell. Fontaine relates that this is the fate reserved for failed peddlers, who, having traveled far, have "nothing to offer but themselves, and nothing to sell but words and a few printed sheets." Seacole joins Fontaine's peddlers in "turning themselves into storytellers, recounting the adventures which had brought them to their current audience and, like Ulysses, describ[ing] the worlds through which they had passed, transporting the villagers to other places."[68] Yet this self-described "female Ulysses" has a different relation to the tale she hawks (11). She is not only looking to achieve fiscal security through the sale of her narrative. She also seeks to pose recognition as an imperial citizen as a just reciprocation for her care work. The publication of her text calls in all of the debts owed to her, all of which are carefully recorded in her "book filled with hundreds of . . . names" of recipients of her care; as on the battlefield, the form of repayment consists more of tokens than of cash. Describing life in London upon her return, she states, "Where, indeed, do I not find friends," continuing:

> In omnibuses, in river steamboats, in places of public amusement, in quiet streets and courts, where taking short cuts I lose my way oft-times, spring up old familiar faces to remind me of the months spent on Spring Hill [in the Crimea]. The sentries at Whitehall relax . . . to give me a smile of recognition; the very newspaper offices look friendly as I pass them by; busy Printing-house Yard puts on a cheering smile, and the *Punch* office . . . sometimes laughs outright. Now, would all this have happened if I had returned to England a rich woman? Surely not. (170)

Such reciprocation does not substitute for fiscal support. Rather, money functions as one specific instantiation of a broader genre of imperial currency— smiles, letters, a lock of hair, cows, the loan of a boat, and so on—all of which facilitate the reproduction of the social. If Seacole were accorded citizenship in the British Empire, and if this empire ran not according to the norms of the market but more as something like the British Hotel, Seacole's lack of money would not matter at all. The affectionate attention she receives would be but a surface sign of the deep social, material, and political security she possesses.

Too Precious

Seacole's memoir had only just been published to much acclaim when she prepared, once again, to depart London for a scene of social crisis. It is as if the British public's reciprocation for the care she had bestowed on the empire's soldiers put her once more in the empire's debt; she had an obligation to discharge. "Give me," Seacole told a newspaper, "my needle and thread, my medicine chest, my bandages, my probe and scissors, and I am off."[69] News of her intention to travel once again had circulated to Jamaica by the time Trollope arrived. He wrote, "'My sister wanted to go to India,' said my landlady, 'with the army, you know.'"[70] She wanted to assist, that is, in the counterinsurgency operations following the rebellion of 1857. Another red cross on her map of the world, another chance to indebt the empire to her.

She never made it. "Queen Victoria," Seacole's sister explains, "would not let her [go to India]; her life was too precious" (12). Her sister is stretching reality a bit. For one thing, it would appear that Seacole had no personal relation with Victoria; they never even met. As Helen Rappaport argues, it is weird that they did not: Victoria served as the patron for a handful of well-known black Britons, and Seacole seems to have been a likely object of sovereign attention. Rappaport convincingly speculates that Seacole's failure to meet Victoria, as well as the minimal public support the queen extended to her faithful subject, were probably the result of a smear campaign conducted by Florence Nightingale. If Seacole's Caribbean cures probably struck Nightingale as so much creole quackery, the British Hotel definitely struck Nightingale as a bawdy house—despite the fact that Nightingale had never visited or spent much time herself at the front. "Anyone who employs Mrs Seacole will introduce much kindness—also much drunkenness and improper conduct wherever she is," Nightingale confided to her brother-in-law Sir Harry Verney, MP, in an letter from 1870 marked with the instruction, "Burn."[71] Referring to the queen's donation of £50 to the Seacole fund, she goes on to comment, "A shameful or ignorant imposture was practiced on the Queen who subscribed to the 'Seacole Testimonial.'"[72] Seacole was not who she and others said she was; she was a well-meaning but ill-doing purveyor of boozy cheer on the Crimean front. Bearing as it does the instructions that it be destroyed, Nightingale's letter allows us to speculate on the illegible activities through which archival and public illegibility is achieved.[73] Her letter's failure to efface its intervention, like Trollope's description of his obscuring Jamaica on the map, reveals neglect to be a practice and illegibility to be an instituted effect. Seacole would more or less be forgotten for a century after her death, and Nightingale certainly facilitated that process.

Nightingale's negative comments to Victoria might have prevented Seacole from gaining permission to provide succor in India. Much more prohibitive was the East India Company's ban on women who might attempt to replicate the Crimean trajectory of Seacole and Nightingale. There were plenty of such women, some veterans of the Crimean campaign. On 21 September 1857, a "nurse in the late war" who had served a "five month's residence in Scutari, under Miss Nightingale," responded to an article in the *Daily News* that had urged women to serve as nurses in India. British women, she responds, were in fact ready and eager to serve: "40 ladies (myself among the rest) have offered their services to Mrs. Seacole." The problem was that the East Indian Company would not let them, as is evident in a letter that the correspondent encloses. Written by James C. Melvill of the East India House, the letter expresses thanks to the would-be volunteers for their benevolence, only to inform them that every station and "force in the field" had a hospital already;

they were not needed. More important, Melvill continues, "No European women would be allowed to follow the camp."[74] Both the British Indian and metropolitan press were awash in tales of white women being raped and murdered by the insurrectionists; the lives and bodily integrity of "European women" could not be risked.[75] Seacole and her band of forty could not go.

Seacole's failed attempt to venture to India evinces her containment within an impossible dialectic. Her instituted inability to achieve robust imperial citizenship in liberal London impels her toward yet another zone of crisis, another place where fellow Britons might care that she cares for them. Yet despite being a few shades too dark, she is too British to be allowed into the scene of war. If only for a moment, she is secured within the pale of "European women." It is in this thin sense that Seacole is "too precious," as her sister claimed, to be risked in India: she is just as precious as any other women who might be legible according to such a minimalist and so expansive definition of the "European." The result is that Seacole's formal inclusion in the empire inhibits her from undertaking the practices that secured her substantive participation as an imperial citizen. Inclusion here functions as a mechanism of exclusion and the concern of the company as an instrument of abandonment. The ascription of a mode of belonging strips her of the means by which she realized that formal identification as a substantive form of life. With no field in which to practice, Seacole could not compel Britain to care that she cared for her sons. The circuit of debt and reciprocation through which she bound herself to empire, and empire to herself, was broken. She became a citizen without citizenship, an imperial subject without an imperial world. It is in this sense, perhaps, that Seacole truly deserves her position as the representative West Indian of the nineteenth century.

Coda

AMERICAS THAT WERE
AND AMERICAS TO COME

Through the era of free trade, Britain never formally abandoned the islands it could only cognize as worthless. As this study has shown, metropolitan Britons offered several reasons for why the imperial relation persisted. For Adam Smith and Anthony Trollope, imperial affects of pride and self-regard blocked Britons from pursuing their interests; for Earl Grey and George Cornewall Lewis, Britain owed its flailing dependencies a white man's debt of civilizing care; for antislavery activists, the islands were beacons of freedom in a world still turned by slavery. Yet to puzzle too much over why Britain never formally abandoned the islands is to miss the point of the great transformation that liberalization effected. The liberal, global order instituted by Britain converted the political tie of empire into an indifferent datum. The formal fact of political relation became negligible alongside the substantive reality of market value. The free-trade world of mid-Victorian Britain inaugurated a new nomos of the earth in which the West Indies were abandoned to a world system that was mostly indifferent to the question of whose flag flew over the islands' government houses.

But Britain's empire of free trade would not prove lasting. As Giovanni Arrighi notes, "The world began abandoning Britain's free trade system almost as soon as this system was established"; the vision of a pacific, postimperial world order, underwritten by free trade, would more or less collapse in the 1870s.[1] As imperial competitors increased in both number and power, as Germany and the United States cut themselves off from the global free market and scrambled for imperial space, the British public and British policy makers began to consider a return to empire as a politico-economic unit. The closing decades of the nineteenth century witnessed a proliferation of groups that supported the extension of preferential tariffs to colonial producers, the federation of empire into a formally instituted state, and a cultural reconceptualization of Britain as a "Greater Britain."[2] West Indians had promoted similar institutional measures as a solution to liberal Britain's rule through neglect, but the integrated empire projected in schemes so much like their own had no place for them within it. Greater Britain was to be a racial empire, a federated polity held together by economic preferences and shared Angloness.

Liberal Britain's swing back to an imperial thinking that nonetheless could not think the West Indies as integral to that empire would decisively shape West Indian thought and letters for decades to come. Indeed, it was in the context of this shift that national independence first emerged, for West Indians, as an imaginable, and even desirable, political future. As West Indians' political horizons slowly shifted from inclusion within empire to a rejection of it, the imaginative function of the Americas changed, as well. As anti-imperial nation-statism recentered empire in West Indians' political imaginaries, and as the nation-state emerged as the desired unit of political life, the West Indies slowly detached from the hemispheric world that Michel Maxwell Philip, George Numa Des Sources, and Mary Seacole began to build. The inchoate hemispheric polity whose emergence I have traced ultimately would prove to be, in Raúl Coronado's phrase, a "a world not to come."[3] The Americas would become a "fact on a map," a place to which one might migrate, yes, but not so much an otherworld of political potentiality.[4] The controversy surrounding James Anthony Froude's famously racist travelogue *The English in the West Indies; or, The Bow of Ulysses* (1888) marks the beginning of this transformation.

Froude was a disciple (and then biographer) of Thomas Carlyle; his discussion of the West Indies traveled in the tracks his master laid in "Occasional Discourse on the Negro Question" (1849). Very simply, the West Indies— and black West Indians—required the strong and active governance of white people so the islands might once more achieve "the days of plantation prosperity."[5] Froude notes that thinking on empire had indeed shifted: "We no longer talk of cutting our colonies adrift; the tone of public opinion is changed, and no one dare to advocate openly the desertion of the least important of them. *But the neglect and indifference continue*" (333; emphasis added). This neglect is emblematized, for Froude, by an estate he has visited: "The house was empty, in charge of servants." The absence of the (presumably) white owner, combined with the spectacle of black servants autonomously running the owner's estate, leads Froude to a melancholic reflection: "What would become of it all, if Jamaica *drifted* after her sisters in the Antilles, as some persons thought she was drifting, and became, like Grenada, an island of small black proprietors? Was such a fate really hanging over her?" Froude would answer negatively: "Not necessarily, not by any law of nature" (220–21; emphasis added). The fate of the island was the responsibility of men—white men. To prevent Jamaica from "drifting" and becoming a de facto self-governing island of blacks, Britons had to "restring the bow of Ulysses" and recommit to empire building in the West Indies.

Froude's barbarous racism—particularly toward Haitians, whom he insisted ate babies—ensured that his volume would receive negative press in the West Indies (55). But barbarous racism alone hardly accounts for the intensity of the responses that Froude would receive; after all, black intellectuals in the islands were accustomed to reading, and responding to, white travelers' publishing of stupid, nonsensical, vile things about the West Indies and West Indians.[6] If racism alone cannot account for the volubility of the responses, it is equally important to consider these antiracist critiques of Froude alongside the fact that Froude's desire for imperial reconsolidation would have found allies—though many of them antiracist, to be sure—in the antiliberal thinkers who peopled the prior century of West Indian letters. Indeed, possible allies still existed. From his adopted home of Boston, the black Kittsian poet George Reginald Margetson would publish a long poem decked out with a *very* Froudean title: *England in the West Indies: A Neglected and Degenerating Empire* (1906). Ornamented with an epigraph from Goldsmith's "Deserted Village" (1770), Margetson's poem complains that the poverty of the islands pushes West Indians out of the empire to seek a livelihood—that "destitution sits o'er all the plain, / Driving her sons to wander o'er the main."[7] For Margetson, imperial neglect was an effect of economic liberalism, just as it had been for his literary forebears and just as it was for Froude.[8] Froude could have been finessed to align with dominant tendencies in West Indian thought.

He was not. The first significant challenge to Froude came from Demerara in the form of "Mr. Froude's Negrophobia; or, Don Quixote as a Cook's Tourist" (1888) by N. Darnell Davis, a Grenada-born imperial civil servant and amateur historian.[9] In 1889, two more responses would follow. Written by a career colonial administrator whose various posts included one in Nevis, Charles Spencer Salmon's *The Caribbean Confederation* included a rebuttal to Froude even as it promoted (yet another) plan to federate the individual islands of the West Indies into a regional state. More famously, the Trinidadian mulatto John Jacob Thomas would publish *Froudacity: West*

Indian Fables by James Anthony Froude. Thomas's text would have a long afterlife, eclipsing the texts of Davis and Salmon. *Froudacity* was republished in 1969 with an introduction by C. L. R. James, and Thomas would come to be remembered as an "important 19th century liberal thinker and Caribbean nationalist."[10] His argument that West Indians were capable of self-government articulated neatly with the "vindicationist" arguments put forth by mid-twentieth-century anticolonial nationalists, as David Scott might put it.[11] Indeed, one scholar would applaud Thomas's "vindication of the cultural singularity and self-directive capabilities of each of the territories in question."[12] Recently, scholars have become far more circumspect regarding the politics of Thomas's text; as Faith Smith has shown, Thomas reinscribes problematic assumptions regarding race, gender, sexuality, and class.[13] Still, *Froudacity* remains a landmark text in the development of creole anticolonialism and anti-imperialism.[14]

Froudacity's monumental status in the history of West Indian thought is intimately linked to the fact that it marks a stark point of transformation in the political unconscious of the West Indies. *Froudacity* did not simply cut ties with empire in the name of an anticolonial nationalism; it also cut ties with the empire-centered political and literary tradition that preceded him. As we have seen, for roughly a century "anticolonial" had served as a term that West Indians deployed to smear the thought and practice of liberal political economy. With *Froudacity*, West Indian intellectuals began to make preparations for what thinkers such as Smith, John Ramsay McCulloch, and Richard Cobden had long desired: the exit of the islands from the empire. Read in the context of this history, the fact that creole elites' aspirations for national sovereignty overtook old desires for a seat at the imperial table marks the creeping adequation of West Indian political imaginaries to the world fashioned by the epistemology and institutional structure of economic liberalism. We can see this transformation at work in the rather bizarre alliance that Thomas made with Salmon through their joint critiques of Froude. What made this alliance so bizarre? The title page of *The Caribbean Confederation* proudly declares Salmon to be a "Member of the Committee of the Cobden Club," and, indeed, Salmon's book would agitate for the wholesale liberalization of all West Indian markets.[15] For perhaps the first time, a creole of color and a Cobdenite would come to substantive agreement on matters of West Indian and imperial policy. Thomas's preface makes a "heartfelt acknowledgement" of Salmon's tract, declaring that it has been "gratefully accepted by myself as an incentive to self-help" (17). Thomas's critique of Froude's imagined empire of white rule displaces several of the principles that organized West Indian political culture during the high era of British liberalism, including a desire for a strong imperial state and a critical refusal of political economic thought. Creole nationalism had absorbed Cobdenite liberal anticolonialism.

In the local terms of Thomas's critique, this absorption occurs in part because Froude's racism is irreducibly linked to his critique of economic liberalism. The incipient black self-rule that Froude fears is an effect of Britain's subordination of the political logics of imperial sovereignty to the logics of political economy. Jamaica will "drift" into the hands of blacks because the islands have been set adrift and abandoned to a world of liberal capitalism. Coming upon a ship full of Jamaicans migrating to "the Darien pandemonium" to labor on the canal, Froude critiques liberal political economy by adopting a position of racialized imperial solicitude: "I found the whole mass of them reduced into the condition of the pigs who use to occupy the foredeck in the Cork and Bristol packets. They were lying in a confused heap together, helpless, miserable, without consciousness apparently, save a sense in each that he was wretched. *Unfortunate brothers-in-law! Following the laws of political economy,* and carrying their labour to the dearest market, where, before a year was out, half of them were to die. They had souls too, some of them, and honest and kindly hearts" (170; emphasis added). Froude's critique of the deleterious consequences of economic liberalism was one that West Indians had made for a century. For Froude, the "laws of political economy" have violated the "laws of nature," and the effects of this violation are figured through these "helpless, miserable" black laborers. Froude's critique also arrives at an identical normative conclusion: imperial intervention. Yet, the racialization of this intervention—Froude's pig-like migrants lack consciousness and even souls—would prevent most West Indians from finding an ally in Froude. Froude wants white Britons to assume their natural position of sovereign solicitude over West Indian blacks to prevent this "drift" unto death, whereas, as we have seen, creoles wanted this solicitude to derive from their recognition as imperial citizens.

In his response to Froude's strong articulation of an antiliberal empire with white supremacy, Thomas's antiracist critique winds up condoning the effects that economic liberalism has had on the islands. Where Seacole laments the fate of migrant workers in the Panama transit zone without attempting to recuperate their losses, Thomas chastises Froude for not recognizing the "heroism of the emigrants to the Canal." Then, in the name of vindicating black laborers, Thomas suggests that black West Indians have been model liberal subjects:

> Apart from Mr. Froude's direct testimony to the fact that from year to year . . . there has been a continuous, scarcely ever interrupted emigration of Negroes to the Spanish mainland, in search of work for a sufficing livelihood for themselves and their families . . . there would be enough indirect exoneration of the Black Man from that indictment in the wail of Mr. Froude and his friends regarding the alarming absorption of the lands of Grenada and Trinidad by sable proprietors. Land cannot be bought without money, nor can money be possessed except through labour, and the fact that so many tens of thousands of Blacks are now the happy owners of the soil . . . ought to silence for ever an accusation, which . . . come[s] from the lips of the Eumolpids who would fain impose a not-to-be-questioned yoke on us poor helots of Ethiopia.[16]

Here, black laborers' modest economic advances are adduced as vindicating evidence for black West Indians' capacity for self-rule. This vindication, however, requires that Thomas reproduce the norms that organize British liberalism: the West Indian migrant laborer comes to resemble the possessive individual of liberal thought. The polity that Thomas projects is not opposed or superordinate to the market; rather, its feasibility is materialized through the successes that blacks have met with as they have sold their labor, saved money, and bought land. The problem, of course, is not black ownership of land; it is, rather, the evidentiary use to which this phenomenon is put. The thin fraternity that Froude decried—the derivation of "brothers-in-law" from the "laws of political economy"—is reinterpreted to provide the basis for black self-rule. By submitting to the "laws of political economy," Thomas's black laborers show their fitness for political self-direction.

Thomas then leverages this figuration of the self-possessive, self-helping black West Indian to critique the imperial state form that Froude would reinvigorate. Given this creole bootstrapping, what was the role of imperial and colonial states? What form should they take? Thomas adduces the colonial magistracy as evidence of the fact that imperial offices and officers only ever interfered with West Indian development. Trinidad's stipendiary magistrates, he argues, "far from being bulwarks to the weaker as against the stronger, have, in their own persons, been the direst scourges that the poor, particularly when coloured, have been afflicted by in aggravation of the difficulties of their lot" (85). For Thomas, the judicial and police powers of the magistracy underwrite the total power of the state; the unaccountability, violence, and oppressive nature of this state apparatus metonymizes that of the existent empire state in general (85). An upstanding middle-class subject, Thomas was hardly a police abolitionist. Rather, his point is that the empire's direct involvement in the organization of West Indian society, figured here through the magistracy, inhibits Trinidadians from inhabiting the narrative arc that begins with wage labor and ends with land ownership. The imperial state blocks West Indian development. The self-possessive, liberal subject of interests implied in the narrative subsequently grounds the state reforms that Thomas advocates: "We, the said Colonies, being an integral portion of the British Empire, and having, in intelligence and every form of civilized progress, outgrown the stage of political tutelage, should be accorded some measure of emancipation therefrom. And thereby we—White, Black, Mulatto, and all other inhabitants and tax-payers—shall be able to protect ourselves against the self-seeking and bold indifference to our interests which seem to be the most cherished expression of our rulers' official existence" (148). Here, Thomas mobilizes the idiom of "indifference" *not* to urge the formation of a more attentive, caring, and egalitarian imperial state, as West Indians had for the century prior. Instead, he mobilizes it to advance a devolution of imperial powers to representative colonial legislatures and to insular elites. (As Roberto Marquez notes, Thomas "replaces Froude's pigmentocratic oligarchy with the gathering colored middle class's notion of meritocracy," envisioning a Trinidad "as democratic as rule by a patriciate of the 'most competent and able' from among the elite will allow.")[17] Thomas is quite vague on the institutional and constitutional fabric of the empire in the wake of such devolution—on what, in short, empire would be. But this vagueness is its own answer: it would not be much of anything at all. Indeed, it is as if the racialization of imperial solicitude evident in Froude's text rendered the idea of a nonracist, egalitarian empire unthinkable. Yet as we saw in chapters 3 and 4, creole empire loyalists through the era of free trade had steadfastly combatted liberal thinkers' equation of colonial subjects' desire for imperial protection with an admission of racial debility. Ironically, it is Thomas's absorption of liberal economic thinking that enables him to call it quits with the cruel optimistic fantasies that his predecessors set to work to contest the constitution of liberal empire. The problem of neglect dissipates as the self-possessive subject becomes, as such a subject must, a self-protecting one, too.

As the principles of economic liberalism began to supply the epistemic and institutional scaffolding for the forms of political autonomy that creoles found imaginable and desirable, it became increasingly impossible to imagine empire as a viable state form. Empire replaced economic liberalism as the antagonistic object that animated creole politics, the condition that West Indians wished to negate. The status of the Americas consequently shifted. As we have seen, when midcentury creoles' cruel optimistic relationship with the empire shattered, they did not move forward toward a nationalist future. They moved laterally—imaginatively and physically—toward the Americas. This lateral movement owed in part to creole thinkers' feeling that a free black state would not be viable within an antiblack state system, that they would leave themselves vulnerable to seizure by the U.S. empire of slavery. More important, the American turn emerged out of West Indians' sense that empire as such was not the irresolvable problem; economic liberalism and the colonial state form was. In this context, the Americas served as a scene not of postimperial sovereignty but of antiliberal poiesis. If the collapse of slavery made a black nation-state practically possible, the liberalization of hegemonic political imaginaries made it all but necessary. As a result, the to-hand form of the autonomous state replaced the improvisatory, hemispheric collectivities forged in days past.[18]

This reconstitution and relocation of the horizon of West Indian political desire would both restructure and be structured by West Indian literature. In the early decades of the nineteenth century, Jamaican writers such as H. G. de Lisser and Thomas MacDermot (alias Tom Redcam) wrote local-color novels intended for consumption by a West Indian reading public; with its yard fiction, the Trinidadian Beacon group wrote similar, if grittier, stories.[19] This localist fiction ultimately gave rise to the anticolonial practice of "writing back" to the imperial metropole, a vindicationist program (in the mode of Thomas) that construes the literary as an antagonistic scene wherein the colonial subject seeks recognition as an autonomous producer of her own culture, history, and people.[20] Crucially, neither the localist nor the vindicationist mode of literary writing required a rejection of Britishness. Indeed, performances of Britishness, assertions of cultural capacity, and rising demands for political autonomy mutually intensified one another, as the pre-Marxist career of C. L. R. James—Arnold devotee, creole nationalist, and colonial Victorian—demonstrates. Emergent anticolonial nationalisms could be accommodated within the framework of empire loyalism, a framework that persisted through the world wars.[21]

As West Indian writers increasingly dedicated themselves to writing (to) the local or back to Britain, the earlier practice of writing with the Americas waned. To be sure, West Indian migration to the Americas only intensified in this period: West Indians traveled to Panama to build the canal and to the United States to work on farms and in cities.[22] West Indian radicals traveled through the Americas, and West Indian writers and artists achieved many successes publishing in the United States.[23] U.S. businesses invested more and more in the islands, and U.S. military interventions throughout the region would only intensify after the publication of *Froudacity*.[24] But the function of the Americas within the West Indian literary and political imaginary had decisively shifted. As West Indian writers increasingly wrote in the horizon of the nation-state, they decreasingly needed the Americas as a site through which to improvise antiliberal, non-nation-statist collectivities. In Thomas's hands, for instance, citations of black uplift in the United States provide analogical grounds for his claims regarding the developmental capacities of black men in the West Indies. As the nation form entrenched itself in West Indian political imaginaries, the Americas signaled economic possibilities or political problems, not political potentialities. On the cusp of independence, V. S. Naipaul would melancholically recover the entangled, hemispheric history of colonial Trinidad, pondering how the islands might change if they oriented their cultural and political desires toward the Americas.[25] But the political fantasies articulated a century earlier were more or less forgotten; George Lamming was not alone in imagining that he and his generation were the West Indies' first novelists, poets, and playwrights.[26] The vagaries of colonial print reception and transmission coupled with the transformed problem-space of West Indian politics to hide most of the authors treated in this study from view.

Of course, there is nothing about the Americas that necessitates that they signal such political potentialities or engender the fantasies I have explored. Geographical contiguity need not yield political, affective, or cultural intimacy, and it is indeed okay if the Americas remain a fact on the map. It is not, however, the hemisphere that matters in this history of occluded hemispheric relation; it is the political poiesis that materialized those relations that we would do well to remember. Liberalization stripped West Indians of the political world to which they nonetheless remained attached, but they were not stripped bare. They repaired their abandonment by one world by building new worlds—ephemeral, fleeting collectivities that were antiliberal, at times anticapitalist, at times antistatist. If few of the subjects I have explored were or considered themselves radicals, their visions and projects were. Circumstance compelled it. Today, as the accumulation requirements of capital convert states throughout the world into instruments of abandonment, as our own cruel optimistic investments in the state bind our political imaginaries to worlds bound to fail, we have much to learn from them. There are other new worlds out there, waiting to be made, if we can learn to want to make them.

$\mathscr{Notes}$

Introduction

1. Smith, *The Wealth of Nations*, 456, *passim*. The very term "mercantilism" has been subjected to analysis—some critical, some recuperative—for more than a century now. Neither Smith nor his predecessors used the term, and scholars tend to agree that it names more a heterogeneous set of practices than a definable economic theory or doctrine. For a recent overview of these debates, see Stern and Wennerlind, *Mercantilism Reimagined*. For the sake of brevity, I refer to Smith's text throughout this book by its popularized, truncated title.

2. The classical text on this moment is Schuyler, *The Fall of the Old Colonial System*. I have also drawn heavily on Howe, *Free Trade and Liberal England*.

3. I am adopting this term from Polanyi, *The Great Transformation*.

4. See Edwards, *The History, Commercial and Civil, of the British West Indies*, 2:567, 2:579.

5. Thomas Hobbes is as good a figure for this conceptualization as any. As Carl Schmitt puts it in a very Hobbesian moment, "The *protego ergo obligo* is the *cogito ergo sum* of the state": Schmitt, *The Concept of the Political*, 52. West Indians tended to reverse the line of this dictum, presenting obligation and dependence as the normative ground of protection. Indeed, Schmitt would himself mark the possibility of a philosophical transaction between the West Indies and Hobbesian thought through a citation to Richard Ligon's *A True and Exact History of the Island of Barbados* (1657). Ligon writes, "And truly these vegetatives, may teach both the sensible and reasonable Creatures, what it is that makes up wealth, beauty, and all harmony in that *Leviathan*, a well governed Commonwealth: Where the Mighty men, and Rulers of the earth, by their prudent and carefull protection, secure them from harmes; whilst they retribute their paynes, and faithfull obedience, to serve them in all just Commands": Ligon, *A True and Exact History of the Island of Barbados*, 20–21. For a broader reading of the political connotations of protection and obligation, see Skinner, *Visions of Politics III*, 264–86. See also Schmitt, *The Leviathan in the State Theory of Thomas Hobbes*. On Ligon and Hobbes, see Parrish, "Richard Ligon and the Atlantic Science of Commonwealths."

6. Williams, *Capitalism and Slavery*, 132.

7. For a general history of Jamaican emancipation attuned to the impact of political economy, see Holt, *The Problem of Freedom*. I discuss this at length in chapter 2.

8. For a description of this shift from an illuminating world-systems perspective, see Tomich, *Through the Prism of Slavery*.

9. Disraeli's description of the "forlorn Antilles" is cited in Williams, *Capitalism and Slavery*, 144. For the "millstone," see Monypenny, *The Life of Benjamin Disraeli*, 385.

10. Koebner and Schmidt, *Imperialism*, 27.

11. See Macpherson, *The Political Theory of Possessive Individualism*; Mehta, *Liberalism and Empire*.

12. I am inspired by Hadley, *Living Liberalism*; Kazanjian, "The Speculative Freedom of Colonial Liberia"; Mantena, *Alibis of Empire*; Sen, *Empire of Free Trade*.

13. See Muthu, *Enlightenment against Empire*; Pitts, *A Turn to Empire*.

14. Pitts, *A Turn to Empire*, 242.

15. For a critique of intentionalist recuperations, see Mantena, *Alibis of Empire*, 188. The history of rescuing liberalism by rescuing liberals' intentions is a far longer historiographical tradition, dating back to the "Adam Smith Problem" in nineteenth-century Germany: see Montes, "Das Adam Smith Problem."

16. See Said, *Culture and Imperialism*, 80–97.

17. Neglect comes from the Latin *ne-* (not) and *legere* (pick up, gather). *Legere* is a cognate of the Greek *legein* or *logos* (neglect, *v.*): *Oxford English Dictionary*, online ed. (Oxford: Oxford University Press, 2003), http://www.oed.com, accessed 18 March 2015.

18. On the contemporary U.S. reception of free trade, see Palen, *The "Conspiracy" of Free Trade*. For an ethnography of banana workers responding to neoliberal initiatives in the 1990s in St. Lucia, see Slocum, *Free Trade and Freedom*.

19. "Former slaves and former masters agreed that the Sugar Duties Act signaled not merely the expansion of free trade but also the empire's abandonment of its Caribbean colonies and its backpedaling on antislavery principles, making a rare moment when the two groups' interests aligned. Their concurrence quickly vanished after 1846": Lightfoot, *Troubling Freedom*, 90.

20. I am indebted to Berlant, *Cruel Optimism*, for help thinking through the ways that subjects manage binding to bad objects.

21. Rancière, *Dissensus*, 33.

22. Key texts in the development of hemispheric studies include Belnap and Fernandez, *Jose Marti's "Our America"*; Brickhouse, *Transamerican Literary Relations and the Nineteenth-Century Public Sphere*; Gruesz, *Ambassadors of Culture*; Saldívar, *The Dialectics of Our America*.

23. I draw the term "surrogation" from Roach, *Cities of the Dead*, 2.

24. For work that thinks through the relationship between the British West Indies and the Americas, see Goudie, *Creole America*; Goudie, "Toward a Definition of Caribbean American Regionalism"; Watson, *Caribbean Culture and British Fiction*.

25. Paul Giles warns us against "simply replacing nationalist essentialism . . . with a geographical essentialism predicated on physical contiguity": Giles, "Commentary," 49. Martha Schoolman has recently argued that scale was itself a problematic that historical subjects—particularly abolitionists—addressed and that literary scholarship should trace these scalar shifts, not impose them: Schoolman, *Abolitionist Geographies*.

26. For other scholarship on this archive, see Cudjoe, *Beyond Boundaries*; Edmondson, *Caribbean Middlebrow*; Rosenberg, *Nationalism and the Formation of Caribbean Literature*; Smith, *Creole Recitations*.

27. From the perspective of canon-forming compendiums such as John Ramsay McCulloch's *A Select Collection of Early English Tracts on Commerce* (1856) or from the vantage of canon-forming narratives offered in texts like Joseph Schumpeter's *History of Economic Analysis* (1954), one could draw the conclusion that West Indians never contributed to economic theory at all.

28. See Burnard, *Mastery, Tyranny, and Desire*, 113. For West Indians' broader involvement in the British polity, see Gauci, *William Beckford*. For their engagements with Enlightenment philosophy and science, see Roberts, *Slavery and the Enlightenment in the British Atlantic*. On West Indians' parliamentary presence, see Franklin, "Enterprise and Advantage"; Higman, "The West India 'Interest' in Parliament"; Ragatz, *Fall of the Planter Class in the British Caribbean*, 52.

29. On reading apparent ignorance as motivated refusal, see Lloyd and Thomas, *Culture and the State*, 81.

30. A smattering of examples includes MacDonnell, *Free Trade*, 464; Premium, *Eight Years in British Guiana*, 58; Telfair, *Some Account of the State of Slavery at Mauritius*, xiii. The term "anticolonial" and the label "anticolonial party" were also extended to abolitionists. See [Anonymous], *Sketches and Recollections*, 256, 259–60; and Barclay, *A Practical View*, 377, 383.

31. Edwards, *The History, Commercial and Civil, of the British West Indies*, 2:482.

32. MacDonnell, *Colonial Commerce*, xii.

33. MacDonnell, *Colonial Commerce*, x.

34. See Drescher, *The Mighty Experiment*, 34–53. I discuss this in chapter 2.

35. As David Beck Ryden notes in his study of abolition, "What is striking about these defenders of the trade in Africans was their conviction that the abolition movement was part of a conspiracy to undermine the 'old colonial system.' From the planters' perspective, then, the abolition of the British slave trade was not simply a threat to their labor supply, but, a challenge to their entire political and economic philosophy": Ryden, *West Indian Slavery and British Abolition*, 7. The defense of the African trade—and, later, slavery—was not only a defense of slavery in itself, but was also a defense of the empire.

36. Smith, *The Wealth of Nations*, 665.

37. Smith, *The Wealth of Nations*, 34.

38. Poovey, *A History of the Modern Fact*, 236–49.

39. I draw the concept of disembedding from Polanyi, for whom the embeddedness of an economic structure marks its nonautonomy and functional reliance on kin and political institutions: Polanyi, *The Great Transformation*.

40. See the work of Jack Greene, who mobilizes the concept of an "imperial constitution" to think regularity in the absence of form: Greene, *Negotiated Authorities*; Greene, *Peripheries and Center*. As Gould writes, "Even within the subordinate polities of Ireland and the British colonies in North America and the Caribbean, Parliament's theoretical supremacy remained hedged about by the competing claims of provincial assemblies and a variety of customary local rights and privileges": Gould, "A Virtual Nation," 482. For recent discussions of the legal and juridical incoherence of Britain's Atlantic empire, see Benton, *A Search for Sovereignty*; Hulsebosch, *Constituting Empire*;

Kostal, *A Jurisprudence of Power*; MacMillan, *Sovereignty and Possession in the English New World*.

41. See Pettigrew, *Freedom's Debt*.

42. See "The Humble Petition of the Poor People of Jamaica and Parish of St. Ann's," in Harvey and Brewin, *Jamaica in 1866*, 101–3.

43. Dumont, *From Mandeville to Marx*, 34.

44. As just one instance of the earlier usage, the Samuel Estwick, agent for Barbados, writes, "To the crown and dignity of the king I owe the firmest loyalty and attachment, and to his person and government all due allegiance; so long as in the judgment of the public, and as by his coronation-oath, as well as by law, he is bound to do, he shall protect, and no longer, the constitutional liberties of his subjects. I say, I owe all *due* allegiance, because allegiance and protection are terms of reciprocal duties only": Estwick, *A Letter to the Reverend Josiah Tucker*, 17. For the use of "protection" in the process of its semantic recentering, see Stephen, *The Slavery of the British West India Colonies Delineated*, 1:xxxviii.

45. For a fantastic account of the generic—and, I would argue, epistemic—separation of economic from literary writing, and literature's counterformation in relation to this separation, see Poovey, *Genres of the Credit Economy*, 87–153.

46. Orderson, *Creoleana*, v.

47. Orderson, *Creoleana*, vi.

48. For a similar claim about the natural scientific work literary genres performed in the black Atlantic, see Rusert, *Fugitive Science*.

49. See, for instance, Lazarus, *The Postcolonial Unconscious*, 36; Quayson, *Calibrations*, xi–xl.

50. See Guru, "How Egalitarian Are the Social Sciences in India?"

51. See Sommer, *Foundational Fictions*. For an overview of how the nineteenth century has largely been expelled from West Indian literary historiography, see Rosenberg, *Nationalism and the Formation of Caribbean Literature*, 1–12.

52. West Indian archives remain woefully underdigitized, inhibiting a broader distribution of the intense primary research work that goes into archival excavation. Exploring the National Archives in Britain and in Trinidad, however, made it clear to me that colonial newspapers from an early period published poetry, serialized stories, and so on—and this is surely true of other islands with presses. Simply collating this material would amply expand the available archive of nineteenth-century West Indian literature. At present, we see only the tip of the iceberg—a handful of republished novels.

53. Cooper, *Citizenship between Empire and Nation*, 1. For another brilliant attempt to think decolonization beyond nation-state formation, see Wilder, *Freedom Time*. For contemporary politics of nonsovereignty in the Caribbean, see Bonilla, *Non-sovereign Futures*.

54. For another take on contingency, imperial breakdown, and nation-state formation, see Adelman, *Sovereignty and Revolution in the Iberian Atlantic*, 258.

55. Sartorius, *Ever Faithful*, 28.

56. Burton, *Empire in Question*, 22.

57. Kelly and Kaplan, "Nation and Decolonization," 427. See also Louis and Robinson, "The Imperialism of Decolonization." For a historically rich, theoretical recovery of anticolonial thinkers' and politicians' attempts to remake the world order in the name of sustaining postcolonial sovereignty, see Getachew, *Worldmaking after Empire*.

58. As Alexander Motyl notes, "Empire, as a distinctly *political* system, has received scant attention from social scientists." Part of the reason, he suggests, is that empire simply became a term of political invective—particularly in the late Cold War—with Ronald Reagan's critique of the "evil empire": Motyl, *Imperial Ends*, 1.

59. Stoler, "On Degrees of Imperial Sovereignty," 137.

60. Wimmer and Schiller, "Methodological Nationalism, the Social Sciences, and the Study of Migration."

61. Indeed, Seeley's attempt to reconceptualize British history as Greater British history was articulated explicitly in the horizon of free trade: Seeley, *The Expansion of England*, 73. For a rather partisan account of free trade, primed by the collapse of the liberal project in the early twentieth century, see Walker-Smith, *The Protectionist Case in the 1840s*.

62. For Polanyi, as for Lenin and then Rosa Luxemburg, imperialism was a means by which nation-states negotiate global crises of accumulation—a falling rate of profit in conditions of monopoly capital, difficulties of realizing surplus in the metropolitan center, and so on. Taking the late-century scramble for Africa as paradigmatic, these accounts accord the nation analytical and ontological precedence over empire. As a consequence, empire itself is never conceived of as a collective or corporate political subject; rather, empire is the institutional scaffolding through which the real collective subjects of the world system (state-backed capitalists in Britain, the United States, Germany, and so on) exercised their power. I do not dispute the adequacy of this analysis to late Victorian imperial expansion. My concern is to stress that the analytic detachability of empire from the nation in these accounts was an epistemic and institutional *effect* of liberalization. Center-left (Polanyi) and Marxist (Lenin, Luxemburg) conceptualizations of empire *as* imperialism share economic liberalism's epistemological frame: See Lenin, *Imperialism, the Highest Stage of Capitalism*; Luxemburg, *The Accumulation of Capital*.

63. See, e.g., Howe, *Free Trade and Liberal England*; Parry, *The Politics of Patriotism*, esp. 184–91. Schonhardt-Bailey, *From the Corn Laws to Free Trade*, rigorously mobilizes incredible data sets to demonstrate how Cobdenites "nationalized the interest" in the repeal of the Corn Law—but nationalizing here marking a scaling *up* from the local, not *down* from the imperial.

64. Gallagher and Robinson, "The Imperialism of Free Trade," 1–15. Following Gallagher and Robinson, Bernard Semmel tracks how the anti-imperial epistemics of political economy rather seamlessly converted into free-trade imperialism: Semmel, *The Rise of Free Trade Imperialism*.

65. Smith, *The Wealth of Nations*, 1028; emphasis added.

66. The phrase is from Richardson, *Moral Imperium*.

67. As Alexandra Franklin remarks, "The year 1833 marked the lowest ebb of West Indian planter power in Britain": Franklin, "Enterprise and Advantage," 257.

68. Cobden, *The Political Writings of Richard Cobden*, 290.

69. See McCulloch, "Colonial Policy," 303.

70. For an exhaustive account of the formation of policies of responsible government, see Ward, *Colonial Self-Government*. On Britain's civilizing mission, see esp. Hall, *Civilising Subjects*. See also chapter 3 of this book.

71. Indeed, as Karuna Mantena argues, the "civilizing" alibi would be dropped after the rebellion of 1857, leading to the emergence of forms of indirect rule—that is, to practices of governance that created even greater distance between ordinary imperial subjects and the British polity: Mantena, *Alibis of Empire*, 11.

72. Stoler, "On Degrees of Imperial Sovereignty," 127.

73. For a detailed overview of these debates, see Ryden, *West Indian Slavery and British Abolition*, 7–33. As Ryden notes, critiques of Williams's argument—or, more accurately, what critics take to be Williams's argument—has had the effect that "the West Indies are written out of the story of the humanitarian victory of 1807": Ryden, *West Indian Slavery and British Abolition*, 12.

74. As Williams put it, "The slave trade was abolished in 1807, slavery in 1833, the sugar preference in 1846. The three events are inseparable": Williams, *Capitalism and Slavery*, 136. The point here—which is missed when critics read Williams's argument from the punctum of a single date, 1807—is that Williams wants to back read a diffuse systemic causality from the vantage of the consequences that attended and accumulated with each legislative moment. To be sure, Williams *does* occasionally inhabit a conspiratorial, intentionalist idiom, one in which a cabal of Manchester Men rigged abolitionism to free capital. (Such conspiratorialism is a frequent politico-methodological recourse of progressive critiques of capitalism that cannot commit to an anticapitalism, which Williams did not.) But his point is rather that abolitionism, emancipation, and then obviously free trade were all *functional* for a form of capital seeking to divest itself of a previous generation's bad investment.

75. "But this industrial development, stimulated by mercantilism, later outgrew mercantilism and destroyed it": Williams, *Capitalism and Slavery*, 106. Earlier, he describes this dialectic of production and destruction as configuring Caribbean history as a "relay race," in which "the first to start passed the baton, unwillingly we may be sure, to another and then limped sadly behind": Williams, *Capitalism and Slavery*, 7.

76. Martin, *An Empire of Indifference*, 131.

77. One might suggest that the forms of life and political imaginations developed by black West Indians were indigenous to empire. I am hesitant to describe this dynamic in such terms; Shona Jackson has importantly shown how creoleness became fashioned into a form of pseudo-indigeneity, and frequently through appropriative erasures of extant indigenous populations: Jackson, *Creole Indigeneity*.

78. Burbank and Cooper, *Empires in World History*, 2.

79. Scott, *Conscripts of Modernity*.

80. For the classical account of racial capitalism, see Robinson, *Black Marxism*.

81. Indeed, the contemporary field of new imperial studies was founded on such reparative maneuvers in relation to economic transformations within the British Commonwealth: see Armitage, "Greater Britain."

82. There were some metropolitan Britons who articulated imperial imaginaries that tracked those developed by black and white West Indians—most notably the systematic colonizers in the form of Edward Gibbon Wakefield, imperial federationists, and Tory protectionists. Yet the racialization of imperial belonging through the 1840s and 1850s had the effect of muting West Indians presence even in projects to unify the empire politically: see Bell, *The Idea of Greater Britain*. Still, there was certainly a gap between metropolitan and colonial understandings as to what imperial belonging entailed. Writing of the period of the American war for independence, P. J. Marshall argues, "The bulk of the British political elite seem to have judged empire in terms of material costs and benefits. . . . A view of the British empire as embodying a common set of values had been much more strongly held in the coloniaes than in Britain itself": Marshall, *Remaking the British Atlantic*, 7.

83. Motyl, *Imperial Ends*.

84. See, among others, Biehl, *Vita*; Povinelli, *Economies of Abandonment*; Standing, *The Precariat*; Wright, *Disposable Women and Other Myths of Global Capitalism*.

85. See, e.g., Goudie, *Creole America*; O'Shaughnessy, *An Empire Divided*; Pares, *Yankees and Creoles*; Rugemer, *The Problem of Emancipation*.

86. Rodrigo Lazo has recently figured this deficit of subjectivity as the "impossibility" of building an archive of the hemisphere: Lazo, "The Invention of America Again," 751–71.

87. O'Shaughnessy, *An Empire Divided*, 238–48.

88. For another narrative along these lines, but centered more on (what becomes) Colombia's ties to, and eventual disentanglement from, the transimperial western Caribbean, see Bassi, *An Aqueous Territory*.

89. See, e.g., Delany, *The Condition, Elevation, Emigration, and Destiny of the Colored People of the United States*, 195–96.

90. In making this argument, I am holding onto the hope that Fred Moten never stops articulating through a long sequence of engagements with the problem of black "social death" first given a name by Orlando Patterson and then rearticulated by Afropessimist scholars such as Jared Sexton. As Moten puts it in a clarification of his position, "What I assert is this: that black life—which is as surely to say *life* as black thought is to say *thought*—is irreducibly social; that, moreover, black life is lived in *political death* or that it is lived, if you will, in the burial ground of the subject by those who, insofar as they are not subjects, are also not, in the interminable (as opposed to the last) analysis, "death-bound," as Abdul JanMohamed . . . would say": Moten, "Blackness and Nothingness," 739. This death to the social, for Moten, opens the possibility of a fundamental reordering of the world. He writes, "[Blackness] instantiates and articulates another way of living in the world, a black way of living together in the other world we are constantly making in and out of this world, in the alternative planetarity that the intramural, internally differentiated presence—the (sur)real presence—of blackness serially brings online as persistent aeration, the incessant turning over of the ground beneath our feet that is the indispensable preparation for the radical overturning of the ground that we are under": Moten, "Blackness and Nothingness," 778–79.

91. Weheliye, *Habeas Viscus*, 131. Along these lines, Christina Sharpe argues, "Even as we experienced, recognized, and lived subjection, we did not *simply* or *only* live *in* subjection and *as* the subjugated": Sharpe, *In the Wake*, 4.

92. Naipaul, *The Loss of El Dorado*, 353.

Chapter 1. The Political Economy of Neglect

1. Torrens, *An Essay on the Production of Wealth*, 229–30.

2. Mill, "Colonies," 31.

3. For a brief overview of Torrens's position on free trade, see Irwin, "The Reciprocity Debate in Parliament."

4. See Semmel, *The Rise of Free Trade Imperialism*.

5. See Hilton, *The Age of Atonement*; Hilton, *Corn, Cash, Commerce*.

6. On this point, see the classic argument in Gallagher and Robinson, "The Imperialism of Free Trade."

7. Arguments in favor of continuity date back at least to Harlow, *The Founding of the Second British Empire*, which is concerned to see Britain's "swing to the East" as a process coextensive with empire building in the Americas. See also Cain and Hopkins, "Gentlemanly Capitalism and British Expansion Overseas. I"; Cain and Hopkins, "Gentlemanly Capitalism and British Expansion Overseas. II. New Imperialism"; Cain and Hopkins, "The Political Economy of British Expansion Overseas"; Marshall, *The Making and Unmaking of Empires*.

8. See Guttridge, "Adam Smith on the American Revolution."

9. See, e.g., McCulloch, "Colonial Policy—Value of Colonial Possessions"; Smith, *The Empire*, 44; Spence, *Britain Independent of Commerce*, 88.

10. For some of these critiques, see Gambles, *Protection and Politics*; Goldman, "The Origins of British 'Social Science.'"

11. I draw this term from Foucault, *Archaeology of Knowledge*, 187.

12. The topic of West Indian decline is vexed within the historiography, due to attempts to locate the logic of emancipation within—or without—structural changes in the British and West Indian economies. For an overview of this historiography, see Ryden, "Does Decline Make Sense?"

13. Tomich, *Slavery in the Circuit of Sugar*, 26. See also Tomich, *Through the Prism of Slavery*.

14. Williams, *Capitalism and Slavery*, 132.

15. See, e.g., Spence, *The Radical Cause of the Present Distresses of the West-India Planters*, 103.

16. Williams, *Capitalism and Slavery*, 144.

17. For an overview of early receptions of Smith's work, see Teichgraeber, "Less Abused Than I Had Reason to Expect."

18. Edwards, *The History, Commercial and Civil, of the British West Indies*, 2:482.

19. Poovey, *Genres of the Credit Economy*, 87–153.

20. Baker, *Securing the Commonwealth*, 5.

21. The classical text on this mode of imperial governance is Henretta, *Salutary Neglect*.

22. [Anonymous], *Jamaica: A Poem*, iv.

23. Smith, *The Wealth of Nations*, 1028.

24. MacDonnell, *Colonial Commerce*, xiii. In a representative critique of political economy's tendency to devalue empirics in favor of abstraction, Lowe writes, "In the prosecution of his researches, the Author has been much aided by Sir William Young's West-India Common-Place Book, and Mr. Bosanquet's Pamphlets on the State of our Colonies. The one affords a valuable collection of documents, accompanied by judicious observation—the other abounds with sound and liberal views. In the former, we perceive how much information may be attained by the national representative, who will collect and digest the instructive material submitted to the Legislature—in the other, we have an example (as yet too rare among our merchants) of the benefits which the theory of commerce may derive from applying a stock of practical knowledge to the formation of general views. How many merchants are rich in experimental information; and how little has political economy, the most important of sciences, profited by their exertions!": Lowe, *An Inquiry into the State of the West Indies*, xviii–xix.

25. Tribe, *Genealogies of Capitalism*, 138.

26. Steuart, *An Inquiry into the Principles of Political Economy*, 1:ix.

27. Pownall, *A Letter from Governor Pownall to Adam Smith*, 3–4.

28. Smith, *Correspondence of Adam Smith*, 257.

29. Milgate and Stimson, *After Adam Smith*, 68.

30. Smith, *The Wealth of Nations*, 34.

31. A fact capitalized on by Arrighi in *Adam Smith in Beijing*.

32. Hume, *Political Essays*, 137; Smith, *The Wealth of Nations*, 573.

33. Smith, *The Wealth of Nations*, 745.

34. Poovey, *A History of the Modern Fact*, 242, 247.

35. Smith, *The Wealth of Nations*, 501.

36. See Milgate and Stimson, *After Adam Smith*, 48, 94.

37. Quoted in Winch, *Classical Political Economy and Colonies*, 6.

38. Winch, *Classical Political Economy and Colonies*, 20.

39. Anderson et al., "Adam Smith in the Customhouse," 755; Smith, *The Wealth of Nations*, 716–17.

40. Smith, *The Wealth of Nations*, 666.

41. Smith, *The Wealth of Nations*, 485.

42. It should be noted that, in terms of concrete policy recommendations, Smith's desires for the postrevolution commercial order of the Atlantic at times jived with the desires of planter elites. For instance, Smith recommended that trade between the recently founded United States and the British West Indies "be allowed to go on as before, arguing, "Any interruption or restraint of commerce would hurt our loyal much more than our revolted subjects": Smith, *Correspondence*, 271. Here, Smith advocates

a free-trade regime between the United States and the West Indies in the name of the latter's imperial attachments.

43. Long, cited in Carrington, *The Sugar Industry and the Abolition of the Slave Trade*, 23. Carrington appears to think that these words originate from Long. Long was most likely extracting quotes from Burke for the preparation of *The History of Jamaica*, although this quotation does not make it into the completed text. His commonplacing slightly alters the original. See Burke, *Observations on a Late State of the Nation*, 48.

44. MacDonnell, *Colonial Commerce*, 59–60. MacDonnell's Yorkshire quip seems to be repurposing James Mill's utilitarian critique of mercantilist restrictions within the empire: "Is it not exactly the same sort of policy, as if Yorkshire were to be drained and oppressed for the benefit of Middlesex?" Mill, "Colonies," 22.

45. See Edwards, *The History, Commercial and Civil, of the British West Indies*, 2:567, 2:579. For a concise history of the origins of tariff protections, see Davis, "The Rise of Protection."

46. Smith, *The Wealth of Nations*, 660–75. This political formalism—which defines the polity through the coherence of institutional forms—would go on to prime the emergence of British legal positivism with John Austin's *The Province of Jurisprudence Determined* (1832). At several key moments, Austin grounds the effectivity of the sovereign's command through reference to the economic structure of the empire, insisting that the political sovereign can unilaterally dissolve economic compacts and even empire itself. Once again, the effect is to delaminate the political from the economic; and, once again, empire is costed out of Britain: see Austin, *The Province of Jurisprudence Determined*, 26, 53–57.

47. McCulloch, *A Statistical Account of the British Empire*, 1:1.

48. McCulloch, "Colonial Policy—Value of Colonial Possessions," 303.

49. Poovey, *Making a Social Body*, 9.

50. Atherton's letter to Gale is published in *The Gale-Morant Papers* (Wakefield, U.K.: Microform Academic Publishers, 1977). All letters to and from Gale in this chapter are drawn from this source; subsequently, I will only cite the name of the author, the addressee, and the date in identifying each letter. This letter is dated 27 January 1783.

51. A position often associated with Eugene Genovese, like whom I will, at certain points, sound: see Genovese, *Roll, Jordan, Roll*.

52. See Tomich, *Through the Prism of Slavery*.

53. See, e.g., Hancock, *Citizens of the World*.

54. For a discussion of formal and real subsumption, see Marx, *Capital*, 1:975–1018. See also Banaji, *Theory as History*, esp. 280, 320, 329–30.

55. Hall, "Incalculability as a Feature of Sugar Production during the Eighteenth Century." Hall's account is Weberian and ideal-typical in outline. Hall's "incalculability" thesis is refined in Best and Polanyi Levitt, *Essays on the Theory of Plantation Economy*.

56. I take the phrase—and much else—from Muldrew, *The Economy of Obligation*.

57. My thinking on Atlantic epistolary culture draws heavily on Bannet, *Empire of Letters*; Pearsall, *Atlantic Families*.

58. Steele, *The English Atlantic*, 265.

59. Derrida, *The Post Card*, 33, 45.

60. It is kind of a late early modern twist on the neoliberal entrepreneurial subject, who, according to Berlant, must "emit desire and identification with the affective ties of collegiality to make networks of shared obligation seem more grounded and permanent than the corporation will support structurally": Berlant, *Cruel Optimism*, 218.

61. Butler, *The Economics of Emancipation*, 92–108.

62. See O'Shaughnessy, *An Empire Divided*.

63. Catherine Harding to William Gale, 10 October 1777.

64. I draw here on Berlant, *The Female Complaint*.

65. Pearsall, *Atlantic Families*, 2.

66. Harding to Gale, 10 October 1777.

67. Pearsall, *Atlantic Families*, 126.

68. Harding to Gale, 8 April 1778.

69. Harding to Gale, 29 July 1780.

70. Higman, *Plantation Jamaica*, 102.

71. Higman, *Plantation Jamaica*, 100.

72. Harding to Gale, 5 October 1780.

73. Harding to Gale, 20 June 1778.

74. Overproduction was thus identified quite early as a key cause of plantations' decline: see, e.g., Spence, *The Radical Cause of the Present Distresses of the West-India Planters*, 17. As Ryden notes, "The defenders of the West Indian interest, such as Edward Long, were correct in highlighting the decentralized nature of the industry. He argued that unlike the 'India house in Lead[e]n hall street, [who are] . . . the sole legal Vendore of Tea,' Jamaican planters enjoyed no such privilege as a single body and were forced to operate in a competitive marketplace. There was no incentive for individual farmers to attempt to raise prices through curbing production": Ryden, "One of the Fertilest Pleasentest Spotts," 40.

75. Conder, *Wages or the Whip*, 44.

76. Indeed, Harding would remark in 1780 that, despite her need for enslaved humans and despite their availability a few months prior to writing, "the general scarcity of provisions" had prevented her from purchasing any: Harding to Gale, 13 May 1780.

77. Harding to Gale, 8 April 1778.

78. Pearson, "The Secular Debate on Economic Primitivism," 5.

79. Polanyi, "Aristotle Discovers the Economy," 73.

80. For a literary analysis of novels of obligation from the period, see Skinner, *Sensibility and Economics in the Novel*. Skinner traces a retrenchment in the narrativization of obligation through the course of the revolutionary period. In effect, new ideologemes of independence pathologized dependence, with the effect that "in the name of independence, all forms of assistance are withdrawn from the poor"—in both imaginative and real ways: Skinner, *Sensibility and Economics in the Novel*, 164. At the same time, the sociality of obligation persisted, even if the citation of obligation became less effective for and from particular subject positions (such as "the poor").

81. Harding to Gale, 5 October 1780.

82. Harding to Gale, 17 April 1783.

83. Blake, *Observations on the Principles Which Regulate the Course of Exchange*, 103.

84. Bosanquet, *Thoughts on the Value to Great Britain, of Commerce in General*, 29.

85. For Drax's manual and a critical introduction, see Thompson, "Henry Drax's Instructions on the Management of a Seventeenth-Century Barbadian Sugar Plantation." Drax's instructions were originally published as an appendix to Belgrove, *A Treatise upon Husbandry or Planting*.

86. Martin, *An Essay upon Plantership*. Gordon Turnbull insisted that his work was "not originally intended for the public eye"; instead, it was intended for the private use of a young planter: Turnbull, *Letters to a Young Planter*, n.p. For a similar example of a private-to-public trajectory, see Anonymous, *Practical Rules for the Management and Medical Treatment of Negro Slaves*, 8.

87. The quote is from Hall, *Civilising Subjects*, 107. In terms of plantation governmentality, Justin Roberts has offered the most robust consideration of the work regimes articulated in these genres, arguing that creole elites harnessed various Enlightenment-era innovations to intensify plantation work. My problem with his approach is that his conception of economic rationality is rather monochromatic: it marks a subjective disposition realized through the adoption of certain technologies (the clock, the calendar, accountancy) that is uninflected by the problem of the valorization process. Weber is not named, but he is there: Roberts, *Slavery and the Enlightenment in the British Atlantic*.

88. "The balance of expressed opinion was usually so heavily against them that merchants and planters preferred to work within the more congenial and conventional network of governmental bureaus and sympathetic ministers": Drescher, *Capitalism and Antislavery*, 96. See also chapter 2 in this book.

89. MacQueen, *The West Indies Colonies*, xvi. Dumas argues that pro-slavery thought was "distributed throughout urban Great Britain for an intended audience of elite, politically active Britons": Dumas, *Proslavery Britain*, 5.

90. See, e.g., MacQueen, *The Colonial Controversy*, 133–72.

91. Gordon Turnbull riffs on Machiavelli so much as to advise, "He [the planter] should, at the same time, endeavour to make the slaves love as well as fear him": Turnbull, *Letters to a Young Planter*, 45.

92. Martin, *An Essay upon Plantership*, 9.

93. Roughley, *The Jamaica Planter's Guide*, 364. Hereafter, page numbers from this work are cited in parentheses in the text.

94. Derrida, *The Beast and the Sovereign*, 94–95.

95. For comparison, see the instructions from Drax appended to Belgrove, *A Treatise upon Husbandry or Planting*, 85–86.

96. Drax, in Belgrove, *A Treatise upon Husbandry or Planting*, 57–58.

97. Drax, in Belgrove, *A Treatise upon Husbandry or Planting*, 62.

98. Turnbull, *Letters to a Young Planter*, 36.

99. Martin, *An Essay upon Plantership*, 10.

100. Martin, *An Essay upon Plantership*, 10.

101. Martin, *An Essay upon Plantership*, 10–11.

102. See O'Shaughnessy, *An Empire Divided*, 247.

103. Martin, *An Essay upon Plantership*, 10.

104. Anonymous, *Marly*, 327. Hereafter, page numbers from this work are cited in parentheses in the text.

105. "From his graphic delineations of scenery and manners, no man who has seen the West Indies will doubt of his having been resident there." Stephen mines "the descriptive passages" from "that new champion of the planters . . . who has assumed the guise of a novelist." As we will see, the question of disguise is central to the narrative of *Marly*: Stephen, *The Slavery of the British West India Colonies Delineated*, 2:106, 2:145.

106. On the importance of the figure of the Bonnie Prince to eighteenth-century novelistic attempts to map spheres of social circulation, see Lynch, *The Economy of Character*, 86–94.

107. Karina Williamson, "Introduction," in Anonymous, *Marly*, xvi.

108. For a discussion of Scottish-Jamaican patronage networks, see Karras, *Sojourners in the Sun*.

109. Watson, *Caribbean Culture and British Fiction in the Atlantic World*, 35.

110. Watson, *Caribbean Culture and British Fiction in the Atlantic World*, 19.

111. Oldroyd et al., "The Culpability of Accounting Practice in Promoting Slavery"; Oldroyd et al., "Monetising Human Life."

112. Bookkeepers were typically drawn from the Atlantic poor, and they functioned as objects of sympathy for both pro-slavery and abolitionist observers of Jamaica's plantation economy. For one first-person account, see M'Mahon, *Jamaica Plantership*.

113. For an analogous scene, see Anonymous, *Montgomery*, 2:100–123.

114. See, e.g., "Mr. Huskisson's Motion for the Reduction of the Sugar Duties," in Huskisson, *The Speeches of the Right Honorable William Huskisson*, 3:595–612.

115. Edwards, *The History, Commercial and Civil, of the British West Indies*, 2:350.

116. MacDonnell, *Colonial Commerce*, x.

Chapter 2. "Them Worthless Ones"

1. "Negro and Stock Accounts 1777–1837," in *The Gale-Morant Papers* (Wakefield UK: Microform Academic Publishers, 1977).

2. These marks are not "ditto" marks, as I initially suspected. To verify this, I calculated the imputed values on the page on which Simon appears (£4,790 total, assigning Simon no value) and subtracted the accumulated total to be carried forward to the page (£11,795) from the accumulated total carried forward to the next (£16,585). Simon had no value. For a reading of the "ditto ditto" of the ever-accumulating archive of black death, see Sharpe, *In the Wake*, 52, 56.

3. "Negro and Stock Accounts 1777–1837," in *The Gale-Morant Papers*.

4. In his discussion of pre- and postemancipation accountancy practices of the Worthy Park estate in Jamaica, Michael Craton writes, "Although the Apprentice work force

of 1834–1838 had already been reduced to those at least potentially capable of work, there was bound to be an immediate further trimming with full emancipation. Unlike the slave lists, which included in work categories many who were temporarily or even permanently unemployable simply because the state was responsible for them, the Worth Park wage books included only those who actually worked": Craton, *Searching for the Invisible Man*, 278–79.

5. This was not universally true. On the York Plantation of Jamaica, for instance, accounts were kept of the free children of apprentices attached to the estate. The status of these children produced a great deal of contention between apprentices (particularly their mothers) and plantation operators: see Vasconcellos, "'To Fit You All for Freedom.'"

6. On possible ugly effects of emancipation in the United States, see Downs, *Sick from Freedom*. For an exploration of valuelessness as it relates to land in the West Indies through the period of emancipation, see Picken, "Rendering Empire," 116–67.

7. Phillips, *West India Question*, 13.

8. *Report of the Proceedings of the Anti-Slavery Meeting*, 7.

9. Williams, *A Narrative of Events*, 17.

10. The phrase is, of course, Foucault's: Foucault, *"Society Must Be Defended,"* 241.

11. On this trope and for a general history of the relationship between the social sciences and emancipation, see Drescher, *The Mighty Experiment*.

12. As Thomas Holt notes, political economy served as a mode of perception: "The ideals of classical political economy shaped what many of the special magistrates observed, what they reported, and how they 'instructed' the freed people"—this insight should be extended to British imperial administrators, antislavery activists, and even the hyper-mediated words of Jamaican ex-slaves themselves: Holt, *The Problem of Freedom*, 77.

13. See Stephen, *Antislavery Recollections*, 213; Tyrell, "The 'Moral Radical Party' and the Anglo-Jamaican Campaign for the Abolition of the Negro Apprenticeship System," 490.

14. Turley, *The Culture of English Antislavery*, 225.

15. I draw this phrase from Thompson, *Models of Value*.

16. See Poovey, *A History of the Modern Fact*. As I argue in the first chapter, Poovey's bracketing of empire from her consideration is an analytically dubious move, insofar as regimes of modern factuality consolidated themselves *against* empire. More to the point here, and as this chapter explores, antislavery liberals made use of the entire apparatus of modern fact production to render legible the ugly effects of emancipatory liberalism.

17. Archibald Palmer, a Scottish physician who served as a special magistrate in Apprenticeship-era Jamaica and as Williams's amanuensis, lamented in 1837 that "hitherto all the efforts made by the friends of the negro, instead of diminishing the amount of suffering, had actually increased it:" *Horrors of the Negro Apprenticeship System in the British Colonies*, 15.

18. Sturge and Harvey, *The West Indies in 1837*, 62. Unlike in most colonies, the legislative assembly in Antigua elected to forgo a period of Apprenticeship and declared full freedom on 1 August 1834.

19. Foucault, *Security, Territory, Population*, 107. On colonial governmentality, see Scott, *Refashioning Futures*.

20. On expressions of gratitude and allegiance, see Eudell, *The Political Languages of Emancipation in the British Caribbean and the U.S. South*, 43; Henry, *Emancipation Day*, 226–27; Sheller, *Citizenship from Below*, 103–4. In the Parliamentary committee on Apprenticeship convened in 1836, special magistrate Richard Robert Madden testified to the desires of ex-slaves to come before the state, but also the *disinclination* of the state to foment this mode of address. "[Chairman.] Has there been any public notification given to the negro population of the readiness of the governor to receive their petitions:— [Madden:] No, certainly not; it would not be desirable to give such a public notification, for if you did you would have all the negroes in the island flocking to Spanish Town": PP, 1836 (560) XV, "Select Committee on Negro Apprenticeship in Colonies," 79. The journals of special magistrates are also invaluable sources: see, e.g., Anderson, *Between Slavery and Freedom*.

21. For the Jamaican case, see Bakan, *Ideology and Class Conflict in Jamaica*. On Demerara, see da Costa, *Crowns of Glory, Tears of Blood*. As da Costa stresses, one of the inciting incidents of the revolt was the belief among slaves that the "good King had sent orders that they should be free" that colonial slaveholders withheld: da Costa, *Crowns of Glory, Tears of Blood*, 216. For a broader black Atlantic take on monarchism and sovereignty, see Landers, *Atlantic Creoles in the Age of Revolutions*; Thornton, "I Am the Subject of the King of Congo."

22. The phrase was common, and even circulated by the imperial state to the emancipated. "The people of England are your friends and fellow-subjects," as the Governor of Jamaica, the Marquess of Sligo, informed newly minted apprentices in a proclamation issued on Emancipation Day: quoted in Madden, *A Twelvesmonth's Residence in the West Indies*, 2:256.

23. Bentham, *Emancipate Your Colonies!* 13.

24. Smith, *The Wealth of Nations*, 299.

25. Bentham, *Emancipate Your Colonies!* 42.

26. Bentham, *Emancipate Your Colonies!* 45.

27. Bentham, *Emancipate Your Colonies!* 42.

28. Wilberforce, *An Appeal to the Religion, Justice, and Humanity of the Inhabitants of the British Empire*, 26–27.

29. Drescher, *The Mighty Experiment*, 35; Schuyler, "The Constitutional Claims of the British West Indies," 3–4. For one contemporary example of assertions of nonactuated sovereignty, see Canning, *Select Speeches of the Right Honourable George Canning*, 423.

30. Fogel and Engerman, *Time on the Cross*.

31. Drescher, *The Mighty Experiment*, 63.

32. Drescher, *The Mighty Experiment*, 64.

33. For this experiment, see Dickson, *The Mitigation of Slavery*.

34. Stephen, *The Slavery of the British West India Colonies Delineated*, 1:xlii.

35. Taylor, *Negro Emancipation and West Indian Independence*, 7.

36. Taylor, *Negro Emancipation and West Indian Independence*, 16.

37. The major possible exception is the Scots-Jamaican mulatto and Spencean socialist Robert Wedderburn, but his politics were less nationalist than radically (and almost anarchically) autonomist. Indeed, the radical free colored press in Jamaica evinced the kind of "empire loyalism" I discussed earlier: see Razi, "Coloured Citizens of the World."

38. The claim and dating are Davis's: see Davis, "James Cropper and the British Anti-Slavery Movement," 161.

39. Davis, "James Cropper and the British Anti-Slavery Movement," 244.

40. Cropper, *Relief for West-Indian Distress*, 16.

41. Cropper, *Relief for West-Indian Distress*, 8–9.

42. Cropper, *Relief for West-Indian Distress*, 29.

43. Cropper, *A Review of the Report of a Select Committee . . .* , 8.

44. *The Correspondence between John Gladstone*, 2.

45. *The Correspondence between John Gladstone*, 6.

46. Cropper, *The Support of Slavery Investigated*, 23.

47. Cropper, *A Review of the Report of a Select Committee . . .* , 22.

48. On the period of "Second Slavery" that followed—and was facilitated by—British liberalization, see Tomich, *Through the Prism of Slavery*, 56–75. I address this more in chapter 3.

49. According to Poovey, for followers of Humean epistemics one came to knowledge "not by moving stepwise from observed particulars to ever greater levels of generalization but by immediately effacing the specificity of the particular in favor of what one believes about the system": Poovey, *A History of the Modern Fact*, 230–31.

50. Indeed, the Statistical Society of London was founded in the same year that emancipation was decreed. As Lawrence Goldman writes, "The real bond [of the society] came from an intellectual contempt for the method of Ricardian economics as it was developed in the 1820s and 1830s and a related desire to base economic and social analysis on inductive procedures": Goldman, "The Origins of British 'Social Science,'" 594. This turn to inductive empiricism, as Anna Gambles notes, was common to Tory imperialists, as well: Gambles, *Protection and Politics*.

51. Similarly, Robert Wilmot-Horton argued about abolitionists' devaluation schemes, "They [abolitionists] reason thus: . . . the poorer the Proprietor of the sugar estate becomes,—the less assistance he is enabled to receive, the greater the difficulties with which he is embarrassed,—the sooner will he be obliged to give up the cultivation of sugar altogether; and in his abandonment of sugar cultivation is involved the interest of his Slaves. But these gentlemen totally forget the misery and wretchedness to which the Slaves must be exposed, when the only chance which remains for the Master to continue that cultivation, which is his sole stake in life, is the keeping himself up to the level of average profits by overworking the Slave, whose extra labour is to supply him with the means of obtaining those profits": Wilmot-Horton, *The West India Question Practically Considered*, 53–54.

52. Cropper, *The Support of Slavery Investigated*, 13.

53. Cropper, *Relief for West-Indian Distress*, 23.

54. As McCulloch would write in the fourth edition of *Principles of Political Economy*, "We are, indeed, strongly impressed with the conviction that, in the end, the cultivation

of the sugar-cane, on a large scale, will have to be abandoned in all those parts of the New World in which slavery is suppressed": McCulloch, *Principles of Political Economy,* 439. This was a new claim based on his interpretation of the results of the emancipation project. For planters' fears of imminent decline, see Curtin, *Two Jamaicas*; Lobdell, "Patterns of Investment and Sources of Credit in the British West Indian Sugar Industry," 32. For a dissenting view, see Ward, "Emancipation and the Planters."

55. See Davis, "James Cropper and the British Anti-Slavery Movement," 256.

56. On the conceptual problem of imperium in imperio and slavery, see Ghachem, *The Old Regime and the Haitian Revolution,* 29–76.

57. Draper, *The Price of Emancipation,* 107.

58. Marquess of Sligo, "To the Newly Made Apprentices of Jamaica," in PP, 1835 (278-I) L, "Papers in Explanation of Measures to Give Effect to Act for Abolition of Slavery," 43.

59. Goodlad, *Victorian Literature and the Victorian State,* 35.

60. Richard, *Memoirs of Joseph Sturge,* 2:279.

61. See Polanyi, *The Great Transformation.*

62. Holt, *The Problem of Freedom,* 53.

63. Marquess of Sligo, "To the Newly Made Apprentices of Jamaica," 43.

64. For an account of the composition of Williams's *Narrative,* see Paton, "Introduction," in *A Narrative of Events,* xxx–xxvii.

65. Williams, *A Narrative of Events,* 2.

66. Williams, *A Narrative of Events,* 26.

67. Madden, *A Twelvemonth's Residence in the West Indies,* 113.

68. The phrase comes from Sligo's anonymous critique of Apprenticeship. An overseer, fined for violating apprentices under his control, responds to the magistrates, " 'It is not me, but the apprentices you are punishing; you don't think I will pay a penny of that myself: oh no; I will sell as much of their allowance fish as will pay it, instead of giving it to them, and they will then be the losers, not I.' This was not uttered from the angry impulse of the moment, but from cool calculation": Browne [Marquess of Sligo], *Jamaica under the Apprenticeship System,* 93.

69. 3 and 4 Will. 4, cap. 73, "An Act for the Abolition of Slavery throughout the British Colonies; for Promoting the Industry of the Manumitted Slaves; and for Compensating the Persons Hitherto Entitled to the Services of Such Slaves," 28 August 1833, available at http://www.pdavis.nl/Legis_07.htm.

70. On the payout structure, see Draper, *The Price of Emancipation,* 104. On the divestment of funds, see Draper, *The Price of Emancipation,* 267–78, 272.

71. Madden, *A Twelvemonth's Residence in the West Indies,* 200.

72. Hall, *Free Jamaica,* 19.

73. See his extended testimony in PP, 1836 (560) XV, "Select Committee on Negro Apprenticeship in Colonies," esp. 79.

74. See Burn, *Emancipation and Apprenticeship in the British West Indies,* 175–76.

75. Paton, *No Bond but the Law,* 59.

76. Mbembe, "Necropolitics," 40.

77. Williams, *A Narrative of Events,* 5.

78. Williams, *A Narrative of Events*, 12.

79. Williams, *A Narrative of Events*, 24.

80. Williams, *A Narrative of Events*, 6.

81. One of James's fellow apprentices, Edward Lawrence, reported to an investigative committee that James "had been a watchman" and that though "old and weakly" he was "working in the field in the great gang at the time he received his flogging": Testimony of Edward Lawrence in "Investigation by the Commissioners of Inquiry into the Case of James Williams, and other Apprenticed Labourers," in PP, 1838 (154-I) XLIX, "Papers Presented to Parliament," 160. James's age is noted in the same text, at p. 156.

82. Williams, *A Narrative of Events*, 6–7.

83. On the saturation of West Indian slave narratives with the idiom of law, see Aljoe, *Creole Testimonies*, 93–118.

84. Williams, *A Narrative of Events*, 13 (italics in the original).

85. Williams, *A Narrative of Events*, 18–19.

86. On the relationship between abolitionist writing and legal forms of address, see DeLombard, *Slavery on Trial*.

87. Prince, *The History of Mary Prince*; Warner, *Negro Slavery Described by a Negro*.

88. See Prince, *The History of Mary Prince*, 2–4, esp. the editorial note on p. 4.

89. Williams, *A Narrative of Events*, 5.

90. Williams, *A Narrative of Events*, 25.

91. Turley, *The Culture of English Antislavery*, 121.

92. *Horrors of the Negro Apprenticeship System in the British Colonies*, 11.

93. See, above all, Hartman, *Scenes of Subjection*, chap. 1.

94. I draw here from Moten, "Knowledge of Freedom," 275.

95. For the general outlines of this history, see Altink, *Representations of Slave Women in Discourses on Slavery and Abolition*.

96. Drescher, *The Mighty Experiment*, 34–53.

97. Drescher, *The Mighty Experiment*, 43.

98. For a general history of the Order, see John, *The Plantation Slaves of Trinidad*, 20–36. As it pertains to the reproduction of the enslaved, see John, *The Plantation Slaves of Trinidad*, 121–59. On a previous order from 1800, see Higman, *Slave Populations in the Caribbean*, 350. For the previous paucity of imperial legal regulations relating to slavery, see Goveia, *The West Indian Slave Laws of the 18th Century*, 19. See also the chapter 1 in this book.

99. The act prohibiting rape was passed in 1826: see Altink, "Deviant and Dangerous," 221.

100. Hall, *Civilising Subjects*, 108.

101. See, e.g., Ramsay, *Essay on the Treatment and Conversion of African Slaves in the British Sugar Colonies*, 75–76. See also Sheridan, *Doctors and Slaves*.

102. The phrase is Foucault's: see Foucault, *Security, Territory, Population*, 79.

103. Drescher, *The Mighty Experiment*, 146.

104. Drescher, *The Mighty Experiment*, 146.

105. See Morgan, *Laboring Women*.

106. Altink, *Representations of Slave Women in Discourses on Slavery and Abolition*, 28.

107. Fortunati, *The Arcane of Reproduction*, 72.

108. Another way to put this, for Marxists, is that enslaved women were not reproducing labor-power; they were reproducing laborers: see Fortunati, *The Arcane of Reproduction*, 7–32.

109. Williams, *A Narrative of Events*, 17

110. For other narratives that indicate the importance of Christianity for self-valorization outside the relations of slavery and Apprenticeship, see Warner-Lewis, *Archibald Monteath*.

111. *A Statement of Facts*, 2.

112. *A Statement of Facts*, 4.

113. For a comparable discussion of the interplay between numerical and nonnumerical strategies of representing black demographic and mortality trends prior to the abolition of the slave trade, see Perry, "A Traffic in Numbers."

114. *A Statement of Facts*, 2.

115. *A Statement of Facts*, 10.

116. *A Statement of Facts*, 10.

117. Altink, *Representations of Slave Women in Discourses on Slavery and Abolition*, 30–31.

118. *A Statement of Facts*, 10.

119. *A Statement of Facts*, 10.

120. *A Statement of Facts*, 10.

121. On treadmills and the scandals they occasioned, see Paton, *No Bond but the Law*, 83–120.

122. *A Statement of Facts*, 10.

123. *A Statement of Facts*, 10.

124. *A Statement of Facts*, 11.

125. For a brilliant study of the social meaning of death in Jamaica, see Brown, *The Reaper's Garden*

126. Spillers, "Mama's Baby, Papa's Maybe," 80.

127. "Investigation by the Commissioners of Inquiry into the Case of James Williams, and Other Apprenticed Labourers," in PP, 1838 (154-I) XLIX, 141.

128. Williams, *Narrative of Events*, 86.

129. "Investigation by the Commissioners of Inquiry into the Case of James Williams," 164.

130. "Investigation by the Commissioners of Inquiry into the Case of James Williams," 166.

131. Williams, *A Narrative of Events*, 96. The letters that follow are included as appendices in the *Narrative*.

132. Williams, *A Narrative of Events*, 96.

133. Williams, *A Narrative of Events*, 97.

134. Williams, *A Narrative of Events*, 98, 100.

Chapter 3. Imperial Abandonment

1. Philip, *Emmanuel Appadocca*, 62. Hereafter, page numbers for this work are cited in parentheses in the text.

2. See Polanyi, *The Great Transformation*. For other work on British free trade from social-science perspectives, see Howe, *Free Trade and Liberal England*; Schonhardt-Bailey, *From the Corn Laws to Free Trade*; Trentman, *Free Trade Nation*.

3. As J. P. Parry puts it, liberalization "suggested the impending end of the formal colonial connection, in line with other departures from *ancien regime* ideals. . . . The fall of the old protectionist colonial system in the 1840s seemed to challenge the value of a formal empire even more": Parry, *The Politics of Patriotism*, 189.

4. Greg, "Shall We Retain Our Colonies?," 220.

5. See Elliot, *The Poetical Works of Ebenezer Elliott*. For an assessment of the broader ways that British culture absorbed and responded to free trade, see Çelikkol, *Romances of Free Trade*.

6. Tomich, *Through the Prism of Slavery*, 63.

7. See Dunckley, *The Charter of the Nations*. In his biography of the protectionist politician Lord George Bentinck, Disraeli describes the debates over free trade as "the great contention between the patriotic and the cosmopolitan system"; patriotism entailed a belief in empire's enduring value. John Barnard Byles would similarly link "anti-colonial and cosmopolitan theories": Disraeli, *Lord George Bentinck*, 379. See also Byles, *Sophisms of Free-Trade*, 108.

8. On the emergent idiom of "imperial reciprocity," see, e.g., *Annual Register* 188 (1846): 189. On the "imperial compact," see chapter 1 in this book.

9. Cobden, *The Political Writings of Richard Cobden*, 1:290.

10. "Petition from the Inhabitants of Trinidad, Interested in the Cultivation of Sugar, Praying for Measures of Relief," *House of Commons Papers* 193 (1848): 2.

11. For this common usage, see, e.g., Premium, *Eight Years in British Guiana*, 15, 60, 70, 72.

12. For an account of political economy and empire, see chapter 1 in this book.

13. Cheryl Schonhardt-Bailey, for instance, describes the Anti-Corn Law League as "nationalizing the interest" in the repeal of the Corn Law—but nationalizing here marks as a scaling *up* from the local, not *down* from the imperial: Schonhardt-Bailey, *From the Corn Laws to Free Trade*, 75–106.

14. Burbank and Cooper, *Empires in World History*, 2.

15. Here I am methodologically borrowing from João Biehl's ethnographic exploration of madness in neoliberal Brazil. For Biehl, the mad speech of his subjects is a form of semiosis split from contextual conventions that would accord such speech semantic value; at the same time, the very articulation of this speech indexes the mad subject's insistence on maintaining a relation to the world. As he puts it, "The overpowering phenomenology of what is generally taken and treated as psychosis lies not in the psychotic's speech but in the actual struggles of the person to find her place in a changing reality vis-à-vis people who no longer care to make her words and actions meaningful." As Biehl stunningly

demonstrates, mad speech in fact offers an agentive mapping of the transformations in discursive convention and worldly structure that produced and abandoned subjects to madness. Mad speech, in other words, faintly indexes the displaced world—the discursive contexts and conventions dissolved through the process of abandonment—in which the speaking subject was once recognized and legible as being a part: Biehl, *Vita*, 18.

16. Cyrus Francis Perkins, "The Planter's Petition," in Perkins, *Busha's Mistress*, 158.

17. My thinking about the creole complaint is heavily indebted to Berlant, *The Female Complaint*.

18. Perkins, "The Planter's Petition," 158. In the published edition, the "grey" is uncapitalized, which is almost certainly an error in transcription. I thank Paul Lovejoy for his help in clarifying this small matter.

19. "Since the era of the Reform Bill, which virtually shut the House of Commons against our colonial proprietors, we are almost totally unrepresented in it. . . . The Reform Bill . . . has closed the only avenue by which the voice of our colonies can reach the ears of the people's representatives, and, as a natural consequence, the feeling of indifference to colonial interests is becoming more and more manifest every succeeding year among Members of Parliament," complained the pseudonymous planter Barton Premium: Premium, *Eight Years in British Guiana*, 196.

20. In writing this section, I have drawn heavily on Blakeley, *The Colonial Office*; Cell, *British Colonial Administration in the Mid-Nineteenth Century*; Hall, *The Colonial Office*. This work is, of course, rather dated, particularly in terms of method. My approach to the papered materiality of governance draws on Burns, *Into the Archive*; Hull, *Government of Paper*; Kafka, *The Demon of Writing*.

21. Cited in Higgins, *Third Letter to Lord John Russell*, 28–29 (italics in the original).

22. Cited in Higgins, *Third Letter to Lord John Russell*, 30–31.

23. Stoler, *Along the Archival Grain*, 106, 138.

24. Stoler, *Along the Archival Grain*, 106.

25. Stoler, *Along the Archival Grain*, 138.

26. As John Cell writes, any Colonial Office response to colonial correspondence "was an abstraction from the reality of time and place, and by the time the governor received it, it was perhaps as irrelevant as his own had been at the time of its consideration in London": Cell, *British Colonial Administration in the Mid-Nineteenth Century*, 42.

27. Miles Taylor brilliantly argues that Britain manipulated empire to displace potential revolutionary disturbances in the metropole to the colonies. Free trade, and therefore the cheapening of key wage goods such as sugar, was one key way in which this displacement occurred: Taylor, "The 1848 Revolution and the British Empire."

28. Peel, *The Speeches of the Late Right Honourable Sir Robert Peel*, 4:780.

29. On this committee, see Morrell, *British Colonial Policy in the Age of Peel and Russell*, 245.

30. On conservative empiricism contra political economy, see Gambles, *Protection and Politics*, 152, 177.

31. For complaints over Parliament's failure to read colonial blue books, see Premium, *Eight Years in British Guiana*, 148, 196.

32. Higgins, *Third Letter to Lord John Russell*, 6.

33. He would thus remark on a report issued by the Committee of the West Indian Merchants and Planters that "such a document should contain much new matter was not to be expected. . . . The facts are palpable and the arguments plain": Higgins, *The Real Bearings of the West India Question*, 37.

34. On the organization of the Record Department in this period, see PP, 1854 (1715) XXVII.33, "Reports of the Committees of Inquiry into Public Offices and Papers Connected Therewith," 47–65.

35. H. C. G. Matthew, "Higgins, Matthew James (1810–1868)," *Oxford Dictionary of National Biography*, online ed. (Oxford: Oxford University Press, 2004), http://www .oxforddnb.com/view/article/13234, accessed 11 July 2017.

36. Cited by Sir William Stirling Maxwell in his "Memoir of Matthew James Higgins," in Higgins, *Essays on Social Subjects*, xlv.

37. Greg, "Shall We Retain Our Colonies?," 221.

38. Grey, *The Colonial Policy of Lord John Russell's Administration*, 1:10.

39. Grey, *The Colonial Policy of Lord John Russell's Administration*, 11, 13.

40. Grey, *The Colonial Policy of Lord John Russell's Administration*, 24.

41. Higgins, *The Real Bearings of the West India Question*, 5.

42. Higgins, *The Real Bearings of the West India Question*, 6.

43. Earl Henry George Grey, quoted in "Parliamentary Intelligence," *The Times*, 28 June 1848, 3.

44. Earl Henry George Grey, quoted in "Parliamentary Intelligence," *The Times*, 28 June 1848, 3.

45. Earl Henry George Grey quoted in "Parliamentary Intelligence," *The Times*, 28 June 1848, 3.

46. Earl Henry George Grey quoted in "Parliamentary Intelligence," *The Times*, 28 June 1848, 3.

47. Higgins, *Third Letter to Lord John Russell*, 4.

48. Higgins, *Third Letter to Lord John Russell*, 12.

49. Higgins, *Third Letter to Lord John Russell*, 6.

50. Benveniste, *Problems in General Linguistics*, 200.

51. As Michael Herzfeld comments, "If one could not grumble about 'bureaucracy,' bureaucracy itself could not easily exist": Herzfeld, *The Social Production of Indifference*, 3.

52. Nyquist, *Arbitrary Rule*.

53. For better or worse, the key point of reference for these debates remains Williams, *Capitalism and Slavery*. On West Indian antislavery societies after 1834, see, e.g., Turnbull, *The Jamaica Movement*.

54. As Higgins put it, Britain was forced to decide between the desire to have "*a commodity at its natural price*" and the desire to "*extinguish a certain method of producing the commodity*": Higgins, *The Real Bearings of the West India Question*, 18.

55. Higgins, *The Real Bearings of the West India Question*, 24.

56. Higgins, *The Real Bearings of the West India Question*, 13.

57. Higgins, *The Real Bearings of the West India Question*, 45.

58. Higgins, *The Real Bearings of the West India Question*, 30 (italics in original).

59. Higgins, *The Real Bearings of the West India Question*, 25.

60. For a world-systems approach to this moment, see Tomich, *Through the Prism of Slavery*, 56–75. For a social historical approach to British capitalists' involvement in Brazilian and Cuban slavery and slave trading, see Fraginals, *The Sugar Mill*; Guenther, *British Merchants in Nineteenth-Century Brazil*.

61. See Huzzey, *Freedom Burning*, 132–76.

62. Laura White offers an anecdote that symbolically and materially articulates liberalism and the slave trade. She writes, "In 1858 [a British consul in the U.S.] told the story of a Charleston mercantile house, E. Lafitte and Company, which proposed to send the ship Richard Cobden of seven hundred and fifty tons, on a voyage to Africa to bring 'free emigrants' to a United States port. The collector of the port appealed to United States Secretary of the Treasury Howell Cobb who pronounced the proposal illegal": White, "The South in the 1850's," 39.

63. Perkins, too, avails himself of this trope: "Oh Daughters of Old England, I wish you could see / The human gore you swallow down in every cup of tea. / The treaties signed long ago are lying in the shade / While Spain and Brazil daringly still carry on their trade, / The bones of murdered millions are bleaching in the sun / While still the coffin slave ship her faithful course doth run": Perkins, "The Planter's Petition," 158.

64. See Huzzey, "Free Trade, Free Labour, and Slave Sugar in Victorian Britain," 77.

65. See James and Lake, "The Second Face of Hegemony," 29; McKeown, "Hegemonic Stability Theory and 19th Century Tariff Levels in Europe."

66. McMichael, "The Crisis of the Southern Slaveholder Regime in the World-Economy," 44–45. Anthony Howe argues that liberals "were aware that Repeal [of protection] would impose costs on British colonies, and that the immediate beneficiary of this change in policy would be the United States . . . the Walker Act of 1846 [was] seen by contemporaries as an early response to Britain's new openness of trade": Howe, *Free Trade and Liberal England*, 22–23.

67. Walker's personal politics tended toward the expansionist. "An annexationist through and through, Walker constantly urged in the Cabinet the acquisition of all the territory the United States could get—which, by the autumn of 1847, meant all of Mexico": Jordan, "A Politician of Expansion," 374.

68. See Rogin, *Subversive Genealogy*, 102–51.

69. For a history of filibustering and slavery, see May, *Manifest Destiny's Underworld*; Obadele-Starks, *Freebooters and Smugglers*, 145.

70. Higgins, *The Real Bearings of the West India Question*, 41.

71. Higgins, *The Real Bearings of the West India Question*, 12.

72. For a set of documents legally linking piracy to slavery and slavery to liberalism, see Turnbull, *The Slave-Trade Treaties and the Suppression of the Slave-Trade*. See also Campbell, *An Empire for Slavery*, 46–66; White, "The South in the 1850's," 32.

73. For a discussion of the trope of "protection" as it relates to U.S. imperialism, see Murphy, *Hemispheric Imaginings*.

74. On protection and civilizationist arguments, see Anonymous, *A Letter on the West India Question*, 16. Uday Mehta has influentially tracked this mutation of political liberalism in colonial India, where the state assumes responsibility for populations declared to be too "helpless" to rule themselves. As Mehta argues of colonial India, the caveats of fitness enabled antiliberal forms of governance to flourish; racial and civilizationist claims enabled the self-perceived superior English colonizers to establish "exclusions" within a purportedly "inclusive" liberal order: see Mehta, *Liberalism and Empire*.

75. Lewis, *An Essay on the Government of Dependencies*, 231.

76. Lewis, *An Essay on the Government of Dependencies*, 336.

77. C. L. R. James, "Michel Maxwell Philip, 1829–1888," in Cudjoe, *Michel Maxwell Philip*, 89.

78. For effects of free trade in Trinidad, see Wood, *Trinidad in Transition*, 59–160. On West Indian migration patterns during the period, see Richardson, "Freedom and Migration in the Leeward Caribbean, 1838–48." For the effects of free trade on Jamaica, see Hall, *Free Jamaica*, 81–120. For Barbados, see Levy, *Emancipation, Sugar, and Federalism*, 103–24.

79. Frye, *The Secular Scripture*, 178–79; Edmondson, *Caribbean Romances*, 4.

80. Heng, *Empire of Magic*, 9.

81. Gould, "Entangled Histories, Entangled Worlds," 767.

82. The phrase is Geraldine Heng's, who writes that romance "must be identified by the structure of desire which powers its narrative . . . rather than by any intrinsic subject matter, plot, style or other content": Heng, *Empire of Magic*, 3–4.

83. See Meer, *Uncle Tom Mania*. On black and brown West Indian reception and use of *Uncle Tom's Cabin*, see Edmondson, *Caribbean Middlebrow*, 63.

84. Its two-volume status aside, *Emmanuel Appadocca* is generically akin to U.S. dime novels, a form usefully treated in Denning, *Mechanic Accents*; Streeby, *American Sensations*.

85. Melville, *Moby-Dick*, 132.

86. I am referring, of course, to Trouillot, *Silencing the Past*. The explosion of interest in the Haitian Revolution on the part of scholars of the transnational Americas and the Caribbean is salutary. However, the scholarly models of disavowal, repression, and silencing through which white hemispheric relations to the revolution are tracked occlude more than they reveal when considering black Caribbean—and, more particularly, West Indian—relations to the event. The risk is that the hunt for traces of Haiti (as a traumatic memory or a source of inspiration) produces a normative demand that historical subjects inhabit a particular horizon of political longing. David Scott's *Conscripts of Modernity* is exemplary for its theorization of how this normative demand emerges and for refusing to be bound by it. While *Conscripts of Modernity* is explicitly directed toward the future of our postcolonial present, it also allows a different orientation to the past, one that looks for alternatives to nationalism that anticolonial norms submerged or erased.

87. See, e.g., Taylor, *Negro Emancipation and West Indian Independence*, 16. See also chapter 2 in this book.

88. The Jamaican mulatto Richard Hill would similarly return to the West Indian history of piracy and privateering to reanimate empire as a political world: see Hill, *Lights and Shadows of Jamaican History*; Hill, *The Picaroons*.

89. On this history, see Murray, *The West Indies and the Development of Colonial Government*; Noel, *Trinidad*.

90. Naipaul, *The Loss of El Dorado*, 170.

91. On such mobilizations of Spanish law, see Taylor, "Most Holy Virgin Assist Me."

92. See Philippe, *Free Mulatto*.

93. Frye, *The Secular Scripture*, 178–79.

94. As Giorgio Agamben writes of melancholia, "Melancholy would be not so much the regressive reaction to the loss of the love object as the imaginative capacity to make an unobtainable object appear as if lost. If the libido behaves *as if* a loss had occurred although *nothing* has in fact been lost, this is because the libido stages a simulation where what cannot be lost because it has never been possessed appears as lost, and what could never be possessed because it had never perhaps existed may be appropriated insofar as it is lost": Agamben, *Stanzas*, 20.

95. Eng and Kazanjian, *Loss*, ix.

96. Here I am thinking of and with the discussion of melancholia and subject formation in Butler, *The Psychic Life of Power*.

97. *The Athenaeum*, 4 March 1854, 398. See also Cudjoe, *Beyond Boundaries*, 119–42.

Chapter 4. Uncle Bolívar's Children

1. On Britishness and habeas corpus, especially for his reading of the Somerset decision and slavery, see Halliday, *Habeas Corpus*, 174–76.

2. Editorial, *The Trinidadian* (Port of Spain, Trinidad), 16 July 1851. Unless otherwise noted, all quotes from *The Trinidadian* are from editorials. Des Sources will repeat this claim in 20 December 1851.

3. For a useful collection of Anti-Toms, see Stephen Railton, "*Uncle Tom's Cabin* and American Culture," http://utc.iath.virginia.edu/proslav/antitoms.html. Accessed December 7, 2016.

4. See Tannenbaum, *Slave and Citizen*. For a good summary of the debate over Tannenbaum's claims, see de la Fuente, "Slave Law and Claims-Making in Cuba."

5. According to Roderick Cave, a subscription to the *Trinidadian* was $10 per annum: Cave, *Printing and the Book Trade in the West Indies*, 275. For a discussion of the difficulties of establishing a critical press in a Crown Colony, see Lent, *Third World Mass Media and Their Search for Modernity*, 25–35.

6. On British colonial fears of francophone Trinidadian subjects, see Brereton, "Haiti and the Haitian Revolution in the Political Discourse of Nineteenth-Century Trinidad." For broader, pan-Caribbean fears of francophone blacks, see Johnson, *The Fear of French Negroes*.

7. Dispatch from Joseph Riddel to Lord John Russell, 4 March 1853, Records of the Foreign Office (hereafter, FO) 99/35.

8. On empire loyalism in black Jamaican print culture, see Razi, "Coloured Citizens of the World."

9. On this history, see Toussaint, "Afro-West Indians in Search of the Spanish Main," 173–216.

10. Edmondson, *Caribbean Middlebrow*, 65.

11. As Fred Moten has recently argued in a critique of cosmopolitan tendencies in diaspora studies, blackness names a form of statelessness that cannot be accommodated by any chronotoping of the Westphalian order. Describing blackness "as an international antinational force," he continues, "statelessness, precisely in its relation to the para-ontological arrangements of populations, is uncontained by the distinction between pre-Westphalian and Westphalian": Moten, "Notes on Passage," 62.

12. See, e.g., Helg, "Simón Bolívar and the Specter of Pardocracia."

13. See Delany, *The Condition, Elevation, Emigration, and Destiny of the Colored People of the United States.*

14. It has long been a truism that Haiti had been more or less isolated within the world system by the midcentury, although Julia Gaffield has recently challenged this position: see Gaffield, *Haitian Connections in the Atlantic World.* It remained the case, nonetheless, that Haiti was in a position of exploitation vis-à-vis the Euro-centered world system. At the same time, successive Haitian states were more or less built on intense wealth and labor extractions from the peasantry. To be sure, some blacks in the hemisphere, such as James Theodore Holly, found much to admire in this state form: see Holly, "A Vindication of the Capacity of the Negro Race for Self-Government and Civilized Progress"; Stinchcombe, "Class Conflict and Diplomacy"; Trouillot, *Haiti.*

15. *Trinidadian*, 20 December 1851; Harris, "A Summer on the Borders of the Caribbean Sea," 170.

16. Iton, *In Search of the Black Fantastic*, 196.

17. Iton, *In Search of the Black Fantastic*, 199.

18. Anderson, *Imagined Communities*, 67.

19. For a very useful and vibrant discussion of transimperial printing culture, see Hofmeyr, *Gandhi's Printing Press.*

20. Mannheim, *Ideology and Utopia*, 193.

21. *Adolphus* was published anonymously, so authorial attribution is uncertain. Based on internal evidence, however, I concur with the assessment of Bridget Brereton and her colleagues that Des Sources was in fact the author: see Bridget Brereton, Rhonda Cobham, Mary Rimmer, Karen Sanchez-Eppler, and Lise Winer, "Introduction," in Des Sources, *Adolphus*, xxiv. I spell Des Sources as I do (as opposed to the convention of "Dessources" adopted by Brereton et al.) because that is the spelling throughout his newspaper.

22. For Berlant, the juxtapolitical marks a space "in proximity to the political because the political is deemed an elsewhere managed by elites who are interested in reproducing the conditions of their objective superiority, not in the well-being of ordinary people or life-worlds": Berlant, *The Female Complaint*, 3.

23. See Armitage, *The Declaration of Independence*; Gould, *Among the Powers of the Earth.*

24. Naipaul, *The Loss of El Dorado*, 353.

25. Wood, *Trinidad in Transition*, 175.

26. See Wood, *Trinidad in Transition*, 121–30.

27. See Paton, *No Bond but the Law*, 104–8.

28. Aside from Wood's account, from which I draw heavily, see also Brereton, "Haiti and the Haitian Revolution in the Political Discourse of Nineteenth-Century Trinidad," 142–43. Brereton says two people were killed: Wood, *Trinidad in Transition*, 175–76.

29. See Wood, *Trinidad in Transition*, 176.

30. In addition to the work of Johnson and Brereton cited earlier, see Pérotin-Dumon, "Révolutionnaires français et royalistes espagnols dans les Antilles."

31. *The Trinidadian*, 13 October 1849.

32. *The Trinidadian*, 10 October 1849.

33. *The Trinidadian*, 6 October 1849.

34. Dicey, *Introduction to the Study of the Law of the Constitution*, 87. See also Hulsebosch, *Constituting Empire*, 40.

35. On the normality of violence, see Kolsky, *Colonial Justice in British India*, 23.

36. *The Trinidadian*, 16 July 1851.

37. I am thinking of Judith Butler's example in Butler and Spivak, *Who Sings the Nation-State?*, 58–67.

38. *The Trinidadian*, 15 August 1849. As he would later assert, "Petitions are forwarded to the Crown by nine-tenths of the population: no mention is made of them by representatives of order of the public rights; and the populations of these countries remain silent, and lower their heads before this mark of contempt like the ox habituated to the yoke": *The Trinidadian*, 30 August 1851.

39. *The Trinidadian*, 15 August 1849.

40. See John, *The Plantation Slaves of Trinidad*; Milette, *The Genesis of Crown Colony Government*; Murray, *The West Indies and the Development of Colonial Government*; Titus, *The Amelioration and Abolition of Slavery in Trinidad*.

41. On the law of conquest, see, e.g., Mills, *Colonial Constitutions*, 265–71. On debates over the mobility of English rights to British colonies, see Black, "The Constitution of Empire." For background on Calvin's Case, a landmark decision for definitions of British citizenship, see Price, "Natural Law and Birthright Citizenship in Calvin's Case (1608)."

42. Fergus, "The Siete Partidas."

43. Philippe, *Free Mulatto*, 40. On early attempts to Anglicize the postconquest law, see John, *The Plantation Slaves of Trinidad*, 20.

44. *The Trinidadian*, 15 August 1849.

45. *The Trinidadian*, 15 August 1849.

46. *The Trinidadian*, 16 July 1851.

47. *The Trinidadian*, 29 March 1851.

48. *The Trinidadian*, 3 September 1851.

49. *The Trinidadian*, 5 April 1851.

50. On this history, see Noel, *Trinidad, Provincia de Venezuela*.

51. Williams, *History of the People of Trinidad and Tobago*, 40.

52. Gould, "Entangled Histories, Entangled Worlds," 767.

53. Horne, *The Counter-Revolution of 1776*; Landers, *Atlantic Creoles in the Age of Revolutions*; Landers, "Spanish Sanctuary"; Scott, "The Common Wind"; Scott and Hébrard, *Freedom Papers*.

54. Landers, *Atlantic Creoles in the Age of Revolutions*, 5, 7.

55. David Kazanjian usefully gives the name "quotidian globalities" to the subjectivities worked out through these transversal movements across the epistemic and territorial divisions of empires. Kazanjian's *The Brink of Freedom* further urges us to consider how subaltern's quotidian globalities gave rise not just to pragmatic, tactical reflections on where freedom might best be secured, but also to theoretical reflection on the nature of freedom itself: Kazanjian, *The Brink of Freedom*, 1–34.

56. Gould, "Entangled Histories, Entangled Worlds," 765.

57. Landers writes, "Africans and Spaniards shared many understandings of the proper relationship between ruler and subject. Loyal subjects generated reciprocal obligations from those they served . . . These cultural similarities allowed even those Africans newly admitted into the Spanish polity to quickly learn Spanish legal and cultural norms . . . As they exercised their freedom, freedom, Atlantic Creoles repeatedly stressed their loyalty, their service, their devotion to the Spanish King and to the 'True Faith' in written documents": Landers, *Atlantic Creoles in the Age of Revolutions*, 7. On black monarchism in the New World, see also Thornton, "I Am the Subject of the King of Congo."

58. *The Trinidadian*, 16 November 1851.

59. Wilkins, "The Slave Son," 107.

60. Wilkins, "The Slave Son," 107.

61. *The Trinidadian*, 20 December 1851.

62. *The Trinidadian*, 20 December 1851.

63. *The Trinidadian*, 6 February 1851.

64. *The Trinidadian*, 7 February 1852.

65. *The Trinidadian*, 7 February 1852.

66. *The Trinidadian*, 7 February 1852.

67. *The Trinidadian*, 7 February 1852.

68. *The Trinidadian*, 13 December 1851.

69. *The Trinidadian*, 28 February 1852.

70. *The Trinidadian*, 13 December 1851.

71. Adelman, *Sovereignty and Revolution in the Iberian Atlantic*, 372.

72. *The Trinidadian*, 17 September 1851.

73. *The Trinidadian*, 17 September 1851.

74. Goodwin, *Social Science and Utopia*, 7, 196.

75. See Graeber, *Direct Action*, 233–34.

76. See, e.g., Owen, *A Development of the Principles and Plans on Which to Establish Self-Supporting Home Colonies*.

77. Moten, "Blackness and Nothingness," 739.

78. I draw the terms "mere life" and "more life" from Honig, *Antigone, Interrupted*, 57.

79. Stollmeyer, *The Sugar Question Made Easy*, 10–11.

80. Eastburn, *Whittier's Relation to German Life and Thought*, 27.

81. Brisbane, *Social Destiny of Man*, 103.

82. Brisbane, *Social Destiny of Man*, 100.

83. Brisbane, *Social Destiny of Man*, viii.

84. Brisbane, *Social Destiny of Man*, vii.

85. These included Francis Joséph Grund's *Aufruf an die deutschen whaler* (1840) and Christian Gotthilf Salzmann's *Der Himmel auf Erden* (1839). On the New York celebration, see Guarneri, *The Utopian Alternative*, 32.

86. As Patrick Ronald Brostowin notes, "There is no extant record of this pamphlet in either Germany or the United States." Brostowin, "John Adolphus Etzler," 7n13.

87. Stoll, *The Great Delusion*, 38.

88. Joel Nydahl, "Introduction," in Etzler, *The Collected Works of John Adolphus Etzler*, xvi.

89. "Industry can be rendered attractive!": Brisbane, *Social Destiny of Man*, vi.

90. Wood, *Trinidad in Transition*, 85.

91. Thoreau, *The Essays of Henry D. Thoreau*, 45.

92. The best overview of free-laborism remains Foner, *Free Soil, Free Labor, Free Men*.

93. Cited in Stoll, *The Great Delusion*, 99.

94. See the dedication in Etzler, *The Paradise within Reach of All Men*, 2:95–96.

95. For a recent fictionalization of this history, see Antoni, *As Flies to Whatless Boys*.

96. John Adolphus Etzler, "Emigration to the Tropical World for the Melioration of All Classes of People of All Nations" (1844), in Etzler, *The Collected Works of John Adolphus Etzler*, 2.

97. Etzler, "Emigration to the Tropical World for the Melioration of All Classes of People of All Nations," 17.

98. Stollmeyer, *The Sugar Question Made Easy*, 7.

99. Stollmeyer, *The Sugar Question Made Easy*, 18.

100. Stollmeyer, *The Sugar Question Made Easy*, 18.

101. For the date of the society's foundation, see Claeys, "John Adolphus Etzler, Technological Utopianism, and British Socialism," 361. On share sales, see Chase, "Exporting the Owenite Utopia," 209. For contemporary reactions to Etzler's network, see TNA HO 45/1609.

102. See Chase, "Exporting the Owenite Utopia," 205.

103. Stollmeyer, *The Sugar Question Made Easy*, 17.

104. As the society put it in its second petition, "They cannot for a moment suppose that, the Republic of Venezuela would dare to publish laws to encourage emigration from Europe to its Territories promising the Protection of its laws and aid in money when wanting, unless it was both able and willing to fulfill the promise": see the consular report from 3 February 1846, TNA HO 45/1609.

105. Foreign Office dispatch dated July 15 1846, compiled in Home Office record TNA HO 45/1609, "Emigration; Colonies."

106. Nydahl, "Introduction," xxvi.

107. Day, *Five Years' Residence in the West Indies*, 2:58.

108. Sewell, *The Ordeal of Free Labor in the British West Indies*, 103.

109. *Trinidad Spectator*, 4 March 1846.

110. *Trinidad Spectator*, 25 April 1846.

111. Des Sources would acknowledge his socialist leanings in January 1852, writing, "As to what relates to socialism, we must confess ourselves infected with this disease, so horrible to the friends of the old abuses. Socialism is, in our view, the progress of mankind": *The Trinidadian*, 24 January 1852.

112. *The Trinidadian*, 1 December 1852.

113. *The Trinidadian*, 2 April 1851.

114. *The Trinidadian*, 7 February 1852.

115. *The Trinidadian*, 7 February 1852.

116. Stollmeyer, *The Sugar Question Made Easy*, 19.

117. *The Trinidadian*, 13 October 1851.

118. Day, *Five Years' Residence in the West Indies*, 2:88.

119. *The Trinidadian*, 1 January 1853.

120. Carey, *The Slave Trade, Domestic and Foreign*, 68.

121. Carey, *The Slave Trade, Domestic and Foreign*, 168.

122. Carey, *The Slave Trade, Domestic and Foreign*, 111.

123. Des Sources, *Adolphus*, 6. Hereafter, page numbers from this work are cited in parentheses in the text.

124. Dillon, *The Gender of Freedom*, 203.

125. As Tim Watson penetratingly remarks, work interested in recovering subaltern pasts "sometimes . . . will be virtually indistinguishable from the paranoid fantasies of the colonial authorities": Watson, *Caribbean Culture and British Fiction in the Atlantic World*, 92.

126. Senior, *American Slavery*, 29.

127. On the relationship between black Caribbean postemancipation politics and the tradition of radical Marxist politics we know as autonomism, see Taylor, "The Refusal of Work."

128. On maroon communities in the West Indies, see Thompson, *Flight to Freedom*.

129. R. J. Boutelle importantly notes that Bolívar is the only character introduced without physiognomic description; his character embodies a post-racial fantasy opposed to the British colonial order of things. Boutelle, "The Race for America," chap. 3.

130. The sidelining of Antonia perhaps also reflects the reality of Des Sources's colonization scheme: only a handful of women accompanied the pioneering settlers.

131. Dispatch from Joseph Riddel to Lord John Russell, 4 March 1853, TNA FO 199/35.

132. Dispatch from Joseph Riddel to Lord John Russell, 4 March 1853, TNA FO 199/35.

133. Quoted in Pocock, *Out of the Shadows of the Past*, 202–3.

134. *The Trinidadian*, 2 April 1853.

Chapter 5. "A Purely 'Mercial Transaction"

1. Trollope, *The West Indies and the Spanish Main*, 322. Hereafter, page numbers from this work are cited in parentheses in the text.

2. I will discuss Seacole's celebrity shortly. Translations included Mary Seacole, *Aventures et voyages d'une créole, Mme Seacole, à Panama et en Crimée*, trans. Victorine

Rilliet de Constant Massé (Paris: Lausanne, Librairie a. Delafontaine, 1858) and Mary Seacole, *Mary Seacole's avonturen in de West en in de Krim, of het belangwek kende leven eener Heldinne der barmhartigheid, door haar zelve verhaald. Voor het publick bewerkt door W. J. S. Meet eene aanprijzende vorrede van W. H. Russell, Esq., correspondent van de "Times" in de Krum. Uit het Engelsch* (Rotterdam: P. C. Hoog, 1857).

3. Classic accounts of the structural work requisite for holding up economic liberalism include Foucault, *The Birth of Biopolitics*; Polanyi, "The Economy as Instituted Process"; Polanyi, *The Great Transformation*."

4. Trollope's sense of "interest" would fit neatly within the intellectual history of interest offered in Hirschman, *The Passions and the Interests*.

5. Burton, *Empire in Question*, 22.

6. Spivak, "Righting Wrongs," 538. Of course, not every residual *is* defective for capitalism,

7. Arrighi, *The Long Twentieth Century*, 23.

8. Weeks, *The Problem with Work*, 40.

9. Gikandi, *Maps of Englishness*, 128. For representative early work on Seacole, see Pouchet, "The Enigma of Arrival"; Robinson, "Authority and the Public Display of Identity." For more recent work sensitive to Seacole's economic concerns, see Goudie, "Toward a Definition of Caribbean American Regionalism"; Gunning, "Traveling with Her Mother's Tastes."

10. On reading Seacole's text as an autoethnography, see Salih, "A Gallant Heart to the Empire."

11. Raphael Dalleo, for instance, writes that Seacole's "desires for modernity [are] embodied by the market": Dalleo, *Caribbean Literature and the Public Sphere*, 64.

12. See, e.g., *Bombay Quarterly Review* 6 (1857): 171; *The Lancet* 1 (1867): 182.

13. See, e.g., Galt, *The Camp and the Cutter*, 148.

14. W. H. Russell, "To the Reader," in Seacole, *The Wonderful Adventures of Mrs Seacole in Many Lands*, 3.

15. I define these terms more fully later. For an overview, see Polanyi, *The Livelihood of Man*, 38–42.

16. Godelier, *The Enigma of the Gift*, 98.

17. For a historiography of these movements reconstructed through literary texts—though dealing with a later period—see Frederick, *Colon Man a Come*. See also Richardson, "Caribbean Migrations"; Richardson, "Freedom and Migration in the Leeward Caribbean"; Senior, *Dying to Better Themselves*.

18. On this point, see Davis, *Planet of Slums*; Denning, "Wageless Life"; Sanyal, *Rethinking Capitalist Development*.

19. Seacole, *The Wonderful Adventures of Mrs Seacole in Many Lands*, 117. Hereafter, page numbers from this work are cited in parentheses in the text.

20. The best work on attempts to articulate a concept of British imperial citizenship is Banerjee, *Becoming Imperial Citizens*. Unlike Des Sources, Seacole does not use this term in relation to Britain; as we will see, the term "citizen" is introduced into the text by a U.S. American in Panama.

21. See, e.g., Damian, "A Novel Speculation"; Gunning, "Traveling with Her Mother's Tastes," 950, 969–70.

22. Put reductively, formalist economic anthropology assumed that economic models generated in the late nineteenth century through the twentieth century (perhaps most importantly, those following the "marginal revolution") could be applied transhistorically and transgeographically; substantivists argued for the "necessity—supposing this formalist position unfounded—of developing a new analysis more appropriate to the historical societies in question": Sahlins, *Stone Age Economics*, xi.

23. Sahlins, *Stone Age Economics*, 186n1.

24. Trollope, *An Autobiography*, 108.

25. On Trollope and Victorian thinking around professionalism, see Dames, "Trollope and the Career." For a short overview of Trollope's long postal career, see Super, *Trollope in the Post Office*.

26. The term "ontogeny of debt" comes from Price, "Credit in the Slave Trade and Plantation Economies," 327.

27. Burnard, *Mastery, Tyranny, and Desire*, 79.

28. As Philip Curtin wrote, "Isolation played a part in creating the West Indian code of hospitality and friendliness": Curtin, *Two Jamaicas*, 53. See also Petley, "Gluttony, Excess, and the Fall of the Planter Class in the British Caribbean."

29. See Bush, "White 'Ladies' Coloured 'Favorites' and Black 'Wenches' "; Kerr, "Victims or Strategists?"

30. On the seeming inevitability of this conscription, see Greeson, "The Prehistory of Possessive Individualism."

31. Whately, *Introductory Lectures on Political Economy*, 6.

32. On capitalist realism, see Fischer, *Capitalist Realism*.

33. Naylor, *Penny Ante Imperialism*, 16, 185; van Alstyne, "The Central American Policy of Lord Palmerston"; Waddell, "British Honduras and Anglo-American Relations"; Waddell, "Great Britain and the Bay Islands."

34. Richard Cobden, for instance, would argue, "Every motive, whether political or politico-economical, prompted an abandonment of the miserable specks of islands, and still more wretched protectorates of the Mosquito Indians": quoted in John Hobson, *Richard Cobden*, 150. The Mosquito Indians had dense historical ties to the British Empire; for an overview of Mosquito long-running negotiations with British and Spanish imperial power, see Offen, "Creating Mosquitia."

35. Clarendon to Palmerston, 30 December 1857, in Bourke, "The Clayton-Bulwer Treaty and the Decline of British Opposition to the Territorial Expansion of the United States," 287–91.

36. On the cultural popularity of filibusters, see Greenberg, *Manifest Manhood and the Antebellum American Empire*, 179; May, *Manifest Destiny's Underworld*; Streeby, *American Sensations*.

37. Dipesh Chakrabarty neatly articulates this line of thinking in his critique of "historicism": "Historicism—and even the modern, European idea of history—one might say, came to non-European peoples in the nineteenth century as somebody's way of

saying 'not yet' to somebody else. . . . That was what historicist consciousness was: a recommendation to the colonized to wait": Chakrabarty, *Provincializing Europe*, 8. My point is not to dispute this claim, but to suggest that temporalities of deferral could be more heterogeneous in their aims and effects than is typically allowed.

38. Polanyi, *The Livelihood of Man*, 42.

39. Polanyi, *The Livelihood of Man*, 40.

40. Polanyi, *The Livelihood of Man*, 38.

41. Browne-Glaude, *Higglers in Kingston*, 2.

42. Browne-Glaude, *Higglers in Kingston*, 65.

43. Browne-Glaude, *Higglers in Kingston*, 48.

44. See, e.g., "An Act to Prevent Hawking and Peddling, and Disposing of Goods Clandestinely" (1735), in *The Laws of Jamaica*, 229

45. Long, *The History of Jamaica*, 537.

46. Price regulation came early to Jamaica. In 1693, for instance, a price schedule for meats was established, which also worked to ground "the public market-place" or "public and open market" as a juridical object subject to regulation: *The Laws of Jamaica*, 63.

47. Browne-Glaude, *Higglers in Kingston*, 77.

48. See Mintz, *Caribbean Transformations*; Mintz, "Peasant Market Places and Economic Development in Latin America"; Mintz, "Peasant Markets"; Mintz and Hall, "The Origins of the Jamaican Internal Marketing System."

49. Scott, *The Moral Economy of the Peasant*, 4. For a classical articulation of this, see Chanyanov, *The Theory of the Peasant Economy*.

50. See Fluhr, "'Their Calling Me "Mother" Was Not, I Think, Altogether Unmeaning,'" 104–5.

51. "The relatively low cost of entering the service economy, combined with the abrupt and dramatically heightened demand for services, meant that there was room for many small, independent operators": McGuinness, *Path of Empire*, 37.

52. Browne-Glaude, *Higglers in Kingston*, 85.

53. Gikandi, *Maps of Englishness*, 128, 130.

54. Roach, *Cities of the Dead*, 2.

55. Goudie, "Toward a Definition of Caribbean American Regionalism," 300.

56. McGuinness, *Path of Empire*, 81.

57. For the details of this negotiation, see *The Contract between the Republic of New Granada and the Panama Railroad Company*. On company sovereignty, see McGuinness, *Path of Empire*, 73–81.

58. Senior, *Dying to Better Themselves*, 30.

59. For a firsthand account of such a fugitive, see Williams, *Life and Adventures of James Williams, a Fugitive Slave*.

60. As McGuinness points out, "The most fearsome of the potential threats to black political power and black freedom in Panama was the possibility of invasion by filibusters": McGuinness, *Path of Empire*, 11.

61. See Delay, "The Watermelon Riot."

62. Polanyi, *The Livelihood of Man*, 39

63. See Marx, *Grundrisse*, 102–3.

64. Quoted in Senior, *Dying to Better Themselves*, 42.

65. For an aligned reading, see Fluhr, "'Their Calling Me "Mother" Was Not, I Think, Altogether Unmeaning,'" 98.

66. Gunning, "Traveling with Her Mother's Tastes," 954, 970.

67. For a recent and decent synthesis of these positions, see Weeks, *The Problem with Work*, 113–74.

68. Fontaine, *History of Pedlars in Europe*, 82.

69. Quoted in Anionqu et al., "New Light on Seacole," 23.

70. Trollope, *The West Indies and the Spanish Main*, 12.

71. Quoted in Rappaport, "The Invitation That Never Came," 12.

72. Quoted in Rappaport, "The Invitation That Never Came," 13.

73. The key text for such considerations remains Trouillot, *Silencing the Past*.

74. *Daily News*, 21 September 1847.

75. For this history, see Sharpe, *Allegories of Empire*.

Coda

1. Arrighi, *The Long Twentieth Century*, 264.

2. For a prehistory of these movements, see Martin, "Empire Federalism and Imperial Parliamentary Union"; Thompson, "Tariff Reform." For an account of how liberal political economy was repurposed to aid imperial integration schemes, see Palen, "Adam Smith as Advocate of Empire."

3. Coronado, *A World Not to Come*.

4. Naipaul, *The Loss of El Dorado*, 353.

5. Froude, *The English in the West Indies*, 220. Hereafter, page numbers for this work are cited in parentheses in the text.

6. N. Darnell Davis would begin his counterpolemic by declaring, "Since Anthony Trollope visited the West Indies and wrote The West Indies and the Spanish Main . . . no Traveller's tale of this part of the Empire has excited such general interest" as Froude's: Davis, "Mr. Froude's Negrophobia," 85.

7. Margetson, *England in the West Indies*, 11.

8. "Against us on all sides are tariff walls, / Whereon long beat in vain our commerce squalls; / Then, turning to thine own, our mother's fold, / We face the competition of the world": Margetson, *England in the West Indies*, 31.

9. For a brief biography, see Friedenberg, "Nicholas Darnell Davis."

10. Lewis, "J. J. Thomas and Political Thought in the Caribbean," 47. The pre-Marxist James himself had written in the key of Thomas, extracting *The Case for West-Indian Self-Government* (1933) in Britain from his earlier *Life of Captain Cipriani* (1932).

11. See Scott, *Conscripts of Modernity*, 55.

12. Marquez, "Nationalism, Nation, and Ideology," 307.

13. See Smith, *Creole Recitations*.

14. Marquez, "Nationalism, Nation, and Ideology," 307.

15. Salmon, *The Caribbean Confederation*, title page.

16. Thomas, *Froudacity*, 205–6.

17. Marquez, "Nationalism, Nation, and Ideology," 308.

18. Adom Getachew has brilliantly argued that West Indian nationalists through the period of decolonization did not seize hold of the nation-state as it existed in some ideal, modular form; they instead radicalized and improvised with the promise of self-determination. My aim here is not to foreclose consideration of such improvisations, but to consider how the anticolonial and early postcolonial periods were themselves structured by prior foreclosures. Getachew, *Worldmaking after Empire*.

19. For an authorial and editorial statement regarding the importance of the local to early twentieth-century Jamaican fiction, see Redcam, *One Brown Girl*, i. See also Morris, *Making West Indian Literature*, 46–51.

20. See Ashcroft et al., *The Empire Writes Back*.

21. See Rush, *Bonds of Empire*; McFee, "Aspirational Nations."

22. This literature is vast, but see Frederick, *Colon Man a Come*; Hahamovitch, *No Man's Land*; Richardson, "Caribbean Migrations."

23. See Ewing, *The Age of Garvey*; James, *Holding Aloft the Banner of Ethiopia*; Stephens, *Black Empire*.

24. See Hudson, *Bankers and Empire*; Neptune, *Caliban and the Yankees*; and Parker, *Brother's Keeper*.

25. "What is needed is access to a society, larger in every sense, where people will be allowed to grow. For some territories this may be Latin America. Colonial rule in the Caribbean defied geography and created unnatural administrative units; this is part of the problem. Trinidad, for instance, was detached from Venezuela. This is a geographical absurdity; it might be looked at again": Naipaul, *The Overcrowded Barracoon*, 274.

26. Lamming, *The Pleasures of Exile*, 38.

Bibliography

Archives

The National Archives, London, U.K. (TNA)
    Home Office, 45/1609 (HO)
    Foreign Office, 199/35 (FO)

Newspapers

The Trinidadian
Trinidad Spectator

Public Documents

Parliamentary Papers (PP). Parliament, House of Commons, Great Britain.
1835 (278-I) L. "Papers in Explanation of Measures to Give Effect to Act for Abolition
    of Slavery: Part II. (Jamaica, Barbadoes. British Guiana and Mauritius. 1833–35)."
1836 (560) XV. "Select Committee on Negro Apprenticeship in Colonies, Report,
    Minutes of Evidence, Appendix, Index."
1837 (521) LIII. "Papers Presented to Parliament, by His Majesty's Command, in
    Explanation of the Measures Adopted by His Majesty's Government, for Giving
    Effect to the Act for the Abolition of Slavery throughout the British Colonies.
    Part V. Jamaica. Barbados. British Guiana."
1838 (154-I) XLIX ."Papers in Explanation of Measures to Give Effect to Act for Aboli-
    tion of Slavery: Part V. (1) Jamaica; Part V. (2) Barbadoes and British Guiana."
1854 (1715) XXVII.33. "Reports of the Committees of Inquiry into Public Offices and
    Papers Connected Therewith."

Primary Sources

Anonymous. *Jamaica: A Poem in Three Parts*. London: William Nicoll, 1777.
Anonymous. *A Letter on the West India Question, Addressed to the British People, by a Free
    Trader*. London: Smith, Elder, 1848.

Anonymous. *Marly; or, A Planter's Life in Jamaica* (1828). Edited by Karina Williamson. Oxford: Macmillan Education, 2005.

Anonymous. *Montgomery; or, The West-Indian Adventurer.* 3 vols. Kingston: Jamaican Chronicle, 1812.

Anonymous. *Practical Rules for the Management and Medical Treatment of Negro Slaves in the Sugar Colonies.* London: Vernor and Hood, 1803.

Anonymous. *Sketches and Recollections of the West Indies.* London: Smith, Elder, and Company, 1828.

Anderson, John. *Between Slavery and Freedom: Special Magistrate John Anderson's Journal of St. Vincent during the Apprenticeship.* Edited by Roderick A. McDonald. Philadelphia: University of Pennsylvania Press, 2001.

Austin, John. *The Province of Jurisprudence Determined* (1832). Edited by Wilfrid E. Rumble. Cambridge: Cambridge University Press, 1995.

Barclay, Alexander. *A Practical View of the Present State of Slavery in the West Indies.* London: Smith, Elder, and Company, 1826.

Belgrove, William. *A Treatise upon Husbandry or Planting.* Boston: D. Fowle, 1755.

Bentham, Jeremy. *Emancipate Your Colonies! Addressed to the National Convention of France.* London: C. and W. Reynell, 1830.

Blake, William. *Observations on the Principles Which Regulate the Course of Exchange; and the Present Depreciated State of the Currency.* London: Edmund Lloyd, 1810.

Bosanquet, Charles. *Thoughts on the Value to Great Britain, of Commerce in General, and the Value and Importance of the Colonial Trade in Particular.* London: S. and C. McDowall, n.d. [1807].

Bourne, Stephen. *The Uncle Toms and St. Clares of Jamaica.* London: Thomas Bosworth, 1853.

Brisbane, Albert. *Social Destiny of Man; or, Association and Reorganization of Industry.* Philadelphia: C. F. Stollmeyer, 1840.

Brougham, Henry. *An Inquiry into the Colonial Policy of the European Powers.* 2 vols. Edinburgh: R. Balfour, Manners, and Miller, 1803.

Browne, Howe. *Jamaica under the Apprenticeship System.* London: J. Andrews, 1838.

Burke, Edmund. *Observations on a Late State of the Nation.* London: J. Dodsley, 1769.

Byles, John Barnard. *Sophisms of Free-Trade and Popular Political Economy Examined* (1850). Manchester: Manchester Reciprocity Association, 1870.

Canning, George. *Select Speeches of the Right Honourable George Canning.* Edited by Robert Walsh. Philadelphia: James Crissy, 1836.

Carey, Henry Charles. *The Slave Trade, Domestic and Foreign: Why It Exists, and How It May Be Extinguished.* Philadelphia: A. Hart, 1853.

Carlyle, Thomas. "Occasional Discourse on the Negro Question." *Fraser's Magazine* 40 (1849): 670–79.

Cobden, Richard. *The Political Writings of Richard Cobden.* 2 vols. London: Ridgway, 1867.

Conder, Josiah. *Wages or the Whip: An Essay on the Comparative Cost and Productiveness of Free and Slave Labour.* London: Hatchard and Son, 1833.

The Contract between the Republic of New Granada and the Panama Railroad Company. New York: John F. Trow, 1856.

The Correspondence between John Gladstone, Esq., M.P., and James Cropper on the Present State of Slavery. Liverpool: West India Association, 1824.

Cropper, James. *Relief for West-Indian Distress, Shewing the Inefficiency of Protecting Duties on East-India Sugar, and Pointing Out Other Modes of Certain Relief.* London: Hatchard and Son, 1823.

———. *A Review of the Report of a Select Committee . . . on the State of the West India Colonies.* Liverpool: Egerton Smith, 1833.

———. *The Support of Slavery Investigated.* Liverpool: George Smith, 1824.

Davis, N. Darnell. "Mr. Froude's Negrophobia; or, Don Quixote as a Cook's Tourist." *Timehri, the Journal of the Royal Agricultural and Commercial Society of British Guiana* 2 (1888): 85–129.

Day, Charles William. *Five Years' Residence in the West Indies.* 2 vols. London: Colburn, 1852.

Delany, Martin. *The Condition, Elevation, Emigration, and Destiny of the Colored People of the United States.* Edited by Toyin Falola. Amherst: Humanity, 2004.

Des Sources, George Numa. *Adolphus: A Tale.* In *Adolphus: A Tale and The Slave Son*, edited by Lise Winer, 1–92. Kingston: University of the West Indies Press, 2003.

Dicey, A. V. *Introduction to the Study of the Law of the Constitution.* London: Macmillan, 1915.

Dickson, William. *The Mitigation of Slavery.* London: R. and A. Taylor, 1814.

Disraeli, Benjamin. *Lord George Bentinck: A Political Biography* (1848). New Brunswick, NJ: Transaction, 1973.

Dunckley, Henry. *The Charter of the Nations; or, Free Trade and Its Results.* London: W. and F. G. Cash, 1854.

Edwards, Bryan. *The History, Commercial and Civil, of the British West Indies* (1793). 5 vols. London: T. Miller, 1819.

Elliot, Ebenezer. *The Poetical Works of Ebenezer Elliott, the Corn-law Rhymer.* Edinburgh: William Tait, 1840.

Engels, Friedrich. *The Condition of the Working Class of England* (1845). Oxford: Oxford University Press, 2009.

Estwick, Samuel. *A Letter to the Reverend Josiah Tucker.* London, 1776.

Etzler, John Adolphus. *The Collected Works of John Adolphus Etzler.* Edited by Joel Nydahl. Delmar, NY: Scholars' Facsimiles and Reprints, 1977.

———. *Emigration to the Tropical World, for the Melioration of All Classes of All People of All Nations.* Surrey: The Condordium, 1844.

———. *The New World; or, Mechanical System: To Perform the Labours of Man and Beast by Inanimate Powers, That Cost Nothing, for Producing and Preparing the Substances of Life.* Philadelphia: C. F. Stollmeyer, 1841.

———. *The Paradise within Reach of All Men, without Labour by Powers of Nature and Machinery.* Pittsburgh: Etzler and Reinhold, 1833.

Froude, James Anthony. *The English in the West Indies; or, The Bow of Ulysses* (1888). New York: Scribner, 1900.

Galt, Edwin. *The Camp and the Cutter; or, A Cruise to the Crimea*. London: Hodgson, 1856.

Greg, William Rathbone. "Shall We Retain Our Colonies?" In William Rathbone Greg, *Essays on Political and Social Science, Contributed Chiefly to the Edinburgh Review*, vol. 2, 219–51. London: Longman, Brown, Green, and Longman, 1853.

Grey, Earl Henry George. *The Colonial Policy of Lord John Russell's Administration*. 2 vols. London: Richard Bentley, 1853.

Harris, J. Dennis. "A Summer on the Borders of the Caribbean." In *Black Separatism and the Caribbean, 1860*, edited by Howard H. Bell, 67–184. Ann Arbor: University of Michigan Press, 1970.

Harvey, Thomas, and William Brewin. *Jamaica in 1866: A Narrative of a Tour through the Island*. London: A. W. Bennett, 1867.

Higgins, Matthew [Jacob Omnium]. *Essays on Social Subjects*. London: Smith, Elder, 1875.

——. *The Real Bearings of the West India Question, as Expounded by the Most Intelligent and Independent Free-Trader of the Day*. London: James Ridgway, 1848.

——. *Third Letter to Lord John Russell*. London: Norman and Skeen, 1848.

Hill, Richard. *Lights and Shadows of Jamaican History*. Kingston: Ford and Gall, 1859.

——. *The Picaroons; or, One Hundred and Fifty Years Ago*. Dublin: John Falconer, 1869.

Hobson, John. *Richard Cobden, the International Man*. New York: Henry Holt and Company, 1919.

Hodgson, Adam. *A Letter to M. Jean-Baptiste Say, on the Comparative Expense of Free and Slave Labour*. London: Hatchard and Son, 1823.

Holly, James Theodore. "A Vindication of the Capacity of the Negro Race for Self-Government and Civilized Progress." In *Black Separatism and the Caribbean, 1860*, edited by Howard H. Bell, 17–66. Ann Arbor: University of Michigan Press, 1970.

Horrors of the Negro Apprenticeship System in the British Colonies, as Detailed at the Public Breakfast Given by the Citizens of Birmingham, to Mr. Joseph Sturge. Glasgow: W. and W. Miller, 1837.

Hume, David. *Political Essays*. Cambridge: Cambridge University Press, 1994.

Huskisson, William. *The Speeches of the Right Honorable William Huskisson*. 3 vols. London: John Murray, 1831.

James, C. L. R. *The Life of Captain Cipriani: An Account of British Government in the West Indies, with the pamphlet The Case for West-Indian Self Government* (1932, 1933). Durham, NC: Duke University Press, 2014.

The Laws of Jamaica: Comprehending All the Acts in Force. St. Jago de la Vega, Jamaica: Alexander Aikman, 1749.

Lewis, George Cornewall. *An Essay on the Government of Dependencies*. London: John Murray, 1841.

Ligon, Richard. *A True and Exact History of the Island of Barbados*. London: Humphrey Moseley, 1657.

Littleton, Edward. *The Groans of the Plantations; or, A True Account of Their Grievous and Extreme Sufferings by the Heavy Impositions upon Sugar*. London: M. Clark, 1689.

Long, Edward. *The History of Jamaica; or, General Survey of the Antient and Modern State of the Island.* 3 vols. London: T. Lowndes, 1774.

Lowe, Joseph. *An Inquiry into the State of the West Indies.* London: C. and R. Baldwin, 1807.

Lowndes, John. *The Coffee-planter; or, An Essay on the Cultivation and Manufacturing of That Article of West-India Produce.* London: C. Lowndes, 1807.

MacDonnell, Alexander. *Colonial Commerce; Comprising an Inquiry into the Principles upon Which Discriminating Duties Should Be Levied on Sugar.* London: John Murray, 1828.

———. *Free Trade; or, An Inquiry into the Expediency of the Present Corn Laws.* London: John Murray, 1826.

MacQueen, James. *The Colonial Controversy, Containing a Refutation of the Calumnies of the Anticolonists; the State of Hayti, Sierra Leone, India, China, Cochin China, etc. etc.* Glasgow: Khull, Blackie, 1825.

———. *The West Indies Colonies; The Calumnies and Misrepresentations Circulated against Them by the* Edinburgh Review, *Mr Clarkson, Mr Cropper, etc.* London: Baldwin, Cradock, and Joy, 1824.

Madden, Richard Robert. *A Twelvesmonth's Residence in the West Indies, during the Transition from Slavery to Apprenticeship.* 2 vols. London: James Cochrane, 1835.

Margetson, George Reginald. *England in the West Indies: A Neglected and Degenerating Empire.* Boston: Blodgett, 1906.

Martin, Samuel. *An Essay upon Plantership, Humbly Inscrib'd to All the Planters of the British Sugar-Colonies in America.* Antigua: T. Smith, 1750.

Martineau, Harriet. "Demerara." *Illustrations of Political Economy.* Vol. 2. London: Charles Fox and Co, 1832.

McCulloch, John Ramsay. "Colonial Policy—Value of Colonial Possessions." *Edinburgh Review* 42, no. 84 (August 1825): 271–303.

———. *Principles of Political Economy.* Edinburgh: Adam and Charles Black, 1849.

———. *A Select Collection of Early English Tracts on Commerce.* London: Printed for the Political Economy Club, 1856.

———. *A Statistical Account of the British Empire: Exhibiting Its Extent, Physical Capacities, Population, Industry, and Civil and Religious Institutions.* 2 vols. London: Charles Knight, 1837.

Melville, Herman. *Moby-Dick; or, The Whale* (1851). New York: Penguin, 1992.

Mill, James. "Colonies." Reprinted from *Supplement to the Encyclopaedia Britannica.* London: J. Innes, n.d. [1828].

Mills, Arthur. *Colonial Constitutions: An Outline of the Constitutional History and Existing Government of the British Dependencies.* London: John Murray, 1856.

M'Mahon, Benjamin. *Jamaica Plantership.* London: Effingham Wilson, 1839.

Orderson, J. W. *Creoleana; or, Social Scenes and Domestic Incidents in Barbados in Days of Yore.* London: Saunders and Otley, 1842.

Owen, Robert. *A Development of the Principles and Plans on Which to Establish Self-Supporting Home Colonies.* London: Home Colonization Society, 1841.

Peel, Robert. *The Speeches of the Late Right Honourable Sir Robert Peel.* 4 vols. London: Routledge, 1853.

Perkins, Cyrus Francis. *Busha's Mistress; or, Catherine the Fugitive: A Stirring Romance of the Days of Slavery in Jamaica* (1855). Edited by Paul E. Lovejoy, Verene A. Shepherd, and David V. Trotman. Kingston: Ian Randle, 2003.

Philip, Michel Maxwell. *Emmanuel Appadocca; or, Blighted Life, a Tale of the Boucaneers* (1854). Edited by Selwyn Cudjoe. Wellesley, MA: Calaloux, 1997.

Philippe, Jean-Baptiste. *Free Mulatto* (1824). Edited by Selwyn Cudjoe. Boston: Calaloux, 1996.

Phillips, Joseph. *West India Question: The Outline of a Plan for the Total, Immediate, and Safe Abolition of Slavery.* London: J. and A. Arch, 1833.

Pownall, Thomas. *A Letter from Governor Pownall to Adam Smith, L.L.D., F.R.S.* London: J. Almon, 1776.

Premium, Barton. *Eight Years in British Guiana: Being a Journal of a Residence in That Province.* London: Longman, Brown, Green, and Longman, 1850.

Prince, Mary. *The History of Mary Prince, a West Indian Slave, Related by Herself.* London: F. Westley and A. H. Davis, 1831.

Ramsay, James. *Essay on the Treatment and Conversion of African Slaves in the British Sugar Colonies.* London: James Phillips, 1784.

Redcam, Tom. *One Brown Girl and—A Jamaica Story.* Kingston: Jamaica Times Printery, 1909.

Report of the Proceedings of the Anti-Slavery Meeting, held at the Town Hall, Birmingham, on Wednesday, October 14th, 1835. Birmingham: B. Hudson, 1835.

Richard, Henry. *Memoirs of Joseph Sturge,* 2 vols. London: S. W. Partridge, 1865.

Roughley, Thomas. *The Jamaica Planter's Guide; or, A System for Planting and Managing a Sugar Estate.* London: Longman, Hurst, Reed, Orme, and Brown, 1823.

Salmon, Charles Spencer. *The Caribbean Confederation.* London: Cassell, 1889.

Say, Jean-Baptiste. *A Treatise on Political Economy; or The Production, Distribution, and Consumption of Wealth.* 2 vols. Translated by C. R. Prinsep. London: Longman, Hurst, Rees, Orme, and Brown, 1821.

Seacole, Mary. *The Wonderful Adventures of Mrs. Seacole in Many Lands* (1857). New York: Penguin, 2005.

Seeley, John Robert. *The Expansion of England: Two Courses of Lectures.* London: Macmillan, 1883.

Senior, Nassau William. *American Slavery.* London: Longman, Brown, Green, Longman, and Roberts, 1856.

Sewell, William Grant. *The Ordeal of Free Labor in the British West Indies.* New York: Harper, 1863.

Smith, Adam. *Correspondence of Adam Smith.* Indianapolis: Liberty Fund, 1987.

———. *The Wealth of Nations* (1776). New York: Random House, 2000.

Smith, Goldwin. *The Empire: A Series of Letters Published in "The Daily News," 1862, 1863.* London: John Henry and James Parker, 1863.

Spence, William. *Britain Independent of Commerce; or, Proofs Deduced from an Investigation into the True Causes of the Wealth of Nations.* London: T. Cadell and W. Davies, 1807.

──────. *The Radical Cause of the Present Distresses of the West-India Planters.* London: T. Cadell and W. Davies, 1807.

A Statement of Facts, Illustrating the Administration of the Abolition Law, and the Sufferings of the Negro Apprentices in the Island of Jamaica. London: John Haddon, 1837.

Stephen, George. *Antislavery Recollections: In a Series of Letters Addressed to Mrs. Beecher Stowe.* London: Thomas Hatchard, 1854.

Stephen, James. *England Enslaved by Her Own Slave Colonies: An Address to the Electors and People of the United Kingdom.* London: Hatchard and Son, 1826.

──────. *The Slavery of the British West India Colonies Delineated.* 2 vols. London: Hatchard and Son, 1824–1830.

Steuart, James. *An Inquiry into the Principles of Political Economy* (1767). 2 vols. Basil: J. J. Tourneisen, 1796.

Stollmeyer, Conrad. *The Sugar Question Made Easy.* London: E. Wilson, 1845.

Stowe, Harriet Beecher. *Uncle Tom's Cabin* (1852). New York: W. W. Norton, 1993.

Sturge, Joseph, and Thomas Harvey. *The West Indies in 1837, Being the Journal of a Visit to Antigua, Montserrat, Dominica, St. Lucia, Barbados, and Jamaica.* London: Hamilton, Adams, 1837.

Taylor, John. *Negro Emancipation and West Indian Independence: The True Interest of Great Britain.* Liverpool: R. Rockliff, 1824.

Telfair, Charles. *Some Account of the State of Slavery at Mauritius.* London: Ridgway, 1830.

Thomas, John Jacob. *Froudacity: West Indian Fables by James Anthony Froude* (1889). Philadelphia: Gebbie, 1890.

Thoreau, Henry David. *The Essays of Henry D. Thoreau.* Edited by Lewis Hyde. New York: North Point, 2002.

Torrens, Robert. *An Essay on the Production of Wealth.* London: Longman, Hurst, Rees, Orme, and Brown, 1821.

Trollope, Anthony. *An Autobiography* (1883). Berkeley: University of California Press, 1978.

──────. *The West Indies and the Spanish Main* (1859). New York: Carroll and Graff, 1999.

Turnbull, David. *The Jamaica Movement, for Promoting the Enforcement of the Slave-Trade Treaties and the Suppression of the Slave Trade.* London: Charles Gilpin, 1850.

──────. *The Slave-Trade Treaties and the Suppression of the Slave-Trade, with Statements of Fact, Convention, and Law.* London: Charles Gilpin, 1850.

Turnbull, Gordon. *Letters to a Young Planter.* London: Stuart and Stevenson, 1785.

Warner, Ashton. *Negro Slavery Described by a Negro: Being the Narrative of Ashton Warner, a Native of St. Vincent's.* London: Samuel Maunder, 1831.

Whately, Richard. *Introductory Lectures on Political Economy.* London: B. Fellowes, 1832.

Wilberforce, William. *An Appeal to the Religion, Justice, and Humanity of the Inhabitants of the British Empire.* London: Hatchard, 1823.

Wilkins, Marcella Noy. *The Slave Son.* In *Adolphus: A Tale and The Slave Son,* edited by Lise Winer, 93–359. Kingston: University of the West Indies Press, 2003.

Williams, James. *Life and Adventures of James Williams, a Fugitive Slave, with a Full Description of the Underground Railroad.* San Francisco: Women's Union Print, 1873.

————. *A Narrative of Events, since the First of August, 1834*. Edited by Diana Paton. Durham, NC: Duke University Press, 2001.

Wilmot-Horton, Robert. *The West India Question Practically Considered*. London: John Murray, 1826.

Winer, Lise, ed. *Adolphus: A Tale and The Slave Son*. Kingston: University of the West Indies Press, 2003.

Secondary Sources

Adelman, Jeremy. *Sovereignty and Revolution in the Iberian Atlantic*. Princeton, NJ: Princeton University Press, 2006.

Agamben, Giorgio. *Stanzas: Word and Phantasm in Western Culture*. Translated by Ronald L. Martinez. Minneapolis: University of Minnesota Press, 1993.

Aljoe, Nicole. *Creole Testimonies: Slave Narratives from the British West Indies, 1709–1838*. London: Palgrave, 2012.

Altink, Henrice. "Deviant and Dangerous: Proslavery Representations of Jamaican Slave Women's Sexuality, ca. 1780–1834." In *Women and Slavery: The Modern Atlantic*, edited by Gwyn Campbell, Suzanne Miers, and Joseph C. Miller, 209–30. Athens: Ohio University Press, 2008.

————. *Representations of Slave Women in Discourses on Slavery and Abolition, 1780–1838*. Oxford: Routledge, 2007.

Anderson, Benedict. *Imagined Communities: Reflections on the Origin and Spread of Nationalism*. Rev. ed. London: Verso, 2006.

Anderson, Gary M., William F. Shughart, and Robert D. Tollison. "Adam Smith in the Customhouse." *Journal of Political Economy* 93, no. 4 (August 1985): 740–59.

Anionqu, Elizabeth, Corry Staring-Derks, and Jeroen Staring. "New Light on Seacole." *Nursing Standard* 27, no. 50 (2013): 22–23.

Antoni, Robert. *As Flies to Whatless Boys*. Brooklyn: Akashic, 2013.

Armitage, David. *The Declaration of Independence: A Global History*. Cambridge, MA: Harvard University Press, 2008.

————. "Greater Britain: A Useful Category of Historical Analysis?" *American Historical Review* 104 (1999): 427–45.

Arrighi, Giovanni. *Adam Smith in Beijing: Lineages of the 21st Century*. London: Verso, 2009.

————. *The Long Twentieth Century: Money, Power, and the Origins of Our Times*. London: Verso, 1994.

Ashcroft, Bill, Gareth Griffiths, and Helen Tiffin. *The Empire Writes Back: Theory and Practice in Post-Colonial Literatures*. London: Routledge, 1989.

Bakan, Abigail B. *Ideology and Class Conflict in Jamaica: The Politics of Rebellion*. Montreal: McGill-Queen's University Press, 1992.

Baker, Jennifer. *Securing the Commonwealth: Debt, Speculation, and Writing in the Making of Early America*. Baltimore: Johns Hopkins University Press, 2005.

Banaji, Jairus. *Theory as History: Essays on Modes of Production and Exploitation.* Chicago: Haymarket, 2013.

Banerjee, Sukanya. *Becoming Imperial Citizens: Indians in the Late-Victorian Empire.* Durham, NC: Duke University Press, 2010.

Bannet, Eve Tavor. *Empire of Letters: Letter Manuals and Transatlantic Correspondence, 1688–1820.* Cambridge: Cambridge University Press, 2005.

Bassi, Ernesto. *An Aqueous Territory: Sailor Geographies and New Granada's Transimperial Greater Caribbean World.* Durham, NC: Duke University Press, 2017.

Bell, Duncan A. *The Idea of Greater Britain: Empire and the Future of World Order, 1860–1900.* Princeton, NJ: Princeton University Press, 2007.

Belnap, Jeffrey, and Raúl Fernandez, eds. *Jose Marti's "Our America": From National to Hemispheric Cultural Studies.* Durham, NC: Duke University Press, 1998.

Benton, Lauren. *A Search for Sovereignty: Law and Geography in European Empires, 1400–1900.* Cambridge: Cambridge University Press, 2010.

Benveniste, Emile. *Problems in General Linguistics.* Translated by Mary Elizabeth Meek. Miami: University of Miami Press, 1971.

Berlant, Lauren. *Cruel Optimism.* Durham, NC: Duke University Press, 2011.

———. *The Female Complaint: The Unfinished Business of Sentimentality in American Culture.* Durham, NC: Duke University Press, 2008.

Best, Lloyd, and Kari Polanyi Levitt. *Essays on the Theory of Plantation Economy: A Historical and Institutional Approach to Caribbean Economic Development.* Kingston: University of the West Indies Press, 2009.

Biehl, João. *Vita: Life in a Zone of Social Abandonment.* Berkeley: University of California Press, 2005.

Black, Barbara A. "The Constitution of Empire: The Case for the Colonists." *University of Pennsylvania Law Review* 124 (1976): 1157–211.

Blakeley, Brian. *The Colonial Office, 1868–1892.* Durham, NC: Duke University Press, 1972.

Bonilla, Yarimar. *Non-sovereign Futures: French Caribbean Politics in the Wake of Disenchantment.* Chicago: University of Chicago Press, 2015.

Bourke, Kenneth. "The Clayton-Bulwer Treaty and the Decline of British Opposition to the Territorial Expansion of the United States, 1857–60." *Journal of Modern History* 31, no. 3 (1961): 287–91.

Boutelle, R. J. "The Race for America: Blackness, Belonging, and Empire in the Transamerican 19th Century." PhD diss., Vanderbilt University, 2016.

Brereton, Bridget. "Haiti and the Haitian Revolution in the Political Discourse of Nineteenth-Century Trinidad." In *Reinterpreting the Haitian Revolution and Its Cultural Aftershocks,* edited by Martin Munro and Elizabeth Walcott-Hackshaw, 123–49. Kingston: University of the West Indies Press, 2006.

Brickhouse, Anna. *Transamerican Literary Relations and the Nineteenth-Century Public Sphere.* Oxford: Oxford University Press, 2004.

Brostowin, Patrick Ronald. "John Adolphus Etzler, Scientific-Utopian during the 1830s and 1840s." PhD diss., New York University, 1992.

Brown, Vincent. *The Reaper's Garden: Death and Power in the World of Atlantic Slavery.* Cambridge, MA: Harvard University Press, 2008.

Browne-Glaude, Winnifred. *Higglers in Kingston: Women's Informal Work in Jamaica.* Nashville, TN: Vanderbilt University Press, 2011.

Burbank, Jane, and Frederick Cooper. *Empires in World History: Power and the Politics of Difference.* Princeton, NJ: Princeton University Press, 2010.

Burn, W. L. *Emancipation and Apprenticeship in the British West Indies.* London: Jonathan Cape, 1937.

Burnard, Trevor. *Mastery, Tyranny, and Desire: Thomas Thistlewood and His Slaves in the Anglo-Jamaican World.* Chapel Hill: University of North Carolina Press, 2003.

Burns, Kathryn. *Into the Archive: Writing and Power in Colonial Peru.* Durham, NC: Duke University Press, 2010.

Burton, Antoinette. *Empire in Question: Reading, Writing, and Teaching British Imperialism.* Durham, NC: Duke University Press, 2011.

Bush, Barbara. "White 'Ladies,' Coloured 'Favorites' and Black 'Wenches': Some Considerations on Sex, Race and Class Factors in Social Relations in White Creole Society in the British Caribbean." *Slavery and Abolition* 2 (1981): 245–62.

Butler, Judith. *The Psychic Life of Power: Theories in Subjection.* Stanford, CA: Stanford University Press, 1997.

Butler, Judith, and Gayatri Chakravorty Spivak. *Who Sings the Nation-State? Language, Politics, Belonging.* Kolkata: Seagull Books, 2011.

Butler, Kathleen Mary. *The Economics of Emancipation: Jamaica and Barbados, 1823–1843.* Chapel Hill: University of North Carolina Press, 1995.

Cain, P. J., and A. G. Hopkins. "Gentlemanly Capitalism and British Expansion Overseas I: The Old Colonial System, 1688–1850." *Economic History Review* 39, no. 4 (1986): 501–25.

———. "Gentlemanly Capitalism and British Expansion Overseas II: New Imperialism, 1850–1945." *Economic History Review* 40, no. 1 (1987): 1–26.

———. "The Political Economy of British Expansion Overseas, 1750–1914." *Economic History Review* 33, no. 4 (1980): 463–90.

Campbell, Randolph B. *An Empire for Slavery: The Peculiar Institution in Texas, 1821–1865.* Baton Rouge: Louisiana State University Press, 1989.

Carrington, Selwyn. *The British West Indies during the American Revolution.* Amsterdam: Brill, 1988.

———. *The Sugar Industry and the Abolition of the Slave Trade, 1775–1810.* Gainesville: University Press of Florida, 2002.

Cave, Roderick. *Printing and the Book Trade in the West Indies.* London: Pindar, 1987.

Çelikkol, Ayşe. *Romances of Free Trade: British Literature, Laissez-Faire, and the Global Nineteenth Century.* Oxford: Oxford University Press, 2011.

Cell, John Whitson. *British Colonial Administration in the Mid-Nineteenth Century: The Policy-Making Process.* New Haven, CT: Yale University Press, 1970.

Chakrabarty, Dipesh. *Provincializing Europe: Postcolonial Thought and Historical Difference.* Princeton, NJ: Princeton University Press, 2000.

Chanyanov, Alexander. *The Theory of the Peasant Economy*. Homewood, IL: American Economic Association, 1966.

Chase, Malcolm. "Exporting the Owenite Utopia: Thomas Powell and the Tropical Emigration Society." In *Robert Owen and His Legacy*, edited by Noel Thompson and Chris Williams, 198–217. Cardiff: University of Wales Press, 2011.

Claeys, Gregory. "John Adolphus Etzler, Technological Utopianism, and British Socialism: The Tropical Emigration Society's Venezuelan Mission and Its Social Context, 1833–1848." *English Historical Review* 101, no. 399 (April 1986): 351–75.

Cooper, Frederick. *Citizenship between Empire and Nation: Remaking France and French Africa, 1945–1960*. Princeton, NJ: Princeton University Press, 2014.

Coronado, Raúl. *A World Not to Come: A History of Latino Writing and Print Culture*. Cambridge, MA: Harvard University Press, 2013.

Craton, Michael. *Searching for the Invisible Man: Slaves and Plantation Life in Jamaica*. Cambridge, MA: Harvard University Press, 1978.

Cudjoe, Selwyn. *Beyond Boundaries: The Intellectual Tradition of Trinidad and Tobago in the Nineteenth Century*. Wellesley, MA: Calaloux, 2003.

———. *Michel Maxwell Philip: A Trinidad Patriot of the 19th Century*. Wellesley, MA: Calaloux, 1999.

Curtin, Philip. *Two Jamaicas: The Role of Ideas in a Tropical Colony, 1830–1865*. Cambridge, MA: Harvard University Press, 1955.

da Costa, Emilia Viotti. *Crowns of Glory, Tears of Blood: The Demerara Slave Rebellion of 1823*. Oxford: Oxford University Press, 1994.

Dalleo, Raphael. *Caribbean Literature and the Public Sphere: From the Plantation to the Postcolonial*. Charlottesville: University of Virginia Press, 2011.

Dames, Nicholas. "Trollope and the Career: Vocational Trajectories and the Management of Ambition." *Victorian Studies* 45, no. 2 (2003): 247–78.

Damian, Jessica. "A Novel Speculation: Mary Seacole's Ambitious Adventures in the New Granada Gold Mining Company." *Journal of West Indian Literature* 16, no. 1 (2007): 15–36.

Davis, David Brion. "James Cropper and the British Anti-Slavery Movement, 1821–1823." *Journal of Negro History* 45, no. 4 (October 1960): 241–58.

———. "James Cropper and the British Anti-Slavery Movement, 1823–1833." *Journal of Negro History* 46, no. 3 (April 1961): 154–73.

Davis, Mike. *Planet of Slums*. London: Verso, 2007.

Davis, Ralph. "The Rise of Protection, 1689–1786." *Economic History Review*, new series, 19, no. 2 (1966): 306–17.

de la Fuente, Alejandro. "Slave Law and Claims-Making in Cuba: The Tannenbaum Debate Revisited." *Law and History Review* 22, no. 2 (Summer 2004): 339–69.

Delay, Mercedes Chen. "The Watermelon Riot: Cultural Encounters in Panama City, April 15, 1856." *Hispanic American Historical Review* 70, no. 1 (1990): 85–108.

DeLombard, Jeannine Marie. *Slavery on Trial: Law, Abolitionism, and Print Culture*. Chapel Hill: University of North Carolina Press, 2007.

Denning, Michael. *Mechanic Accents: Dime Novels and Working-Class Culture in America.* London: Verso, 1987.

———. "Wageless Life." *New Left Review* 66 (2010): 79–97.

Derrida, Jacques. *The Beast and the Sovereign,* vol. 1. Translated by Geoffrey Bennington. Chicago: University of Chicago Press, 2009.

———. *The Post Card: From Socrates to Freud and Beyond.* Translated by Alan Bass. Chicago: University of Chicago Press, 1987.

Dillon, Elizabeth Maddock. *The Gender of Freedom: Fictions of Liberalism and the Literary Public Sphere.* Palo Alto, CA: Stanford University Press, 2004.

Downs, Jim. *Sick from Freedom: African-American Illness and Suffering during the Civil War and Reconstruction.* Oxford: Oxford University Press, 2013.

Draper, Nicholas. *The Price of Emancipation: Slave Ownership, Compensation and British Society at the End of Slavery.* Cambridge: Cambridge University Press, 2010.

Drescher, Seymour. *Capitalism and Antislavery: British Mobilization in a Comparative Perspective.* Oxford: Oxford University Press, 1987.

———. *The Mighty Experiment: Free Labor versus Slavery in British Emancipation.* Oxford: Oxford University Press, 2002.

Dumas, Paula. *Proslavery Britain: Fighting for Slavery in an Era of Abolition.* London: Palgrave, 2016.

Dumont, Louis. *From Mandeville to Marx: The Genesis and Triumph of Economic Ideology.* Chicago: University of Chicago Press, 1977.

Eastburn, Iola Kay. *Whittier's Relation to German Life and Thought.* Philadelphia: University of Pennsylvania Press, 1915.

Edmondson, Belinda. *Caribbean Middlebrow: Leisure Culture and the Middle Class.* Ithaca, NY: Cornell University Press, 2009.

———, ed. *Caribbean Romances: The Politics of Regional Representation.* Charlottesville: University of Virginia Press, 1999.

Eng, David, and David Kazanjian, eds. *Loss: The Politics of Mourning.* Berkeley: University of California Press, 2003.

Eudell, Demetrius L. *The Political Languages of Emancipation in the British Caribbean and the U.S. South.* Chapel Hill: University of North Carolina Press, 2002.

Ewing, Adam. *The Age of Garvey: How a Jamaican Activist Created a Mass Movement and Changed Global Black Politics.* Princeton, NJ: Princeton University Press, 2014.

Fergus, Claudius. "The Siete Partidas: A Framework for Philanthropy and Coercion during the Amelioration Experiment in Trinidad, 1823–34." *Caribbean Studies* 36, no. 1 (2008): 75–99.

Fischer, Mark. *Capitalist Realism: Is There No Alternative?* Winchester: Zero, 2014.

Fluhr, Nicole. "'Their Calling Me "Mother" Was Not, I Think, Altogether Unmeaning': Mary Seacole's Maternal Personae." *Victorian Literature and Culture* 34, no. 1 (2006): 95–113.

Fogel, Robert, and Stanley Engerman. *Time on the Cross: The Economics of American Negro Slavery.* New York: W. W. Norton, 1974.

Foner, Eric. *Free Soil, Free Labor, Free Men: The Ideology of the Republican Party before the Civil War*. Oxford: Oxford University Press, 1995.

Fontaine, Laurence. *History of Pedlars in Europe*. Durham, NC: Duke University Press, 1996.

Fortunati, Leopoldina. *The Arcane of Reproduction: Housework, Prostitution, Labor and Capital*. Translated by Hilary Creek. Brooklyn: Autonomedia, 1995.

Foucault, Michel. *Archaeology of Knowledge*. New York: Vintage, 1982.

———. *The Birth of Biopolitics: Lectures at the College de France, 1978–1979*. London: Picador, 2010.

———. *Security, Territory, Population: Lectures at the Collège de France, 1977–78*. New York: Picador, 2007.

———. *"Society Must Be Defended": Lectures at the College de France, 1975–1976*. London: Picador, 2003.

Fraginals, M. Moreno. *The Sugar Mill: The Socioeconomic Complex of Sugar in Cuba*. Translated by C. Belfarge. New York: Monthly Review Press, 1976.

Franklin, Alexandra. "Enterprise and Advantage: The West India Interest in Britain, 1774–1840." PhD diss., University of Pennsylvania, 1992.

Frederick, Rhonda. *Colon Man a Come: Mythographies of Panama Canal Migration*. Lexington, MA: Lexington Books, 2005.

Friedenberg, Albert M. "Nicholas Darnell Davis." *Publications of the American Jewish Historical Society* 25 (1917): 148–49.

Frye, Northrop. *The Secular Scripture: A Study of the Structure of Romance*. Cambridge, MA: Harvard University Press, 1976.

Gaffield, Julia. *Haitian Connections in the Atlantic World: Recognition after Revolution*. Chapel Hill: University of North Carolina Press, 2015.

Gallagher, John, and Ronald Robinson. "The Imperialism of Free Trade." *Economic History Review* 6, no. 1 (1953): 1–15.

Gambles, Anna. *Protection and Politics: Conservative Economic Discourse, 1815–1852*. London: Boyden and Brewer, 1999.

Gauci, Perry. *William Beckford: First Prime Minister of the London Empire*. New Haven, CT: Yale University Press, 2013.

Genovese, Eugene. *Roll, Jordan, Roll: The World the Slaves Made*. New York: Vintage, 1976.

Getachew, Adom. *Worldmaking after Empire: The Rise and Fall of Self-Determination*. Princeton, NJ: Princeton University Press, forthcoming.

Ghachem, Malick W. *The Old Regime and the Haitian Revolution*. Cambridge: Cambridge University Press, 2012.

Gikandi, Simon. *Maps of Englishness: Writing Identity in the Culture of Colonialism*. New York: Columbia University Press, 1996.

Giles, Paul. "Commentary: Hemispheric Partiality." *American Literary History* 18, no. 3 (July 2006): 648–55.

Godelier, Maurice. *The Enigma of the Gift*. Translated by Nora Scott. Cambridge: Polity, 1999.

Goldman, Lawrence. "The Origins of British 'Social Science': Political Economy, Natural Science and Statistics, 1830–1835." *Historical Journal* 26, no. 3 (September 1983): 585–616.

Goodlad, Lauren. *Victorian Literature and the Victorian State: Character and Governance in a Liberal Society*. Baltimore: Johns Hopkins University Press, 2003.

Goodwin, Barbara. *Social Science and Utopia: Nineteenth-Century Models of Social Harmony*. Sussex, U.K.: Harvester, 1978.

Goudie, Sean X. *Creole America: The West Indies and the Formation of Literature and Culture in the New Republic*. Philadelphia: University of Pennsylvania Press, 2006.

———. "Toward a Definition of Caribbean American Regionalism: Contesting Anglo-America's Caribbean Designs in Mary Seacole and Sui Sin Far." *American Literature* 80, no. 2 (June 2008): 293–322.

Gould, Eliga. *Among the Powers of the Earth: The American Revolution and the Making of a New World Empire*. Cambridge, MA: Harvard University Press, 2012.

———. "Entangled Histories, Entangled Worlds: The English-Speaking Atlantic as a Spanish Periphery." *American Historical Review* 112, no. 3 (June 2007): 764–86.

———. "A Virtual Nation: Greater Britain and the Imperial Legacy of the American Revolution." *American Historical Review* 104, no. 2 (April 1999): 476–89.

Goveia, E. V. *The West Indian Slave Laws of the 18th Century*. Barbados: Caribbean University's Press, 1970.

Graeber, David. *Direct Action: An Ethnography*. Oakland, CA: AK Press, 2009.

Greenberg, Amy. *Manifest Manhood and the Antebellum American Empire*. Cambridge: Cambridge University Press, 2005.

Greene, Jack. *Negotiated Authorities: Essays in Political and Constitutional History*. Charlottesville: University of Virginia Press, 1994.

———. *Peripheries and Center: Constitutional Development in the Extended Polities of the British Empire and the United States, 1607–1788*. Athens: University of Georgia Press, 1986.

Greeson, Jennifer Rae. "The Prehistory of Possessive Individualism." PMLA 127, no. 4 (2012): 918–24.

Gruesz, Kirsten Silva. *Ambassadors of Culture: The Transamerican Origins of Latino Writing*. Princeton, NJ: Princeton University Press, 2002.

Guarneri, Carl J. *The Utopian Alternative: Fourierism in Nineteenth-Century America*. Ithaca, NY: Cornell University Press, 1991.

Guenther, Louise H. *British Merchants in Nineteenth-Century Brazil: Business, Culture, and Identity, 1808–50*. London: Centre for Brazilian Studies, 2004.

Gunning, Sandra. "Traveling with Her Mother's Tastes: The Negotiation of Gender, Race, and Location in *Wonderful Adventures of Mrs. Seacole in Many Lands*." *Signs* 26, no. 4 (2001): 949–81.

Guru, Gopal. "How Egalitarian Are the Social Sciences in India?" *Economic and Political Weekly* 37, no. 50 (2002): 5003–9.

Guttridge, G. H. "Adam Smith on the American Revolution: An Unpublished Memorial." *American Historical Review* 38 (1933): 714–20.

Hadley, Elaine. *Living Liberalism: Practical Citizenship in Mid-Victorian Britain*. Chicago: University of Chicago Press, 2010.

Hahamovitch, Cindy. *No Man's Land: Jamaican Guestworkers in America and the Global History of Deportable Labor*. Princeton, NJ: Princeton University Press, 2013.

Hall, Catherine. *Civilising Subjects: Metropole and Colony in the English Imagination, 1830–1867*. Chicago: University of Chicago Press, 2002.

Hall, Douglas. *Free Jamaica, 1838–1865: An Economic History*. New Haven, CT: Yale University Press, 1959.

———. "Incalculability as a Feature of Sugar Production during the Eighteenth Century." *Social and Economic Studies* 10 (1961): 340–52.

Hall, Henry. *The Colonial Office: A History*. London: Longmans, Green, and Company, 1937.

Halliday, Paul D. *Habeas Corpus: From England to Empire*. Cambridge, MA: Harvard University Press, 2010.

Hancock, David. *Citizens of the World: London Merchants and the Integration of the British Atlantic Community, 1735–1785*. Cambridge: Cambridge University Press, 1995.

Harlow, Vincent. *The Founding of the Second British Empire, 1763–1793*. London: Longmans, Green, 1952.

Hartman, Saidiya. *Scenes of Subjection: Terror, Slavery, and Self-making in Nineteenth-Century America*. Oxford: Oxford University Press, 1997.

Helg, Aline. "Simón Bolívar and the Specter of Pardocracia: Jose Padilla in Post-Independence Cartagena." *Journal of Latin American Studies* 35, no. 3 (2003): 447–83.

Heng, Geraldine. *Empire of Magic: Medieval Romance and the Politics of Cultural Fantasy*. New York: Columbia University Press, 2003.

Henretta, James A. *Salutary Neglect: Colonial Administration under the Duke of Newcastle* (1972). Princeton, NJ: Princeton University Press, 2015.

Henry, Natasha. *Emancipation Day: Celebrating Freedom in Canada*. Toronto: Natural Heritage, 2010.

Herzfeld, Michael. *The Social Production of Indifference: Exploring the Symbolic Roots of Western Bureaucracy*. Chicago: University of Chicago Press, 1993.

Higman, Barry. *Plantation Jamaica, 1750–1850: Capital and Control in a Colonial Economy*. Kingston: University of the West Indies Press, 2005.

———. *Slave Populations in the Caribbean, 1807–1834*. Baltimore: Johns Hopkins University Press, 1984.

———. "The West India 'Interest' in Parliament, 1807–1833." *Historical Studies* 13, no. 49 (1967): 1–19.

Hilton, Boyd. *The Age of Atonement: The Influence of Evangelicalism on Social and Economic Thought, ca. 1795–1865*. Oxford: Clarendon, 1985.

———. *Corn, Cash, Commerce: The Economic Policies of the Tory Governments, 1815–1830*. Oxford: Oxford University Press, 1977.

Hirschman, Albert. *The Passions and the Interests*. Princeton, NJ: Princeton University Press, 1997.

Hofmeyr, Isabel. *Gandhi's Printing Press: Experiments in Slow Reading*. Cambridge, MA: Harvard University Press, 2013.

Holt, Thomas. *The Problem of Freedom: Race, Labor, and Politics in Jamaica and Britain, 1832–1938*. Baltimore: Johns Hopkins University Press, 1992.

Honig, Bonnie. *Antigone, Interrupted*. Cambridge: Cambridge University Press, 2013.

Horne, Gerald. *The Counter-Revolution of 1776: Slave Resistance and the Origins of the United States of America*. New York: New York University Press, 2014.

Howe, Anthony. *Free Trade and Liberal England, 1846–1946*. Oxford: Oxford University Press, 1997.

Hudson, Peter. *Bankers and Empire: How Wall Street Colonized the Caribbean*. Chicago: University of Chicago Press, 2017.

Hull, Matthew. *Government of Paper: The Materiality of Bureaucracy in Urban Pakistan*. Berkeley: University of California Press, 2012.

Hulsebosch, David. *Constituting Empire: New York and the Transformation of Constitutionalism in the Atlantic World, 1664–1830*. Chapel Hill: University of North Carolina Press, 2005.

Huzzey, Richard. *Freedom Burning: Anti-Slavery and Empire in Victorian Britain*. Ithaca, NY: Cornell University Press, 2012.

———. "Free Trade, Free Labour, and Slave Sugar in Victorian Britain." *Historical Journal* 53, no. 2 (June 2010): 359–79.

Irwin, Douglas. "The Reciprocity Debate in Parliament, 1842–6." In *Free Trade and Its Reception, 1815–1960: Freedom and Trade*, vol. 1, edited by Andrew Marrison, 129–44. London: Routledge, 1998.

Iton, Richard. *In Search of the Black Fantastic: Politics and Popular Culture in the Post–Civil Rights Era*. Oxford: Oxford University Press, 2008.

Jackson, Shona. *Creole Indigeneity: Between Myth and Nation of the Caribbean*. Minneapolis: University of Minnesota Press, 2012.

James, Scott C., and David A. Lake. "The Second Face of Hegemony: Britain's Repeal of the Corn Laws and the American Walker Tariff of 1846." *International Organization* 43, no. 1 (Winter 1989): 1–29.

James, Winston. *Holding Aloft the Banner of Ethiopia: Caribbean Radicalism in Early Twentieth Century America*. London: Verso, 1999.

John, A. Meredith. *The Plantation Slaves of Trinidad, 1783–1816: A Mathematical and Demographic Enquiry*. Cambridge: Cambridge University Press, 1988.

Johnson, Sara E. *The Fear of French Negroes: Transcolonial Collaboration in the Revolutionary Americas*. Berkeley: University of California Press, 2012.

Jordan, H. Donaldson. "A Politician of Expansion: Robert J. Walker." *Mississippi Valley Historical Review* 19, no. 3 (December 1932): 362–81.

Kafka, Ben. *The Demon of Writing: Power and Failures of Paperwork*. New York: Zone, 2012.

Karras, Alan L. *Sojourners in the Sun: Scottish Migrants in Jamaica and the Chesapeake, 1740–1800*. Ithaca, NY: Cornell University Press, 1992.

Kazanjian, David. *The Brink of Freedom*. Durham, NC: Duke University Press, 2016.

———. "The Speculative Freedom of Colonial Liberia." *American Quarterly* 63, no. 1 (2011): 863–93.

Kelly, John D., and Martha Kaplan. "Nation and Decolonization: Toward a New Anthropology of Nationalism." *Anthropological Theory* 1, no. 4 (2001): 419–37.

Kerr, Paulette. "Victims or Strategists? Female Lodging-House Keepers in Jamaica." In *Engendering History: Caribbean Women in Historical Perspective*, edited by Verene Shepherd, Bridget Brereton, and Barbara Bailey, 197–212. New York: St. Martin's, 1995.

Knight, Franklin, and Colin Palmer. *The Modern Caribbean*. Chapel Hill: University of North Carolina Press, 1989.

Koebner, Richard, and Helmut Schmidt. *Imperialism: The Story and Significance of a Political Word, 1840–1960*. Cambridge: Cambridge University Press, 1961.

Kolsky, Elizabeth. *Colonial Justice in British India: White Violence and the Rule of Law*. Cambridge: Cambridge University Press, 2011.

Kostal, R. W. *A Jurisprudence of Power: Victorian Empire and the Rule of Law*. Oxford: Oxford University Press, 2005.

Lamming, George. *The Pleasures of Exile* (1960). Ann Arbor: University of Michigan Press, 1992.

Landers, Jane. *Atlantic Creoles in the Age of Revolutions*. Cambridge, MA: Harvard University Press, 2010.

———. "Spanish Sanctuary: Fugitives in Florida, 1687–1790." *Florida Historical Quarterly* 62, no. 3 (January 1984): 296–313.

Lazarus, Neil. *The Postcolonial Unconscious*. Cambridge: Cambridge University Press, 2011.

Lazo, Rodrigo. "The Invention of America Again: On the Impossibility of an Archive." *American Literary History* 25, no. 4 (Winter 2013): 751–71.

Lenin, Vladimir I. *Imperialism, the Highest Stage of Capitalism: A Popular Outline*. Moscow: International Publishers, 1969.

Lent, John A. *Third World Mass Media and Their Search for Modernity: The Case of the Commonwealth Caribbean, 1717–1976*. Cranbury, NJ: Associated University Press, 1977.

Levy, Claude. *Emancipation, Sugar, and Federalism: Barbados and the West Indies, 1833–1876*. Gainesville: University Presses of Florida, 1980.

Lewis, Rupert. "J. J. Thomas and Political Thought in the Caribbean." *Caribbean Quarterly* 36, nos. 1–2 (1990): 46–58.

Lightfoot, Natasha. *Troubling Freedom: Antigua and the Aftermath of British Emancipation*. Durham, NC: Duke University Press, 2015.

Lloyd, David, and Paul Thomas. *Culture and the State*. London: Routledge, 1998.

Lobdell, Richard A. "Patterns of Investment and Sources of Credit in the British West Indian Sugar Industry, 1838–97." *Journal of Caribbean History* 4 (May 1972): 31–53.

Louis, William Roger, and Ronald Robinson. "The Imperialism of Decolonization." *Journal of Imperial and Commonwealth History* 22, no. 3 (1994): 462–511.

Luxemburg, Rosa. *The Accumulation of Capital*. London: Routledge, 2003.

Lynch, Deidre. *The Economy of Character: Novels, Market Culture, and the Business of Inner Meaning*. Chicago: University of Chicago Press, 1998.

MacMillan, Ken. *Sovereignty and Possession in the English New World: The Legal Foundations of Empire, 1576–1640*. Cambridge: Cambridge University Press, 2006.

Macpherson, C. B. *The Political Theory of Possessive Individualism: From Hobbes to Locke*. Oxford: Oxford University Press, 1962.

Mannheim, Karl. *Ideology and Utopia: An Introduction to the Sociology of Knowledge*. Translated by Louis Wirth and Edward Shils. New York: Harcourt, 1936.

Mantena, Karuna. *Alibis of Empire: Henry Maine and the Ends of Liberal Imperialism*. Princeton, NJ: Princeton University Press, 2010.

Marquez, Roberto. "Nationalism, Nation, and Ideology: Trends in the Emergence of Caribbean Literature." In *The Modern Caribbean*, edited by Franklin Knight and Colin Palmer, 293–340. Chapel Hill: University of North Carolina Press, 1989.

Marrison, Andrew, ed. *Free Trade and Its Reception, 1815–1960: Freedom and Trade*, vol. 1. London: Routledge, 1998.

Marshall, Peter. *The Making and Unmaking of Empires: Britain, India and America c. 1750–1783*. Oxford: Oxford University Press, 2004.

———. *Remaking the British Atlantic: The United States and the British Empire after American Independence*. Oxford: Oxford University Press, 2012.

Martin, Ged. "Empire Federalism and Imperial Parliamentary Union, 1820–1870." *Historical Journal* 16, no. 1 (1973): 65–92.

Martin, Randy. *An Empire of Indifference: American War and the Financial Logic of Risk Management*. Durham, NC: Duke University Press, 2007.

Marx, Karl. *Capital*, vol. 1. Translated by Ben Fowkes. London: Penguin, 1990.

———. *Grundrisse: Foundations of the Critique of Political Economy*. Translated by Martin Nicolaus. New York: Penguin, 1993.

May, Robert E. *Manifest Destiny's Underworld: Filibustering in Antebellum America*. Chapel Hill: University of North Carolina Press, 2002.

Mbembe, Achille. "Necropolitics." Translated by Libby Meintjes. *Public Culture* 15, no. 1 (2003): 11–40.

McFee, Mollie. "Aspirational Nations: Language, Intimacy, and the Twentieth-Century Caribbean." PhD diss., University of Chicago, 2017.

McGuinness, Aims. *Path of Empire: Panama and the California Gold Rush*. Ithaca, NY: Cornell University Press, 2009.

McKeown, Timothy J. "Hegemonic Stability Theory and 19th Century Tariff Levels in Europe." *International Organization* 37, no. 1 (Winter 1983): 74–91.

McMichael, Philip. "The Crisis of the Southern Slaveholder Regime in the World-Economy." In *Rethinking the Nineteenth Century: Contradictions and Movement*, edited by Francisco O. Ramirez, 43–60. Westport, CT: Greenwood, 1988.

Meer, Sarah. *Uncle Tom Mania: Slavery, Minstrelsy, and Transatlantic Culture in the 1850s*. Athens: University of Georgia Press, 2005.

Mehta, Uday Singh. *Liberalism and Empire: A Study in Nineteenth-Century British Liberal Thought*. Chicago: University of Chicago Press, 1999.

Milette, James. *The Genesis of Crown Colony Government: Trinidad, 1783–1810.* Port of Spain, Trinidad: Moko Enterprises, 1970.

Milgate, Murray, and Shannon C. Stimson. *After Adam Smith.* Princeton, NJ: Princeton University Press, 2009.

Mintz, Sidney. *Caribbean Transformations.* New York: Columbia University Press, 1974.

———. "Peasant Market Places and Economic Development in Latin America." Occasional Paper no. 4, Graduate Center for Latin American Studies, Vanderbilt University, 1964, 1–8.

———. "Peasant Markets." *Scientific American* 203, no. 2 (1960): 112–22.

Mintz, Sidney, and Douglas Hall. "The Origins of the Jamaican Internal Marketing System." *Yale University Publication in Anthropology,* no. 57 (1960): 3–26.

Montes, Leonidas. "Das Adam Smith Problem: Its Origins, the Stages of the Current Debate, and One Implication for Our Understanding of Sympathy." *Journal of the History of Economic Thought* 25, no. 1 (2003): 63–90.

Monypenny, William Flavelle. *The Life of Benjamin Disraeli.* New York: Macmillan, 1910.

Morgan, Jennifer. *Laboring Women: Reproduction and Slavery in New World Slavery.* Philadelphia: University of Pennsylvania Press, 2004.

Morrell, W. P. *British Colonial Policy in the Age of Peel and Russell.* Oxford: Clarendon, 1930.

Morris, Mervyn. *Making West Indian Literature.* Kingston: Ian Randle, 2005.

Moten, Fred. "Blackness and Nothingness (Mysticism in the Flesh)." *South Atlantic Quarterly* 112, no. 4 (2013): 737–80.

———. "Knowledge of Freedom." *New Centennial Review* 4, no. 2 (Fall 2004): 269–310.

———. "Notes on Passage (The New International of Sovereign Feelings)." *Palimpsest* 3, no. 1 (2014): 51–74.

Motyl, Alexander J. *Imperial Ends: The Decay, Collapse, and Revival of Empires.* New York: Columbia University Press, 2001.

Muldrew, Craig. *The Economy of Obligation: The Culture of Credit and Social Relations in Early Modern England.* New York: Palgrave, 1998.

Munro, Martin, and Elizabeth Walcott-Hackshaw, eds. *Reinterpreting the Haitian Revolution and Its Cultural Aftershocks.* Kingston: University of the West Indies Press, 2006.

Murphy, Gretchen. *Hemispheric Imaginings: The Monroe Doctrine and Narratives of U.S. Empire.* Durham, NC: Duke University Press, 2005.

Murray, D. J. *The West Indies and the Development of Colonial Government, 1801–1834.* Oxford: Clarendon, 1965.

Muthu, Sankar. *Enlightenment against Empire.* Princeton, NJ: Princeton University Press, 2003.

Naipaul, V. S. *The Loss of El Dorado: A Colonial History.* New York: Vintage, 1969.

———. *The Overcrowded Barracoon.* Harmondsworth, U.K.: Penguin, 1976.

Naylor, Robert. *Penny Ante Imperialism: The Mosquito Shore and the Bay of Honduras, 1600–1914, a Case Study in British Informal Empire.* Cranbury, NJ: Farleigh Dickinson University Press, 1989.

Neptune, Harvey. *Caliban and the Yankees: Trinidad and the United States Occupation.* Chapel Hill: University of North Carolina Press, 2007.

Noel, Jesse A. *Trinidad, Provincia de Venezuela: Historia de la Administración Española de Trinidad.* Caracas, Venezuela: Academia Nacional de la Historia, 1972.

Nyquist, Mary. *Arbitrary Rule: Slavery, Tyranny, and the Power of Life and Death.* Chicago: University of Chicago Press, 2013.

Obadele-Starks, Ernest. *Freebooters and Smugglers: The Foreign Slave Trade in the United States after 1808.* Fayetteville: University of Arkansas Press, 2007.

Offen, Karl H. "Creating Mosquitia: Mapping Amerindian Spatial Practices in Eastern Central America, 1629–1779." *Journal of Historical Geography* 33 (2007): 254–82.

Oldroyd, David, Richard K. Fleishman, and Thomas N. Tyson. "The Culpability of Accounting Practice in Promoting Slavery in the British Empire and Antebellum United States." *Critical Perspectives on Accounting* 19 (2008): 764–84.

———. "Monetising Human Life: Slave Valuations on U.S. and British West Indian Plantations." *Accounting History* 9, no. 2 (July 2004): 35–62.

O'Shaughnessy, Alexander Jackson. *An Empire Divided: The American Revolution and the British Caribbean.* Philadelphia: University of Pennsylvania Press, 2000.

Palen, Marc-William. "Adam Smith as Advocate of Empire, c. 1870–1932." *Historical Journal* 57, no. 1 (2014): 179–98.

———. *The "Conspiracy" of Free Trade: The Anglo-American Struggle over Empire and Economic Globalisation, 1846–1896.* Cambridge: Cambridge University Press, 2016.

Pares, Richard. *Yankees and Creoles.* London: Longmans, 1956.

Parker, Jason C. *Brother's Keeper: The United States, Race, and Empire in the British Caribbean, 1937–1962.* Oxford: Oxford University Press, 2008.

Parrish, Susan Scott. "Richard Ligon and the Atlantic Science of Commonwealths." *William and Mary Quarterly* 67, no. 2 (April 2010): 209–48.

Parry, J. P. *The Politics of Patriotism: English Liberalism, National Identity and Europe, 1830–1886.* Cambridge: Cambridge University Press, 2007.

Paton, Diana. *No Bond but the Law: Punishment, Race, and Gender in Jamaican State Formation, 1780–1870.* Durham, NC: Duke University Press, 2004.

Pearsall, Sarah. *Atlantic Families: Lives and Letters in the Later Eighteenth Century.* Oxford: Oxford University Press, 2011.

Pearson, Harry W. "The Secular Debate on Economic Primitivism." In *Trade and Market in the Early Empires: Economies in History and Theory,* edited by Karl Polanyi, Conrad M. Arensberg, and Harry W. Pearson, 3–11. Glencoe, IL: Free Press, 1957.

Pérotin-Dumon, Anne. "Révolutionnaires français et royalistes espagnols dans les Antilles." *Revue Française d'Histoire d'Outre-Mer* 76 (1989): 125–58.

Perry, Amanda T. "A Traffic in Numbers: The Ethics, Effects, and Affect of Mortality Statistics in the British Abolition Debates." *Journal for Early Modern Cultural Studies* 12, no. 4 (Fall 2012): 78–104.

Petley, Christer. "Gluttony, Excess, and the Fall of the Planter Class in the British Caribbean." *Atlantic Studies* 9, no. 1 (2012): 75–106.

Pettigrew, William. *Freedom's Debt: The Royal African Company and the Politics of the Atlantic Slave Trade, 1672–1752.* Chapel Hill: University of North Carolina Press, 2013.

Picken, Cassidy. "Rendering Empire: Rent and the Writing of Liberal Imperialism, 1776–1833." PhD diss., University of Chicago, 2016.

Pitts, Jennifer. *A Turn to Empire: The Rise of Imperial Liberalism in Britain and France.* Princeton, NJ: Princeton University Press, 2005.

Pocock, Michael Rogers. *Out of the Shadows of the Past.* Port of Spain, Trinidad: Self-published, 1993.

Polanyi, Karl. "Aristotle Discovers the Economy." In *Trade and Market in the Early Empires: Economies in History and Theory,* edited by Karl Polanyi, Conrad M. Arensberg, and Harry W. Pearson, 64–96. Glencoe, IL: Free Press, 1957.

———. "The Economy as Instituted Process." In *Trade and Market in the Early Empires: Economies in History and Theory,* edited by Karl Polanyi, Conrad M. Arensberg, and Harry W. Pearson, 243–270. Glencoe, IL: Free Press, 1957.

———. *The Great Transformation: The Political and Economic Origins of Our Time* (1944). Boston: Beacon, 2001.

———. *The Livelihood of Man.* Edited by Harry W. Pearson. New York: Academic Press, 1977.

Poovey, Mary. *Genres of the Credit Economy: Mediating Value in Eighteenth- and Nineteenth-Century Britain.* Chicago: University of Chicago Press, 2008.

———. *A History of the Modern Fact: Problems of Knowledge in the Sciences of Wealth and Society.* Chicago: University of Chicago Press, 1998.

———. *Making a Social Body: British Cultural Formation, 1830–1864.* Chicago: University of Chicago Press, 1995.

Pouchet, Sandra Paquet. "The Enigma of Arrival: *The Wonderful Adventures of Mrs. Seacole in Many Lands.*" *African American Review* 26, no. 4 (1992): 651–63.

Povinelli, Elizabeth. *Economies of Abandonment: Social Belonging and Endurance in Late Liberalism.* Durham, NC: Duke University Press, 2011.

Price, Jacob M. "Credit in the Slave Trade and Plantation Economies." In *Slavery and the Rise of the Atlantic System,* edited by Barbara Solow, 293–340. Cambridge: Cambridge University Press, 1991.

Price, Polly. "Natural Law and Birthright Citizenship in Calvin's Case (1608)." *Yale Journal of Law and the Humanities* 9 (1997): 73–138.

Quayson, Ato. *Calibrations.* Minneapolis: University of Minnesota Press, 2003.

Ragatz, Lowell Joseph. *Fall of the Planter Class in the British Caribbean, 1763–1833* (1928). New York: Octagon, 1977.

Ramirez, Francisco O., ed. *Rethinking the Nineteenth Century: Contradictions and Movement.* Westport, CT: Greenwood, 1988.

Rancière, Jacques. *Dissensus: On Politics and Aesthetics.* Translated by Steven Corcoran. London: Continuum, 2010.

Rappaport, Helen. "The Invitation That Never Came: Mary Seacole after the Crimea." *History Today* 55, no. 2 (2005): 9–15.

Razi, Alpen. "'Coloured Citizens of the World': The Networks of Empire Loyalism in Emancipation-Era Jamaica and the Rise of the Transnational Black Press." *American Periodicals* 23, no. 2 (November 2013): 105–24.

Richardson, Bonham C. "Caribbean Migrations, 1838–1985." In *The Modern Caribbean*, edited by Franklin Knight and Colin Palmer, 203–28. Chapel Hill: University of North Carolina Press, 1989.

———. "Freedom and Migration in the Leeward Caribbean, 1838–48." *Journal of Historical Geography* 6, no. 1 (1980): 391–408.

Richardson, Ronald Kent. *Moral Imperium: Afro-Caribbeans and the Transformation of British Rule, 1776–1838.* Westport, CT: Greenwood, 1987.

Roach, Joseph. *Cities of the Dead: Circum-Atlantic Performance.* New York: Columbia University Press, 1996.

Roberts, Justin. *Slavery and the Enlightenment in the British Atlantic, 1750–1807.* Cambridge: Cambridge University Press, 2013.

Robinson, Amy. "Authority and the Public Display of Identity: *Wonderful Adventures of Mrs. Seacole in Many Lands.*" *Feminist Studies* 20, no. 3 (1994): 537–57.

Robinson, Cedric. *Black Marxism: The Making of the Black Radical Tradition* (1983). Chapel Hill: University of North Carolina Press, 2000.

Rogin, Michael. *Subversive Genealogy: The Politics and Art of Herman Melville.* Berkeley: University of California Press, 1985.

Rosenberg, Leah Reade. *Nationalism and the Formation of Caribbean Literature.* London: Palgrave, 2007.

Rugemer, Edward Bartlett. *The Problem of Emancipation: The Caribbean Roots of the American Civil War.* Baton Rouge: Louisiana State University Press, 2008.

Rusert, Britt. *Fugitive Science: Empiricism and Freedom in Early African American Culture.* New York: New York University Press, 2017.

Rush, Anne Spry. *Bonds of Empire: West Indians and Britishness from Victoria to Decolonization.* Oxford: Oxford University Press, 2011.

Ryden, David Beck. "Does Decline Make Sense? The West Indian Economy and the Abolition of the British Slave Trade." *Journal of Interdisciplinary History* 31, no. 3 (Winter 2001): 347–74.

———. "'One of the Fertilest Pleasentest Spotts': An Analysis of the Slave Economy in Jamaica's St. Andrew Parish, 1753." *Slavery and Abolition* 21, no. 1 (June 2001): 32–55.

———. *West Indian Slavery and British Abolition.* Cambridge: Cambridge University Press, 2009.

Sahlins, Marshall. *Stone Age Economics.* Hawthorne, NY: Aldine de Gruyter, 1972.

Said, Edward. *Culture and Imperialism.* New York: Vintage, 1993.

Saldívar, José David. *The Dialectics of Our America: Genealogy, Cultural Critique, and Literary History.* Durham, NC: Duke University Press, 1991.

Salih, Sarah. "'A Gallant Heart to the Empire': Autoethnography and Imperial Identity in Mary Seacole's *Wonderful Adventures.*" *Philological Quarterly* 83, no. 2 (2004): 171–95.

Sanyal, Kalyan. *Rethinking Capitalist Development: Primitive Accumulation, Governmentality and Post-Colonial Capitalism*. New Delhi: Routledge India, 2007.

Sartorius, David. *Ever Faithful: Race, Loyalty, and the Ends of Empire in Spanish Cuba*. Durham, NC: Duke University Press, 2014.

Schmitt, Carl. *The Concept of the Political*. Translated by George Schwab. Chicago: University of Chicago Press, 1996.

———. *The Leviathan in the State Theory of Thomas Hobbes: Meaning and Failure of a Political Symbol*. Translated by George Schwab and Erna Hilfstein. Chicago: University of Chicago Press, 2008.

Schonhardt-Bailey, Cheryl. *From the Corn Laws to Free Trade: Interests, Ideas, and Institutions in a Historical Perspective*. Cambridge, MA: MIT Press, 2006.

Schoolman, Martha. *Abolitionist Geographies*. Minneapolis: University of Minnesota Press, 2015.

Schumpeter, Joseph. *History of Economic Analysis* (1954). Oxford: Oxford University Press, 1996.

Schuyler, Robert Livingston. "The Constitutional Claims of the British West Indies." *Political Science Quarterly* 40, no. 1 (1925): 1–36.

———. *The Fall of the Old Colonial System: A Study in British Free Trade, 1770–1870*. Oxford: Oxford University Press, 1945.

Scott, David. *Conscripts of Modernity: The Tragedy of Colonial Enlightenment*. Durham, NC: Duke University Press, 2004.

———. *Refashioning Futures: Criticism after Postcoloniality*. Princeton, NJ: Princeton University Press, 1999.

Scott, James. *The Moral Economy of the Peasant: Rebellion and Subsistence in Southeast Asia*. New Haven, CT: Yale University Press, 1976.

Scott, Julius S. "The Common Wind. Currents of Afro-American Communication in the Era of the Haitian Revolution." PhD diss., Duke University, 1986.

Scott, Rebecca, and Jean M. Hébrard. *Freedom Papers: An Atlantic Odyssey in the Age of Emancipation*. Cambridge, MA: Harvard University Press, 2012.

Semmel, Bernard. *The Rise of Free Trade Imperialism: Classical Political Economy, the Empire of Free Trade and Imperialism, 1750–1850*. Cambridge: Cambridge University Press, 1970.

Sen, Sudipta. *Empire of Free Trade: The East India Company and the Making of the Colonial Marketplace*. Philadelphia: University of Pennsylvania Press, 1998.

Senior, Olive. *Dying to Better Themselves: West Indians and the Building of the Panama Canal*. Kingston: University of the West Indies Press, 2014.

Sharpe, Christina. *In the Wake: On Blackness and Being*. Durham, NC: Duke University Press, 2016.

Sharpe, Jenny. *Allegories of Empire: The Figure of Woman in the Colonial Text*. Minnesota: University of Minnesota Press, 1993.

Sheller, Mimi. *Citizenship from Below: Erotic Agency and Caribbean Freedom*. Durham, NC: Duke University Press, 2012.

Shepherd, Verene, Bridget Brereton, and Barbara Bailey, eds. *Engendering History: Caribbean Women in Historical Perspective*. New York: St. Martin's, 1995.

Sheridan, Richard. *Doctors and Slaves: A Medical and Demographic History of Slavery in the British West Indies, 1680–1834*. Cambridge: Cambridge University Press, 1985.

Skinner, Gillian. *Sensibility and Economics in the Novel, 1740–1800*. London: Macmillan, 1999.

Skinner, Quentin. *Visions of Politics III: Hobbes and Civil Science*. Cambridge: Cambridge University Press, 2001.

Slocum, Karla. *Free Trade and Freedom: Neoliberalism, Place, and Nation in the Caribbean*. Ann Arbor: University of Michigan Press, 2006.

Smith, Faith. *Creole Recitations: John Jacob Thomas and Colonial Formation in the Late Nineteenth-Century Caribbean*. Charlottesville: University of Virginia Press, 2002.

Solow, Barbara, ed. *Slavery and the Rise of the Atlantic System*. Cambridge: Cambridge University Press, 1991.

Sommer, Doris. *Foundational Fictions: The National Romances of Latin America*. Berkeley: University of California Press, 1991.

Spillers, Hortense. "Mama's Baby, Papa's Maybe: An American Grammar Book." *Diacritics* 17, no. 2 (1987): 64–81.

Spivak, Gayatri Chakravorty. "Righting Wrongs." *South Atlantic Quarterly* 103, nos. 2–3 (2004): 523–81.

Standing, Guy. *The Precariat: The Dangerous New Class*. London: Bloomsbury Academic, 2011.

Steele, Ian. *The English Atlantic, 1675–1740*. Oxford: Oxford University Press, 1986.

Stephens, Michelle Ann. *Black Empire: The Masculine Global Imaginary of Caribbean Intellectuals in the United States, 1914–1962*. Durham, NC: Duke University Press, 2005.

Stern, Philip J., and Carl Wennerlind, eds. *Mercantilism Reimagined: Political Economy in Early Modern Britain and Its Empire*. Oxford: Oxford University Press, 2013.

Stinchcombe, Arthur L. "Class Conflict and Diplomacy: Haitian Isolation in the 19th-Century World System." *Sociological Perspectives* 37, no. 1 (1994): 1–23.

Stoler, Ann Laura. *Along the Archival Grain: Thinking through Colonial Ontologies*. Princeton, NJ: Princeton University Press, 2009.

———. "On Degrees of Imperial Sovereignty." *Public Culture* 18, no. 1 (2006): 125–46.

Stoll, Steven. *The Great Delusion: A Mad Inventor, Death in the Tropics, and the Utopian Origins of Economic Growth*. New York: Hill and Wang, 2008.

Streeby, Shelley. *American Sensations: Class, Empire, and the Production of Popular Culture*. Berkeley: University of California Press, 2002.

Super, R. H. *Trollope in the Post Office*. Ann Arbor: University of Michigan Press, 1981.

Tannenbaum, Frank. *Slave and Citizen: The Negro in the Americas*. New York: Random House, 1947.

Taylor, Christopher. "'Most Holy Virgin Assist Me': Subaltern Transnationalism and Positively Possible Worlds." *History of the Present* 4, no. 1 (Spring 2014): 75–96.

———. "The Refusal of Work: From the Postemancipation Caribbean to Post-Fordist Empire." *Small Axe* 44 (2014): 1–17.

Taylor, Miles. "The 1848 Revolution and the British Empire." *Past and Present* 166, no. 1 (February 2000): 146–80.

Teichgraeber, Richard F. "'Less Abused Than I Had Reason to Expect': The Reception of the *Wealth of Nations* in Britain, 1776–1790." *Historical Journal* 30, no. 2 (June 1987): 337–66.

Thompson, Alvin. *Flight to Freedom: African Runaways and Maroons in the Americas.* Kingston: University of the West Indies Press, 2006.

Thompson, Andrew S. "Tariff Reform: An Imperial Strategy, 1903–13." *Historical Journal* 40, no. 4 (1997): 1033–54.

Thompson, James. *Models of Value: Eighteenth-Century Political Economy and the Novel.* Durham, NC: Duke University Press, 1996.

Thompson, Peter. "Henry Drax's Instructions on the Management of a Seventeenth-Century Barbadian Sugar Plantation." *William and Mary Quarterly*, 3rd series, 66, no. 3 (July 2009): 565–604.

Thornton, John K. "'I Am the Subject of the King of Congo': African Political Ideology and the Haitian Revolution." *Journal of World History* 4, no. 2 (Fall 1993): 181–214.

Titus, Noel. *The Amelioration and Abolition of Slavery in Trinidad, 1812–1834: Experiments and Protests in a New Slave Colony.* Bloomington, IN: Self-published, 2009.

Tomich, Dale. *Slavery in the Circuit of Sugar: Martinique and the World-Economy, 1830–1848.* Baltimore: Johns Hopkins University Press, 1990.

———. *Through the Prism of Slavery: Labor, Capital, and World Economy.* Lanham, MD: Rowman and Littlefield, 2004.

Toussaint, Michael Ferguson. "Afro-West Indians in Search of the Spanish Main: The Trinidad-Venezuela Referent in the Nineteenth Century." PhD diss., University of the West Indies, 2000.

Trentman, Frank. *Free Trade Nation: Commerce, Consumption and Civil Society in Modern Britain.* Oxford: Oxford University Press, 2008.

Tribe, Keith. *Genealogies of Capitalism.* Atlantic Highlands, NJ: Humanities Press, 1981.

Trouillot, Michel Rolph. *Haiti: State against Nation.* New York: Monthly Review Press, 1990.

———. *Silencing the Past: Power and the Production of History.* Boston: Beacon, 1997.

Turley, David. *The Culture of English Antislavery, 1780–1860.* London: Routledge, 1991.

Tyrell, Alex. "The 'Moral Radical Party' and the Anglo-Jamaican Campaign for the Abolition of the Negro Apprenticeship System." *English Historical Review* 49, no. 342 (July 1984): 481–502.

van Alstyne, Richard. "The Central American Policy of Lord Palmerston, 1846–1848." *Hispanic American Historical Review* 16, no. 3 (1936): 339–59.

Vasconcellos, Colleen A. "'To Fit You All for Freedom': Jamaican Planters, Afro-Jamaican Mothers and the Struggle to Control Afro-Jamaican Children during Apprenticeship, 1833–40." *Citizenship Studies* 10, no. 1 (February 2006): 55–75.

Waddell, David. "British Honduras and Anglo-American Relations." *Caribbean Quarterly* 5, no. 1 (1957): 50–59.

———. "Great Britain and the Bay Islands, 1821–1861." *Historical Journal* 2, no. 1 (1959): 59–77.

Walker-Smith, Derek. *The Protectionist Case in the 1840s*. Oxford: Oxford University Press, 1933.

Ward, John Manning. *Colonial Self-Government: The British Experience, 1759–1856*. Toronto: University of Toronto Press, 1976.

Ward, J. R. "Emancipation and the Planters." *Journal of Caribbean History* 22, no. 1 (January 1988): 116–37.

Warner-Lewis, Maureen. *Archibald Monteath: Igbo, Jamaican, Moravian*. Kingston: University of the West Indies Press, 2007.

Watson, Tim. *Caribbean Culture and British Fiction in the Atlantic World, 1780–1870*. Cambridge: Cambridge University Press, 2008.

Weeks, Kathi. *The Problem with Work: Feminism, Marxism, Antiwork Politics, and Postwork Imaginaries*. Durham, NC: Duke University Press, 2011.

Weheliye, Alexander. *Habeas Viscus: Racializing Assemblages, Biopolitics, and Black Feminist Theories of the Human*. Durham, NC: Duke University Press, 2014.

White, Laura A. "The South in the 1850's as Seen by British Consuls." *Journal of Southern History* 1, no. 1 (1935): 29–48.

Wilder, Gary. *Freedom Time: Negritude, Decolonization, and the Future of the World*. Durham, NC: Duke University Press, 2015.

Williams, Eric. *Capitalism and Slavery* (1944). Chapel Hill: University of North Carolina Press, 1994.

———. *History of the People of Trinidad and Tobago*. Brooklyn: A and B Publishers Group, 1942.

Williamson, Karina. Introduction to Anonymous, *Marly; or, A Planter's Life in Jamaica* (1828). Oxford: Macmillan Education, 2005.

Wimmer, Andreas, and Nina Glick Schiller. "Methodological Nationalism, the Social Sciences, and the Study of Migration: An Essay in Historical Epistemology." *International Migration Review* 37, no. 3 (Fall 2003): 576–610.

Winch, Donald. *Classical Political Economy and Colonies*. Cambridge, MA: Harvard University Press, 1965.

Wood, Donald. *Trinidad in Transition: The Years after Slavery*. Oxford: Oxford University Press, 1968.

Wright, Melissa W. *Disposable Women and Other Myths of Global Capitalism*. London: Routledge, 2006.

Index

Wilberforce, William, 58, 79, 95; and the Slave Registry Bill of 1815, 79

Wilkin, Marcella Noy, 24; *The Slave Son* (1854), 24, 161

Williams, Eric, 1, 18–19, 33, 71, 125, 128, 239n6, 244n74; *Capitalism and Slavery* (1944), 19–19

Williams, James, 27, 87, 103–4; *A Narrative of Events since the First of August, 1834* (1837), 27, 74, 87, 91–93, 97–99, 103–4

Willmington, James, 107

"worthless life," 72–77, 89, 94, 97–98